Activating Urban Waterfronts

Activating Urban Waterfronts shows how urban waterfronts can be designed, managed and used in ways that can make them more inclusive, lively and sustainable. The book draws on detailed examination of a diversity of waterfronts from cities across Europe, Australia and Asia, illustrating the challenges of connecting these waterfront precincts to the surrounding city and examining how well they actually provide connection to water. The book challenges conventional large scale, long-term approaches to waterfront redevelopment, presenting a broad re-thinking of the formats and processes through which urban redevelopment can happen. It examines a range of actions that transform and activate urban spaces, including informal appropriations, temporary interventions, co-design, creative programming of uses, and adaptive redevelopment of waterfronts over time. It will be of interest to anyone involved in the development and management of waterfront precincts, including entrepreneurs, the creative industries, community organizations, and, most importantly, ordinary users.

Quentin Stevens is an Associate Professor in the School of Architecture and Urban Design at RMIT University in Melbourne, Australia. He has professional degrees in Architecture and Urban Planning and previous taught at the Bartlett School of Planning, University College London. He has published widely on the social uses of public spaces, including the books *Transforming Urban Waterfronts: Fixity and Flow*, *The Ludic City*, and *Loose Space*. His current areas of research interest include temporary and tactical urbanism, the contribution that public space design makes to social cohesion, and the role of memorials in national identity.

Activating Urban Waterfronts

Planning and Design for Inclusive, Engaging and Adaptable Public Spaces

Quentin Stevens

NEW YORK AND LONDON

First published 2021
by Routledge
52 Vanderbilt Avenue, New York, NY 10017

and by Routledge
2 Park Square, Milton Park, Abingdon, Oxon, OX14 4RN

Routledge is an imprint of the Taylor & Francis Group, an informa business

© 2021 Taylor & Francis

The right of Quentin Stevens to be identified as author of this work has been asserted by him in accordance with sections 77 and 78 of the Copyright, Designs and Patents Act 1988.

All rights reserved. No part of this book may be reprinted or reproduced or utilised in any form or by any electronic, mechanical, or other means, now known or hereafter invented, including photocopying and recording, or in any information storage or retrieval system, without permission in writing from the publishers.

Trademark notice: Product or corporate names may be trademarks or registered trademarks, and are used only for identification and explanation without intent to infringe.

Library of Congress Cataloging-in-Publication Data
Names: Stevens, Quentin, 1969–
Title: Activating urban waterfronts : planning and design for inclusive, engaging and adaptable public spaces / Quentin Stevens.
Identifiers: LCCN 2020029509 (print) | LCCN 2020029510 (ebook) | ISBN 9780367473259 (hardback) | ISBN 9780367473242 (paperback) | ISBN 9781003034872 (ebook)
Subjects: LCSH: Urban renewal. | City planning. | Waterfronts.
Classification: LCC HT170 .A29 2021 (print) | LCC HT170 (ebook) | DDC 307.3/416—dc23
LC record available at https://lccn.loc.gov/2020029509
LC ebook record available at https://lccn.loc.gov/2020029510

ISBN: 978-0-367-47325-9 (hbk)
ISBN: 978-0-367-47324-2 (pbk)
ISBN: 978-1-003-03487-2 (ebk)

Typeset in Univers
by KnowledgeWorks Global Ltd.

Contents

List of Contributors   *vii*
Acknowledgements   *ix*

Introduction   1

Part I   Plugging the Waterfront into the City   **15**

1   Three 'Southbanks'   17
Quentin Stevens

2   Postcolonial Waterfronts: Global Imagery and Local Realities   52
Quentin Stevens, Marek Kozlowski and Norsidah Ujang

3   Tracing the Shifting Waterfront   72
Quentin Stevens

4   Artificial Waterfronts   92
Quentin Stevens

Part II   Switching the Waterfront On   **113**

5   Appropriating the Spectacle   115
Quentin Stevens and Kim Dovey

6   The 'City Beach' as a New Waterfront Development Model   132
Quentin Stevens

7   Post-Fordist Placemaking   155
Quentin Stevens and Mhairi Ambler

Contents

8 Sandpit Urbanism   180
      Quentin Stevens

9 A Temporary Waterfront: Prompting Public Engagement   197
      *Jacob Bjerre Mikkelsen, Quentin Stevens, Catherine Hills
      and Florian 'Floyd' Mueller*

    Conclusion   *221*
    Bibliography   *231*
    Index   *241*

Contributors

Mhairi Ambler In 2008, Mhairi undertook a Masters in European Urban Cultures, a multi-disciplinary programme which crossed the boundaries between the arts, design, urban planning, public policy, artistic creativity and cultural management and concluded with a transnational comparative analysis of urban beaches. Upon graduating from the Masters, she led the European and International team at Bristol City Council where she was involved in securing Bristol's role as the only UK signatory of the EU China Partnership on Sustainable Urbanisation (2014), being awarded European Green Capital (2015) and becoming an active member of the Global Parliament of Mayors (2015). Mhairi is currently living within walking distance of a natural beach where she is co-ordinating Falmouth University's Research Excellence Framework (REF) submission.

Kim Dovey Kim Dovey is Professor of Architecture and Urban Design at the University of Melbourne, where he is also Director of *InfUr-* the Informal Urbanism Research Hub. He has published and broadcast widely on social issues in architecture, urban design and planning. Books include *Framing Places, Fluid City Becoming Places, Urban Design Thinking* and *Mapping Urbanities*. He leads research projects on urban morphology and informal settlements.

Catherine Hills Catherine is an academic in the School of Design at RMIT University. Her specialisations include human-centered design (HCD), service design, user experience (UX) design, organisational design, software development, business model design and value proposition innovation. Catherine has established experience both in academia and in the design and technology sector over the course of two decades, recently leading experience at Publicis Sapient Australia in Experience Strategy. Catherine is a regular presenter at events such as UX Australia, First and Last Conferences. Her recent major thesis and Masters' project has just been published -- Contributing Factors to the User Experience of e-Commerce Websites: Usability, User Expectations and the Designer Perspective (2019). Catherine is a regular contributor and reviewer of product, design and UX writing and publications. Her next research interests currently are focused on time-based UX, artificial intelligence, decision making and moral relativity.

Marek Kozlowski Marek Kozlowski is currently a Senior Lecturer at the Faculty of Design and Architecture, University Putra Malaysia (UPM). He graduated from the University of Queensland as an Urban Planner and completed his master's in architecture at the Technical University in Krakow, Poland. He received his PhD at the University of Queensland. He has worked as an urban planner in Brisbane and Gold Coast City Councils and as an architect/urban designer for private consultancies in Australia, Malaysia, Poland, United Arab Emirates, Oman and Saudi Arabia. He has recently published a book with Routledge, *'Kuala Lumpur: Community, Infrastructure and Urban* Inclusivity'.

Jacob Bjerre Mikkelsen Jacob Bjerre Mikkelsen is a Danish urban designer and scholar who has conducted research on urban design, urban transformation and mobilities in the United States, Australia and Europe. He has a profound interest in the transformation of urban waterfronts and has worked with this field through his PhD project, as a visiting scholar and through urban design and planning practice in the private and public sector.

Florian 'Floyd' Mueller Florian 'Floyd' Mueller is Professor of Future Interfaces in the department of Human-Centred Computing at Monash University in Melbourne, Australia, directing the Exertion Games Lab that investigates the coming together of technology, the human body and play. Previously, Floyd was a Fulbright Scholar at Stanford, led 12 researchers at CSIRO and researched at RMIT, Stanford, University of Melbourne, Microsoft Research, Media Lab Europe, Fuji-Xerox Palo Alto Labs, Xerox PARC and MIT's Media Lab.

Norsidah Ujang Norsidah Ujang is an Associate Professor at the Department of Landscape Architecture, Faculty of Design and Architecture, Universiti Putra Malaysia. Her research areas include urban design, environmental attachment, and environmental behaviour focusing on urban regeneration, place attachment, place identity, social urbanism, and sustainable pedestrian environment. She was a visiting scholar at the Department of Planning and Urban Studies, MIT under the UTM-MIT Sustainable Cities Program.

Acknowledgements

I wish to give particular thanks to Dagmar Meyer-Stevens, who suggested that I undertake a wider study of waterfronts, David Gordon, who inspired me to continue, and Nathalie Boucher, who encouraged me to gather it all together.

Thank you to my seven co-authors, who contributed so much to this work and to my knowledge and thinking about waterfront development. Thanks also to collaborators Gene Desfor, Jennefer Laidley, Dirk Schubert, Zhugen Wang, and research assistants See Chin Lim, Amanda Claremont, Patricia Aelbrecht, Shanti Sumartojo, Birgit Billinger, Felix Fehr, Ha Thai, Miza Moreau and Jonathan Daly. Thank you to Djamila Vilcsko for the translation and transcription of interviews.

Thank you for valued critique, input and support from Karen Franck, Julia Lossau, Peter Hall, Claire Colomb, Matthew Carmona, Denise Meredyth, Britta Timm Knudsen, Jeremy Nemeth, Bernardo Jiménez-Dominguez, Shuhana Shamsuddin, Laurent Vernet, Christian Heinrich, Martin Klamt, Mathew Aitchison, John Macarthur, Louisa Carter, and many editors and referees at journals and conferences. Thank you also to the numerous interviewees.

This research was supported by funding from the University of Queensland School of Geography, Planning and Architecture; the Alexander von Humboldt Foundation; the Bartlett School of Planning at University College London; RMIT University School of Architecture and Urban Design; and in-kind support from the Geographisches Institut at Humboldt University Berlin and the Faculty of Design and Architecture at Universiti Putra Malaysia.

This book is an assemblage of more than twenty years of research into how open spaces in urban waterfront leisure precincts are developed, used and managed. The original descriptions of individual sites have largely been retained, and there is thus some anachronism, overlap and disjuncture among the examples and critiques that are presented here. Some analyses that were based on past conditions have been updated to examine later changes, or expanded to provide additional comparisons between

Acknowledgements

projects. Earlier versions of the material collected here have previously been published in the articles and books listed below:

Chapter 1: Stevens, Q. (2006) 'The design of urban waterfronts: a critique of two Australian "Southbanks"', *Town Planning Review,* 77(2).

Chapter 2: Stevens, Q. Kozlowski, M. and Ujang, N. (2016) 'Contrasting global imagery to local realities in the postcolonial waterfronts of Malaysia's capital cities', *ArchNet-IJAR: International Journal of Architectural Research*, 10(1).

Chapter 3: Stevens, Q. (2010) 'Conclusion: patterns of persistence, trajectories of change', in Desfor, G., Laidley, J., Stevens, Q. and Schubert, D. (eds) *Transforming Urban Waterfronts: Fixity and Flow*, New York, Routledge.

Chapter 4. Stevens, Q. (2009) 'Artificial waterfronts', *Urban Design International,* 14(1).

Chapter 5: Stevens, Q. and Dovey, K. (2004) 'Appropriating the spectacle: play and politics in a leisure landscape', *Journal of Urban Design,* 9(3)

Chapter 6: Stevens, Q. (2011), 'Characterising Germany's artificial "city beaches": distribution, type and design', World Schools of Planning Congress, Perth.
and
Stevens, Q., (2010) 'The German "city beach" as a new waterfront development model', in Desfor, G., Laidley, J., Stevens, Q. and Schubert, D. (eds) *Transforming Urban Waterfronts: Fixity and Flow*, New York, Routledge.

Chapter 7: Stevens, Q. and Ambler, M. (2010) 'Europe's city beaches as post-fordist placemaking', *Journal of Urban Design* 15(4).

Chapter 8: Stevens, Q., (2015) 'Sandpit urbanism', in Knudsen, B., Christensen, D. and Blenker, P. (eds) *Enterprising Initiatives in the Experience Economy: Transforming Social Worlds*, New York, Routledge.

Chapter 9: Mikkelsen, J, Stevens, Q., Hills, C. and Mueller, F. (2018) 'Exploring how urban waterfronts can encourage visitors' active engagement with water through a temporary design installation', *Archnet-IJAR: International Journal of Architectural Research*, 12(1).

Introduction

This book has its origins in my doctoral research, which examined the many playful ways that people use public spaces (Stevens 2007a, 2007b). I noticed then that people were appropriating various spaces along Melbourne's Southbank Promenade to play in many ways other than what the precinct's political proponents, developers, designers and managers may have intended. Since that time, I have remained interested in why people come to the Southbank: how do they get there, what attracts them there, what special experiences are possible in that space; and equally interested in the myriad ways that people animate these kinds of public waterfront areas.

The book provides a critical and comparative examination of the design, management and use of new urban waterfront leisure areas like Melbourne's Southbank that have been developed in recent decades in former industrial areas, with a particular focus on their open spaces. It seeks to go beyond the many existing publications on such waterfronts, which typically provide either admiring accounts of the high-quality architecture, infrastructure and landscaping of many showpiece waterfronts worldwide, or focus on detailed critiques of the political economy of single cases. The book contests the assumption that the world's urban waterfronts all have been, and should be, transformed following the physical, economic and managerial examples of Baltimore and other post-industrial US cities. This book seeks to challenge the perception that new urban waterfronts are a singular and incontrovertible global success story, and to identify a range of specific ways that existing urban waterfronts can be managed, re-designed and occupied to make them more inclusive, lively and sustainable. The book aims to bring critical insights from the social sciences about the problems and opportunities of existing waterfronts together with detailed illustration and analysis of their design features at a range of scales. It draws on examination of a diverse range of case studies from urban waterfronts in the UK, Germany, France, the Netherlands, Australia, South Korea and Malaysia, bringing these together into a comparative analysis that aims to identify more broadly-applicable principles that can inform design and policymaking for various types of new urban precincts.

Introduction

Existing Research on Urban Waterfront Transformations

Industry began moving away from inner-urban waterfront areas 50 years ago, and there is now a sizeable academic literature on the post-industrial redevelopment of urban waterfronts. Studies of urban waterfront redevelopment first started emerging after major technological changes and economic restructurings in the mid-1970s had started to transform inner-cities, ports and industrial areas. Books illustrating and analysing waterfront redevelopments have continued to appear as ever more cities redevelop former industrial port areas for housing, offices, leisure and open space uses, or extend or change earlier redevelopment schemes, as has occurred in both London's and Melbourne's Docklands. The first generation of research into urban waterfront transformation is thus now over 30 years old, the cases and contexts these books examined have changed, and their insights been overtaken by examples and innovations elsewhere. In particular, the social uses of waterfront spaces have changed dramatically since these first books came out, in line with broader increases in the use of urban public spaces and broader re-investment into inner cities.

Since the 1980s, many new books illustrating and analysing waterfront transformations have continued to appear. These studies fall into two distinct categories: critical scholarly analyses of the political, social and economic contexts within which waterfront redevelopments happen, which say little about the design or use of the places, and professionally-oriented illustrative catalogues, which give limited insight into how these places came about or function.

Collective Perspectives

Critical social science analyses of urban waterfronts began with edited collections by Hoyle et. al. (1988) and Malone (1996). Such books have mostly been collections of geographically-spread individual case studies. More recent collections have continued to follow the same general format, although they have tended to take a specific geographical and/or conceptual focus.

Desfor et al.'s *Transforming Urban Waterfronts* (2010), for which I was one of the editors and contributors, and which I discuss in detail in Chapter 3, is a set of studies from academics across urban geography, sociology, and planning. These are all framed around the theme of transient relationships between 'fixed' elements (built environment, regulatory structure and cultural practices) and 'fluid' elements (labour, capital, energy, information) of urban waterfronts. The book critiques the redevelopment of former industrial waterfronts into 'spaces of opportunity' for the 'creative class', and the consequent impacts on the civic nature of these precincts. The analyses are supported by theoretical discussion about capitalism, Nature, work, social relations and identity, which is in most cases not connected through to the small scale of physical waterfront sites or human experiences.

Smith and Ferrari's *Waterfront Revitalization: Experience in Citybuilding* (2012) is the outcome of an action-research collaborative project involving academic institutions and local authorities in nine cities around the North Sea. It examines the inclusion of various stakeholders in waterfront redevelopments, and presents a conceptual framework for studying waterfront revitalizations that combines institutionalist analysis with spatial political economy. It does not examine physical characteristics of waterfront settings, or everyday human experience of them.

Most recently, Carta and Ronsivalle's *The Fluid City Paradigm* (2016) is the result of another research network that seeks to rethink waterfront renewal strategies for the coastal areas of the central Mediterranean, also including some North Sea examples. It largely focuses on port areas and functions, with a secondary focus on contemporary leisure uses. While this study's ambition is to develop common guidelines and principles, it remains a disparate set of authors, case studies, and conceptualisations of the characteristics and potentials of waterfronts.

The selection of cases, quality, and themes covered within these edited collections varies, depending on the conferences and funded research collaborations that have precipitated them. Each tends to cover a wide geographical scope of waterfront cities, usually mixing well-known cases with less-well-known examples. These books tend to focus on examining waterfronts as historical case studies that illustrate broader social problems, of politics, globalization and neoliberalism, economic and property development, industrial restructuring, transport, and ecological sustainability. Their authors are mostly from the social sciences, particularly geography and the policy and strategy areas of urban planning. They rarely have much description or critique of the fine-scale design and public use of redeveloped waterfront spaces, and they tend not to have many close-up illustrations of waterfront landscapes. These studies have given relatively little attention to the important social and cultural dimensions of urban waterfront change. There is also rarely any synthesis or comparison across case studies or between chapters.

Beginning with Malone (1996), the critical studies of waterfront redevelopment have often emphasised the significant role played by deregulated planning and finance capital. Collectively, they have thus traced the significant cycles of economic boom and bust that have played out in different parts of the world over the last 30 years, and especially within Europe. Given the major impact of the Global Financial Crisis of 2007–08, the related European debt crisis, and the worldwide economic contraction that is unfolding at time of writing in response to the COVID-19 pandemic, it is timely to examine a range of ways that waterfront development and management can respond to a scarcity of resources. This is one of my key objectives in Part 2 of this book.

Detailed Individual Case Studies

Deeper, richer insights into waterfront redevelopment processes and outcomes have been achieved by in-depth single case studies. The largest number of such books focus on the quite untypical example of New York City, an exceptionally large and economically significant city. The first, David Gordon's *Battery Park City: Politics and Planning on the New York Waterfront* (1997), tells a story spanning several decades, through the experience of the state public-benefit corporation in charge of delivering the project. It thus gives limited attention to the experience of other actors, in particular the

Introduction

general public who use this precinct. With its main focus on political struggles, strategic planning processes and financing, there is little coverage of urban design or the qualities and functions of the public spaces of the waterfront as it was eventually built. Gastil's *Beyond the Edge* (2002) provides a far broader critical account of the cultural, functional, and ecological evolution of New York's extensive and diverse waterfront areas. He compares the New York case against other well-known waterfront redevelopments elsewhere, such as London, Amsterdam, Barcelona and Bilbao. His book focuses on design considerations, rather than political economy, but this is primarily generalized at the scale of master planning, and does not address everyday experiences at the human scale. Despite offering a detailed account of various land uses, plans, and programs associated with these waterfronts, Gastil does not engage with how these waterfront areas are experienced and used by the public.

Daniel Campo's *The Accidental Playground: Brooklyn Waterfront Narratives of the Undesigned and Unplanned* (2013), in contrast, does focus in on everyday uses and appropriations of New York's waterfront. It limits its physical scope to one waterfront area in Brooklyn, the site of a former railway-harbor transfer terminal. Campo focuses on the myriad of uses that emerged informally on this abandoned site, and the ways that space functioned as an incidental park, prior to its redevelopment through formal planning efforts. Each chapter of his study is dedicated to a specific user group, including skateboarders, street performers, environmental artists, workers in need of leisure space, and homeless, undocumented migrants. Their informal appropriations of the waterfront are discussed in relation to official planning efforts by government agencies and organized community groups. The book provides a rich empirical account of the waterfront's uses and users. The one limitation is that, as a study of an undeveloped site, there are relatively few detailed insights that can be taken forward into the design, planning and management of future waterfront redevelopment.

There have been several detailed case studies of waterfront design and use outside the context of New York. Kim Dovey's *Fluid City* (2005) is probably the most readily comparable work to what I am attempting in this book. Dovey discusses the transformation of the waterfront in Melbourne, Australia, examining a range of different waterfront precincts developed there during the 1980s and 1990s: the earliest redevelopment, Southbank (discussed here in Chapters 1 and 5), the Docklands, and a stretch of urban beachfront along Port Philip Bay. The book studies the political, economic, and cultural forces that shaped Melbourne's waterfront, as well as its informal and unplanned adaptations by the public. While *Fluid City* frames the discussion of Melbourne's waterfront transformation through a theoretical lens, it remains empirically grounded.

Jasper Rubin's *A Negotiated Landscape: The Transformation of San Francisco's Waterfront Since 1950* (2016) similarly provides a chronological narrative of the transformation of that city's waterfront. It charts the circumstances leading to the port's commercial decline, the revitalization of the waterfront as public space, its recent gentrification pressures, and emerging future directions. The case of San Francisco's waterfront redevelopment is rather unique for its focus on public space, without large-scale new residential and commercial development. Yet even so, Rubin's book does not examine the experience of that public space in terms of human activity patterns and everyday experiences.

Alasdair Jones's *On South Bank: The Production of Public Space* (2014) focuses specifically on London's South Bank area, also discussed here in Chapter 1. Jones examines how a waterfront open space is socially produced as 'public', rather than its physical production. He pursues this through the study of a range of micro-spatial practices, focusing on informal appropriations and activities such as skateboarding, BMX riding, and street performers. These activities are examined in relation to the existing context of urban design and architecture, and the institutional management of these spaces. There is, surprisingly, no discussion in *On South Bank* of any activities that are related to the actual water of the adjacent Thames River – an all-too-common shortcoming of waterfront studies that I seek to address in this book. Jones uses field observations and interviews with users of the South Bank to examine how its public space is managed and experienced. But these observations are not translated into practical insights about the design of waterfront spaces. The discussion remains largely conceptual, focussing on changing definitions of publicness and 'the right to the city' (Lefebvre 1996). Jones shows how the activation of waterfront areas can contribute to urban life, but does not identify how their design can also play a role.

While each of the works discussed above are excellent reads in their own right, they each focus in on the story of one specific waterfront. The unique physical, cultural, political and economic conditions of that case limit the transferability of the research. Theoretical critiques of wider political, economic, social and environmental issues are generally confined to the background, in order to maintain focus on the empirical case study.

This book seeks to provide a similar depth of analysis to these single case studies, but to also extend beyond their approach in two key ways. Firstly, it explores a range of cases studies from different cities around the globe within a single overarching framework, and examines various points of convergence and divergence among these different cases. Secondly, it has a much stronger focus on detailed observation and analysis of the design and use of the physical settings. While Gordon, Gastil, Dovey and Rubin offer insightful critical accounts of the first wave of waterfront redevelopment, where large-scale developers and state actors were responsible for re-purposing and re-shaping large urban areas, my aim in this book is more similar to the accounts of Campo and Jones, who examine more recent practices where public space is continually re-shaped through a myriad of human-scale, informal and temporary modifications.

Spectacular Design-Oriented Catalogues of 'Waterfront Success Stories'

The second broad category of studies of urban waterfront transformation focuses on the new physical designs of their architecture, landscaping and infrastructure. These books are generally large-format, professionally-oriented illustrative catalogues, providing a global overview without detailed analysis. The panoramic images are generally accompanied by short descriptive articles, which are in many cases written by individual projects' local political sponsors, developers and planners. Several of these books

Introduction

provide prescriptive approaches to design, with little reflection on what does not work well in waterfront design and management, and why.

This type of book began with Bruttomesso's *Waterfronts: A New Frontier for Cities on Water* (1993) and Breen and Rigby's lavish *Waterfronts: Cities Reclaim their Edge* (1994) and *The New Waterfront: A worldwide urban success story* (1996). The cases in Bruttomesso's book are arranged geographically, with no attempt to analyse or compare their contexts and outcomes. Both of Breen and Rigby's volumes largely organise their examples according to functional types – residential, commercial, recreational, cultural – although as with urban design generally, it is the mixing of such uses in waterfronts that inherently underpins their success.

Marshall's *Waterfronts in Post-industrial Cities* (2001) has its case study chapters organised into larger thematic sections that have wider applicability. This includes, importantly, the connection between a waterfront area and the city around it – a topic addressed here throughout Part 1. In Marshall's book, description of the physical design of waterfront projects is mixed with some critical analysis of them. But it retains the format of a large number of short, specific, illustrative case studies which are isolated from other examples and wider issues. Marshall introduces each section with an overview essay, but these do not link the specific case studies and their varied critical approaches together into a coherent overall statement. The individual chapters' authors were in many cases directly involved in the creation of these projects. While the chapters can therefore offer insight into the background objectives and processes behind these waterfronts, they lack critical distance on their challenges and lack comparisons across cases. Only three of the accompanying essays are written by academics, all of them designers, and all focussing on design practice rather than evaluating outcomes. Problematically, Marshall's book has a very simplistic definition and use of the concept 'post-industrial'; apart from one chapter on Genoa and Las Palmas, little is learned about the political contexts and the economic actors that shape waterfront development. The book, like most of its ilk, makes very little use of primary research findings or references. These are mostly affirmative accounts, emphasizing success and over-emphasizing the transferability of development solutions.

Waterfront Landscapes, by Chloe Fang (2012), refines the approach of cataloguing prize-winning design examples. It primarily serves as an image sourcebook, with little first-hand observation or critical analysis. It presents 46 waterfront revitalization projects, mostly in Europe, with some from North America and Australia, through photographs and site plans, with single-paragraph summaries of their design elements, and listings of each project's designers, clients, dates, and awards. The book focuses exclusively on landscape design, organizing the cases into three sections according to spatial types: waterfront promenades, squares, and parks. One can learn here what a specific waterfront project looked like, but little about what lessons it might offer for other contexts.

Two recent books both provide up-to-date catalogues of a large number of recent best-practice waterfront examples, as well as providing detailed recommendations on design and planning principles. Thorbjorn Andersson's *Waterfront Promenade Design: Urban Renewal Strategies* (2017) and Elizabeth Macdonald's *Urban Waterfront*

Promenades (2018) each illustrate and review at least 30 urban waterfront revitalization projects from across the globe. Andersson's opening chapters include many tables and bullet lists of standards and design objectives. These have been drawn together from the planners who developed the individual projects, rather than from direct empirical observation of what works and why. Macdonald provides cross-section drawings of the waterfront promenades and figure-ground maps of their wider urban contexts, in addition to the customary photographs. She often mentions specific physical dimensions, pedestrian counts and water levels. But there is little analysis of how these influence individual human experience and use of these places. Both these books group their examples into sections, according to either geographical contexts (beachfronts, riverfronts, promontories) or planning contexts (formerly industrial, suburban new town, incrementally-built, eco-district). But these themes are only briefly introduced. The cases are not put to work to draw specific comparative, analytical insights about these contexts and the different kinds of responses that have been developed for them.

Indeed, considering the problem-solving nature of design practice, none of the numerous catalogues of waterfront design identify or analyse the specific, often complex design problems that waterfront settings present, or the functional, aesthetic and management problems that waterfront redevelopment schemes themselves sometimes produce. They give limited attention to issues of climate change, sea level rise, and environmental degradation, or to how approaches that are intended to address these issues might be modified to suit different topographical and geographical contexts. To be fair, these catalogues are not intended as research studies. Most problematically, the focus of all these design catalogues remains strongly on the waterfront landscapes, not the people in them. They say little about how management approaches, both formal and informal, enliven these showpiece urban spaces. My key aim in this book is to combine the detailed, critical post-occupancy evaluation of the human use and management of waterfronts that is provided by the in-depth single case studies of Dovey (2005), Jones (2016) and Campo (2013) with the attention to physical design details and the broader geographical and spatial scope of the designerly collections discussed above.

There are two existing books that go some way to providing this kind of mix. Han Meyer's *City and Port* (1999) has a quite different focus to most of the other books about the transformation of urban waterfronts that have been discussed thus far. It devotes 314 of its 424 pages to detailed, extensively-illustrated spatial histories of the waterfronts of four of the Western world's greatest port cities: London, Barcelona, New York, and Rotterdam. Each case is discussed separately; each is structured in a thematic chronology from pre-modern times through early modern, modernist and postmodern eras. The book examines the changes in the form, accessibility and use of waterfront spaces over time. But Meyer has a very macro focus, in terms of both the physical scale of the four cities and their ports (all very large), and his analysis of 'culture', which is broad and theoretical. The book's long introductory essay discusses changes in the public life of the cities and their waterfront areas, in terms of a shift from industrial production to the consumption of commerce, of cultural productions, and the consumption of public life and public space itself. But this is not grounded in any fine-grained empirical detail about people's individual experiences and actions on the four waterfronts. Meyer provides very detailed stories about the planning, construction and management of each of the four individual cases, and many details about specific sites, landscape conditions, functions, and projects, but these all remain subservient to the overarching historical narratives. Unfortunately, Meyer does not draw his extensive knowledge of these four cases together to glean more general insights into urban waterfront spaces and their uses, except in the broad-brush sense of comparing the variations and changes in the scale, shape and commercial role of the four ports. The book focuses more on large-scale strategic planning and infrastructure development than on small-scale redesign and management of spaces. The other limitation is that Meyer's histories end in the 1980s, after which significant further changes have occurred along these four cities' waterfronts.

Riverscapes: Designing Urban Embankments (2008), by the foundation Montag Stiftung Urban Räume and Regionale 2010, is a handsome 575-page volume that illustrates and discusses almost 100 different waterfront redevelopment examples from across Western Europe, with a particular focus on the Rhine (39 projects). The examples are meticulously cross-referenced according to three spatial typologies (promenades and public squares, urban quarters and buildings, and parks and landscapes); strategic planning at three spatial scales (region, city, and individual masterplanned projects); and four key functional objectives (new access, 'water adventures', revitalisation, and flood protection). The first two of these objectives – improving connections to rivers and providing direct contact with the water itself – are two of the main themes that also animate this book, particularly in Chapters 1, 4 and 9. Appendices in *Riverscapes* also index its case studies according to 38 rivers, lakes and seas where they are sited, and 81 thematic keywords, from *arts* to *mixed use* to *water quality*. In addition to the case study descriptions, the book includes a 100-page summation of insights from four design workshops involving design experts and stakeholders, which examined the 'Riverscapes on the Rhine'. These focused around four themes: industry, residence, leisure, and the Rhine's specific economic and climatic identity. This section offers impressively varied, detailed and critical analysis. But the bulk of the book remains a catalogue.

Like these two books, my book seeks to combine insights into the architecture, landscape design and physical planning of a range of waterfront examples with a critical examination of a range of social, economic, political and management issues surrounding them. Like Meyer's book, and Dovey's, I aim to give a sense of historical progression (and regression) in the planning and activation of urban waterfront areas, rather than presenting contemporary waterfront masterplans as perfect, finished exemplars of what is currently believed to be good design practice.

This Book's Approach

Malone's (1996) book, one of the first critical studies of urban waterfronts, was in fact developed as an explicit critique of the limitations of Bruttomesso's illustrative, descriptive volume from 1993. My book similarly aims to critique the continued presentation of 'best practice' designs, which rarely acknowledges or examines their limitations and problems, particularly in terms of access, social experience, and management.

Introduction

This book seeks to advance knowledge about urban waterfronts in three ways. Firstly, it aims to bridge between analysis of the processes used to plan and manage waterfronts and analysis of the physical design outcomes. Secondly, I wish to give focussed attention to the ways that people actually use waterfront open spaces once they have been constructed, building on the approaches of Campo (2013) and Jones (2014). Thirdly, I aim to pursue these aims by drawing together insights from across a variety of different kinds of studies of a range of waterfront cases. My approach can, I hope, show better than most existing books on waterfronts how the lessons of individual cases, both positive and negative, might be applied to other waterfronts. Where Marshall's *Waterfronts in Post-industrial Cities* (2001) praises the neo-liberal development approach that created the first wave of new projects, this book focuses more on the ways that waterfronts are subsequently being made into valuable public spaces through their integration with the wider city, informal activities, and their appropriation by broad publics.

This book highlights a range of different approaches to designing, developing and managing urban waterfronts, and the multiplicity of actors who are involved in them. The book also utilises a range of different analytical techniques and theories to study different cases and processes in individual chapters. It draws these together into a larger set of arguments about how waterfronts can be activated with urban life. The analytical methods used here include site analysis at varied scales, material analysis of landscape settings and their components, analysis of waterfront plans and policies, post-occupancy evaluation through behavioural observation, photography and mapping, discourse analysis, in-depth interviews with a range of actors involved in designing and managing waterfront spaces, and experimental design research. Some of the case studies examined in this book, such as Melbourne's Southbank, are explored through several different methods across several chapters. Some methods are used to study and contrast several different cases. This is in line with the book's overarching focus on being critical and comparative, to highlight different ways of examining the design, use and management of waterfronts, and to identifies similarities and differences in the contexts and factors shaping individual examples, and different formal and managerial solutions. That makes this book different from most other books on waterfronts, which either use a uniform approach to briefly document a large number of examples, or a range of theories to understand just one example.

The Book's Structure

This book gathers together a range of detailed case studies of individual waterfront projects, comparisons between cases, and focused studies of specific aspects of waterfront design, management, and use, within two overarching thematic Parts.

Part 1 of the book, *Plugging the waterfront into the city*, explores the challenges of connecting new urban waterfront leisure precincts on formerly-isolated sites to the spaces, flows and life of their surrounding cities, in terms of pedestrian linkages, visibility, the scope of their land uses and activity settings, their atmosphere

Introduction

and symbolism, and the mix of users that they attract. It also examines a matter very often overlooked in both the design and critique of new urban waterfronts: how well, and in what ways, they actually provide connection between the existing city, the waterfront precincts, and the actual water of adjoining rivers, bays and lakes, whether through their interface with adjacent natural watercourses or through artificial landscape designs that shape encounters with water.

Part 2 of the book, *Switching the Waterfront on*, responds to a set of challenges that are highlighted by critiques of new urban waterfront precincts, and most public spaces, as being isolated, overly controlled, socially stratified, uniform, predictable, static and lacking in authentic urban life. This Part explores how new urban waterfront precincts that have been connected to inner city areas can be enlivened by a wide range of formal and informal processes. It presents a range of 'post-industrial' – and to some extent 'post-planning' – models for managing, activating and re-shaping waterfront public spaces and the land uses that surround them. These include informal appropriations, temporary interventions, co-design, programming, and adaptively developing and redeveloping waterfronts over time. These processes involve diverse collectives of entrepreneurs, designers and others from the creative industries, community organizations, and, most importantly, users. These models present a challenge to the conventional approach to waterfront redevelopment, which involves large special-purpose government agencies, large budgets, large permanent buildings and landscapes, long timeframes, and fixed investments, contracts and governance arrangements. As such, the book also presents a wider re-thinking of the formats and processes through which large-scale urban redevelopment can happen. In this context, the book's main intended conceptual and methodological innovation is its focus on the everyday social activities that occur within waterfront spaces. It applies post-occupancy evaluation to examine the diversity of the actual uses and users of completed waterfront projects, as a means to better understand design, and examines the interrelation between long-term physical design and the ongoing, changing management and use of urban spaces.

Plugging the Waterfront into the City

Chapter 1 examines and compares the urban design of three inner-city riverfront cultural and leisure precincts in Melbourne, Brisbane and London, which are all called 'Southbank'. It identifies four key dimensions of leisure experience on these contemporary urban riverfronts: escaping the everyday, mixing with strangers, consuming spectacle, and exploring new forms of bodily activity. The chapter explores the tensions between attempts to carefully manage activities and imagery in these leisure zones, and the messy diversity of everyday life which actually takes place in and around them. It highlights the importance of the waterfronts' orientations to the sun, and of their connections to the wider development and life of their respective cities.

Chapter 2 shows how this kind of global waterfront model has been adopted to project an image of a modern, developed, postcolonial urban lifestyle in Malaysia through three waterfront projects in two cities – Kuala Lumpur, and the new national capital, Putrajaya – where the climatic, economic and urbanistic circumstances are very different. It explores how these waterfront landscapes are intended to contribute to their cities' image, to economic development, and to ecological performance. It evaluates the projects' success by drawing on policy documents, interviews with local policymakers, designers and academics, field observation of social activity, and a mental mapping survey of users' cognitive images of how these precincts fit within people's overall image of the cities. The chapter suggests several waterfront spaces and uses within the three projects that indicate a more authentic local paradigm for urban waterfront development.

Chapter 3 draws upon a large set of individual studies of waterfront redevelopments by other scholars, in 16 cities across 8 countries worldwide. It identifies many commonalities and differences in waterfront change under varying circumstances. The chapter explores the 'where', 'when', and 'who' of waterfront change, and contrasts these against other aspects of waterfronts that remain relatively fixed, lending continuity, stability, connection and resistance. The chapter discusses the wide range of concepts and transdisciplinary methodologies that are used to interpret waterfront transformation, and highlights several distinct directions and questions that these studies suggest for future research. These include the transferability of development approaches between different geographical, climatic, and economic contexts, and the social and environmental impacts of urban redevelopment in waterfront areas.

Chapter 4 closes the first part of the book by shifting attention from the waterfront's connection (or lack of connection) with its surroundings, to the connection between waterfront urban spaces and the actual water. It draws attention to the importance, role and condition of water in these urban settings, and the distinctive physical, sensory experiences that waterfront landscapes can enable. It explores designers' careful geographic, climatological, hydrological and urbanistic shaping of the land/water interface, aiming to optimise consumptive leisure. A range of forms of 'artificial' waterfronts are discussed, including artificial beaches, lagoons, rivers and even indoor waterscapes. This analysis foregrounds four aspects of the artificiality of urban waterfronts: taming the landscape to provide comfort and safety; augmenting the landscape to provide varied sensory stimulation; carefully positioning the waterfront within a wider climatic, thematic and functional context; and managing the temporal dimension of visitor experience.

Switching the Waterfront On

Chapter 5 begins the book's second part by returning to Melbourne's 'Southbank'. It contrasts the contrived spectacle of its signature architecture, corporate headquarters, casino, and fountains with observations on many unplanned and unexpected uses of the waterfront promenade. This highlights that complex uses and meanings can emerge within the spectacular, choreographed landscape, because its design is not seamless and its uses cannot be controlled.

Chapters 6, 7 and 8 all draw on one particular type of artificial waterfront, the 'city beach', to illustrate a wide range of different sets of spaces, actors and actions that can bring urban waterfront areas to life. The artificial beach presents a new kind of open

Introduction

space for urban waterfront areas, as well as several new models for waterfront development and management processes, which all contrast strongly with the traditional 'spectacular', large-scale, big-budget waterfront revitalization approaches that originated in Baltimore in the 1970s and that have been reproduced in Melbourne, Brisbane, Kuala Lumpur, and hundreds of other cities.

Chapter 6 analyses the variations within the city beach approach, in terms of the kinds of sites used, the development contexts, the kinds of material components they are assembled from, their varying physical contents, design approaches, and programming. This chapter closes by identifying two distinct forms of city beach ownership and management which are then examined in Chapters 7 and 8: independent entrepreneurs from the hospitality industry, and local non-profit community groups. This characterization of flexibility and variety among city beaches and their makers highlights a range of broader possibilities for the activation of waterfronts, and for many other kinds of under-utilised urban sites.

Chapter 7's analysis of four European city beaches created by entrepreneurs in Paris, Amsterdam, Bristol and Berlin emphasizes the diverse, complex, highly flexible, temporary networks of people, materials and resources that are combined to produce them. It focuses on the 'soft' content that switches these waterfronts on – their services, programmes, themes, atmosphere – rather than on large, inflexible built forms. The chapter also suggests what new policies, tools and management approaches these kinds of waterfront schemes require.

Chapter 8 focuses on city beaches which have been initiated, designed, produced and operated by local citizens. While these projects look similar to commercial beach bars, the chapter highlights the considerable differences in their social functions and meanings, and how their production processes require even more initiative, learning, and improvisation. The chapter examines how these informal landscaping projects provide opportunities for citizens to become actively engaged in imagining future forms and uses for waterfront spaces, and to be 'hands-on' in physically making, inhabiting and managing them. The chapter also shows how citizen-led city beaches often draw upon formal models that were pioneered by artists and businesspeople, re-performing these models to meet specific social objectives.

Chapter 9 presents another, rather different model for activating waterfronts, by reporting on a temporary design intervention created to investigate various potential ways of prompting people to interact playfully with the actual water, through a range of spatial prototypes and devices. Observations of visitor interactions with this intervention provide insights into users' desires for water engagement, in three respects: people's bodily engagement with the water and the marine life within it, the multiple behavioural affordances of the water's edge, and the adaptability of waterfront spaces. This study indicates the potential of temporary installations to test hypotheses and design possibilities, and thereby inform larger permanent waterfront urban design projects.

The book's Conclusion draws together the diverse waterfront case studies, methodologies, scales of analysis and issues that have been explored across the chapters, to clarify and extend the book's two core organising themes: physically connecting the waterfront to the surrounding city, and activating waterfronts' open spaces. The conclusion explores four inter-related aspects of urban waterfront development that all influence their vitality: visibility and access between waterfronts and other urban activity areas; the fine-scaled design of the interface between the land and water; land uses, amenities and programming that encourage broad, diverse public use; and empowerment of new actors and new forms of collaboration among governments, private landowners and users. This summary identifies a range of potential solutions to the challenges of putting the flat, formerly industrial landscape of urban waterfronts 'on the map', and getting more actors involved in developing, resourcing and managing them.

References

Andersson, T. (ed.) (2017) *Waterfront Promenade Design: Urban Renewal Strategies*, Mulgrave, Australia: The Image Publishing Group.
Breen, A. and Rigby, D. (1994) *Waterfronts: Cities Reclaim their Edge*, New York: McGraw Hill.
Breen, A. and Rigby, D. (1996) *The New Waterfront: A Worldwide Urban Success Story*, London: Thames and Hudson.
Bruttomesso, R. (1993) *Waterfronts: A New Frontier for Cities on Water*, Venice: International Centre 'Cities on Water'.
Campo, D. (2013) *The Accidental Playground: Brooklyn Waterfront Narratives of the Undersigned and Unplanned*, New York: Fordham University Press.
Carta, M. and Ronsivalle, D. (eds) (2016) *The Fluid City Paradigm: Waterfront Regeneration as an Urban Renewal Strategy*, Cham, Switzerland: Springer.
Desfor, G., Laidley, J., Stevens, Q. and Schubert, D. (eds) (2010) Transforming Urban Waterfronts: Fixity and Flow, New York: Routledge.
Dovey, K. (2005) *Fluid City: Transforming Melbourne's Urban Waterfront*, London: Routledge.
Fang, C. (2012) *Waterfront Landscapes*, Shenyang, China: Liaoning Science and Technology Publishing House.
Gastil, R. (2002) *Beyond the Edge: New York's New Waterfront*. New York: Van Alen Institute & Princeton Architectural Press.
Gordon, D. (1997) *Battery Park City: Politics and Planning on the New York Waterfront*, Amsterdam: Gordon and Breach Publishers.
Hoyle, B., Pinder, D. and Husain, M. (Eds) (1988) *Revitalising the Waterfront*, London: Belhaven.
Jones, A. (2014) *On South Bank: The Production of Public Space*, Ashgate: Farnham.
Lefebvre, H. (1996) *Writings on Cities*, Oxford: Blackwell.
Macdonald, E. (2018) *Urban Waterfront Promenades*, London: Routledge.
Malone, P. (ed) (1996) *City, Capital and Water*, London: Routledge.
Marshall, R. (ed) (2001) *Waterfronts in Post-industrial Cities*, London: Spon.
Meyer, H. (1999) *City and Port: Urban Planning as a Cultural Venture in London, Barcelona, New York and Rotterdam*, Utrecht: International Books.
Montag Stiftung Urban Räume and Regionale 2010 (eds.) (2008) *Riverscapes: Designing Urban Embankments*, Birkhäuser: Basel.
Rubin, J. (2016) *A Negotiated Landscape: The Transformation of San Francisco's Waterfront Since 1950*, 2nd edition. Pittsburgh: The University of Pittsburgh Press.
Smith, H. and Ferrari, M. (eds) (2012) *Waterfront Revitalization: Experience in Citybuilding*, London: Routledge.
Stevens, Q. (2007a) *The Ludic City: Exploring the Potential of Public Spaces*, London: Routledge.
Stevens, Q. (2007b) 'Betwixt and Between: Building Thresholds, Liminality and Public Space' in Franck, K. and Stevens, Q. (eds) *Loose Space: Diversity and Possibility in Urban Life*, New York: Routledge, pp. 73–92.

Part I
Plugging the Waterfront into the City

Chapter 1
Three 'Southbanks'

Quentin Stevens

During the last few decades, the waterfront areas of many 'post-industrial' cities in North America, Britain, Europe, Australia and elsewhere have undergone a remarkable transformation. Emerging from industrial degradation and from burial under transportation infrastructure, inner-urban harbours and riverfronts have been reborn as showpiece cultural and leisure precincts (Pinder et.al. 1988; Meyer 1999). This waterfront redevelopment has gone hand-in-hand with a broader renaissance of inner cities after decades of suburban dispersion. Urban waterfronts have become key drawcards for foreign tourists, visitors from the suburbs, and new upmarket residents. They are locus for a variety of cultural institutions, ranging from elitist (concert halls and art galleries) to populist (casinos, movie theatres and aquariums). They provide extensive new areas of high-quality public open space in precisely those parts of the city where land values are highest and social life at its most dense. In their elongated form, they also establish new linkages between existing inner-city areas, intensifying the interconnectedness of urban functions. They have dramatically increased the activity in inner cities during evenings and weekends. The opening up of the urban riverfront has brought about an extensive re-orientation of the entire city, both spatially and behaviourally.

A Common History of Waterfront Regeneration

In London, Melbourne and Brisbane, three former industrial waterfront areas which were all redeveloped into leisure precincts called 'Southbank' each lie on the opposite side of the river to their cities' central activities districts. These Southbanks have historically been relatively poorly connected by transport infrastructure to their north riverbanks. A brief historical introduction reveals the similarities of planning approaches and design in the three cases, as well as differences in the opportunities framed by each context (Figure 1.1).

Three 'Southbanks'

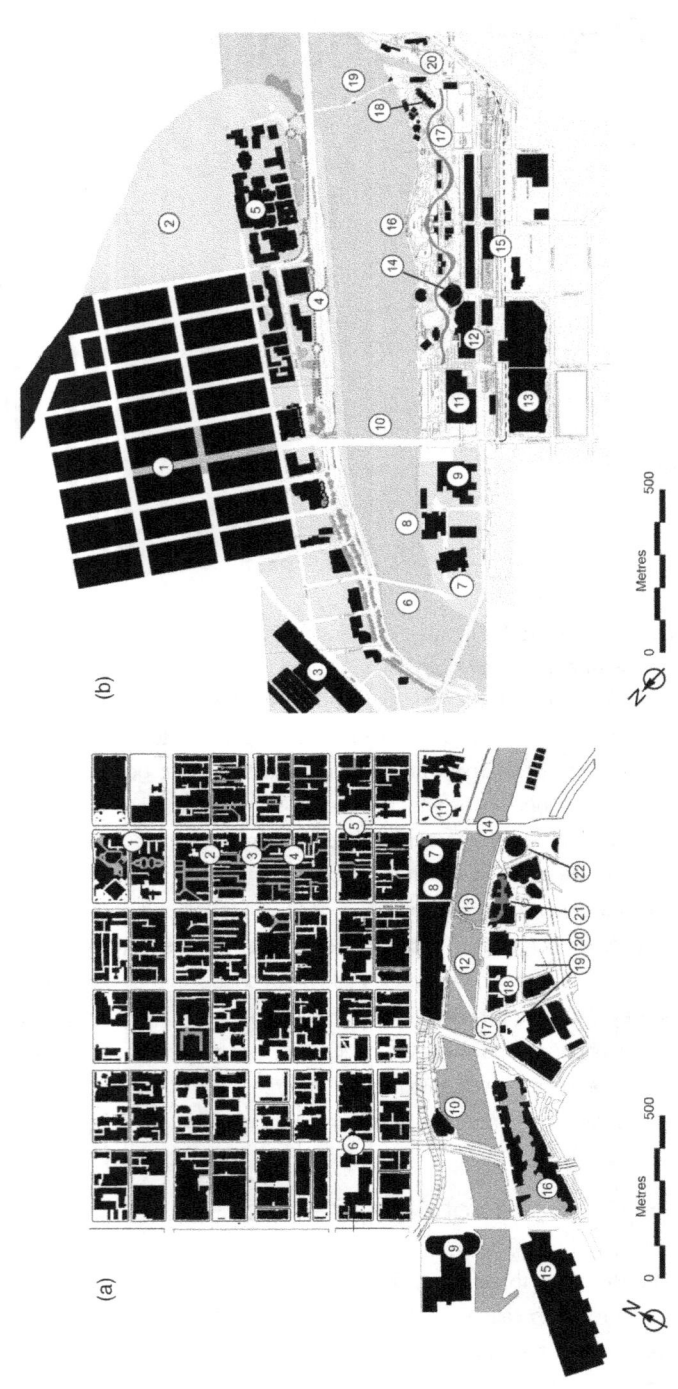

Melbourne
1. Indoor shopping mall with pedestrian through routes 2. Main department stores with pedestrian through routes 3. Bourke St Mall (pedestrianised street block) 4. Numerous mid-block private arcades and public laneways 5. Swanston Walk (transit mall) 6. Kings St nightclub precinct 7. Flinders St Railway Station 8. Pedestrian underpass 9. World Trade Centre 10. Aquarium 11. Federation Square 12. Sandridge Railway Bridge (redeveloped as pedestrian-only) 13. Princes Bridge (vehicular) 14. Princes Bridge (vehicular) 15. Exhibition Centre 16. Casino complex showing internal public circulation areas 17. Queensbridge Square 18. Low-rise office buildings 19. 200-300-metre high apartment towers (under development) 20. Esso Headquarters 21. SouthGate shopping mall 22. Concert Hall (part of Arts Centre complex)

Brisbane
1. Queen St Mall 2. Botanic Gardens 3. Roma St Railway Station 4. Queensland Parliament 5. Queensland University of Technology 6. Kurilpa Bridge (pedestrian only) 7. Gallery of Modern Art 8. State Library 9. Queensland Art Gallery and Museum 10. Victoria Bridge (vehicular) 11. Performing Arts Centre 12. Convention Centre 13. Queensland Conservatorium 14. Suncorp Piazza (roofed amphitheatre) 15. Axis of elevated railway line and dedicated busway 16. Swimming lagoon and artificial beach 17. Energex Arbour 18. Pre-existing apartment complex 19. Goodwill Bridge (pedestrian only) 20. Maritime Museum

Figure 1.1 (*Continued*)

London

1. Trafalgar Square 2. Charing Cross Railway Station 3. Houses of Parliament 4. Westminster Bridge 5. former London County Council offices 6. London Eye observation wheel 7. Jubilee Gardens 8. Shell Centre 9. Hungerford Bridge and Jubilee Bridges 10. South Bank Centre (Festival Hall, Queen Elizabeth Hall and Hayward Gallery) 11. Waterloo Bridge 12. National Theatre 13. Gabriel's Wharf 14. Bernie Spain Gardens 15. OXO Tower 16. Sea Containers House 17. Blackfriars Bridge 18. Tate Modern Gallery 19. Globe Theatre (new) 20. Millennium Bridge (pedestrian only) 21. St Paul's Cathedral 22. Southwark Bridge 23. London Bridge 24. City Hall (Greater London Authority headquarters) 25. Tower Bridge 26. Tower of London

Figure 1.1 Maps of Southbanks in Melbourne (a), Brisbane (b) and London (c) to the same scale, showing their connections to their respective central city areas on the opposite riverbanks.

Source: Quentin Stevens and Ha Thai

Three 'Southbanks'

In London, the Thames River only had its one original crossing point until the Westminster Bridge opened in 1750. The south riverbank, opposite the City, has always been very low-lying, and it was only in the 1860s with the construction of the Albert Embankment that the land here was stabilised and new landfill extended into the width of the river. This neighbourhood, Southwark, had, like many medieval suburbs outside cities' walls, long been a place of noxious industries and 'low' entertainment such as bull rings, bear pits, wrestling and brothels. A theatre district, including the famous Globe Theatre, developed here in the 1580s and '90s to serve the rapid growth of Elizabethan London, burgeoning when seditious theatre was barred from the City (Hall 1998). By the 1800s, an increasing number of bridges and the rapidly increasing number and size of ships and cargoes led to London's port moving downriver, and the South Bank's many warehouses fell into decline (Ball and Sutherland 2001). The 1943 London Plan formally designated the area a cultural precinct. After extensive wartime bombing, many remaining warehouses were demolished for the 1951 Festival of Britain, a large temporary exposition. The remaining Festival Hall was joined in the 1960s by the Brutalist, inward-facing Hayward Gallery and Queen Elizabeth Hall, and numerous new, insular Modernist office buildings monopolised the riverfront (Simões Aelbrecht 2017). The Globe Theatre was rebuilt in 1996 by private investors. The revival in both government and private investment in British cities through the 'Urban Renaissance' agenda of Tony Blair's New Labour (1997–2010) drove extensive re-investment in the Southwark waterfront, including a major refurbishment of the cultural venues in the Southbank Centre, the new Tate Modern art gallery (2000) in the renovated Bankside Power Station, and two new pedestrian bridges in 2002. The Millennium Bridge linked the Tate Modern to St. Paul's Cathedral. Two broad new Jubilee bridges were suspended alongside the Hungerford Bridge that carried trains into Charing Cross Station, replacing very cramped older footbridges.

The Southbank of Melbourne's Yarra River also has a long history of use for leisure functions such as temporary fun parks. In 1964, the state government built a major public art gallery on the south side of the main Princes Bridge which linked the city to its southern suburbs. Beginning in 1982, a new government acquired 100 hectares of land stretching more than 1km along the water's edge and produced a long-term planning framework. The art gallery was expanded into an Arts Centre with a concert hall and theatres by 1984. A museum was planned for the other, western end of the precinct to provide a second anchor for a new 15m-wide publicly-accessible riverfront promenade. The first private investment was a set of medium-rise office buildings on the suburban office-park model. A new pedestrian bridge which linked across to the precinct opened in 1989, followed in 1992 by SouthGate, a shopping, dining and hotel complex backed by two office towers. These two developments started to realise and expand the leisure potential of the area.

Another new government after 1992 brought deregulation of the planning function and more commercially-driven investments on the waterfront from both private and public sectors. The Esso corporate headquarters filled the remaining site in the eastern part of the Southbank in 1995. The partially-built museum to the west was converted and completed in 1996 as the largest exhibition centre in the Asia-Pacific region. The 500m of remaining frontage between the two precincts was filled in 1997 by the Crown Casino, a single 500,000m² building on an eight hectare site, encompassing gaming tables, cinemas, nightclubs, restaurants, shops and a 43-storey hotel tower. A new public square was constructed in the middle of the length of Southbank, as were several apartment towers set back behind the river frontage, the tallest being 200m and 300m high (Sandercock and Dovey 2002; Dovey 2005).

Brisbane's South Bank had previously been the site of the city's wharves, cold storage, fish market, and interstate rail freight terminal. The area contained numerous cheap hotels and boarding houses, as well as live theatres, cinemas, dance halls and nightclubs which made it the city's entertainment quarter. With the wharves falling into disuse during the 1960s, the State Government of Queensland first began large-scale redevelopment of the area in 1977 with plans for a multi-venue Cultural Centre at the south end of the Victoria Bridge connection to the Central Business District (CBD), and the reclamation of 1.9 hectares of the river. The first stage, the Queensland Art Gallery, was completed in 1982, with the Queensland Museum, State Library and Performing Arts Centre all finished by the mid-1980s. These brutalist buildings are all by the same architect, Robin Gibson, and are linked by elevated pedestrian concourses. A small privately-run maritime museum had opened on a disused wharf approximately 1.5km south along the riverfront in 1979 (Longhurst 1992; Fagence 1995; Mullins et.al. 1999).

In 1983 Brisbane was awarded the right to host the 1988 World Expo, the year of Australia's bicentennial celebrations, and legislation was passed to acquire a 500m-wide strip of derelict riverfront between the Cultural Centre and the Maritime Museum to use as the Expo site. These 16 hectares were raised above the 100-year floodplain (Craik 1992; Fagence 1995; Mules 1998). After Expo, a 1989 Act of Parliament created a public corporation for redevelopment of the site as public parklands, plus 27 hectares of surrounding land for a mixture of commercial and residential uses. An approved development plan was gazetted in 1990, and a new public riverfront park, which incorporated a rainforest and an artificial beach at the edge of a freshwater swimming 'lagoon', was opened in 1992. Apartments, a convention and exhibition centre and associated hotels were completed during the mid 1990s (Queensland Government 1990; Mules 1998; Mullins et.al. 1999). A new pedestrian bridge connecting the south end of the South Bank precinct to the CBD was opened in 2001 at a cost of AUD $35 million (Wanna 2001). The Queensland Gallery of Modern Art, at the north end of the Cultural Centre, was opened late 2006, and another pedestrian bridge was designed to connect this end of South Bank to the CBD and to redevelopment of the north bank opposite (Department of Public Works 2005). The South Bank Parklands currently attract more than 5 million visitors each year (Mullins et. al. 1999).

These three case studies follow a typical pattern where decades of disinvestment and the undesirable image of remaining land uses had lowered waterfront property values, creating opportunities for government intervention, large-scale recapitalisation and speculative gain. Yet this success was only possible because of a much broader shift in value: people became newly attracted to the city centre and to the water's edge. The question of what makes inner-urban waterfronts special, valuable sites for public leisure is the focus of this chapter. Answers focus on the potential which such sites provide for a range of experience and leisure behaviour.

Three 'Southbanks'

Table 1.1 Five key stratagems for the successful planning and design of urban waterfronts

- Improving image and imageability
- Learning from what exists and adaptively re-using existing built form
- Improving public accessibility and connectivity, integrating waterfronts with their urban surroundings and with the water
- Thinking small and planning in increments
- Coordinating public and private investments in order to create a coherent urban environment which maximises value (rather than internalised 'malling')

Source: Gordon (1996), drawing on Eckstut (1986).

Gordon (1996) suggests a number of key stratagems for the successful planning and design of urban waterfronts (see Table 1.1). The last four of the five issues Gordon presents all speak to a concern with the creation of an inclusive social leisure environment, a place where different people and activities can come together and mix. The first three of the listed issues highlight the strong emphasis on visual quality and legibility, which is a product of the high visibility of waterfront sites, their commonly degraded appearance, and the wider 'thematisation' of urban leisure environments (Sorkin 1992; Loukaitou-Sideris and Banerjee 1998). These two larger themes – leisure space as urban diversity and leisure space as image – form the focus of the current analysis.

Gordon highlights the importance for all investors in waterfronts of having design guidelines which ensure high quality. However, questions remain as to what can actually provide the measure for design quality. This chapter attempts to provide a framework for considering quality in urban waterfront redevelopment which is both informed by a robust theory of leisure behaviour and linked to the study of the actual everyday function, sensory experience and use of waterfront spaces. The chapter seeks to identify how the pursuit of the design objectives listed above give shape to the scope of people's leisure behaviour 'on the ground' in urban waterfront precincts.

Dodson and Kilian (1998) move the critique of waterfronts beyond their simplistic depiction as spectacularised theme parks (Harvey 1989; Sorkin 1992) to examine the proposition that urban waterfronts are in fact contested 'sites of control and resistance', where consumers (sic) are actively involved in the ongoing production of the meaning of place, bringing with them different identities, values, perceptions and practices (Dodson and Kilian 1998, 156). They find that visitors are drawn to the urban waterfront chiefly because of the diversity of other people and experiences on offer, and they critique the frequent use of design, marketing and management to achieve racial and class exclusivity. They note some users' resistance to the consumption orientation of the waterfront, through such activities as protest marches which are 'antithetical to the purposes of the designers' (Dodson and Kilian 1998, 160). Unfortunately, Dodson and Kilian's own data is limited to a visitor survey conducted by the Cape Town waterfront's managers and newspaper reports, and provides few specifics about environment-behaviour relations.

Relatively little research on waterfront leisure precincts has involved going down to these sites and observing how various groups of people actually use them, particularly during the times when there are no scheduled events to stimulate activity, and trying to understand how design characteristics of the waterfront leisure landscape shape and support perceptions and behaviour. This chapter seeks to identify some of the critical behavioural issues which can inform research and, in turn, future design and management decisions.

Passive and Active Leisure Experience on Urban Waterfronts

This chapter pursues a structured examination of the physical conditions, behaviour and imagery of urban leisure precincts, using a comparison between the inner-urban riverfronts of London and two of Australia's largest cities, Melbourne and Brisbane, all three of which are called 'Southbank'. The aim is to analyse how the design characteristics of these urban precincts serve different leisure patterns and practices, both intended and unintended. The study starts from a definition of urban leisure drawn in the first instance from Lefebvre (1991, 1996), and developed through sociological and anthropological literature. This dialectical definition of urban leisure experience draws together four key aspects of the relation between behaviour and space.

Table 1.2 shows the four aspects of environmental experience which form the focus of this study. The first column identifies the two broad dimensions of urban leisure experience under investigation: firstly, the experience of a novelty and variety of settings and people, and secondly exposure, whether visual or bodily. The horizontal axis differentiates people's levels of engagement. The two passive modes of difference and staging are the generally expected condition of the global waterfront model. But leisure waterfronts are not just places of escape, relaxation and consumption. Following Dodson and Kilian (1998), the chapter attempts to illustrate more complex and active experience, and to explore how people's various passive and active leisure activities continue to develop over time through their spatial confrontations and combinations. Table 1.3 shows the theoretical sources of the four factors under investigation, as well

Table 1.2 Four environmental experiences of leisure: their dialectical tensions

Dimension of urban leisure experience	Passive experience	Active experience	Dialectical tension between passive and active forms of experience
Difference	ESCAPE FROM THE EVERYDAY	MIXING WITH STRANGERS	Escape vs Contact
Staging	CONSUMING SPECTACLE	EXPLORATORY FORMS OF BODILY ACTION	Watching vs Doing

Three 'Southbanks'

Table 1.3 Four environmental experiences of leisure: theoretical sources and spatialisation on the urban riverfront

Environmental experience of leisure	Origin in broader theories of leisure and urbanity	Sources	Spatial context of the urban riverfront
ESCAPE FROM THE EVERYDAY	The theory of play as existing in a 'world apart'	Huizinga (1970) Lyman and Scott (1975) Cohen and Taylor (1976)	Across the river
MIXING WITH STRANGERS	Theories of behaviour in public space	Goffman (1963) Sennett (1971) Lofland 1998	Pools (of uses) and Flows (of people)
CONSUMING SPECTACLE	'The society of the spectacle', city as theme park	Sorkin (1992) Debord (1994) Dodson and Kilian (1998)	The riverbank stage
EXPLORING LANDSCAPE THROUGH THE BODY	Theorisation of the forms and objectives of play	Caillois (1961) Borden (2001)	On the edge

as providing a general conceptualisation of their particular spatial manifestation in the context of urban riverfront precincts. These spatial concepts provide the organisation for the analysis of the three case studies which follows.

The hypothesis is that such urban leisure environments, though 'global' in their inspiration and objectives (Sandercock and Dovey 2002), can provide a wide variety of different kinds of leisure opportunities for different users; some opportunities are commonly and intentionally well served by the design of waterfront precincts, other activities can be supported if appropriate design approaches are employed (although they not always are), whilst still other activities occur despite poor design, despite designer's and managers attempts to prevent them, or indeed because of poor design. The chapter draws upon two sets of empirical findings. Semi-structured behavioural observations of the four kinds of leisure activities outlined in Tables 1.2 and 1.3 provide a focused opportunity sample which is the basis for an evaluation of how the three study sites allow or facilitate those behavioural outcomes. Secondly, evaluation of the planning and design of the sites themselves against the theorisation of leisure, as well as mainstream urban design thinking about how public space functions generally, is the basis for an analysis of what leisure-related perceptions and experiences are enabled or prevented by design factors such as patterns of land uses, urban morphology, the pedestrian network and solar orientation. Both kinds of data aid in understanding the environmental affordances (Gibson 1979) which are presented by these spaces, for human action as well as for visual perception.

Across the River

The most elementary organising principle which defines these three urban riverfront leisure precincts is that the river separates them from their city's central business district. 'Southbank' is thus a distinctive typology among redeveloped waterfronts, with a somewhat different image and function than 'Docklands'.

In these three cities, the concentration of urban uses into one main central district on one side of the river has led to the riverbank opposite becoming defined as a 'place apart' (Huizinga 1970) for functions not desired or permitted in the city centre. The spatial separation of the river enables an escape from everyday experiences, from roles and rules which are institutionalised in work settings. One could speak of a 'social geology', with governance and business taking the high, solid (moral) ground on one bank, and other functions left low in the swamp opposite. In the case of Brisbane's South Bank, 'other' functions meant industry, port and trading facilities (with their transient population), as well as the local Aborigines (Noble 2001). It is perhaps no coincidence that the boundary of exclusion for Brisbane's non-white population, West End's Boundary Street, became the centre of the city's most vibrant community, enlivened even today by a fine-grained interplay of traditional and migrant cultures; the edge which joins being more robust than that which separates.

Like noxious industry, many forms of leisure have in history been banished *extra muros*, or escaped there to secure their own freedom of operation (Kostof 1992). Leisure presents problems for the urban mix which require spatial management; it is by its nature a diverse, inclusive, messy 'function'; it often has a transgressive mien, sometimes even with overtones of vice (Goodale and Godbey 1988; Lefebvre 1991). It does not sit easily with the notions of order and predictability which govern planning. Time and space for leisure, particularly in protestant cultures, has always been an uncertain virtue, and it is thus safer to isolate it from serious activity.

The physical juxtaposition of work and leisure does much to enliven the potential of the waterfront, in both pragmatic and experiential terms. This is particularly clear in both London and Melbourne, where the nearby Southbanks are destinations for a high volume of people who empty out of the city's office precincts on weekday evenings. In London, as noted, this linking of work and authority in the City with the pleasure venues of the South Bank has a very long history.

The distinctiveness of the character of the opposite riverbank has been compromised in the redevelopment of Melbourne Southbank, in its first stage because government plans promoted office development, and also later as government policy reoriented the city to centre on its river (Dovey 2005), spreading the CBD into the wider Southbank area beyond the water's edge. Though now mixed-use, Melbourne's Southbank retains a sense of difference to the city centre through its relatively new architecture and open space design, its primary leisure focus, and its planned and accessible water frontage, which contrasts to the main railway station's platforms which dominate the north embankment. The distinction is more easily preserved in the case of Brisbane, which has a less-densely built-up city centre (Fagence 1995b), a much wider river, a much larger riverfront site under public management, and a conscious aim of maintaining its park-like character, which is significant to the popular tourist image of Brisbane (Macarthur 1999).

Jan Gehl rates the eastern half of Melbourne's Southbank Promenade highest amongst ten of the city centre's main public spaces, in terms of environmental conditions which enhance the prospects for people to spend their free time there (Gehl and City of Melbourne 1994). The precinct gets his highest rating for shelter from wind, noise, pollution and traffic, exposure to sunshine, and quality of view (i.e. across to the city skyline): in summary, all conditions which arise through its separation from the city. Being in the Southern Hemisphere, Melbourne's and Brisbane's Southbanks have the virtue of superior solar exposure. London's South Bank suffers by comparison because in the Northern Hemisphere, at a relatively high latitude, this embankment receives less sunshine, a problem exacerbated by that South Bank's very tall and rectilinear industrial and Brutalist buildings, many of which overshadow the water's edge.

It would be tempting to believe that difference to and segregation from the working city helps sustain a vital leisure zone. Yet a further criterion in his list is that high-quality spaces have lively edges. Gehl also distinguishes between 'necessary' and 'optional' activities, and 'resultant' social activities which evolve out of these two categories, 'occur(ing) spontaneously as a direct consequence of people moving about and being in the same spaces' (Gehl 1987, 11–16). In this context, unplanned and informal leisure activities in public spaces such as waterfronts are in part prompted by the closeness of their juxtaposition with planned activities, both work and leisure. This leads to the question of how else waterfront precincts might link in with other inner-city activity, functionally, temporally and spatially.

The second factor which shapes the range and type of leisure activities which occur on these three inner-urban riverfronts is their potential for facilitating the mixing together of strangers, whether passive or active (Lofland 1998). This will be examined at two scales: the pools of uses which exist within the precincts (Jacobs 1961) and the flows of people who move into and through the riverfront from other areas (see Table 1.3).

Pools of Use

Whilst the separation of the Southbank from the everyday, serious space of the city centre helps to give it a special atmosphere, leisure theory suggests that the diversity and vitality of each participant's leisure experience can be enhanced by adopting a more inclusive notion of leisure activity (Rojek 1995; Lefebvre 1991) and by design solutions which connect and interweave various activity sites within the precinct. Urban leisure precincts, by their very nature, have typically been places of reduced social stratification, where high and low, refined and base enjoyments mix together. Perhaps the greatest functional potential of urban leisure waterfronts is indicated by their capacity to embrace both high culture and low culture: the definition of 'free time' which they support is itself loose and inclusive. They can be spaces where rock concerts, art galleries, opera and waterskiing contests exist side-by-side.

The openness of Brisbane's South Bank is in part due to its low density and soft landscaping. Its loose park-like setting weaves together numerous different zones

Figure 1.2 Interface between riverfront promenade and edge of free public swimming pool, Brisbane South Bank.

and facilities, framing opportunities for interactions between people pursuing a wide range of activities, both passive and active; commercial and free; solitary and group. Picnic shelters with public barbecues are wedged between an artificial beach with a free public swimming pool and a riverside promenade which permits cycling and skating. The pool is built to enable eye-level interaction between swimmers and passers-by, and steps and a sittable edge leads up from the promenade (Figure 1.2), often encouraging a spontaneous dip.

Public investments at South Bank Brisbane, including lockers and free showers, enhance the prospects for free public enjoyment by people of varied backgrounds and interests, in forms of their own choosing. The success of the approach can be gauged from extended family gatherings who utilise the barbeque areas near the pool (Figure 1.3). Children play nearby on sand or in the water and interact with other children; women supervise, chatting and preparing lunch whilst men play rugby football in the pool nearby. Such users are typically large working-class minorities from the suburbs, a demographic for whom inner-urban waterfront housing is unattainable. The setting provides a rare opportunity to participate in the public leisure life of the inner city. They bring cold-storage boxes filled with food and drink; costs are minimised. Such users may never purchase items on-site or visit paid entertainments like the theatre or even the (free) cultural venues like the Art Gallery. Many international tourists come merely to swim or lie in the sun and watch the passing show. Unlike managed theme parks, the design of South Bank does not segregate a particular stratum of audiences and performers; quite the opposite.

Three 'Southbanks'

Figure 1.3 Family using barbecue shelter adjacent to swimming pool, Brisbane South Bank.

Source: Photomontage

In London, potential for diversity of uses and users on the South Bank has been preserved by the area's long and piecemeal history of development and destruction. This has left numerous 'loose spaces' between the large-scale buildings, which people can appropriate for a wide range of informal leisure (Franck and Stevens 2007). These spaces include the dark, reverberating undercroft of the elevated Queen Elizabeth Hall. Its smooth, sloping concrete surfaces, designed to be uninviting and unusable, has been permanently appropriated by skateboarders who do tricks that explore the challenging terrain (Figure 1.4). For the skaters, the very public nature of this skate-spot, in the

Figure 1.4 Skateboarders using the undercroft of the Queen Elizabeth Hall, London South Bank.

Quentin Stevens

Figure 1.5 Gabriel's Wharf, London South Bank.

midst of other leisure-seekers, is part of its attraction and value, something lacking in planned, out-of-the-way skate parks (Jones 2014). A similar opportunity for public expression is illustrated in the treatment of the undercroft's blank walls with graffiti. A second leftover space nearby is Jubilee Gardens, the former site of the Festival of Britain, which lay vacant and undeveloped with a simple cover of grass from 1977 until its redesign in 2012. Further east is Gabriel's Wharf (Figure 1.5), a 'pop-up' market of independent restaurants and art stores that occupy a row of old car garages. It was initiated in 1988, presaging the wider redevelopment of the South Bank. Next to this lies Bernie Spain Gardens, a park that replaced derelict warehouses demolished in the 1980s.

The wide riverfront promenade along London's South Bank provides the dense inner city with breathing space and an atmosphere of openness. There is, similarly, much un-programmed space around the Tate Modern, which was closed off when it was a power station. Additionally, the buildings of the formal cultural venues on London's Southbank Centre have been renovated to make their facades more transparent and accessible, to better connect their internal circulation with the surrounding public realm, and to introduce a wider range of commercial and public amenities that are active at different times. The previously blank spaces around the Brutalist buildings have been enlivened with a range of temporary installations that encourage active participation, softening up the concrete landscape, making it more sensuous (Simões Aelbrecht 2017). All along the London South Bank, the undercroft spaces under the many road and rail bridges provide shelter from the sun and rain and good acoustics, supporting a wide range of uses, including many that are informal and unofficial.

London's riverfront spaces are, then, not monopolized by high-end commercial activities. It benefits from two approaches: conscious planning for diversity, and significant underdeveloped areas which allow diversity to flourish. It mixes high and low culture, and commercial and free forms of leisure. These diverse amenities along London's South Bank are fed by dense flows of pedestrians, from numerous major railway stations nearby and by the density of residential and commercial areas surrounding it.

Melbourne's Southbank promenade is rather more rigid than Brisbane's and London's in both form and content. Gehl rates the natural advantages of the site very highly, and notes a large number of both formal and informal, secondary places to sit, such as low walls. These extend people's visits, and hence the likelihood of them becoming involved in optional and resultant (social) activities (Gehl and City of Melbourne 1994, Wang and Stevens 2020). However, much of the landscaping is quite hard and formal, promoting only promenading and relatively short rest breaks. There is a shortage of comfortable places to settle in and spend time in the public realm. High levels of patron amenity inside the buildings which face the river comes at a price: In the SouthGate shopping centre, the various floors offer a selection of eating opportunities, ranging from cheap take-away counters on the ground floor to elegant restaurants on the second. Such stratification mitigates against social mixing.

The long bulks of the casino and the exhibition centre at the west end of Melbourne's Southbank prohibit the flourishing of truly urban diversity. At the east end of the Southbank precinct, however, building footprints are much smaller in scale; similar in fact to the Melbourne CBD's block structure with its network of pedestrian laneways. Management of public circulation space and of building tenancy is also at a smaller scale. The piecemeal, incremental development of this older part of the precinct, and the inclusion of some land uses along the waterfront which aren't very public, including corporate offices, leave a variety of 'loose' spaces, particular during evenings and weekends when Southbank is at its busiest.

Members of the public and informal performers can, at their leisure, appropriate such riverfront sites because they are free from control by retail businesses. It is easy to introduce new uses into the leisure mix, because there are places where none have been prescribed, including loading docks, closed entrances, the superstructure of bridges and perpendicular laneways. Alongside its commercial offerings – in fact between them – Melbourne Southbank provides pools of 'not use'. The creative uses of these leftover spaces will be discussed in Chapter 5.

Brisbane's, London's and Melbourne's Southbanks thus provide contrasting approaches to social inclusiveness: in the first through consciously planned social space and the ample provision of basic comforts and amenities, in the last through under programming, and in London due to the rich mixing of both.

Flows of People

The diversity of users and uses which can be experienced on urban riverfronts, and the functional integration of riverfronts with surrounding areas, can both be served by enhancing connectivity and permeability. Whilst waterfronts may be drawcards in themselves, they are also, like all urban districts, secondary destinations within other orbits of activity. They can sustain a greater diversity within themselves when they optimise their interactions with surrounding attractions and market catchments. Four distinct elements of connectivity are discussed below: building bridges to connect the Southbank to the CBD; the design of those bridges; the continuity of riverfront paths through the precincts; and connection of the Southbank to the wider neighbourhood surrounding it.

Flows 1: New Links to the City Centre

The relation between the leisure waterfront and the CBD opposite is clearly a significant factor. The city centre can be considered a very large shopping mall: primary attractions are located at the extremities of the viable pedestrian realm and at key nodes; these various primary uses provide flows of people at different times which makes smaller-scale secondary facilities between them viable (Jacobs 1961). In a shopping mall these intervening uses are invariably shops. In outdoor public settings, they may also include open spaces for unregimented activity, community facilities (like barbecues), unofficial art installations and performance spaces which do not by themselves have guaranteed audience pulling power.

In Melbourne's CBD, the core pedestrian circuit links through numerous arcades and laneways between the Bourke Street Mall, with its major department stores, and Flinders Street Railway Station (Figure 1.1). This was extended by the construction of a new pedestrian bridge early in the redevelopment of Southbank, forming an additional loop beyond the station, across the river to the Victorian Arts Centre, the SouthGate shopping mall, the casino and Melbourne Exhibition Centre. The shops and cinemas of Southgate and the casino were an essential element of the successful malling of the city centre (Crawford 1992). These primary attractors at each end of Southbank also allow the riverfront to itself function much like the dumb-bell of a shopping mall, drawing pedestrians along the promenade (Sandercock and Dovey 2002).

The new pedestrian bridge split the first phase of the waterfront redevelopment into 300m and 350m sections and linked them across to the CBD's major north-south shopping streets, Elizabeth and Swanston. Southbank Promenade lies approximately 200m beyond the CBD edge at Flinders Street, which it parallels. This stretch of Southbank is thus effectively scaled as a two-by-one-block extension of the Melbourne CBD's 200m standard block pattern. The later western section of the promenade, in front of the impermeable casino, is also split by King Street into 200m and 300m blocks. The near end of King Street is the city's traditional nightclub strip, and newer venues inside the casino complex have thus effectively extended this pre-existing precinct.

Garreau (1992) notes that mall shoppers in America will willingly walk no more than 200m. He suggests a pleasant and attractive walking environment may increase the maximum to 500m. Lynch and Hack (1985) note that recreation planning standards require a major open space to be located within 500m of home: ten minutes' walk at a comfortable, leisurely pace. Transit Oriented Development similarly aims to locate a mix of land uses and open spaces within a 600m radius (Calthorpe 1993). Melbourne's Southbank illustrates a similar achievement for a retail and office area, its strategic new bridges provide a model for integrating new large-scale special-use precincts into existing pedestrian-scaled urban areas.

Three 'Southbanks'

In London, the Millennium Bridge, opened in 2002, halved the 700m distance between the existing pedestrian river crossing points at the Blackfriars and Southwark Bridges. It thereby reduced from 1300m to 600m the total walking distance between two major tourist attractions, St. Paul's Cathedral and the Tate Modern gallery – now on a wide, safe pedestrian-only pathway with low railings and spectacular views across the river, up the river, and down it to the iconic Tower Bridge and the skyscrapers of Canary Wharf. The new Jubilee Bridges, located 450m west of Waterloo Bridge and 600m east of Westminster Bridge, similarly reduce from 1200m to 800m the walking distance between the cultural amenities of the South Bank and those of Trafalgar Square and London's West End. The walking is both shorter and more enjoyable.

In Brisbane, the task is more difficult. The separation between the city's core retail area and the South Bank is greater (300m across the river, as with London, and a further 100m to the start of the Queen Street Mall). The pedestrian path connecting across the Victoria Bridge is of limited width and quality due to heavy vehicular traffic. CBD block dimensions are far narrower in the direction facing the river, at only 100m (Siksna 1998). The zone of highest CBD pedestrian activity stretches away from the river, and is concentrated across only two blocks of river frontage, 100m either side of the axis of the Victoria Bridge and the Queen Street Mall beyond it. The two precincts thus only have one point of linkage; their circulation patterns are effectively connected end-to-end.

An extremely large new pedestrian bridge was built at the far south-east end of Brisbane's South Bank in 2001. 'Together with Victoria Bridge to the north, (this) Goodwill Bridge encloses South Bank Parklands in a circuit' (Musgrave 2002). However, the minimum walking distance between the bridges along Brisbane's South Bank is 1100m. The bridge itself stretches 450m, and the total loop is thus over 3km. The north bank pathway has poor pedestrian amenity and safety and few facilities, and lies buried at the bottom of a long steep embankment beneath the Riverside Expressway. In 2006, a new Gallery of Modern Art was built at the north-west end of the South Bank Cultural Centre. The 470m-long Kurilpa pedestrian bridge was constructed nearby in 2009, 450m north-west of the Victoria Bridge. It connects this end of the South Bank to the north end of Brisbane's CBD and its inter-city railway station at Roma Street. The Kurilpa Bridge has a distinctive, complex structure composed of 36 angled steel masts and almost 7km of tensile steel cables.

Enhancing connectivity does not in itself necessarily increase the functional interaction of the city and the opposite riverfront. Primary attractions are needed, to draw people back and forth along all sections of the pathway system. The two established foci of the Queen Street Mall and Cultural Centre need to be complemented with further nodes toward the eastern end of the dumb-bell, so that the path is occupied by those who stroll, and not only by joggers and walkers out for strenuous exercise.

Flows 2: The Design of New Cross-River Links

New bridges can clearly enhance urban permeability, but flows of pedestrians will only shift if these new connections become part of users' image of the city (Lynch 1961) and are easy to use. Fundamental problems persist for both Melbourne's and Brisbane's Southbanks in their legibility and accessibility from their city centres. Although both precincts provide wide, dramatic views back to their respective cities (which heightens the sense of escape promoted by their leisure function), neither Southbank is easily seen from its CBD. The design of the connections between new bridges and the riverbanks also presents difficulties.

In Melbourne, two landmark office towers which form a backdrop to the SouthGate complex are visible from the major CBD shopping precinct along Elizabeth Street: a signal that this urban axis continues beyond the intervening barrier of Flinders Street Railway Station. The station's subway entry also forms a link through to Southbank, but this is neither obvious nor clearly marked, and the path is narrow, compromised also through its mixing with hordes of commuters. From this subway, one emerges suddenly on the north bank of the Yarra River at a panoramic viewing point. From here on, the journey to the other side has a sense of drama. A wide pedestrian bridge arches across to Southbank Promenade (Dovey 2005). The relative narrowness of Melbourne's River and a long history of low bridge clearances has allowed this new bridge to have low springing points. It opens directly onto the promenade at a wide junction which provides a natural social meeting point.

In Brisbane, the south end of the Queen Street Mall, approaching the river, terminates awkwardly at the blank portal of the bus tunnel running below it and a wide road intersection (Figure 1.6). Whilst the bulk of the Performing Arts Centre can be glimpsed ahead across the river, the angle of the Victoria Bridge itself reduces the legibility of the pedestrian circulation. A sufficiently broad and direct pedestrian pathway which could itself draw people across the river and '(add) to the anticipation' (Jinnai 1995, 98) is

Figure 1.6 Poor visibility and obstructed access to South Bank, Brisbane from end of Queen Street pedestrian mall (foreground).

Three 'Southbanks'

Figure 1.7 Kurilpa Bridge, Brisbane.

Source: Image by Kgbo – https://creativecommons.org/licenses/by-sa/4.0/deed.en

sacrificed in the name of facilitating complex vehicular movements. The more recent pedestrian Kurilpa Bridge provides a much clearer link; its canopied pathway extends 150m inland, over the northern riverbank's expressway, to connect directly at-grade onto an existing city centre footpath and bike lane (Figure 1.7).

London's Jubilee Bridges are suspended from rows of tall structural pylons that make the bridges both highly visible and memorable. Like Melbourne's pedestrian bridge, they also connect directly into a major railway terminus. Their generous scale and views make them natural stopping and meeting places. They are wide enough for buskers, hawkers (often illegal), for tourists to take photos, even for sitting on. The Millennium Bridge connects directly onto a new, extended pedestrian link which is aligned between the 111m-high dome of St. Paul's and the 99m-high chimney of the Tate Modern gallery. More than just being functional paths, these new bridges are visible, attractive landscapes and landmarks in themselves.

Also particularly difficult is the design of junctions between pre-existing bridges and the waterfront path systems of these precincts. High bridgeheads on the CBD side of the major roadways leading to each of the Australian Southbanks (Victoria Bridge in Brisbane, Princes Bridge in Melbourne) are at-grade, allowing a smooth transition out of the city. However, the waterfront promenades themselves are considerably lower, in the order of ten to 15 metres, and earlier road bridges passed high above both the water and the riverfront industrial area, their primary function being to enhance metropolitan-scale connectivity. There are benefits to this disjuncture. It enhances the sense of separation from everyday urban space. More pragmatically, it allows for continuity of the riverfront path underneath the road. However, the critical vertical connections down to the water are in all cases indirect, indistinct, and of insufficient width, particularly given the mix of pedestrian and bicycle traffic they must handle. Such slow points and junctions are natural stopping and meeting places; as such they should be of generous dimensions, whereas in fact they are far narrower than the promenades.

Brisbane's new pedestrian Goodwill Bridge skilfully negotiates a complexity of clearances and level changes defined by the existing transport network to create a new linkage. However, its great height and existing private property ownership has led to a bridgehead on the south side which is well over 100m inland and separated more than 300m from the South Bank precinct by the bulk of an apartment complex. This layout compromises the central objective of looping the riverfront path. As Garreau (1992, 464) argued, with such a distended experience, 'there is a significant chance that (pedestrians) will say forget the whole thing and go home'. The bridge spills out onto a large empty plaza which leads away from the South Bank precinct. The entry to the Maritime Museum, which predates the Expo '88 development, is located back and underneath the bridge, but with this alone there are too few adjacent attractions to animate the node. Whilst 40,000 persons per week use the new Goodwill Bridge (Hazel and Parry 2004), the links which it does most to improve are those between the South Brisbane neighbourhood, the Queensland University of Technology campus and the Botanical Gardens. Whilst the need to enhance the connectivity to and from the South Bank promenade may have been a major impetus for the bridge's construction, this has perhaps not been its major benefit.

London's cross-river links also show the difficulties of making horizontal and vertical pedestrian connections deeper into the urban fabric. The northern Thames embankment slopes significantly, and London's South Bank is a very low-lying terrain. As in Brisbane, bridges that have to be high enough to allow river traffic therefore have to extend far inland from the river on viaducts, in some cases several hundred metres, in order to link up to ground-level streets, and its numerous bridges and elevated causeways thus all have to have complex connections down to the riverside level, which take up scarce and valuable pedestrian space, and which are sometimes cramped and hard to find. These key transition points are often congested by clusters of tourists taking cross-river photographs. The wide, straight, open staircases linking the Jubilee Bridges to London's South Bank show a generosity and elegance in pedestrian infrastructure which is all too rare (Figure 1.8).

Flows 3: Longitudinal Pathways

The sheer scale of the pedestrian loop on the Brisbane riverfront presents a near intractable problem. This suggests the desirability of paying greater attention to internal matters of circulation, grain size and scope of use. The new Energex Arbour (Figure 1.9) is in many ways a step in the right direction. The first real destination attraction on South Bank, the artificial beach, lies about 500m beyond the new Goodwill Bridge. The Arbour is a necessary wayfinding device to lead pedestrians around the obstructing apartment complex and back onto the main pathway of the leisure precinct itself. Whilst its winding form adds further to the walking distance, this is artfully disguised by bending the path

Three 'Southbanks'

Figure 1.8 Staircase connecting Golden Jubilee Bridge to South Bank, London.

Figure 1.9 Energex Arbour, Brisbane South Bank.

around buildings and by screening with bougainvillea. The Arbour links together the precincts' numerous attractions, also framing a range of viewpoints and trajectories and opening up future development sites which did not previously have much exposure.

The piecemeal development and redevelopment of London's South Bank has generated a broad mix of building sizes, style and uses, although there are still a significant number of post-war office buildings with dead, inaccessible frontage onto the river, and several buildings that stand right on the water's edge, with either no or very indirect pedestrian access along the waterfront. The precinct's piecemeal character and the many bridges passing over the waterfront pathway also mean that it lacks continuity and consistency. As a public space, it is very fragmentary.

In Melbourne, the redevelopment of Southbank was based on maintaining a continuous, high-quality 14m-wide public waterfront promenade for its full length (City of Melbourne 1997). Problems relate to the land use pattern fronting onto this pathway, particularly later phases of development further downstream. The Crown Casino complex lacks any public control over the mix of uses, whilst the Melbourne Exhibition Centre is a monofunctional, access-controlled space. Each building occupies 500m of frontage (City of Melbourne 1997; Sandercock and Dovey 2002). As with all urban streets, the most fundamental threat to pedestrian vitality on the waterfront is the permitted maximum frontage given over to a single use and sole management (Gehl and City of Melbourne, 1994) – essentially the monopolisation of spatial experience within what is supposed to be a public realm. Eckstut (1986) argues for the need to design waterfronts on the same principles as inner-urban streets, as coherent, mixed-use pedestrian environments. As Jacobs (1961) noted, small scale blocks and a fine-grained mixing of primary and secondary uses are both necessary to maintain vitality; flows of people and pools of uses mutually underpin each other.

Flows 4: Beyond the Riverfront

In addition to studying the relation of riverfront precinct to the city, we need to critically examine its other edges and links. At both Melbourne's and Brisbane's Southbanks, buildings are quite sensibly scaled down toward the water's edge, ensuring solar penetration to waterfront promenades and to Brisbane's artificial beach. Less thought seems given to the importance of the reverse view, back away from the waterfront and through to other neighbourhoods, and whether here too scale and permeability might be important factors affecting both legibility and vitality.

Macarthur (1999, 180–1) notes that South Bank Brisbane 'is disconnected in a completely uninteresting way from... South Brisbane behind it; it is planned in thin slivers of water/path/water... and (has a) maniacal directionality to the city'. The relatively high frequency of pedestrian through-routes from South Bank through to Grey Street immediately behind does little to enliven a streetscape there which itself has little activity. One side of Grey Street is loomed over by the dull blank backsides of the four masses of the Queensland Art Gallery and Museum, Performing Arts Centre (Figure 1.10), Conservatorium and College of Art. Here is an abject example of Art emasculating Life. On its opposite side, Grey Street is cut off from the remainder of South

Three 'Southbanks'

Figure 1.10 Queensland Performing Arts Centre creates an impermeable barrier between waterfront (left) and Grey Street and residential neighbourhoods behind (right), Brisbane South Bank.

Brisbane, Brisbane's most vital and diverse neighbourhood, by an elevated railway, two train stations, an elevated, dedicated busway and a major bus interchange, the 400m-long bulk of the Brisbane Convention and Exhibition Centre, the walled precincts of South Bank College of TAFE and several busy traffic arteries which link the precinct to nearby expressways. There are some 3700 on-site parking spaces in the immediate vicinity (Southbank Development Corporation 2002).

One of the key potential pedestrian paths and sightlines through the back of Brisbane's South Bank, Glenelg Street, lies obscured behind the large Piazza building, where it serves primarily as a loading bay, and is narrowed and bent to suit car traffic and to negotiate elevated stanchions. Designing for the needs of the South Bank tourist enclave undermines the viability of its interaction with urban space surrounding it. Footpath connections to South Brisbane, including the main axis of Melbourne Street, are either awkward, invisible or entirely absent. Although both Melbourne's and Brisbane's Southbanks prosper in their image as ideal pedestrian environments, this success is in part built on major investments in heavy transport infrastructure which compromise the viability of a wider pedestrian network. All these changes which enhance connectivity at the larger scale also reduce it locally, marginalizing these settings as a whole, and making it difficult for people to wander, explore and mix. The qualities of the riverfront promenade are in a sense traded off against the quality and range of transport options in adjoining neighbourhoods.

Similarly at Southbank Melbourne, the SouthGate shopping and restaurant complex presents a 'split personality' (City of Melbourne 1997, 30). The project has several levels of active frontage to its water side, but to the rear is a lifeless elevated plaza lacking in sunlight and active uses. Multi-level parking structures, truck bays, expanses of solid wall and widened roads on the inland frontage of this precinct kill off potential adjacency synergies. Behind the promenade, in the wider Southbank district, the car predominates. Roadways are extremely wide, and overshadowed by coarse-grained, high-rise buildings lacking setbacks or active frontages. London's Millennium Bridge addresses this issue by extending deep into the urban fabric on the northern riverside, connecting directly to St. Paul's Cathedral.

In addition to good pedestrian connectivity and solar exposure, the three Southbank leisure precincts all exhibit conscious artifice in the choice of architectural forms which provide a strong mental image that contrasts to their CBDs. This is most clearly illustrated in London, where the serious, morally upright city with its historic seats of power is counterposed across the Thames River to a new landscape of high-tech, democratic, fun spaces with unusual geometries, with iconic individual structures forming at least three direct pairings of 'dialectical images' connected by bridges (Buck-Morss 1991): the Houses of Parliament and the London Eye; St. Paul's Cathedral and the Tate Modern gallery; and the Greater London Authority headquarters and the Tower of London (Figures 1.11–1.13). These arrangements nicely draw together imagery, wayfinding, connectivity and oppositions of function. The current landmarks have antecedents and inspiration in earlier generations of icons on London's South Bank: The 91m high aluminium 'skylon' at the 1951 Festival of Britain (Figure 1.14), and before that, the round theatres in the 1700s. Alongside the many cultural venues and more recent 'landmark' waterfront office and residential towers on London's, Melbourne's and Brisbane's Southbanks, the spectacular structural forms of their new pedestrian bridges have also helped to make these urban waterfronts more prominent, giving these predominantly horizontal landscapes strong and distinctive vertical profiles. The bridges contribute to reorienting the gaze and to reframing the mental Image of the City around the river and its leisure offerings (Lynch 1961).

The Riverbank Stage

The high visibility of the three case study Southbanks is crucial to their success in attracting both visitors and tenants. Within the space of the precincts themselves, wide promenades, ample open spaces, multiple levels and interconnections between different functions also provide excellent opportunities for 'seeing and being seen', a relatively passive but very important form of social engagement (Lofland 1998; Sennett 1974). But beyond the social amenity of this form of leisure, the redevelopment of these three riverfronts was driven by the desire to attract leisure spending, especially by outside tourists. These Southbanks are places of spectacle not only they emphasise the visual, but because they package leisure and culture into forms which can be sold and passively consumed (Debord 1994).

One great danger of waterfront redevelopment is the potential of creating a 'tourist bubble' (Judd 1992), a discrete enclave with a layout and mix of uses which meets only the desires of out-of-town tourists, suburban residents, commuting white-collar city workers, and upper-income inner-city residents. Redeveloped waterfronts

Three 'Southbanks'

Figures 1.11 – 1.13 Dialectical pairings of landmark structures across the Thames River (top-bottom): the Houses of Parliament and the London Eye; St. Paul's Cathedral and the Tate Modern; and the GLA headquarters and the Tower of London.

Source: Fig. 1.13: Dronepicr - https://500px.com/dronepicr - https://creativecommons.org/licenses/by/3.0/deed.en

Figure 1.14 Festival of Britain buildings with Royal Festival Hall to left, and the 'Skylon', 1951.

Source: © Harold Dilworth Crewdson – geograph.org.uk/p/3099083 – https://creativecommons.org/licenses/by-sa/2.0/

are part of (and often a display case for) a 'trophy collection' of formulaic urban visitor attractions including hotels, convention centres, stadia, aquaria and casinos (Judd 1992, citing Frieden and Sagalyn 1989). For the Australian cases, we could add museums and galleries. The practical logical behind the clustering of such attractions is to provide economies of scale and agglomeration which make possible high levels of investment in the public realm and maximise patronage.

A case study of the shortcomings of the 'trophy collection' approach to planning is the Queensland Cultural Centre, a master-planned hard-edged cluster of large-scale institutional buildings hogging the waterfront. Inside, culture is framed as a spectacle, experience is carefully managed as a series of fixed impressions. Clearly such institutions are important for urban culture as a whole. However, their contribution to the possibilities of experience of place, the river's edge, is rather negative. The river is also treated as spectacle, a distant, architecturally-framed pictorial backdrop, unavailable to more active experiences. The Art Gallery turns inward to its own pools and fountains.

These cultural attractions are introduced and arranged on the waterfront to optimise their interrelations, rather than their connections to the wider urban landscape and the economy and cultural life of adjoining neighbourhoods. The synergies of placing them together are managerial and aesthetic, and are seldom experienced in patterns of use by the public (Alexander 1965). The Gallery of Modern Art (2006) extended culture's monopoly to 850m of riverfront. As a whole, South Bank Brisbane is highly polarised, not at all a dumb-bell: at one end, a massive, tight cluster of similar high-culture artefacts, and at the other, an overabundance of open space with too few primary attractors.

Such staple tourist diversions as casinos, aquariums and IMAX cinemas are of value to waterfront leisure precincts not merely because of tax revenues or their multiplier effect on tourist spending, but fundamentally because they help generate sufficient densities and flows of people to make a visit to the urban waterfront into a worthwhile and varied social experience. Vital urban places have diversified, complex economies (Jacobs 1961; 1970).

The former industrial use of riverfronts had a clear rational basis; they had an instrumental dependence on the river as a source of power, for industrial processes of heating, cooling and washing, and for the transport of heavy materials. The clustering of cultural and leisure uses on riverfronts, regardless of their need for water, suggests a need to reflect critically upon what actually qualifies as a 'waterfront use' and contributes to its vitality. Melbourne's Southbank is enlivened and made more informal by the difference between the customer bases and activities gathered together by its various facilities. Yet many buildings on all three Southbanks have uses which are neither public nor leisure-oriented, including Griffith University College of Art and Theiss Construction Company in Brisbane, the headquarters of Philip Morris and Esso in Melbourne, and numerous modernist office buildings in London. Such buildings are purely visual spectacles, billboards which advertise their tenants (Sandercock and Dovey 2002, see also Chapter 5). The unbuildable width of the river and height controls on buildings close to the water's edge are critical as they provide monopoly conditions for advertising on taller buildings behind. Indeed, most of the former Festival of Britain site had remained empty for decades because of a restrictive covenant that prevented any construction on the 160m setback between the river's edge and the 27-storey office tower of the Shell Centre (1962). The river-facing façade of that building was regularly used for commemorative light projections.

Some of the many large, formerly non-public modernist buildings along London's South Bank have been converted to leisure uses, including its two former power stations. One of them, long used as a factory producing OXO stock cubes, was transformed into apartments, art shops and galleries in 1997. The other, far larger one was renovated as the Tate Modern art gallery in 2000. That building was subsequently expanded and its southern façade opened up to facilitate better pedestrian links through to the adjoining Southwark neighbourhood behind it. These developments have encouraged further investment and transformations of land use along London's riverside. In 2014, the bulk of Sea Containers House, operating as an office building since the 1980s, was party converted to its originally-planned function as a luxury hotel. The Shell Centre is currently being redeveloped as luxury housing. The risk is that high-rise, high-end housing and cultural venues combined can crowd out all other uses of the waterfront and close out views to the river.

On the Edge

Leisure is not only about looking at something. As argued in the broader methodology of this chapter, users of urban waterfronts play an active role in producing their own personal leisure experiences. The careful theming and programming of these Southbanks and their behavioural controls have not actually killed off public life. In fact, these manipulations also frame distinctive prospects for free, active and creative social activity. Commercial entertainment spaces and programmed events on waterfronts are mixed in with a range of sensory stimuli provided by the spectacular leisure landscape itself, such as lighting, sculpture and music; not to forget of course water.

Carefully sited, such elements can actually enhance and promote possibilities for informal socialisation and bodily experiences of the open landscape on the river's edge. A number of illustrations will be briefly sketched out.

Even though Brisbane's 'Breaka Beach' is artificially constructed, with no physical link to the real river, going into the water is still a rich bodily, sensory activity (Macarthur 1999). River bridges become sites of freedom and novel experience. Brisbane's Goodwill Bridge is articulated into various sections, 'teasing out and amplifying a series of experiences' (Musgrave 2002). The bridge incorporates semi-private seating areas and layers of screens which conceal and frame views.

The approach path to Melbourne's Southbank pedestrian bridge begins with a tight, dimly-lit pedestrian tunnel under Flinders Street Station and emerges suddenly onto the open riverbank. Several shifts in elevation and axis intensify sensory and bodily engagement with the landscape. The bridge frames a range of experiences which stimulate play. Its platform rises in a continuous arc which lends itself to smooth acceleration on the descent. Its surface of narrow transverse boards provides a pleasant vibration and subtle rasping hum underneath the wheels of cycles and skates. Tyre marks from in-line skates and graffiti far up the curve of the arch reveal that people's path across the bridge sometimes leads over the top of the structure, 20 metres above the water: people perceive and act out a bodily challenge latent in the bridge's form. The bridge was frequently repainted to remove the evidence of such transgressions, with a grooved surface later added to make scaling it more difficult (Figures 1.15 and 1.16). People also

Figure 1.15 Southbank pedestrian bridge, Melbourne, with graffiti.

Figure 1.16 Southbank pedestrian bridge, after modifications to prevent climbing.

Three 'Southbanks'

Figure 1.17 South Bank Brisbane: note people at right dangling legs over the water.

Figure 1.18 Teenagers kissing on lower concourse, Southbank Melbourne.

jump over the low triangular stanchions at the ends of the arch and slide down the other side. People are clearly highly aware of opportunities for playful exploration which are available around them.

On Brisbane's South Bank, plenty of comfortable seating is provided on the inland side of the broad promenade. Nonetheless, many people choose to sit on the low concrete barrier wall on the edge of the embankment, either cross-legged on top of it, or with their legs dangling 'outboard', to feel the breezes and to have an uninterrupted view of the river (Figure 1.17). Lastly, Melbourne's Southbank promenade is split. A lower concourse, which can't easily be seen from above, is often quite empty. It's a place apart from surveillance and control (Lynch 1981). Teenagers often hang out here, smoking, kissing or wrestling (Figure 1.18). These mild acts of passion and violence hint at the escapism which urban space on the edge of the flowing water might offer (Jinnai 1995). These marginal spaces of transgression on Melbourne's Southbank will be explored further in Chapter 5.

Similarly on London's Thames embankment adjacent to Gabriel's Wharf, stone staircases lead down to a small sandy beach exposed at low tide on the river's edge. This is used for planned and impromptu public dance parties. Groups of young men jump from the open edge of the stairs, doing flips and somersaults before landing feet-first in the soft sand. The varying step heights create incremental, manageable risks that they can test themselves against. Lower steps are less scary to jump from, but also allow less time to complete a flip, and are thus actually more challenging (Figure 1.19). The significance of

Figure 1.19 Teenagers jumping from steps onto sand at the river's edge, London.

Source: Photomontage

Three 'Southbanks'

the beach for urban play will be explored further in Chapter 6. Not only teenagers come to London's South Bank seeking escapist play on the edge. One summer evening, a middle-aged couple climb over the railing with wine glasses and a portable barbecue, to enjoy a sheltered space on an unfenced landing 10m above the river with a direct view onto the water (Stevens 2007). The fenced-off piers supporting the new Jubilee Bridges are strewn with cigarette butts and empty alcohol bottles, evidencing people's illicit leisure uses of these small edge spaces set apart from the main pedestrian flows.

Improving Waterfront Image and Integration

Table 1.4 provides a summary of the key findings obtained from the comparative examination of the three Southbanks, drawing on the evidence of both positive and negative outcomes. Many of these principles might productively be applied to other kinds of leisure precincts, although others highlight the specificities of riverfronts.

Three further suggestions for design practice on riverfronts emerge when several of the environmental dimensions of leisure discussed here are considered in combination – a task of synthesis with which all designers and planners must engage. The specific historical and spatial contexts of the three built case studies preclude their use to irrefutably demonstrate these points. These further recommendations are, then, an interpolation between the various factors outlined in the methodology, projecting knowledge gained from the analysis.

The first point is that the experience of arriving at and moving through a leisure precinct like Southbank can itself a fundamental part of its magic. The location, planning and design of bridges and pathways which move people to and through riverfronts are all critical to their liveliness. Bridges are more than investments in transport, and road bridges which provide access to riverfront leisure areas may need to be budgeted and programmed to take account of their crucial contribution to legibility, delight and leisure activities.

The second related issue is the nature of those key nodal points where pedestrian bridges meet riverfront promenades. Placing a diversity of active, publicly-accessible land uses adjacent to such nodes can also contribute to their liveliness, increasing the time people spend lingering at them and making them sites where more people's paths will cross.

Thirdly, many different facets of the two fundamental dimensions of leisure considered here – difference and visibility – appear to point toward the importance of an urban design framework which optimises land use mix as well as permeability to and from the water's edge. Subdivision planning and staged site release with narrow and relatively deep lots running perpendicular to waterfronts would be one way to ensure this. This could enliven major promenades by bringing different user groups on and off them at more points, creating more intersections for pausing and interaction, as well as providing economic incentive for active frontages to spread along the minor perpendicular frontages. Perhaps a sufficient number of such through-routes could support commercial activities on a second route paralleling the waterfront, provided these block depths were

Table 1.4 How does the design of 'Southbanks' serve people's diverse needs for leisure?

Dimension of urban leisure experience	Passive experience	Active experience
Difference	Across the river • Adjacent to places of work • Low-lying, shifting, malleable landscapes • Good solar exposure • Different histories, cultures • Differently regulated	Pools (of uses) • Planned for diverse use • Underdesigned • Provide basic amenities Flows (of people) • Connected into existing orbits of activity • Urban structure scaled to the pedestrian • Legible – part of the image of the city • Bridges as distinctive, enjoyable environments in their own right • Careful and ample design of vertical connections • Pathways weave activity sites together • Pathways offer a variety of uses • Connected to local space and everyday life
Staging	The riverbank stage • Highly visible and accessible sites • Spectacular attractions generate crowds • Tourist bubble = economies of scale and agglomeration • E+nsure that public institutions do not 'privatise' urban space	On the edge • Highly-designed, themed environments can still provide diverse opportunities for users • Links to water (land use, visual, behavioural) • Engages people's bodies with landscape forms and materials • Spaces set apart from close surveillance and control, but still highly visible and connected

Three 'Southbanks'

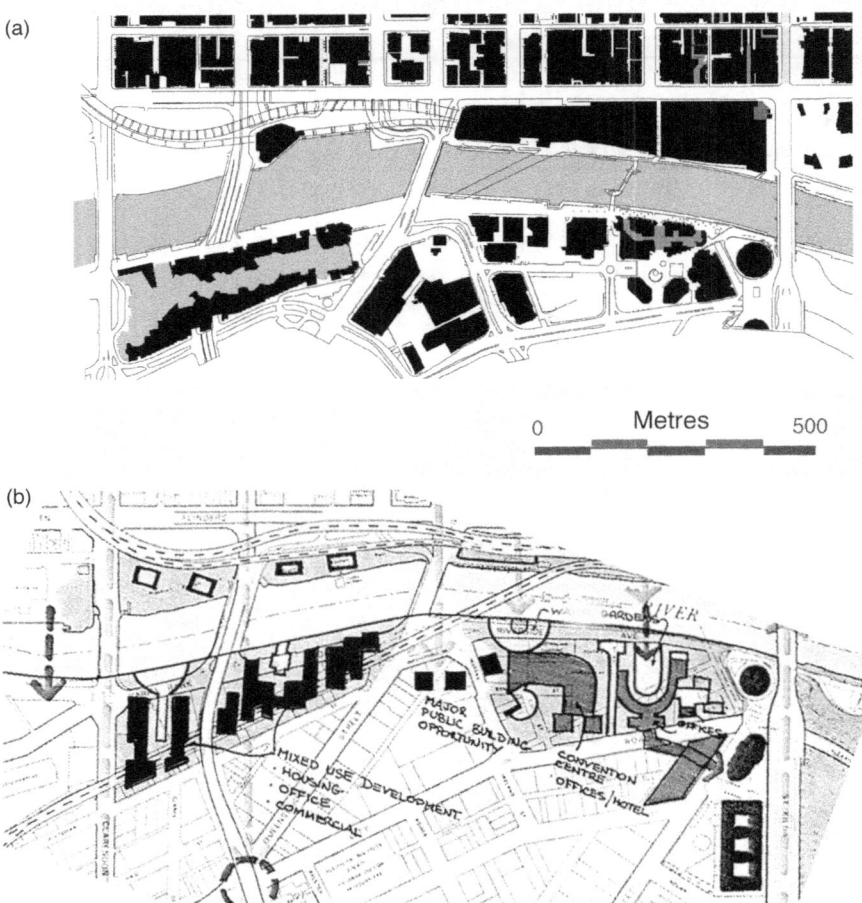

Figure 1.20 Melbourne Southbank figure-ground map from 2000 (a), compared to unpublished Victorian state government proposal, circa 1984 (b).

themselves no further than 200m from the waterfront path. Such a strategy would also be more likely to achieve a richer mix of uses and development form along the water's edge.

The two latter strategies, placing major public building at visible, accessible nodes and running mixed-use blocks perpendicular to the river, are well illustrated by an unapproved, unpublished sketch proposal prepared in the early years of Melbourne Southbank (Figure 1.20), discovered, as in legend, abandoned on a dusty shelf in the offices of the state government planning department many years later. This scheme also suggests construction of a wide pedestrian link away from the river and south over the top of the vehicular corridor of City Road, connecting the riverfront to the National Gallery (lower right) and the wider neighbourhood.

Having used the four-part theoretical framework of leisure outlined in Table 1.3 to explore these somewhat lesser-known examples of waterfronts, it is also useful to return to reconsider the applicability and scope of the five key urban design principles drawn from Gordon (see Table 1.1).

On the topic of difference, Gordon does not mention the issue of separation from 'the city'. It was noted that riverfronts are a distinctive typology, in this respect quite unlike many redeveloped urban harbours, docklands or piers, and also unlike riverbanks in city centres which have always straddled their rivers, and thus do not present a new 'face' to these post-industrial leisure precincts.

In terms of social mixing, the three Southbanks illustrated Gordon's call for improved public accessibility and connectivity, at least in terms of developing high-quality links to the city centre and along the riverfront (see 'Flows' 1–3). They were less successful in the integration of the riverfronts with their wider urban surroundings. The case studies also highlighted that urban vitality relied on combining 'pools of uses' and was confounded by single-function buildings with massive footprints. Gordon's injunction to coordinating public and private investments in order to create a coherent urban environment, 'to design streets not buildings', implies that careful urban design and property management can deliver mixed use and permeability (Gordon 1996, 287). But in contrast, all three Southbanks are also partial demonstrations that such goals can actually be served by Gordon's stratagem of thinking small and planning in increments. London's South Bank in particular has proved to be an open zone for experimentation, where many new built forms and uses can be trialled temporarily. Interestingly, some of its main attractions, "the Young Vic, Gabriel's Wharf, and the London Eye were all planned as temporary structures; they now define the South Bank' (Bosetti and Colthorpe 2018, 8).

The development of these riverbanks as carefully-managed spectacles tallies well with Gordon's focus on image and imageability. Gordon's main contribution on the topic of bodily experience requires an extrapolation of his broad concern that waterfront redevelopment should integrate with the water; an obvious objective, but one often strangely overlooked. He provides few specifics about the perceptual, behaviour or social affordances of waterfronts for users, and this point gives the chief impetus for the present chapter.

Gordon's fifth point is to learn from what exists and adaptively re-use existing built form. The one clear example of this in the Australian cases was the extension of Melbourne's existing urban block structure across the river, imitating its robustness. The idea of adaptively re-using buildings had limited relevance for the Melbourne and Brisbane sites because almost all pre-existing buildings had been cleared when both were redeveloped. In Brisbane, some renovated nineteenth-century pubs have formed the basis for the creation of a new urban block within the South Bank precinct. Though this sub-area functions well, it is not closely connected to the river's edge. The leisure uses are unchanged and no different to elsewhere in the city. The example thus offers little new insight into riverfront design, except to highlight the persistence of leisure lifestyles. London's South Bank, in contrast, is a vital space largely because its plans and uses keep changing. Many of its buildings and spaces have been reconfigured and re-used to adapt them for increased publicness, pedestrian circulation, and a new mix of leisure functions. The Bankside power station only operated for 20 years, and has now served as an art gallery for almost as long. The OXO Tower, the offices of the abolished London County Council, Sea Containers House and the Shell Centre have also all changed their function. In recent years, a changing program of outdoor art and play installations have enlivened the London South Bank's public spaces, bringing visitors back to the place more often.

In conclusion, people come to an urban riverfront to escape from everyday responsibilities. This escapism takes many forms. The ideologies driving waterfront renaissance and the design objectives which organise these leisure settings can run counter to the tremendous diversity of people, activities and ideals which we find gathered together by the water. As sites designed for consumption, they also enable a wide range of creative, productive and even destructive practices. It should be recognised that instruments of culture and consumption and systems of transport intended to serve desirable, profitable and camera-friendly forms of leisure may also support, or even encourage, many other possibilities. Observing and interacting with a diversity of spaces and other people are the crux of urban leisure. Design and planning for public riverfront leisure precincts must aspire to that ambition.

References

Alexander, C. (1965) 'The city is not a tree', *Architectural Forum*, 122 (1), pp. 58–62, and 122 (2), pp. 58–61.
Ball, M. and Sutherland, D. (2001) *An Economic History of London 1800-1914*, London: Routledge
Borden, I. (2001) Skateboarding, *Space and the City: Architecture and the Body*, Oxford: Berg.
Bosetti, N. and Colthorpe, T. (2018) *Meanwhile, in London: Making use of London's Empty Spaces*, London: Centre for London, available from https://www.centreforlondon.org/publication/meanwhile-use-london/, accessed 20 May 2019.
Buck-Morss, S. (1991) *The Dialectics of Seeing: Walter Benjamin and the Arcades Project*, Cambridge MA: MIT Press.
Caillois, R. (1961) *Man, Play and Games*, New York: Free Press of Glencoe.
Calthorpe, P. (1993) *The Next American Metropolis: Ecology, Community, and the American Dream*, Princeton: Princeton Architectural Press.
City of Melbourne (1997) *Grids and Greenery Case Studies*, Melbourne: City of Melbourne.
Cohen, S. and Taylor, L. (1976) *Escape Attempts: The Theory and Practice of Resistance to Everyday Life*, London: Allen Lane.
Craik, J. (1992) 'Expo 88: Fashions of sight and politics of site', in Bennett, T., Buckridge, P., Carter D. and Mercer C. (eds) *Celebrating the Nation: A critical study of Australia's Bicentenary*, St. Leonards (Australia): Allen and Unwin.
Crawford, M. (1992) 'The world in a shopping mall', in Sorkin, M. (eds) *Varations on a Theme Park: The New American City and the end of Public Space*, New York: Hill and Wang, pp. 3–30.
Debord, G. (1994) *The Society of the Spectacle*, New York: Zone Books.
Department of Public Works (Queensland, Australia) (2005) *State Budget 05-06: Budget Highlights*, available from http://www.publicworks.qld.gov.au/about/publications.cfm
Dodson, B. and Kilian, D. (1998) 'From port to playground: The redevelopment of the Victoria and Albert waterfront, Cape Town', in Tyler, D., Guerrier, Y. and Robertson, M. (eds), *Managing Tourism in Cities*, Chichester: John Wiley.
Dovey, K. (2005) *Fluid City: Transforming Melbourne's Urban Waterfront*, London: Routledge.
Eckstut, S. (1986) 'Solving complex urban design problems', in Fitzgerald, A. R. (ed), *Waterfront Planning and Development*, New York: American Society of Civil Engineers, pp. 54–57.
Fagence, M. (1995), 'Episodic progress toward a grand design: Waterside redevelopment of Brisbane's South Bank', in Smith, J. C. and Fagence, M. (eds), *Recreation and Tourism as a Catalyst for Urban Waterfront Redevelopment*, London: Praeger, pp. 71–87.
Franck, K. and Stevens, Q. (2007) 'Tying down loose space', in Franck, K. and Stevens, Q. (eds), *Loose Space: Possibility and Diversity in Urban Life*, London: Routledge.
Frieden, B. and Sagalyn, L. (1989) *Downtown, Inc.: How America rebuilds cities*, Cambridge MA: MIT Press.
Garreau, J. (1992) *Edge City: Life on the New Frontier*, New York: Anchor Books.
Gehl, J. (1987) *Life Between Buildings*, New York: Van Nostrand Reinhold.
Gehl, J. and City of Melbourne (1994) *Places for People*, Melbourne: City of Melbourne.
Gibson J. (1979) *The Ecological Approach to Visual Perception*, Boston: Houghton Mifflin.

Goffman, E. (1963) *Behaviour in Public Places*, Westport CT: Greenwood.
Goodale, T. and Godbey, G. (1988) *The Evolution of Leisure: Historical and Philosophical Perspectives*, State College PA: Venture.
Gordon, D. (1996) 'Planning, design and managing change in urban waterfront redevelopment', *Town Planning Review*, 67 (3), pp. 261–290.
Hall, P. (1998) *Cities in Civilization: Culture, Technology and Urban Order*, London: Weidenfeld and Nicolson.
Harvey, D. (1989) *The Condition of Postmodernity*, London: Blackwell.
Hazel, G. and Parry, R. (2004) *Making Cities Work*, Chichester: John Wiley.
Huizinga, J. (1970) *Homo Ludens: A Study of the Play Element in Culture*, London: Temple Smith.
Jacobs, J. (1961) *The Death and Life of Great American Cities*, New York: Vintage.
Jacobs, J. (1970) *The Economy of Cities*, London: Cape.
Jinnai, H. (1995) *Tokyo: A Spatial Anthropology*, Berkeley: University of California Press.
Jones, A. (2014) *On South Bank: The Production of Public Space*, Ashgate: Farnham.
Judd, D. (1992), 'Constructing the tourist bubble', in Judd, D. and Fainstein, S. (eds), *The Tourist City*, New Haven: Yale University Press, pp. 35–53.
Kostof, S. (1992) *The City Assembled: The Elements of Urban Form Through History*, London: Thames and Hudson.
Lefebvre, H. (1991) *Critique of Everyday Life*, Vol. 1, 2nd. ed., London: Verso.
Lefebvre, H. (1996) *Writings on Cities*, Oxford: Blackwell.
Lofland, L. (1998) *The Public Realm: Exploring the City's Quintessential Social Territory*, Hawthorne NY: Aldine de Gruyter.
Longhurst, R. (1992) *South Bank: An Historical Perspective from then Until Now*, Brisbane: State Library of Queensland and South Bank Corporation.
Loukaitou-Sideris, A. and Banerjee, T. (1998) *Urban Design Downtown: Poetics and Politics of Form*, Berkeley: University of California Press.
Lynch, K. (1961) *The Image of the City*, Cambridge MA: MIT Press.
Lynch, K. (1981) *Good City Form*, Cambridge MA: MIT Press.
Lynch, K. and Hack, G. (1985) *Site Planning*, 3rd Ed, Cambridge MA: MIT Press.
Lyman, S. and Scott, M. (1975) *The Drama of Social Reality*, New York: Oxford University Press.
Macarthur, J. (1999) 'Tactile simulations: Architecture and the image of the public at Brisbane's Kodak Beach', in Barcan, R. and Buchanan, I. (eds) *Imagining Australian Space: Cultural Studies and Spatial Inquiry*. Nedlands, Australia: University of Western Australia Press.
Meyer, H. (1999) *City and Port: Urban Planning as a Cultural Venture in London, Barcelona, New York and Rotterdam*, Utrecht: International Books.
Mules, T. (1998), 'Events tourism and economic development in Australia', in Tyler, D., Guerrier, Y. and Robertson, M. (eds), *Managing Tourism in Cities*, Chichester: John Wiley, pp. 195–214.
Mullins, P., Natalier, K., Smith, P. and Smeaton, B. (1999), 'Cities and consumption spaces', *Urban Affairs Review*, 35 (1), pp. 44–71.
Musgrave, E. (2002), 'Goodwill overture', *Architecture Australia*, 91.
Noble, L. (2001) 'South Bank dreaming', *Architecture Australia*, 90, pp. 86–93.
Pinder, D.A., Hoyle B.S. and Husain, M.S. (eds) (1988), *Revitalising the Waterfront: International Dimensions of Dockland Redevelopment*, London: Belhaven.
Queensland Government (1990) *Queensland Government Gazette*, 28 April 1990, CCXCIII (111).
Rojek, C. (1995) *Decentering Leisure: Rethinking Leisure Theory*, London: Sage.
Sandercock, L. and Dovey, K. (2002), 'Pleasure, politics and the public interest: Melbourne's waterfront revitalization', *Journal of the American Planning Association*, 68, 151–64
Sennett, R. (1971) *The Uses of Disorder: Personal Identity and City Life*, Harmondsworth: Penguin.
Sennett, R. (1974) *The Fall of Public Man*, Cambridge: Cambridge University Press.
Siksna, A. (1998) 'City centre blocks and their evolution: A comparative study of eight American and Australian CBDs', *Journal of Urban Design*, 3 (3), pp. 253–283.
Simões Aelbrecht, P. (2017) 'The complex regeneration of post-war modernism: London's Southbank Centre's Masterplan', *Urban Design International*, 22 (4), pp. 331–348.
Sorkin, M. (ed.) (1992) *Variations on a Theme Park*, New York: Hill and Wang.
South Bank Development Corporation (Brisbane) (2002), *South Bank Development '97 Plan (amended)*.
Stevens, Q. (2007) *The Ludic City: Exploring the Potential of Public Spaces*, London: Routledge.
Wang, Z. and Stevens, Q. (2020) 'How do open space characteristics influence open space use? A study of Melbourne's Southbank Promenade', *Urban Research and Planning*, 13 (1), pp. 22–44.
Wanna, J. (2001), 'Political Chronicles: Queensland', *Australian Journal of Politics and History*, 48 (2), pp. 259–267.

Chapter 2
Postcolonial Waterfronts
Global Imagery and Local Realities

*Quentin Stevens, Marek Kozlowski and
Norsidah Ujang*

The redevelopment of urban waterfront areas for non-industrial uses has been driven by a wide range of economic, social, and environmental objectives (Breen and Rigby 1996). It also has aesthetic and representational aims. Existing research into flagship waterfront development projects in Western cities highlights three key representational aims. Firstly, it often emphasises the key role these areas can play in transforming the wider image of cities, both literally and metaphorically (Marshall 2001, Dovey 2005). Secondly, the redevelopment of waterfronts for new residential, commercial, and leisure uses typically aims to both display and facilitate a transition to a post-industrial economy. Waterfront plans tend to be driven by economic imperatives that prioritise real estate investment and leisure and tourism uses, both internationally focused (Sandercock and Dovey 2002, Desfor et al. 2010). Thirdly, this is often coupled with ambitions to demonstrate environmental remediation and enhanced ecological sustainability in formerly-industrial waterfront areas, although there are criticisms of the limited environmental benefits of such transformations and which socio-economic groups they serve (Hagerman 2012, Bunce 2009).

For newly-developing countries in the global East and South, flagship waterfront redevelopments also often seek to showcase nations' transitions away from their colonial pasts; urban ports were typically a key locus of exploitative colonial-era trade. Studies of waterfront transformation projects in Hong Kong (Law 2002), Singapore (Chang et al. 2004) and the Caribbean (Dodman 2007, Gidel 2010) suggest that waterfront projects that try to assert a new, local identity and a new economic trajectory for a city and a nation paradoxically often draw upon international consultants, international planning approaches and architecture, and international financing. Locally-driven waterfront transformations appear to privilege the interests, activities and self-image of newly-dominant local elites and ignore the needs of existing waterfront residents and workers (Dodman 2007). Projects that ostensibly seek to reintegrate the city and its waterways and to create new, socially-inclusive urban spaces often paradoxically increase social and spatial fragmentation. There is broad agreement that the imagery of waterfront redevelopments in Southeast Asia and elsewhere is largely generic, inauthentic, and detached from their cities' wider economic vitality (Savage et al. 2004, Chang et al. 2004, Dovey 2005, Chang and Huang 2011).

There is growing international interest in the environmental remediation aspects of contemporary urban waterfront development (Desfor and Laidley 2010). But many waterfront projects involve the creation of entirely new, artificial landscapes, often by filling into waterways. These landscapes are carefully tailored to particular consumer interests, and have little connection to either local history or ecology. In tropical regions, the redevelopment of waterfront areas for new urban leisure uses is often argued to be a desirable makeover of 'unhealthy, repulsive swamps and mangroves' (Gidel 2010, 35). However, Savage et al. (2004, 218) emphasise that while Singapore's, redeveloped river "has become a more ecologically viable and sustainable environment, the motivation was not primarily environmental, but more to sustain a new economic lifeline for... tourism... Keeping the River... aesthetically pleasing". There is little literature examining the environmental benefits or impacts of urban waterfronts (Savage et al. 2004). Gidel (2010) highlights that goals of improving environmental cleanliness often become entwined with goals of social cleansing. Existing research emphasises tensions between traditional local waterfront spaces and activities that are 'authentic' but unsustainable and insufficiently profitable, and global waterfront transformations that bring investment but obliterate local character.

Within the Southeast Asian context, Malaysia's waterfronts differ from those in the more widely studied island city-states, Hong Kong and Singapore. In those cases, significant population and economic pressures drive the production of new waterfront land, which has been going on for many decades. Singaporean respondents in a survey by Chang and Huang (2010) cited the Malaysian waterfronts of Malacca and Kuching as having retained local image and lifestyle better than Singapore's efforts to present a 'world class' waterfront. The inland waterfronts of Malaysia's largest urban area, Kuala Lumpur, have developed later and more quickly than Hong Kong's and Singapore's.

Malaysia's Two Capital Cities

Kuala Lumpur was founded in 1857 at the confluence of the Klang and Gombak Rivers. Historically, the Malay settlement concentrated northeast of the junction. The city's oldest mosque, Masjid Jamek (1909), was built at the rivers' confluence, on the site of the city's first Malay burial ground. The Chinese neighbourhood was to the south, around Petaling Street. The British administration occupied the Klang River's west bank. As the rivers' role as transport corridors declined after 1911, squatter developments spread along the derelict riverbanks. Major floods in 1925 and 1971 killed thousands. Planners relocated the squatters. Concrete channelling for flood mitigation blocked visual and physical

Figure 2.1 Masjid Jamek (Mosque) at confluence of Gombak (left) and Klang (right) Rivers, Kuala Lumpur, April 2014.

access to the rivers – a problem shared by many large cities in China and throughout Asia. Later, new elevated highways, light rail tracks and their stations spanned large sections of the rivers. In the early 1990s, the riverfront pedestrian walkways around Masjid Jamek were improved (Figure 2.1) and urban design guidelines encouraged new buildings to face the river (Shamsuddin et al. 2013, Abdul Latip et al. 2009).

In the 1990s, Malaysia's economy grew rapidly. The federal government began developing Putrajaya, a new administrative capital city 25km south of Kuala Lumpur. This sat within the new Multimedia Super Corridor that stretches a further 40km south to the new international airport. Malaysia's parliament remains in Kuala Lumpur. The MSC was intended to relieve existing metropolitan growth pressures to the west along the Klang River valley. Putrajaya was intended to be a showplace of post-colonial Malaysian identity (King 2008). The city has 72,000 residents, predicted to increase to 350,000 by 2025. Most federal ministries have relocated there (Putrajaya Holdings 2014).

Analysing Malaysia's Showpiece Waterfronts

This article examines the three largest mixed-use waterfront projects developed in the greater Kuala Lumpur metropolitan area over the past twenty years. The mixed use projects include Kuala Lumpur City Centre (KLCC) and River of Life in Kuala Lumpur, and Lake Putrajaya in Putrajaya. All the three projects are located in the Kuala Lumpur Metropolitan Area.

Kuala Lumpur City Centre (KLCC) (Figures 2.2 and 2.3) is a new high-rise downtown area, incorporating the landmark Petronas Towers, a mosque, convention centre, high-end 6-storey shopping mall, Suria KLCC, prestige apartment and hotel towers, and a 20 ha public park with a children's playground and a botanical garden built over underground carparking (Bunnell 1999). The park was the last major project by renowned Brazilian landscape architect Roberto Burle Marx. The design retained mature trees and contains many indigenous plants (Bunnell 1999). A 'Symphony Lake' features fountains programmed to music, and a children's wading pool. Kuala Lumpur's planned River

Figure 2.2 KLCC Park, Kuala Lumpur. Wading pool, Suria KLCC mall and Petronas Towers.

Postcolonial Waterfronts

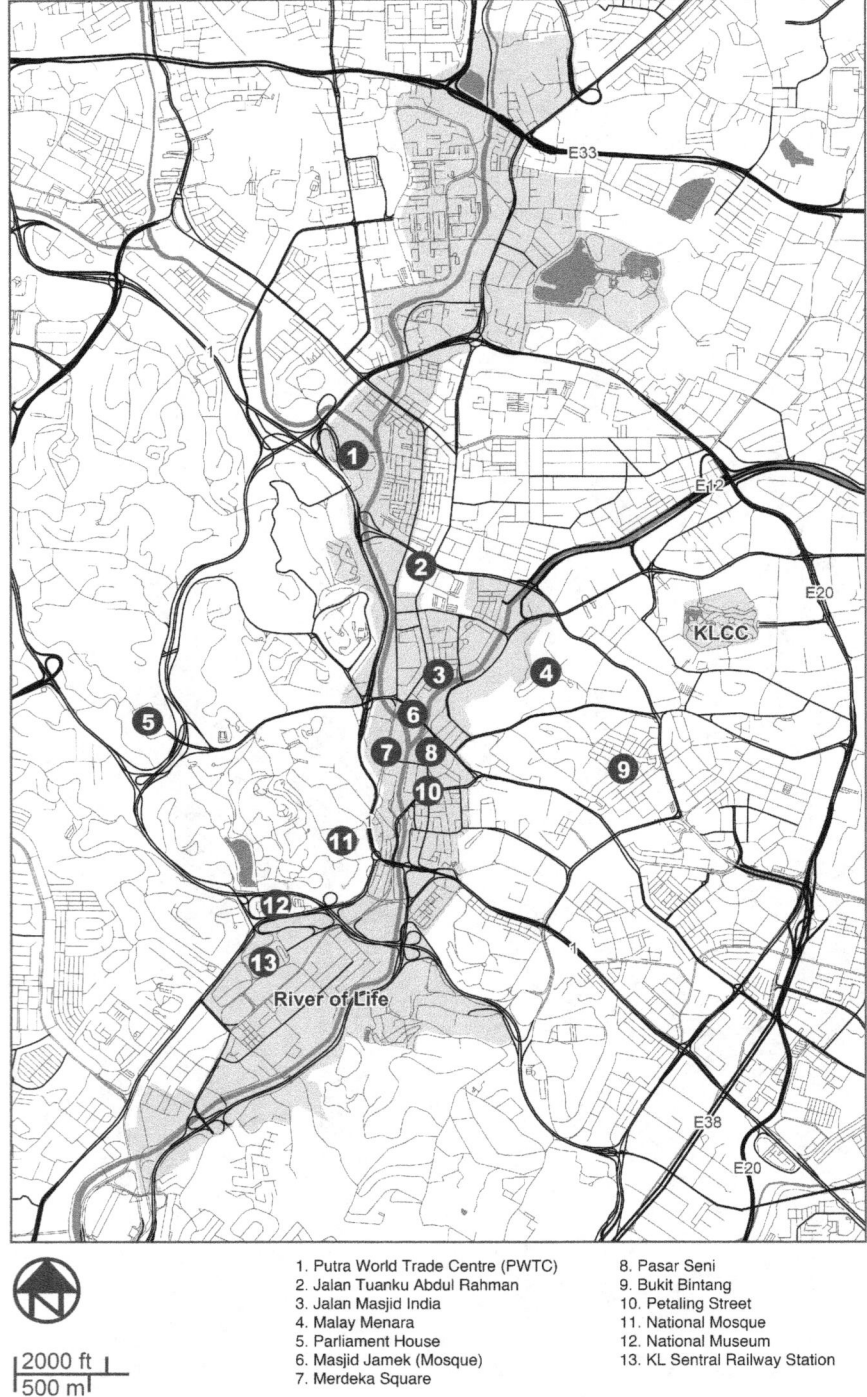

Figure 2.3 Map of central Kuala Lumpur, showing River of Life area and KLCC.

Source: Felix Fehr

1. Putra World Trade Centre (PWTC)
2. Jalan Tuanku Abdul Rahman
3. Jalan Masjid India
4. Malay Menara
5. Parliament House
6. Masjid Jamek (Mosque)
7. Merdeka Square
8. Pasar Seni
9. Bukit Bintang
10. Petaling Street
11. National Mosque
12. National Museum
13. KL Sentral Railway Station

of Life (ROL) project (Figure 2.3), integrated within the Kuala Lumpur City Plan 2020 (DBKL 2012), seeks to revitalise the Gombak and Klang riverfronts in the city centre as a means to stimulate national economic development. EUR 900 million invested in improving aesthetic quality and amenity aims to leverage economic transformation when government waterfront land is ultimately tendered to private developers (MFT 2014). ROL embraces key cultural destinations Kampung Bharu, Masjid India, Masjid Jamek, Pasar Seni (the oldest city market), Petaling Street, and Malaysia's national space, Merdeka Square. AECOM's Master Plan (AECOM 2013a) foregrounds ecological, social and economic principles, creating a pedestrian-friendly environment, retaining existing natural landscapes and increasing native tropical vegetation (AECOM 2013b).

Lake Putrajaya was developed as the heart of Malaysia's new capital city (Figures 2.4 and 2.5) on a former oil palm plantation. Its master plan by a consortium of Malay consultants and government planners includes 200 ha of terraced wetlands (Moser 2010). Development is regulated by the local authority, Putrajaya Corporation (PP 1997). The technocratic plan segregated land uses. A purely administrative central precinct, essentially a large master-planned office park for government, lines the 4km formal central boulevard, Persiaran Perdana, terminated by the Prime Minister's office and an International Convention Centre on two large hills. Putrajaya's masterplan provides significant public recreational space along the lake foreshores, including the Botanical Gardens and Taman Wawasan, 'Vision Park', Putrajaya's central park, its name linked to former Prime Minister Mahathir's vision for Malaysia to attain developed country status by 2020. There is a water-sports complex at the lake's south end.

Our analysis examines the distinctive aims, forms and impacts of these three waterfront schemes. It identifies what international waterfront images and formal models have been chosen as exemplars, from where, and why, and what messages about Malaysian identity and national development these schemes present. The article examines these new Malaysian waterfronts in relation to three leading critiques of the imagery of waterfront redevelopment worldwide, which were identified in our Introduction's review of the recent literature: waterfronts' contribution to reshaping the overall city image; the use of waterfront redevelopment visions to attract private-sector investment in real estate and in service industries; and presenting the appearance of improved environmental performance. These facets of contemporary waterfront development in Malaysia indicate that visions of urban form, development and environmental management are perceived as important both for expressing the country's shifting identity as a postcolonial nation and for impelling its further development.

The article draws together the limited existing data and first-hand analysis to assess the effectiveness of these waterfront landscapes in both representational and performative terms. The evaluation contrasts the representational aspirations of these three waterfront projects against empirical realities of their performance in shaping the urban image, attracting further urban development and employment, and enhancing ecological sustainability. The aesthetic, representational, economic and environmental objectives underpinning the projects and the formal models that inspired them were gleaned from policy documents, project plans, and interviews with local planners, policymakers, designers and academics who are closely engaged with the projects.

Postcolonial Waterfronts

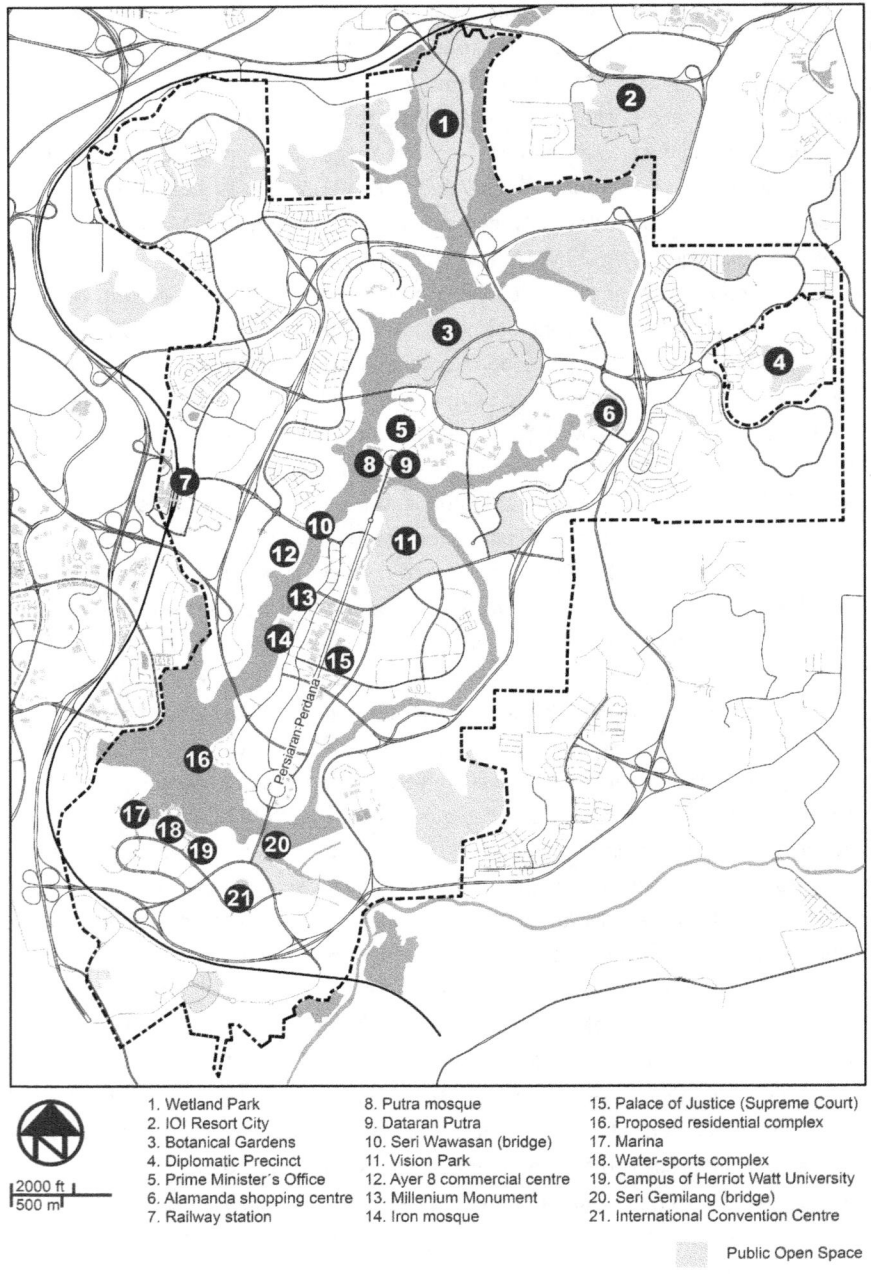

1. Wetland Park
2. IOI Resort City
3. Botanical Gardens
4. Diplomatic Precinct
5. Prime Minister's Office
6. Alamanda shopping centre
7. Railway station
8. Putra mosque
9. Dataran Putra
10. Seri Wawasan (bridge)
11. Vision Park
12. Ayer 8 commercial centre
13. Millenium Monument
14. Iron mosque
15. Palace of Justice (Supreme Court)
16. Proposed residential complex
17. Marina
18. Water-sports complex
19. Campus of Herriot Watt University
20. Seri Gemilang (bridge)
21. International Convention Centre

Public Open Space

Figure 2.4 Map of Putrajaya.

Source: Felix Fehr

As Savage et al. (2004) note, quantitative and qualitative data and assessments of urban waterfronts are generally limited. In recently-developed nations such as Malaysia, there is a paucity of published historical and current information to track rapid urban and economic changes. Our analysis of the actual impacts of these

Figure 2.5 Putra Mosque and the Prime Minister's Office as seen from Lake Putrajaya.

Source: © CEphoto, Uwe Aranas/CC-BY-SA-3.0

three Malaysian waterfronts draws together the limited existing empirical studies of the three precincts (Siong et al. 2013, Hassan and Hanif 2012, Shamsuddin et al. 2012, Moser 2010, King 2008, Bunnell 1999). The analysis was extended through first-hand field surveys of the current physical development, land use, social use, and open space management regimes of the sites. These surveys identified the number of existing hotel rooms adjacent to KLCC, the number of eating establishments facing Lake Putrajaya, and the orientation of entry points to major buildings on Putrajaya's main street. A mental mapping survey of users' perceptions of central Kuala Lumpur and Putrajaya was also undertaken to determine the significance of the waterfront areas within the overall city image. This involved thirty random pedestrians in each location, including local residents, workers and visitors. At each site respondents were asked to sketch a simple map of the respective city centre area identifying the most recognisable geographical and built form elements. They were also invited to note the elements they recognised within each area.

Analysis of this data identifies tensions between the images and objectives that Malaysia's governments and property developers pursue through flagship waterfront schemes, and the local nuances of the case studies' urban fabric, landscape, climate, vegetation, management practices, and the consequent local uses of waterways and open spaces. The conclusion of the chapter draws these findings together to reflect on the successes and shortcomings of these three waterfront projects in promoting an authentic post-colonial Malaysian cityscape.

Our analysis explores three aspects of the urban waterfront image, and how that image responds to international influences and local conditions and customs, considering in turn the contributions these waterfront projects make to the overall city image, to an image of economic development, and to an image of ecological sensitivity. The three paradigms cover issues related to aesthetic qualities, placemaking, people's perception, economic performance, political decision making and environmental and sustainability aspects.

City Image

These three waterfronts in the Malaysian capitals have important roles in placemaking and place marketing, and in this respect they are consciously similar in purpose and form to waterfront projects in developed countries, which transform inner-urban, previously-industrial areas to present a new image of a city focused on new 'world class' residents, businesses and cultural and leisure amenities (Desfor et al 2010, Marshall 2001). Each of these Malaysian waterfronts is proposed as the centrepiece of a wider urban area, fundamental to its image.

Our mental mapping survey for Kuala Lumpur (Table 2.1) revealed a majority of respondents identified the Petronas Towers as the city's main landmark. Only two respondents included the KLCC Park's lake in their mental sketches. Most identified the

Table 2.1 Summary of elements drawn in cognitive maps of Kuala Lumpur and Putrajaya

Kuala Lumpur (n = 30)			Putrajaya (n = 30)		
	Frequency of depiction	Percent of users depicting		Frequency of depiction	Percent of users depicting
River	7	23	–	–	–
KLCC Lake	2	7	Lake	17	57
Drainage	1	3	–	–	–
Landmark • Building • Bridge	28	93	Landmark • Building • Bridge	29	97
Path/Street	23	77	Path/Street	25	83
Edge–Railway	8	27	Edge–Railway	0	
Nodes • Junction • Square	24	80	Nodes • Junction • Square	18	60
Others: • Bus Station • Landscape • Parking	2 2 1	7 7 3	Others: • Bus Station • Landscape • Parking • Trees	1 4 2 2	3 13 7 7

Major landmarks identified for Kuala Lumpur:
KLCC Petronas Tower
KL Tower
National Mosque
Jamek Mosque
Central Station
KL Sentral Station

Major nodes identified for Kuala Lumpur:
Merdeka Square
Bukit Bintang

Major landmarks identified for Putrajaya:
Putra Mosque
Iron Mosque
Premier's Department
Putrajaya International Convention Centre
Lake Putrajaya

Major Paths identified for Putrajaya:
Persarian Perdana (main boulevard)

Major Nodes identified for Putrajaya:
Putra Square

shopping area Bukit Bintang and major traditional streets such as Jalan Tuanku Abdul Rahman and Jalan Masjid India (see Figure 2.3). Despite strong local publicity for the River of Life project, only 23% of respondents identified the two rivers as elements. They were usually drawn in isolation from the street network, and only the historic mosque Masjid Jamek (see Figure 2.1) and Light Rail Transit (LRT) stations were shown connected to them. This corroborates the findings of earlier surveys of the city image that modern high-rise buildings dominate lower historic buildings, and that the rivers are perceived as boundaries isolated from the neighbourhoods that they demarcate, not as integrating pathways within them (Kum and Ujang 2012). For Putrajaya, 93% of respondents identified the Putra Mosque, the Prime Minister's Office (see Figure 2.5), the International Convention Centre and the main boulevard Persiaran Perdana (see Figure 2.4). Most identified the major node Dataran Putra fronting the Putra Mosque. Almost 60% sketched Lake Putrajaya as a key feature, although most showed it detached from any streets or buildings. It appears that KLCC's Petronas Towers and Putrajaya's axial boulevard of large Islamic-styled buildings generate strong images, and the waterfronts are peripheral elements.

The Symphony Lake and wading pool at KLCC Park have an important role in the image making of the Petronas Towers and shopping mall by providing a visually, aurally, and bodily pleasing, animated foreground that attracts tourists and families and provides a comfortable setting free from traffic, an 'oasis' within the 'concrete jungle' (Bunnell 1999, 13), where they can linger, look at, photograph, and then visit the Towers and the Mall (Figure 2.2).

Lake Putrajaya was intended as the city's central feature. The Prime Minister wanted to 'put the water in front of the people' (PP 2014). But Putrajaya's main axis of government office complexes is set approximately 400m back from the lake, separated by car parks (Figure 2.6). A survey of the 11 buildings lining this axis's western side shows all of their public entries face the boulevard; the rear facades only have minor staff entrances. Pedestrian access from the boulevard to the lake along transverse streets is hampered by the use of these frontages as access points for cars and service vehicles. Putrajaya's streets and buildings are not oriented to enjoy lakeside views and breezes. Visual connectivity to the lake from the city is limited. Most other residential and office areas also turn their backs on the lake. Putrajaya's two large mosques stand

Figure 2.6 Government office buildings in Putrajaya set well back from lake edge and facing away from it onto Persiaran Perdana. Vacant lots currently used as temporary car parks.

off-axis near the lake. Their picturesque minarets and domes dominate the city image from the lake, foregrounding the government's desired image of Malaysia as a modern Muslim state (Figure 2.5).

A comparison of Putrajaya's layout (Figure 2.4) with that of other master-planned post-colonial capitals – Washington, New Delhi, Canberra, Brasilia, and Sri Jayawardhanapura Kotte in Sri Lanka – confirms its designers were keen to redeploy and appropriate the strong colonial image of an urban axis of power (Vale 2008). But there are significant contrasts between Putrajaya and the other capitals planned around lakes. The lake does not contribute any obvious symbolism to the meaning of the government or the nation, unlike Sri Lanka's 'floating' island parliament near Colombo, which draws upon ancient cultural precedents, or Brasilia, with its lake conceived as the headwaters of the country's three great river systems spreading north, south and east (Vale 2008). Unlike axially-planned Canberra and Brasilia, Putrajaya does not symbolically link its irregularly-shaped lake into the spatial framework that represents national identity and its connection to the wider landscape. Putrajaya's planning is more comparable to Washington D.C. in being a postcolonial capital designed to proclaim an independent identity by employing the urbanism and architecture of other, older, imperial cultures. Putrajaya's architecture does not draw upon specifically Malaysian precedents, but primarily seeks to evoke the history, modernity and wealth of the contemporary Middle East (King 2008, Moser 2010). Much of the Putrajaya lakefront remains vacant and underutilised (author survey). There are few attractions or facilities near the lake that might promote activities and attract pedestrians, and little residential development within walking proximity of the shoreline. A similar survey conducted five years later in 2019 revealed that new lakeside residential neighbourhoods and Ayer 8 commercial complex located along the western side of the lake have contributed to increased recreational activities along its foreshore.

Economic Development

The KLCC Park is an amenity to encourage companies to make economic and symbolic investments in the KLCC's 'new downtown'. The precinct is now home to many other leading multinational and Malaysian companies including Exxon, Maxis and Mitsubishi, and several leading international hotels (Hassan and Hanif 2012). Our own survey identified 2250 hotel rooms and serviced apartments nearby. Public investment in the site has had a significant role in attracting such businesses. Twenty-seven of the site's 39 ha were public land on leasehold, but the entire site was sold in untransparent circumstances to a former director of Petronas with close links to the then Prime Minister (Bunnell 1999). The new 20 ha park is in principle owned by the city government, but the council granted the property developers a 21-year lease to manage the park, so they could ensure high maintenance standards to optimise the value of the surrounding commercial investments (Hassan and Hanif 2012). This management regime admits the prospect of controls that go beyond mere maintenance, to optimise amenity value for commercial consumption. This includes posted rules prohibiting eating and drinking near the wading pool and adults wearing swimsuits, the right to close the pool to public use without prior notice, and construction of a leasable waterfront pavilion to re-capture the value of the lake view. The pavilion's daily rental fee is 16,000 EUR, restricting it to high-end business users. The KLCC Park serves primarily as an amenity that has helped attract wealthy tourists, shoppers and residents to the Suria KLCC mall and Petronas Towers, and is attracting significant further property development (JUBM and Langdon Seah 2014).

The larger-scale River of Life project was first and foremost conceived as an investment in national economic development, as part of Malaysia's aim to attain developed-country status by 2020. The two rivers (Gombak and Klang) which played such an important role in the history and development of Kuala Lumpur have been transformed into two industrial drains, buried under the city's transport and road infrastructure (King 2008). The current landscape along the rivers in central Kuala Lumpur is constituted by blank flood walls and empty pedestrian walkways. The only points of interest are the flood walls' informal murals (Figure 2.7). DBKL's deputy director of planning put it frankly: when the national government looked at what quality of life assets cities in advanced economies had, they all had revitalised urban waterfronts (DBKL 2014). Waterfront revitalisation was thus made an element of the wider development goal within Malaysia's Economic Transformation Plan (ETP) to enhance urban development in the Klang Valley. For the ROL project, which was launched in 2012, economic impact was difficult to measure and very long-term, compared to industry

Figure 2.7 Informal murals painted on the concrete flood walls of the Klang River in central Kuala Lumpur. Note also transport infrastructure cutting river off from surrounding city.

investments in other sectors (DBKL 2014). The other ETP projects all involve exploiting existing natural or human resources. The Klang and Gombak rivers were seen as assets degraded through relatively low-value uses, underexploited and requiring public-sector recapitalisation to leverage private investment in more up-market housing and offices. The Economic Report supporting the ROL Master Plan indicated that the project aimed to trigger as much as 5,000,000m^2 of new development on private and government owned land, including 20,000 new apartments to house 66,000 residents (23% of Kuala Lumpur's total predicted growth), and 100,000 new jobs (AECOM 2013c, DBKL 2012). What the River of Life primarily sought to emulate from the world's most liveable cities and their waterfront redevelopments was not improvements in ecology or quality of life, but demonstrating and advertising the municipal government's entrepreneurial competence in neoliberal management of an existing resource, recovering its potential as an asset to stimulate private-sector real estate investment (Desfor et al. 2010). The project clearly has an indirect, promotional role in the Klang Valley's economic development. But to date it has been difficult to determine the viability of the ROL's economic predictions.

The construction commenced in 2015 and the first phase of the ROL project, a 500 metre stretch between Masjid Jamek and the Central Market, was opened in 2017. The new riverfront comprises landscaped areas including walkways, sunken gardens, water fountains and several sitting and resting areas. A new pedestrian and cycling bridge linking two sides of the river was also constructed. The Blue Pool Project, a dancing water fountain, blue-lit corridor, plus sound and lighting effects, became the evening attraction of the riverfront (Nita Jay 2017). However, the project has not fulfilled its main objectives. The new riverfront is not a thriving and vibrant area popular with locals and visitors. The project is not physically and visually integrated with the surrounding areas. A majority of the heritage buildings along the River have not been revitalised and are still empty and obsolete. A multi-level joint government project to clean the river has not been fully successful. The water quality remains poor, it still looks muddy and polluted, and floating rubbish is common (Babulal 2019). Engineering failures in the creation of new weirs across the river also undermined the success of the project's first phase (Bavani 2019).

Compared to ROL, Putrajaya's waterfront lacks potential to directly stimulate economic development. There was no pent-up demand for the land of the existing oil palm plantation. Like the River of Life, Putrajaya's lake and surrounding green spaces are an amenity intended to attract white-collar residents to the city, promote a leisure lifestyle that makes use of public settings, and thus stimulate domestic consumption. But Putrajaya's development is strongly shaped by state regulation and state investment; it is not a real estate venture. Tight constraints on a private-sector land market have limited the prospects for significant outside economic investment. This approach is slowly changing (Kozlowski 2014). But few sites near the waterfront are open to private-sector land development or to commercial activities. The government's emphasis on preserving water quality restricts the range and intensity of waterfront and water-based uses. A dearth of permits for restaurants and food vending means few attractors to draw people regularly to the lake edge and keep them there for an extended time. Poor wayfinding and poor pedestrian connection to most of the lake edge also limits its attractiveness for commercial uses.

Putrajaya's waterfront recreation complex is at present disconnected from the government spine. Most food venues near Lake Putrajaya have views onto it but no direct physical connection, limiting prospects for complementary pools of mixed uses that would attract other consumption venues and keep the waterfront lively (see Chapter 1). Although the lakeside bicycle path is illuminated at night, public bicycle rental facilities close at 5pm, limiting evening cycling, the optimal time for active outdoor recreation in this perennially tropical climate. Our field survey of cafés and restaurants in the eight Precincts surrounding Lake Putrajaya revealed only 12 of 43 outlets are located along the 38km of lakeshore.

Putrajaya's two central mosques potentially provide focal points for catalysing a mix of urban activities near the lake. But they are set very high above the lake edge, and are entered from the land side, along sub-axes connecting to the city spine. There is a missed opportunity to harness the potent symbolic connection between the clean lake and the ritual of washing before entering a mosque to pray. As a point of comparison, the historic mosque Masjid Jamek in the centre of Kuala Lumpur, at the junction of the city's two main rivers, was originally entered from a grand staircase leading up from the water's edge. Putrajaya's largest completed shopping centre, Alamanda, sits adjacent to the lake. Although it is too far from the city's main axis to walk, it is potentially within walking distance of several dense residential clusters. Like the Suria KLCC, the Alamanda mall has a large pond with dancing fountains outside its inland, roadway front entrance, and a smaller one at the lake end of its main spine. But like most malls, it is very internalised. The outdoor dining area is elevated 3.5m above the foreshore, and has poor connection to its lake frontage. A 3m high blank wall on the lake frontage of the adjacent Everly Hotel also discourages evening pedestrian activity along the lake.

Only in recent years has the Putrajaya Corporation begun encouraging residential and commercial development facing the lake. A new lakeside commercial complex, Ayer 8 has recently opened across from the Iron Mosque. It incorporates some retail and dining premises fronting the water. But the public waterfront right-of-way has not been upgraded to support these uses (Figures 2.8 and 2.9); there is a lack of coordination between private and public investments. New waterfront developments recently

Figure 2.8 Open-sided waterfront restaurant in Taman Seri Empangan, a park adjacent to the dam at the south end of Lake Putrajaya.

Figure 2.9 Ayer 8 commercial development, Putrajaya. Weak pedestrian connection to the lake edge.

opened include the Putrajaya Marina recreational complex and a 2.6 ha local campus of Scotland's Heriot Watt University catering for 5000 students, deliberately sited within walking distance of the marina and resort. It was envisaged that the campus should enhance pedestrian vitality, economic vibrancy and commercial development along the Lake (Heriot-Watt University 2014). However, by 2019 Heriot-Watt had still not reached its full student capacity, and its contribution towards increased activity along the Lake is minimal. In 2014 there were still 1746 ha of vacant land suitable for development in Putrajaya. Sixty percent of this is located along the Lake or ancillary waterways (Putrajaya Holdings 2014). This illustrates the significant scope for further waterfront investment in Malaysia's administrative capital.

Ecological Performance

The managers of KLCC Park advertise its preservation of mature trees and its planting of a range of indigenous species, and its potential as a haven for native birds and small wildlife. But its purported role as a 'green lung' (Bunnell 1999) has to be seen chiefly in visual, psychological and promotional terms. Kuala Lumpur's hilly terrain retains adequate amounts of undeveloped, densely-forested land. The KLCC Park is an idealised, thematic construction of a tropical Malaysian landscape for leisure consumption, placed in a sublime oppositional pairing with high-tech, high-rise urban forms. It is not the riparian reconstitution of an endogenous water body; it has little capacity to improve air quality or protect biodiversity.

The creation of Lake Putrajaya and its wetlands has served practical purpose in controlling runoff and purifying the water. Putrajaya's lakefront botanical gardens and Vision Park help support biodiversity. There are numerous green fingers and reservations providing a wider green network throughout Putrajaya's built-up area. The area has a far richer diversity of plant and animal species than the palm plantation it replaced. The lake's extensive, sophisticated system of retention and filtration ponds advertise Malaysia's ecological ambitions, showcase contemporary best practice in sustainable drainage systems, and educate the public about the importance of water quality; at least for those who venture upstream of the lake to inspect them. These are certainly all significant steps forward.

But the overall visual rhetoric of Putrajaya as a 'green lung' (Siong et al. 2013) and these specific investments in ecological protection and their touted benefits should not be seen in isolation (PP 2012). As a whole, Putrajaya is a relatively carbon-intensive urban development. The city's carbon emissions have increased six-fold over the period 2007–11, and the local authority is now pursuing policies aiming to reverse this growth (Ho et al. 2013). Putrajaya's buildings are mostly air-conditioned; only the mosques and pavilions utilise the lake breezes. The most popular outdoor waterfront places for social interaction in Putrajaya are the two major bridges that span the lake (Figure 2.10). Out of 48 buildings in Putrajaya's core surrounding Persiaran Perdana (Precincts 1, 2, 3 and 4), only two buildings, the Premier's Department and the Energy Commission Building are certified as having efficient use of energy, water and materials (Green Building Index 2014). The distances between workplaces, residences and leisure areas in Putrajaya are too large for walking in the hot humid climate, and so are the distances between individual buildings; most people use cars, taxis or busses.

King (2008) critiqued Kuala Lumpur's as lacking any of the kind of ecological management and education provided by Putrajaya's wetlands and botanical garden. The

Figure 2.10 People socialising in the evening on Seri Wawasan (Bridge), Lake Putrajaya.

Source: Chee.Hong/Flickr – https://creativecommons.org/licenses/by/2.0/

River of Life responds to this lack, developing an image of ecological sensitivity. Like Putrajaya, the ROL reinforces its implicit message of ecological awareness through educational facilities such as publicly-accessible demonstration detention and filtration facilities along the embankments. But these investments are not concentrated in significant, useful enhancements in ecological performance. The ROL is, rather, a carefully managed image composed from natural elements, overlaid on a thoroughly urbanised, manufactured landscape, functioning as an advertisement for the government.

Despite the high internal environmental standards of these three waterfront projects, and their appealing images as ecologically rich, vibrant, clean environments, none has the capacity to provide significant improvements in overall environmental quality for their wider urban areas, except to the extent that Lake Putrajaya provides a source of clean, drinkable water. Nor has this necessarily been intended. These are urban waterfronts, carefully designed to fit within a context of intense development and use of land and high-volume transportation infrastructure. All three of these waterfront landscapes are highly cultivated, even to the extent of reforming drainage channels and basins. The wider urban development surrounding these signature set-pieces seldom makes any attempt to yield to natural landforms and vegetation or traditional practices of managing them (King 2008).

Learning from the Local Waterfront

The waterfront precincts examined here contribute significantly to the portrayal of Putrajaya and Kuala Lumpur as post-industrial cities that have moved beyond a colonial heritage of resource extraction and dependence, and that can compete for residents, global visitors and high-end real estate investment on the basis of high-quality landscapes tailored to consumption and displays of environmental responsibility. The KLCC and Putrajaya waterfronts also follow similar projects overseas in being largely segregated from existing mixed-use pedestrian precincts that could potentially make these waterfronts lively, inclusive social settings. Rather than reconnecting urban areas with the water, KLCC and Lake Putrajaya establish new enclaves. The ROL project's effort to re-integrate the city centre and the rivers by emphasising connectivity to, across and along the river corridor is a step in the right direction. However, lack of integrated planning and design, poor water quality, and engineering problems have failed to deliver the desired outcomes.

Despite critiques of its origins and ethnic exclusion, the Islamic-inspired architecture of Putrajaya and the Petronas Towers has been quite successful in presenting a distinctive new Malaysian identity (Moser 2010, Bunnell 1999). The same cannot be said for the waterfront landscapes that these buildings sit within, which reproduce generic international ideas about the appearance and uses of waterfront open space. These settings are strongly influenced by both Western and Eastern exemplars with colonial heritage: green oases within shopping malls, aquatic play zones, riverside promenades, restored colonial buildings, artificial beaches, educational demonstrations of ecological restoration, spectacular road bridges. None of the three projects reflect the local context of hilly, tropical jungle (except by selecting choice tree specimens from it), and there is little attention to traditional local ways of managing and using waterfront landscapes.

While urban waterfront redevelopment in most countries involves remediating the toxic heritage of former sea and river ports, none of these three Malaysian sites were industrial precincts. While Lake Putrajaya and the River of Life, like other urban waterfront re-naturalisation schemes, clearly provide aesthetic benefits that attract tourists and residents, there is no evidence that the three projects significantly enhance overall environmental indicators such as air and water quality. Also in representational terms, these three projects do not engage directly with the particular history of their landscape of colonisation, immigration and development – the tin mines, the plantation, the horseracing club, the Chinese commercial zone. Putrajaya's grand new urban architecture largely ignores the Malay vernacular housing or mosque forms with their tiered roofs and open walls and their intimate relation to water. In terms of appearance, use and development process, these waterfront projects are formulaic, similar to urban waterfront redevelopments elsewhere. The use of international design consultants to shape KLCC Park and the River of Life suggests this was actively sought.

These three projects conform to King's (2008) assessment of Malaysian urban landscapes generally as being collages of contradictory, largely exogenous influences and objectives. Such contradictions are perhaps at odds with the very idea of an 'ecology', undermining any prospect that sets of forces can be brought into balance. Malaysia's planners and designers are clearly seeking to forge distinctive outcomes by drawing on a range of external exemplars, but the predominantly Western models, which are mostly former industrial areas in temperate climates, are of questionable relevance to the Malaysian context. The greatest lack seems to be in Malaysia's new urban waterfronts learning from their own local spaces and traditions and developing new, distinctive paradigms. Four more authentic possibilities for Malaysian waterfronts are suggested by existing sites within our study areas. The first is the numerous street-art murals currently lining the concrete flood walls around Kuala Lumpur's river junction (Figure 2.7). The very inaccessibility of this riverfront has made it a sheltered site for this rare kind of contemporary public expression. There is little public art in Kuala Lumpur and Putrajaya, especially not depicting people. The second locally-derived waterfront public space is the numerous modern, open-sided pavilions facing onto Lake Putrajaya, such as the large fish restaurant overlooking the lake's remote southern end, next to its retaining wall (Figure 2.8). Third, Putrajaya's two main lake bridges (Figure 2.10) are very popular locations for evening socialising because of their breezes, views and night-time illumination. More could be made of the opportunities for public life encouraged by these predominantly-vehicular bridges. The fourth is the steps that lead up from the river to Kuala Lumpur's first mosque, Masjid Jamek, now being reinstated (Figure 2.11). This links the intimate religious practice of washing the feet to the city's founding location. These latter examples encourage people to have prolonged, frequent engagement with the river in their everyday lives. Rather than jet-ski rentals, high-rise luxury apartments and school visits to retention ponds, these seem to be activities that Malaysians readily associate with urban waterfronts.

Figure 2.11 Reinstatement works on stairs leading down to the river confluence, Masjid Jamek (Mosque), Kuala Lumpur, October 2014.

References

Abdul Latip, N.S., Heath, T., and Liew, M.S. (2009) 'A morphological analysis of the waterfront in City Centre', *Kuala Lumpur INTA-SEGA Bridging Innovation, Technology and Tradition Conference Proceedings*.
AECOM (2013a) *Master Plan Report for the River of Life (ROL) Project*, Kuala Lumpur: AECOM.
AECOM (2013b) *Technical Report for the River of Life Project: Environmental Study*, Kuala Lumpur: AECOM.
AECOM (2013c) *Technical Report for the River of Life Project: Economic Report*, Kuala Lumpur: AECOM.
Babulal, V. (2019) 'River of Life project has fallen short of objectives', *New Straits Times*, 7 October, available from https://www.nst.com.my/news/nation/2019/10/527674/river-life-project-has-fallen-short-objectives, accessed 15 April 2020.
Bavani, M. (2019) 'KL's Venetian dream collapses', *The Star*, 22 May. https://www.thestar.com.my/metro/metro-news/2019/05/22/kls-venetian-dream-collapses/. Accessed 15 April 2020.
Breen, A. and Rigby, D. (1996) *The New Waterfront: A Worldwide Urban Success Story*, London: Thames and Hudson.
Bunce, S. (2009) 'Developing sustainability: Sustainability policy and gentrification on Toronto's waterfront', *Local Environment*, 14 (7), pp 651–667.
Bunnell, T. (1999) 'Views from above and below: The Petronas Twin Towers and/in contesting visions of development in contemporary Malaysia', *Singapore Journal of Tropical Geography*, 20 (1), pp 1–23.
Chang, T. C. and Huang, S. (2011) 'Reclaiming the city: Waterfront development in Singapore', *Urban Studies*, 48 (10), pp. 2085–2100.
Chang, T. C., Huang, S., and Savage, V. (2004) 'On the waterfront: Globalization and urbanization in Singapore', *Urban Geography*, 25 (5), pp. 413–436.
DBKL = Dewan Bandaraya Kuala Lumpur (Kuala Lumpur City Hall) (2012) *Kuala Lumpur City Plan 2020*.
DBKL = Dewan Bandaraya Kuala Lumpur (2014) *Personal interview with staff from the city planning department*, 16 April.
Desfor, G. and Laidley, J. (2010) 'Introduction: Fixity and flow of urban waterfront change', in Desfor, G., Laidley, J., Stevens, Q. and Schubert, D. (eds) *Transforming Urban Waterfronts: Fixity and Flow*, New York: Routledge, pp. 1–13.
Desfor, G., Laidley, J., Stevens, Q. and Schubert, D. (eds) (2010) *Transforming Urban Waterfronts: Fixity and Flow*, New York: Routledge.
Dodman, D. (2007) 'Post-independence optimism and the legacy of waterfront redevelopment in Kingston, Jamaica', *Cities*, 24 (4), pp. 273–284.

Dovey, K. (2005) *Fluid City: Transforming Melbourne's Urban Waterfront*, London: Routledge.
Gidel, M. (2010) 'Fragmentation on the waterfront: Coastal squatting settlements and urban renewal projects in the Caribbean', in Desfor, G., Laidley, J., Stevens, Q. and Schubert, D. (eds) *Transforming Urban Waterfronts: Fixity and Flow*, New York: Routledge, pp 35–53.
Green Building Index (2014) www.greenbuildingindex.org, accessed 14 November 2014.
Hagerman, C. (2012) 'Shaping neighborhoods and nature: Urban political ecologies of urban waterfront transformations in Portland, Oregon', *Cities*, 24 (4), pp 285–297.
Hassan, N. and Hanif, N.R. (2012) 'Privatization of urban space: The Kuala Lumpur City Centre' City Innovation case Study Brief', available from https://pdfs.semanticscholar.org/5bc1/c909a35ace8de994f375207949b39f1be989.pdf, accessed 9 August 2020.
Heriot-Watt University (2014) 'Our Campus', available from http://www.hw.ac.uk/malaysia/about/campus.htm, accessed 14 November 2014.
Ho, C. S., Azeez, A. and Adeyemi, J. (2013) 'Low carbon cities – The way forward in real estate development in Malaysia', *International Journal of Real Estate Studies*, 8 (1), pp 50–59.
JUBM and Langdon Seah (2014) *Construction Cost Handbook*, available from www.langdonseah.com.
King, R. (2008) *Kuala Lumpur and Putrajaya: Negotiating Urban Space in Malaysia*, Copenhagen: NIAS Press.
Kozlowski, M (2014) 'Revisiting Putrajaya', *Architecture Malaysia*, 26 (3), pp. 72–75.
Kum, T. L. and Ujang, N. (2012) 'The application of mental mapping technique in identifying the legible elements within historical district of Kuala Lumpur city centre', *Alam Cipta*, 5 (1), pp. 55–62.
Law, L. (2002) 'Defying disappearance: Cosmopolitan public spaces in Hong Kong', *Urban Studies*, 39 (9), pp 1625–1645.
Marshall, R. (ed) (2001) *Waterfronts in Post-industrial Cities*, London: Spon.
MFT = Ministry of Federal Territories (2014) *EPP5: River of Life*, Putrajaya: Ministry of Federal Territories, available from http://app.kwpkb.gov.my/greaterklkv/entrypoint- project-river, accessed 20 May 2014.
Moser, S. (2010) 'Putrajaya: Malaysia's new federal administrative capital', *Cities*, 27 (4), pp 285–297.
Nita Jay, B. (2017) 'Najib launches River of Life, Blue Pool projects', *New Straits Times*, 28 August, available from https://www.nst.com.my/news/nation/2017/08/273894/najib-launches-river-life-blue-pool-projects, accessed 15 April 2020.
PP = Perbadanan Putrajaya (1997) 'Master plan for Putrajaya'.
PP = Perbadanan Putrajaya (2012) 'Putrajaya draft structure plan: Sustainable Putrajaya 2025: From Garden to Green'.
PP = Perbadanan Putrajaya (2014), *personal interview with staff from the Lake Management department*, 14 April.
Putrajaya Holdings (2014) *Putrajaya Facts and Figures*, available from http://www.pjh.com.my/corporate/putrajaya-facts/
Sandercock, L. and Dovey, K. (2002), 'Pleasure, politics and the public interest: Melbourne's waterfront revitalization', *Journal of the American Planning Association*, 68, 151–64
Savage, V., Huang, S. and Chang, T. (2004) 'The Singapore river thematic zone: Sustainable tourism in an urban context', *The Geographical Journal*, 170 (3), 212–225.
Shamsuddin, S., Abdul Latip, N., and Sulaiman, A.B. (2013) *Regeneration of the Historic Waterfront: An Urban Design Compendium for Malaysian Waterfront Cities*, Kuala Lumpur: ITBM.
Shamsuddin, S, Abdul Latip, N.S, Ujang, N., Sulaiman, A.B., and Alias, N.A. (2012) 'How the city lost its waterfront: Tracing the effects of policies on the sustainability of the Kuala Lumpur waterfront as a public place', *Journal of Environmental Planning and Management*, 56 (3), pp. 378–397.
Siong, H. C., Abdul-Azeez, I. A. and Adeyemi, I. (2013) 'Low carbon cities – The Way forward in real estate development in Malaysia', *International Journal of Real Estate Studies*, 8 (1), pp. 50–59.
Vale, L. (2008) *Architecture, Power and National Identity*, 2nd ed., London: Routledge.

Chapter 3
Tracing the Shifting Waterfront

Quentin Stevens

This chapter gathers together general insights gleaned from a collection of single and comparative studies of the physical, social and economic changes that urban waterfronts have undergone over recent decades, *Transforming Urban Waterfronts* (Desfor et al. 2010). This collection has a particular focus on the interactions between their various fixities and flows. The contributions in this volume examine the ongoing development of waterfronts in urban areas from the tropics to the cool temperate regions, both north and south, from the Pacific to the Atlantic and Caribbean and on the Great Lakes, as well as along rivers both large and small. The developmental contexts range from incipient industrialisation to decline and through one or more cycles of reinvestment.

    This chapter identifies a range of common themes and concerns that flow through that book, and discerns the key social, economic, political and urbanistic variations within those themes. This chapter's opening section summarises the kinds of fixities and flows that captured the interest of that book's contributors. The case study chapters in that book provide the detail of *why* and *how* specific waterfronts become fixed or are brought in flow. The focus of this chapter's synopsis is on three interlinked variables through which the contributors try to understand the fixities and flows of waterfront change, and the problems therein: the *where*, *when* and *who*. The question of *where* reflects the varying scales and directions of waterfront development and governance. To address *when* requires charting different histories of growth, stagnation and decline. The subject of *who* involves the scope of actors who shape waterfront change, as well as those affected by it, and the divergent interests they pursue. Because the question of *who* is always political, this conclusion also explores the diverse political and governance structures and processes that give shape to waterfront development, and in particular the recent popularity of neoliberalism as an approach to both developing and critiquing waterfronts, to see how this philosophy is actually manifested on particular waterfronts and in specific fixities and flows. Each of this chapter's thematic sections draws upon the detail of the book's case studies and theorisations to illustrate commonalities and diversities in waterfront change under differing circumstances, to critically compare a range of actions and outcomes, and to identify persistent problems which still require practical resolution. The final section of this chapter reflects upon the concepts and methodologies through which the book's contributors interpreted waterfront change, and highlights several distinct directions and questions that these studies and findings suggest for future research into urban waterfronts within the social sciences.

What Is Flowing and What Is Fixed?

The contributions in *Transforming Urban Waterfronts* do not only study the physical space of the waterfront, and do not treat this space as a fixed given. They examine what moves through the space, and what makes the space itself change: goods, people and vehicles; information, money and political power. But which aspects are fixed, and which flow? The contributors critically prise open the question of whether any dimensions of waterfronts and their development are definitively permanent or transient. The land itself is not necessarily fixed. It is created and removed, contaminated and rectified, by human intervention but also by tides and floods. Much of the waterfront is liminal, a 'both-and' margin between land and water: floodway, floodplain, marsh, swamp or beach. It can be concreted or renaturalised, although generally not forever. The legal tenure of waterfront land is also often in flux, and this is not only true of informal settlements. Land can sometimes be sold to investors by agencies that do not technically own it, private railroad companies struggle with public port authorities for dominance of freight transport, and even large government authorities that control entire port regions are dissolved, created or replaced.

The 'fixing' of urban waterfronts through planning and construction does not always mean their spatial reintegration into cities or economic security for everyone: in London, Dublin, Antwerp and Port of Spain, we see new fragmentation, whether through exclusionary intentions or inadvertently through the multiplicity of governance arrangements. Enhancing flows of global trade often involves building fences, walls and uncrossable roadways that restrict access to waterfronts. Ports themselves move, historically flowing away from the cities to which they were previously fixed, usually downstream toward the river mouth, onto land that was less stable and harder to 'fix.' Some people, equipment and investment move with them. Some things are left behind: communities, memories, buildings and contaminants. In those cases where a waterfront environment does remain fixed, one has to ask whether this is due to political success or merely neglect. Fixity does not always mean power; in Vancouver, Fort-de-France, and still-industrial Brooklyn, it has meant disconnection. When ports move, their former links to inner-city commerce and residents are transformed. Wonneberger (2010) observes that redevelopment also threatens the wider social capital that has been built up over time in communal institutions such as the church, community centres and informal social venues. Gidel (2010) and Kane (2010) both question who it is that defines and preserves particular identities for waterfront areas, and to what ends.

New people and activities continue flowing into waterfronts. In the Caribbean, the poorer residential populations who now resist change have themselves not always been so fixed in place; they are part of a continuing rural-to-urban drift. Similarly, those who were once blue-collar immigrants to an industrialising Seattle now struggle against an influx of apparently more skilled 'creative' workers. Some people are more mobile and less fixed to place than others. This can be seen positively as 'cosmopolitan' or negatively as 'nomadic'. But is there social mobility *upward* on the waterfront? Despite all the physical, economic and social changes occurring there, the urban social strata generally seem to be very fixed. Lurking behind many waterfront redevelopment proposals there seems to be a strong class consciousness, belied by the obsession with 'world class' facilities. Antagonism and segregation seem endemic. Change on urban waterfronts often happens very swiftly, with new people and buildings tending to displace the old, instead of an upgrading in place. Enticing wealthier residents to Dublin's waterfront involved the creation of gated housing enclaves, which have limited social mixing. Rotterdam illustrates attempts to define a more mixed-use, mixed income, balanced waterfront community. Yet neighbourhoods inevitably continue to grow, and their demography changes.

These manifold shifts highlight that the study of 'the waterfront' is not just about one isolated strip of land, but rather about a wide range of flows that pass across the interface between a city and its waterways. These flows often have their own complex structure and regularity, such as the standardisation of shipping containers and their handling.

The Scale and Direction of Fixities and Flows

Scale is a central concern for both Hall and Clark (2010) and Schubert (2010). Restructuring continues at local, metropolitan and regional scales. Regional changes in the economic geography of ports and port cities are driven by global forces. Gidel (2010) differentiates between colonial and regional dynamics shaping Caribbean ports. Desfor (2010) notes how the nineteenth-century growth of Toronto and its waterfront were driven by the increasing development of its hinterland and by competition with other cities and regions. In this context, it would be interesting to examine the regional landscape surrounding the other case study cities presented in this book, to consider, as Hall and Clark and Schubert do, the contrasting fixities and flows of their neighbouring ports: Puerto Nuevo near Buenos Aires, Tacoma near Seattle, Oakland near San Francisco, and New Jersey near New York – this last pair being jointly managed. Originally smaller, less urban, cheaper to develop and less widely-known, these ports were often better suited to containerisation as it developed in the 1960s. As Schubert notes, these ports have grown tremendously while the waterfronts of their urban cousins have undergone redevelopment.

At a much smaller scale, Gidel (2010) and Wonneberger (2010) both study disadvantaged communities who are largely excluded from waterfront economies, but who have to contend with these economies' external impacts. In both large and small contexts, many contributors to this volume highlight the importance of broadening the research focus to examine what is adjacent to the waterfront, because there is a risk for researchers and planners, as for developers and politicians, of fetishising the water's edge (see also Chapter 1). As Ramsey (2010, 117) notes of Seattle,

> debate concerned only one segment of roadway along Seattle's waterfront. Focusing only on the waterfront area prompted a polarizing debate between those seeking benefits for the waterfront and those whose concerns were for impacts outside the study area. A more comprehensive consideration ... would have avoided this conflict and could therefore have helped in building creative alliances ... in pursuit of common goals.

Researchers need to be alert to the ways that waterfronts are integrated into – or detached from – a wide variety of forces operating at differing scales. In terms of natural geography, the Plate River Basin adjacent to Buenos Aires is affected by thousands of factories illegally dumping waste into its tributaries. The construction of Toronto's port physically expanded the city's geography and also expanded its economic importance and power. Many contributors examine waterfronts as social geographies (neighbourhoods) and political geographies (jurisdictions). While many studies within *Transforming Urban Waterfronts* illustrate the importance of waterfronts' links to surrounding activity patterns (see Chapter 1), Gidel (2010) critiques waterfront schemes for their frequently 'ad hoc', 'exceptional' status: politically and economically as well as physically detached from the flows and the constraints of their urban surroundings. This ambition also perhaps underlay Margaret Thatcher's vision of London Docklands as 'an exceptional place' (Lee 1992, 7). Hall and Clark (2010) illustrate the usefulness of Cox's (1998) distinction between 'spaces of dependence' and 'spaces of engagement': actors must engage in political processes at a variety of scales to protect or improve local waterfront spaces where they have relatively fixed social, political and financial investments. The recurring question is whether they can. Gidel documents different scales at which changes on waterfronts are actually put into practice, depending on what decisions are made, by whom, and in whose interest, emphasising not just shifting scales of external forces for change, but also the different links between local and global in different cases.

For both shipping and post-industrial uses, the physical development of waterfronts generally continues to increase in scale and intensity. Development grows even when available space does not, and as a result intervening green spaces become smaller. Wonneberger (2010) documents many such 'micro-level effects' of port construction in Dublin on the local environment, as waterfront buildings keep getting taller. In Boston's Inner Harbor, eleven of thirteen new buildings are taller than proposed height limits. Height increases on waterfronts are even offered to leverage private investment in infrastructure – infrastructure for which this intensive development actually creates the need. This approach could be conceived as an unconstitutional selling of the State's police power; such is the scale of the interests being negotiated. One might ask what height limits seek to protect. Gidel (2010), Wonneberger (2010), Rubin (2010) and Schaller and Novy (2010) all suggest a fundamental incompatibility between high-rise development and waterfront sites: it overshadows their unique open spaces, and its construction often destroys the sensitive inter-tidal zone. On Buenos Aires's waterfront, a giant silo remains, an icon of Argentina's standing as 'the Granary of the World', and of an earlier, more liberal industrial era (Kane 2010). Other waterfront transformations progress through very small-scale interventions, although their cumulative impact can nonetheless be substantial.

The development of waterfront spaces is regulated through plans and planning approaches with differing geographical scopes and differing degrees of sensitivity and inclusivity. Planning sometimes neglects or homogenises the waterfront's existing diversity. In Brooklyn, zoning is too blunt a planning instrument to guarantee compatibility between existing industrial uses and intense demands for new housing and office space. In other cases, the waterfront is fragmented to maximise profits, as with Antwerp's 1990s proposal to subdivide port land for private investment, without a comprehensive plan. On marginal land along Berlin's Spree River, fragmentation allows new, low-budget projects to find a foothold and flourish. Heeg (2010) draws on Swyngedouw et al. (2002, 215) to contrast comprehensive planning of waterfronts against the contemporary focus on projects: 'Against the crisis of the comprehensive *Plan* – the classic policy instrument of the Fordist age – the large, emblematic *Project* has emerged as a viable alternative, allegedly combining the advantages of flexibility and targeted actions with a tremendous symbolic capacity.' Heeg also critiques the use of Planned Development Areas that support deviation from general zoning regulations: whatever their other merits in terms of flexibility, they restrict community involvement and influence in the planning process. In most cases it is clear that policy for urban waterfront development is primarily, though not exclusively, shaped at the urban level, and thus according to the needs of urban populations that are typically large and culturally and economically diverse. Waterfronts are local spaces where a wide range of social issues and needs are concentrated, and where there is also scope for them to be addressed.

In addition to examining the scale of waterfront flows and changes it is important to consider their direction. As Kane (2010, 213) observes: 'Flows are multidirectional, rivers flow out to sea, brackish tidal waters flow upstream … people, goods, money, music, text and image move and settle in diverse, interlinking and layered channels, networks and niches'. Many contributors to *Transforming Urban Waterfronts* see the waterfront as a place of high mobility, defined by many different systems of connectivity: for ships, for vehicles, for pedestrians. Hall and Clark (2010), Schubert (2010) and Desfor (2010) all document shifts in the dominance of transport modes, from water to rail to truck, and shifts in competition and coordination among them. There are also changes in the direction of goods being shipped: formerly from the West, now increasingly from the East. In numerous chapters, waterfront transport infrastructure provides an important conceptual and empirical link between directional flows and fixed characteristics. In Rubin's (2010, 145–6) summation, the key characteristic of a waterfront is that it is an edge ... crossing it frequently requires large capital investments in wharfs, piers, quays, cranes, railroads, roads, etc. And both the use and exchange value of the water's edge depends very much on those capital investments. Although the edge is a relatively fixed feature, its precise location will vary as a result of both human interventions and biophysical forces.

In Vancouver and Seattle, improving flows in one direction (for local residents and businesses) has a negative impact on flows in another (for port trucking). San Francisco's elevated Embarcadero Freeway ostensibly served the latter but in reality benefited the former. Barcelona's new pedestrian links over the vehicular flows to Port Vell predominantly foster flows of tourists and their Euros. Taşan-Kok and Sungu-Eryilmaz (2010, 262) argue Rotterdam's Erasmus Bridge to Kop van Zuid 'has succeeded in linking socially, economically, and physically separate parts of the city'. More than transport infrastructure, the bridge is also a landmark that fixes local identity. Kane (2010) brings anthropological insight to the significance of bridges for cultural identity: authenticity is reflected in the technological necessity of La Boca's mobile industrial bridge, but absent from Calatrava's Bridge of Womankind in Puerto Madero. In Willetts Point, Brooklyn, the 'barriers' of heavyweight transport infrastructure are part of the character that defines the area, sustains its 'unique auto-related industry cluster'. and separates it from pedestrian networks (Schaller and Novy 2010, 176). In Buenos Aires, Rotterdam and Hamburg, bridges are proud symbols of the conquest of natural divisions and flows and the creation of new connections. In London Docklands, local underinvestment in transport infrastructure parallels fluctuations in the flow of inward investment. In many cases, major waterfront transport investments are resisted, to protect relatively fixed patterns of urban social and economic life.

The rhetoric of change on waterfronts is almost always about 'opening up' the city to the water. This is usually linked to a metaphoric opening up of property, trade and governance to external markets; hence the frequent construction of International Waterfront Centres (e.g. Port of Spain), International Financial Services Centres (e.g. Dublin), and the like. This is an unassailable positivist rhetoric, in which physical expansion necessarily goes together with being outward-looking and forward-looking. Rubin writes of the expansion of San Francisco's crowded downtown out into the water, on piers and landfill. Proposed waterfront mega-projects showed a patent disregard for their physical and environmental context, especially the water. The result of such real-estate-focused schemes is typically degradation of coastal and riverine ecologies, and reduction of public amenity and public access. Heeg (2010, 279) notes the large-scale projects in South Boston 'seem to develop a life of their own: in terms of design, social and economic structure, many are scarcely integrated into their surrounding neighbourhoods'. Desfor (2010) argues that new, solid waterfront land in Toronto was produced through social, and therefore political, processes, which thus largely reflect the interests of economically dominant groups. Reshaping of the land responds to shifting markets and also reshapes local economic fortunes.

Time and Tide

There is an important historical perspective to most of the changes documented in *Transforming Urban Waterfronts*, from Desfor describing the creation of industrial ports, to Hall and Clark and Schubert examining their recent transformations. Some constructed fixities generate new flows over long timespans, such as the Panama Canal did for Vancouver. Containerisation was clearly a major shift, a long-term investment in technology that has restructured port geography. The typically large scale of waterfront changes usually means long time frames, in terms of physical developments, but also the politics and financing that drive them. Brownhill examines the fixities and flows of the London Docklands development process, not its object and image. As Heeg (2010, 274) emphasises, 'the focus on the built environment comprises more than providing visible signs, urban spectacle, flagship developments, design and images. It is first and foremost about facilitating constant change in the urban landscape to meet new economic requirements'. Rubin (2010) traces an extended history of struggle between the interests of capital accumulation and local community on San Francisco's waterfront. Brownhill (2010) also portrays shifting, evolving dynamics; waterfront development does not necessarily have tidy eras. Seldom do we see the planning and management of waterfronts flowing smoothly, through continuous, well-managed and inclusive development. Schubert (2010) presents Hamburg's 'String of Pearls' as a market-sensitive strategy whereby spectacular projects could proceed according to lumpy flows of financing and site availability. He contrasts this with HafenCity's phased implementation of developments in sub-districts: a fine solution, provided the public development company remains financially liquid and investment flows support it.

In many cases, we see recurring shifts between periods of intense investment interest and periods of economic decline. Schubert highlights that these waves often reflect wider markets for housing and office space. While contemporary governance strategies are often premised on inbound flows of private capital, these flows cannot always be ensured. Periods of neglect can last for decades: not all deindustrialised urban waterfront land in Berlin and Buenos Aires has investors ready and waiting. Uneven historical development can also vary across different parts of a single waterfront, differentiated by social investments and perceptions even in cases where its underlying geography is uniform. Gidel (2010) notes that development on one waterfront site can at the same time degrade others: Port of Spain gains an international flagship, but this reduces the quality of the local environment. Schaller and Novy (2010, 168) note that despite all the talk of spectacle and public access, much of a city's waterfront land is unsightly, home to 'waste sites, hazardous manufacturing facilities and highways'. These disparities aid subsequent revaluation of waterfront land, and thus speculative profits.

Several contributors to *Transforming Urban Waterfronts* question the formulation of 'blight requiring improvement.' Ramsey critiques the teleology of waterfront 'development' as 'progress', the belief that proposed redevelopments are inevitably technologically, socially, environmentally and economically better than what came before. Drawing on Flyvbjerg (1998) and Gidel (2010) notes that development decisions often flow more quickly than the wider logic that should sustain them. Schaller and Novy (2010) argue that not all industrial waterfronts are necessarily in need of redevelopment and changes in land uses; the small-scale industrial landscapes of Brocklyn's Willets Point and Gowanus Canal are still economically viable, even vibrant, with low vacancy rates, and they serve the needs of immigrant groups. Waterfront planning and investment should support rather than displace them.

The unevenness of waterfront development needs to be understood in terms of political, social and environmental objectives, as well as economic ones. Economic growth cannot always be used as a justification for physical development, and it cannot always be expected as an outcome. Fort-de-France, economically the poorest waterfront studied here, pursues a long-term strategy of inclusive social development. Rotterdam's plans also involve developing the community as well as the port. Rubin (2010, 150) highlights that San Francisco's 25 years without waterfront development reflected conscious priorities, wherein a lack of commercial pressure allowed the city scope to promote 'adaptive re-use, moderately-scaled, contextual development, access to the water and provision of other public amenities'. It was projects with a strong public interest component, such as fishing piers and open spaces, that eventually brought new flows of users to the waterfront. Heeg's (2010) conclusion from South Boston is that an economic downturn may be just the time when urban governments can push forward their agendas for housing and other social needs on waterfronts. There is much scope for further research focusing on new kinds of movements on waterfronts.

Role and Interests in Waterfront Change

Wonneberger (2010) demonstrates that Dublin's waterfront is not just a contaminated industrial brownfield, but a community, or more precisely a heterogeneous set of communities. Schubert (2010) notes that historically, urban waterfronts were defined by the 50 of a centrally-managed, specialised single-purpose area. Yet a scan across the chapters reveals a near-inexhaustible list of interested and affected parties who have knowledge to share and who struggle for attention on waterfronts.

Politicians at national, regional and local levels are involved in waterfront change, with their wide array of professional and bureaucratic staffs as well as relatively independent public bodies such as environmental agencies. These organs of the State themselves have tremendously varied interests. This applies as well to port officials and redevelopment agencies, such as the DDDA, LDDC, LTGUDC, BRA, and THC (the Dublin Docklands Development Authority, London Docklands Development Corporation, London Thames Gateway Urban Development Corporation, Boston Redevelopment Authority, and Toronto Harbour Commissioners, respectively), which appear to often be publicly unaccountable, with their own budgets and unelected management.

These organisations ostensibly represent and serve the interests of the general public, within which there are often differing interests among local residents, local workers, residents from elsewhere in the region, and visitors. Wonneberger (2010), Gidel (2010) and Taşan-Kok and Sungu-Eryilmaz (2010) draw our attention to the specific needs – often underserved – of low-income residents. Such underprivileged groups sometimes have their own skilled advocates for 'social justice', however defined. Taşan-Kok and Sungu-Eryilmaz (2010, 270) refer to the representation of public interest(s) undertaken by 'resident groups ... labour unions, environmental groups, affordable housing groups, school districts, faith-based organisations'.

Schaller and Novy (2010,167) distinguish among 'specific interests such as environmentalism, labor rights, affordable housing and industrial retention'. Kane (2010, 214) explores the involvement of a wider group of actors who bring specific expertise, including 'activists and artists, scholars, and experts in universities and non-governmental organisations'. These intermediaries may or may not come from the 'grass-roots,' and seldom speak for everyone. Ramsey (2010) differentiates among activists favouring particular transportation needs and systems, highlighting the fine fragmentation of the public good.

Private interests range from property owners, investors, and developers with their armies of professional consultants, to the wide range of tenants utilising waterfront property. The scope of production uses ranges from the obvious shipping and fishing to maritime industries such as fish processing, manufacturing, and recently in Boston life sciences and biotechnology. Waterfronts are home to re-locating corporate offices and new retailers, as well as existing local retailers (in Rotterdam, New York and Seattle) who suffer from the new competition. And there are leisure uses, both entertaining and edifying, which typically serve city-wide audiences. Of particular interest for researchers is the frequency and extent of vacant land on waterfronts, often disguised as parking lots, being held by speculators.

These various actors' interests in the future of waterfronts span a wide range of ecological, economic and social agendas. In Brownhill's review of the different rationalities underpinning and coordinating these interests, she emphasises that there can be mutually exclusive objectives. Ramsey concurs that new plans are not always 'win-win'. But discourses are hybrid and dynamic, and it is important to examine the detail of how needs and ideas change or become embedded over time. Gidel (2010), for example, observes formal acceptance of informal waterfront dwellings; new flows of residents are destined to become fixed and normalised. Brownhill (2010, 138) notes that 'the tensions between these different discourses played themselves out in different ways in different projects and strategies'.

Having noted earlier the frequent imperative to 'open up' the waterfront, research should examine what is opened up, and for whom. Taşan-Kok and Sungu-Eryilmaz (2010), Ramsey (2010) and Heeg (2010) all highlight that local governments have attempted to – or are compelled to – make waterfront areas attractive for higher-income groups to increase local tax revenues and thereby diminish existing or potential fiscal and social problems. Taşan-Kok and Sungu-Eryilmaz's (2010, 262) critique of Antwerp's waterfront proposals could apply to many other waterfronts featured in *Transforming Urban Waterfronts* and in earlier books: 'The plan simply provided housing and entertainment for well-paid upper-middle class professionals'. Schubert suggests Barcelona's 'sanitising' approach with 'gentrified gastronomy' and attractive new public spaces have become a European template. Ramsey (2010, 102) depicts the new activities Seattle's waterfront might have to accommodate: 'ambling pedestrians, sidewalk cafes, street performers, tour buses, sightseeing cruises, police surveillance and jogging'. His analysis of the rhetoric of class warfare draws our attention to the unequal distributive impacts, costs and benefits of these transformations. Several contributors depict a central, polarised conflict between the new, 'creative' knowledge workers, bankers, realtors and tourists flowing into waterfronts, and blue-collar workers and underemployed residents who are staying put. The existing residents, workers and businesses are usually expected to adapt and be flexible, whether the resources and supports for them to do this exist or not.

The shift away from primary industry and manufacturing toward the service sector brings a different residential base with a very different relationship to the water. Gidel (2010) laments a 'forgotten maritimity' (Desse 1996): oceans and rivers used to be a source of work, food and income, not just nice views. As contrast, Fort-de-France, Dublin and San Francisco illustrate upgrading of existing housing, fixing of minimum standards, and 'proportionality principles' for ensuring housing affordability, as well as improving job prospects for existing residents and sustaining local heritage. Gidel's conclusion cautions that such upgrading can inadvertently foster gentrification. Economic development broadly defined remains of considerable interest to local politicians and campaigners, although it is not nearly as photogenic as property development and is of little interest to architects.

The Turning of the Political Tide

The question of *who* fixes or changes the waterfront needs to be examined within a political context. Heeg (2010, 275) notes that 'transformation is triggered in the *relationship* between urban planners, local politicians and the private real estate sector... and non-governmental stakeholders, including residents'. The actors outlined in the previous section are examined throughout the book building alliances of varying durability at different scales and around different waterfront problems and ambitions. Policy and development outcomes are always a product of struggles among a great multiplicity of parties and forces. Brownhill (2010, 126) provides a useful review of how 'different modes of governance and different practices and strategies have developed over time, and how these have constantly interacted, collided, repelled and intersected with each other'. Ramsey's (2010) analysis highlights new and unexpected alignments of interests, sometimes united by their common opposition to official plans. All the contributors' case studies emphasise processes, rather than fetishising the landscape as a fixed object. Antwerp's failings indicate the limitations of design-oriented waterfront plans that lack innovative economic and social policies and implementation instruments.

Providing an historical and philosophical context to the political dimension, Desfor (2010, 197) writes of an essentialising, state-sponsored 'politics of improvement', a belief that 'what was good for the waterfront was always what was good for all of Toronto', which short-circuits the very complex politics actually determining waterfront transformations. Seen positively, Taşan-Kok and Sungu-Eryilmaz (2010, 271) believe the 'top down' approach at Kop van Zuid in Rotterdam suggests 'macro-scale policies for achieving social sustainability are necessary for success in creating social integration in cities'. In Belgium and the Netherlands, municipal ownership of land allows control in the public interest, for example by building affordable housing. Desfor (2010) presents the case that State control allows development to proceed 'gradually and economically according to plans framed in the public interest' (Bryce 1892, 4). Yet the Toronto City Commissioner's campaign for State-led and State-managed growth for 'business too important to leave to private capital' (Desfor 2010, 204) also has later echoes in the State's top-down facilitation of private enterprise in the London Docklands in the 1980s and in New York City and Boston today. In this vein, Schaller and Novy (2010) suggest that plans for New York's waterfront had to wait for a mayor with 'vision and resolve', a comprehensive and 'interventionist' agenda for urban planning and economic development, a 'return of urban renewal' *a la* Robert Moses (Fainstein 2005). Their critique is that Bloomberg's vision was mostly linked to the extrinsic aims of bidding for the 2012 Olympics and promoting private-sector investment. Interestingly, Paris's temporary waterfront project from 2002, the city beach *Paris Plage* (see Chapter 7), also served as a form of city marketing to tourists and to support Paris' competing bid for the 2012 Olympics (Gale 2009). Large-scale, rigid plans, designs and management systems tend to imply State control, but whether in its Fordist or entrepreneurial guise, the State is one of the fixities that can potentially hinder flows of new ideas, materials, forms and activities through the urban waterfront.

Desfor (2010) documents the creation, expansion and regulation of the powers available to those that implement waterfront change: 'the right to raise capital, to expropriate land and to operate largely independently of city, provincial and national governments'. Heeg (2010) and Rubin (2010) caution that even when public agencies are politically autonomous, they are often not financially autonomous, either because their hands are tied on raising capital or increasing land value, or because they are beholden to private property owners and investors to actually realise anything on the ground. Desfor also highlights that the relation and accountability of port authorities to different levels of democratic government is sometimes unclear, and often contested and modified. Different case studies in this volume show port authorities that own land or only manage it, that develop it themselves or only regulate it, in different combinations, and with different kinds of successes or failures. Taşan-Kok and Sungu-Eryilmaz (2010) critique Antwerp's overlapping of jurisdictional responsibilities. They also highlight very different relationships between the port authority and the municipality in Belgium versus the Netherlands: fragmentary projects arise in the former, making it difficult to deliver on complex goals like affordable housing, whereas cooperation exists in the latter, with clear task definitions. Gidel (2010, 43) finds that 'coordination and cooperation between so many actors and bodies remain complicated'. Schubert (2010) notes London Docklands 'had advisory committees, planning committees, inter-relating committees and even discussion committees – but nothing happened' (Michael Heseltine in Thornley [1991, 181]). In San Francisco, much development was stifled by regulations – perhaps representing success (Rubin 2010). More attention can be given in research and policy to how management arrangements relate to development outcomes, and what flexibilities are feasible.

Hall and Clark (2010) identify new cleavages of political power, such as local politicians contesting the actions of regional and national governments from the same party. Scaling of governance is a complex topic, for what is rigid at one level may be up for grabs at another, and different scales of government may fill the same role in different locations and different eras. On Boston's waterfront, the state-level agency Massport is not obliged to follow urban plans. Brownhill (2010) notes the trickle-down of devolved governance may only mean a shift from national to local government, without necessarily improving citizen engagement or empowerment. In London, public planning power flowed from the State to 'quangos' such as Urban Development Corporations – an influential model of 'state investment to create land and property markets' (Brownhill 2010, 129). In Toronto, creating local special-purpose agencies did not clearly provide more accountability or serve broader interests than political bodies and legislation at the national level. In San Francisco, however, the early devolution of port authority (1969) was actually driven by local campaigning; this was not a neo-liberalisation by higher-order government. We see a contrary shift 'up' to a newly-conceived regional scale of waterfront governance for Vancouver, Barcelona and London's Thames Gateway. Sometimes this shift is in pursuit of sustainability, but often it is merely done in the service of economic competitiveness.

In many chapters, institutional fixities are contrasted against flows of new ideas, new visions of what the waterfront could be and who it could serve – 'An Open Waterfront for All'. Gidel (2010), Brownhill (2010) and Ramsey (2010) all document the creation of new institutions. Brownhill (2010, 125) is sceptical, observing that 'politicians have sought to move away from the past while promoting seemingly similar agendas'. In London's Docklands, she sees constant flows and modifications of institutional arrangements in 'waves'; the pendulum swings between top-down governance and consensus – and back again. Sometimes local authorities that stand in the way of new waterfront flows are dissolved.

Whither Neoliberalism

The chapters in Sections II and IV of *Transforming Urban Waterfronts* have a common focus on a particular shift in the politics of urban waterfronts development, namely neoliberalism, and its manifestation in the field of urban planning as property-led development. Harvey's (1989) articulation of a shift from urban managerialism to entrepreneurialism is a touchstone for many contributors: since the 1970s there has been a move away from objective, rational, long-range state-led planning in the general public interest, often accompanied by state ownership of land, to placing the interests of private-sector investors at the centre of urban policy, leading to a boosterish 'speculative construction of place' which has led to more fluidity (Harvey 1989, 8). Rubin (2010) charts the currents of this entrepreneurial flow: deregulation and a freeing-up of markets, the devolution of government functions and responsibilities to the local level, the creation of quasi-public management entities, the outsourcing of government activities to private contractors, and the privatisation of public resources. As Schaller and Novy (2010, 127) note, citing Peck and Tickell (2002), the scale and complexity of the desired changes often engenders a 'roll-out' neoliberal approach, where 'the state takes on a more aggressive role through the introduction of new institutions, policies and governmentalities'.

Within this agenda, Heeg (2010; 275) provides a tighter focus on property-led development strategies, 'the role of the built environment as a policy tool for generating socioeconomic growth'. In Taşan-Kok and Sungu-Eryilmaz's (2010) formulation, Western cities perceive that their core problem is not producing enough of the right kinds of real estate in the right places to meet market needs, to keep rents down and facilitate growth. This is mostly because cities lack investment capital, but also because of physical, institutional, political and social impediments to new development. Through rezonings, joint urban redevelopment ventures, and improvements to transport infrastructure and public spaces, municipalities seek to make their cities more attractive and provide financial incentives to highly-mobile external investors, firms, upper-income residents and visitors, and thereby spur economic flows to help fund their existing services and their future development aspirations. Heeg (2010) critiques such approaches as 'a last-ditch attempt to shape and mobilise urban potentials when there is a limited scope for endogenous, independent strategies'. Within this context, cities often seek to create and stimulate waterfront property markets. Waterfronts, as large, highly visible areas that are politically relatively weak, are choice resources in the neoliberal transmutation of public-sector planning into city marketing. These themes of dependence on inward investment, state mediation of private profiteering and subjugation of the local are not new. Hall and Clark (2010), Gidel (2010), Desfor (2010) and Kane (2010) reveal the long and widespread legacy of colonialism and postcolonialism for New World waterfronts. As Desfor (2010) notes, 'during the development of colonial capitals under mercantilism, waterfronts served as port areas where political, economic and ecological relationships were intertwined with the sale of African slaves, the trading of natural resources, the development of cartels, and the institutionalisation of colonial power'. The Emperor has new clothes.

Many contributors to *Transforming Urban Waterfronts* identify the particular consequences of the neoliberal shift for waterfront development processes and outcomes. The perceived dependence of cities on global flows of finance capital is writ large in the expansion into former industrial waterfront areas of the Financial Districts of London, San Francisco and Boston. Taşan-Kok and Sungu-Eryilmaz (2010, 257) highlight a range of consequent problems: 'elite dominated decision-making mechanisms, social polarisation and spatial fragmentation'. Their observation that 'social inequality in and around the newly regenerated waterfront project area increases and social discontinuity is experienced because of the dominance of high-end land-use and high-income residents' (*ibid.*, 258) clearly applies in Antwerp, Dublin, Seattle, New York, Boston, Buenos Aires and the Caribbean. While Taşan-Kok and Sungu-Eryilmaz study the integration of private real-estate interests into European urban planning processes in Antwerp and Rotterdam, this tendency is strongest in the U.S., where cities depend primarily on the local property tax base for their own operating budgets. Such cities have a great incentive to expand revenues by expanding the amount of urban land (often into waterways) and increasing its development value through rezonings and incentives.

Heeg (2010) highlights that although property-led development approaches can stimulate the cooperation of private actors, it is unclear how the 'invisible hand' can turn this to public advantage. Coordinating public- and private-interests remains problematic. Property-led initiatives generally lead to waterfronts having an undersupply of housing and other socially beneficial uses with low exchange values. Even the utilitarian trickle-down ambition is often compromised, as cities use tax abatements to provide an incentive to land developers. South Boston's District Increment Financing means the increased tax revenues from property-led waterfront development are unavailable to democratic re-allocation, being diverted to pay off the bonds that financed the infrastructure that incentivised the development. Ironically, this means that a tool originally designed for improving poor neighbourhoods is being used to prevent government resource redistribution to poorer neighbourhoods. In Antwerp, the Port Authority was tasked by city government with using income from property development to finance pensions, not for the general public good.

By contrast, San Francisco demonstrates the incremental, 'intensely deliberated' development of policies and procedures to more smoothly guide the flow of investment to maximise public benefit. Rubin (2010, 143) presents San Francisco's waterfront planning as a relative fixity, 'a bulwark against the pressures of contemporary neoliberal urbanisation'. San Francisco (and California generally) illustrates the State moving a range of social and environmental agendas forward, rather than rolling them back; 'an example of the assertion of state power to restrict investment, quite contrary to devolution of responsibilities associated with neoliberalism' (Rubin 2010, 157). San Francisco's more equitable solutions have come through carefully steering the flow of public tax funds to authorities charged with delivering public benefits along the waterfront. The urban waterfront is shown in this and several other chapters to be an important site of resistance and struggle, and not only of accumulation.

Taşan-Kok and Sungu-Eryilmaz (2010) identify two specific techniques through which U.S. communities redistribute the financial flows from property-led development more equitably: Community Land Trusts ensure public capture of property value increases and inclusive governance; Community Benefits Agreements are well-suited to large-scale projects involving what Desfor (2010, 204) terms 'business too important to leave to private capital'. Kop van Zuid's Mutual Benefits Program provides a European waterfront example. Both solutions involve project-specific negotiations between the developer and 'the local community', which builds power through 'bottom-up mobilisations' (Moulaert et al. 2007), addressing a very wide range of matters: project design, scale, mix of uses, local employment, community services and amenities, rent and tenant mix regulation, and environmental mitigation. One concern about such negotiations: they mostly occur outside of and prior to the mainstream, city-wide, public planning process. Another concern noted by Wonneberger (2010) is that the social ties of community only operate locally; they cannot easily be 'scaled up'. In any case, it is refreshing to view the U.S. as a source of solutions rather than problems. Further studies of international policy transfer in waterfront development would be welcome.

Heeg (2010) notes that the development of waterfront land does not necessarily meet the neoliberal aim of driving the economic cycle forward; instead, its development becomes dependent upon those cycles, leading to a destabilisation of the flow of development, due to over- and under-investment during economic booms and busts. The cyclical changes in waterfront development mean that *Transforming Urban Waterfronts* is a timely update on the work of previous decades (Malone 1996; Hoyle et al. 1988), but it also suggests the need for regular reviews and longitudinal studies.

Desfor (2010) illustrates that within the realm of 'capital', there have long been rival interests and claims on waterfronts: Toronto's Board of Trade, the Canadian Manufacturers' Association and the Civic Guild of Toronto reflected 'contrasting political economies' and thus developed competing visions for change. Drawing on Brenner and Theodore (2002) and Rubin (2010) counsels us to look to the detail of 'actually existing neoliberalisms' on waterfronts, as they vary across locations, scales and times. Brownhill's (2010) study of London Docklands highlights that neoliberalism in its current form will probably not always hold sway over waterfronts: history shows that over a longer time frame there are tidal shifts between increasing and decreasing State involvement and leadership in waterfront development. Schaller and Novy (2010, 167) call for us to see waterfront development and planning under neoliberalism as inherently dynamic: 'seemingly top-down development plans and projects are reworked in and through local policy environments, as well as through oppositional practices'.

Interpreting Waterfront Change

In addition to the thematic contents outlined thus far, much can also be learned from the diverse contributions presented in *Transforming Urban Waterfronts* about how to study and understand the fixities and flows of waterfront development, and urban development generally, both methodologically and conceptually. The contributions illustrate a wide range of data-gathering and analytical methods for understanding waterfront change, involving both single case studies and wide geographical comparisons. Three main categories of data are involved. Much work involves analysing existing documentation: historical archives, development plans, promotional literature, policy documents, economic data, and wider public discourse, both textual and graphic. Analysis of such materials ranges from political analysis of power relations and network analysis of social relations generally, to discourse analysis, to quantitative study of property values and goods traffic. Site analysis of built environments is also critical. Although Wonneberger's (2010) approach is anthropological, she also examines the Dublin waterfront's architectural forms and public spaces because these long-term fixed investments make community change visible; the fixed forms reflect the social flows, and stabilise them. New building types such as museums, offices and apartments represent changing demographics. Public spaces are linked to community activities, the development of sense of place and sense of self. Kane (2010) similarly reads a social history of activity patterns and cultural meanings through Buenos Aires's bridges. A second type of data is first-hand accounts from the people involved in and affected by waterfront change.

This means interviews and detailed oral histories, but also surveys, mental mapping by users, and walking tours to visually document users' experiences. The third distinct kind of data, which greatly enlivens and enriches the critique of waterfront change, is first-hand observation and participant observation in the lives of those involved, attending formal and informal community meetings and festivals as well as being engaged in everyday life. From this embedded perspective, the waterfront is not just an abstract image, value or process.

This is not to discount the importance of concepts for understanding, critiquing and shaping waterfront change. The contributors to this volume use a wide range of metaphors to describe and interpret the waterfront and its constituent fixities and flows. Within the case studies themselves, concepts are also deployed by actors to either fix or transform the future of waterfront spaces – most notably in Ramsey's (2010) study of Seattle.

Looking across the chapters within *Transforming Urban Waterfronts* at specific conceptualisations, we can discern a certain ambivalence about the waterfront: about natural forces, about the waterfront's economic and social role, and its connection to various social groups and activities. On Toronto's waterfront, 'Nature provided both an advantage and an obstacle'. (Desfor 2010, 203). While Gidel's (2010) metaphor of mangroves suggests particular conditions of stability, sensitivity, flexibility and variability, Desfor (2010) discusses swamps as unproductive, degraded, and unhygienic, in need of refashioning, 'rationalisation' to speed up or slow down flows. Schubert (2010) describes the 'cleansing' and 'sanitising' of Barcelona; Kane (2010) documents the ongoing contamination of Buenos Aires. In all these cases, biophysical health, economic health and physical orderliness become linked.

The Introduction to *Transforming Urban Waterfronts* and Wonneberger's (2010) chapter both draw upon Cresswell's (2006) distinction between sedentarist and nomadic metaphysics. Waterfronts are obviously places characterised by flows: of water, traffic, goods, people, ideas and diseases. There are also contra-flows, from tidal backwash to grassroots mobilisation. This makes for highly dynamic systems. As noted earlier, the directions of flow also shift. The research presented in the book investigates whether fixity is always orderly, and whether flow necessarily implies change. Waterfronts' fixed elements are often disorderly. Landforms, watercourses, old roads, old factories and old ways of thinking often seem to get in the way; they compromise the capacity of particular waterfronts to remain vital, to stay linked into the wider flows of society and economy.

Another theme frequently encountered is progress, or, as the book's Introduction puts it, 'modernisation.' Desfor (2010) critiques the often-unquestioned belief in the teleological improvement of nature, to increase productivity. The 'natural' waterfront is an asset, but its unpredictable fluidities also make it an obstruction. Its potential is waiting to be imagined by planners and realised by developers. This productive ethic seems to be starkly counterposed by the consumption emphasis of many contemporary urban waterfronts, but neoliberalism appears to have turned consumption into a productive asset. Gidel, Wonneberger, Brownhill, Rubin, Schaller and Novy, Kane, and Heeg all discern stark metaphysical contrasts of the shiny and new against the old and dirty (Desfor et al. 2010). In the Caribbean, Dublin, Rotterdam and London, taller is also considered better. Seen negatively, newness is sterile, faceless, anonymous, a rupture with the past. For Kane (2010, 221), Puerto Madero's architectural optimism, its 'steel and glass architecture, emboldened by repainted cranes', cannot dispel a troubled political history. The existing is positively seen as 'heritage': gasometers and old pubs provide links to Dublin's past, although its cranes must be re-imported from other waterfronts where they still exist. Schaller and Novy (2010, 179) critique the nostalgic re-imagining of the Gowanus Canal, 'one of the most polluted urban waterways in the country', as 'New York's Little Venice' (Prete et al. 2001). Depictions of new and old span across a range of imaginaries: waterfront architecture and infrastructure are often valued for its functional and economic importance and progressiveness rather than its spectacular aesthetics. Ramsey presents cases for and against a progressive reading of several waterfront transport infrastructure options. The chapters show that newness and progress are value-laden distinctions which are politically expedient. The sustainability of change – or stasis – remains an open question. The new is not always durable or flexible. Its benefits are not always widely distributed. Such metaphysical conflicts are sidestepped by the UK use of the term 'urban renaissance' (Schubert 2010; Carmona 2009).

Looking Forward... and Backward... and Eastward and Northward

There is ample scope for both new and revisited studies of urban waterfront change following the methods and employing the concepts outlined above, and engaging with the key issues laid out earlier in this chapter: the scale and direction of development; how development changes over time; the roles and interests of various players; and the political structures and processes through which they interact. In all these respects, further research will inevitably chart continuing shifts in what is flowing and what is fixed about urban waterfronts. In terms of research approaches, the diverse case studies presented in *Transforming Urban Waterfronts*, and the wide variety of disciplinary and transdisciplinary approaches employed by the contributors, suggest that the future research agenda should be transdisciplinary and encompass comparative perspectives.

The clear evidence that waterfront development progresses unevenly and often furthers social inequalities suggests that waterfront researchers should be sceptical of the modernist notion that current design proposals and management approaches are necessarily improvements on the past. As its name suggests, neoliberalism is not a new panacea; it has its roots in the brutish early industrial era that now defines the prehistory of contemporary urban waterfront development. It is important to dig beneath the rhetoric to look at detailed qualitative and quantitative data of what is happening and to compare that with what has happened before.

Looking to Rubin's elucidation of neoliberalism, we are led to ponder whether we do in fact currently live in a neoliberal age. Schaller and Novy (2010, 182) end on an optimistic note that even in New York, 'a "poster child" city of neoliberal urbanism', struggles between the Bloomberg administration and local community interests have led to the retention of and reinvestment in Brooklyn's working waterfronts of Red Hook and Sunset Park. Is this a triumph of advocacy, or is it just economic expediency in a slowed economy? The context and resources for property investment and development have already changed significantly since the International Network of Urban Waterfront Research conference in Hamburg in October 2008, where the contributions to *Transforming Urban Waterfronts* originated. In both the Americas and Europe, research will need to chart the changing fate of neoliberal thinking and practice after the global financial crisis. In some cases, the State may feel compelled to reassert leadership in investment and development. San Francisco's patient custodianship suggests this is not the only way forward. The emergence of neoliberalism should perhaps be seen as one part of a broader search for workable approaches to fixing waterfronts and making them flow, and ongoing struggles between competing philosophies.

Reflecting on Taşan-Kok and Sungu-Eryilmaz's (2010) speculations about the future of development practice, the transfer of policy tools from the U.S. such as CLTs and CBAs (Community Land Trusts and Community Benefits Agreements) makes sense if Europeans are also adopting the Americans' understanding of the problem of neo-liberalism. Researchers will need to look at how such political and economic approaches become locally inflected, and become 'actually existing', given the differing institutional contexts, patterns of land ownership, investment markets, and so forth. Widening the geographic perspective, research could also examine what the rapidly-developing port cities of the East and Middle East can learn from the relatively slow centuries of rise and decline of waterfronts in Europe and the Americas (see also Chapter 2 and Graf and Beng Huat 2007).

In terms of the physical landscape, too, research is needed to assess the geographical variation among, and transferability of, waterfront development approaches. Toronto's waterfront is cold for many months of the year, with a lot of ice, snow and wind. Hamburg and Dublin are less icy but even less sunny. Despite warming climates, cities probably should not always be trying to apply the same 'Barcelona model'. We need to consider the particularities of wet and wintry waterfronts. Chapter 4 which follows shows many ways that the designs of contemporary urban waterfronts can be highly artificial, consciously separating the city from the natural climatic cycles, risks and discomforts of waterways. But design should also explore ways of accommodating and adapting to water-edge conditions in cities that have different climates as well as varied challenges of rising water levels, and addressing different contexts of urban, economic and technological development, different political priorities, and different cultural roles for waterfront areas. Climate sensitivity is inevitably bound up with a range of other contextual factors that shape waterfront design and management. This brings us to a close on two wide-open questions where much research is needed, and where social scientists may wish to make connections to technical expertise in the natural sciences. First, what are the environmental implications of de-industrialised waterfronts, and of the urban redevelopment schemes that have transformed them? Ecological systems keep flowing, and they also keep changing, which requires regular study. And second, how can waterfront developments that are equitable and economically viable also be sustainable? Ramsey's account of the discourse in Seattle suggests a pure antagonism between environmentalism and social justice. We need to consider what kinds of relationships and actions can move both agendas forward.

References

Brenner, N. and Theodore, N. (2002) *Spaces of Neoliberalism: Urban Restructuring in North America and Western Europe*, Oxford: Blackwell.
Brownhill, S. (2010) 'London Docklands revisited: The dynamics of waterfront development', in Desfor, G., Laidley, J., Stevens, Q. and Schubert, D. (eds) *Transforming Urban Waterfronts: Fixity and Flow*, New York: Routledge, pp. 121–142.
Bryce, P. H. (1892) 'Letter to John Hendry, The Globe, 3 September', in *The River Don and Ashbridge's Bay*, Toronto Port Authority Archives: SC 26, box 4, folder 4.
Carmona, M. (2009) 'The isle of dogs: Four development waves, five planning models, twelve plans, thirty-five years, and a renaissance… of sorts', *Progress in Planning*, 71(3), pp. 87–151.
Cox, K. (1998) 'Spaces of dependence, spaces of engagement and the politics of scale, or: Looking for local politics', *Political Geography*, 17(1), pp. 1–23.
Cresswell, T. (2006) *On the Move: Mobility in the Modern Western World*, New York and London: Routledge.
Desfor, G. (2010) 'Deep Water and Good Land: Socio-nature and Toronto's Changing Industrial Waterfront', in Desfor, G., Laidley, J., Stevens, Q. and Schubert, D. (eds) *Transforming Urban Waterfronts: Fixity and Flow*, New York: Routledge, pp. 191–210.
Desfor, G., Laidley, J., Stevens, Q. and Schubert, D. (eds) (2010) *Transforming Urban Waterfronts: Fixity and Flow*, New York: Routledge.
Desse, M. (1996) 'L'inégale Maritimité des villes des Départments d'outre-mer Insulaires', in Péron F. and Rieucau J. (eds.) *La Maritimé Aujourd'hui*, Paris: L'Harmattan, pp. 241–249.
Fainstein, Susan. (2005) 'The return of urban renewal: Dan Doctoroff's grand plans for New York City', *Harvard Design Magazine*, 22, pp. 1–5.
Flyvbjerg, B. (1998) *Rationality and Power: Democracy in Practice*, Chicago: University of Chicago Press.
Gale, T. (2009) 'Urban Beaches, Virtual Worlds and 'The End of Tourism'', *Mobilities*, 4(1), pp. 119–138.
Gidel, M. (2010) 'Fragmentation on the waterfront: Coastal squatting settlements and urban renewal projects in the Caribbean', in G. Desfor, J. Laidley, Q. Stevens, and Schubert D. (eds) *Transforming Urban Waterfronts: Fixity and Flow*, New York: Routledge, pp. 35–53.
Graf, A. and Beng-Huat C. (eds) (2007) *Port Cities: Asian and European Transformations*, Oxford: Routledge.
Hall, P. and Clark, A. (2010) 'Maritime ports and the politics of reconnection', in Desfor, G., Laidley, J., Stevens, Q. and Schubert, D. (eds) *Transforming Urban Waterfronts: Fixity and Flow*, New York: Routledge, pp. 17–34.
Harvey, D. (1989) 'From managerialism to entrepreneurialism: The transformation in urban governance in late capitalism', *Geografiska Annaler*, 71(1), pp. 3–17.
Heeg, S. (2010) 'Flows of capital and fixity of bricks in the built environment of Boston: Property-led development in urban planning?', in Desfor, G., Laidley, J., Stevens, Q. and Schubert, D. (eds) *Transforming Urban Waterfronts: Fixity and Flow*, New York: Routledge, pp. 274–294.
Hoyle, B., Pinder, D. and Husain, M. (Eds) (1988) *Revitalising the Waterfront*, London: Belhaven.
Kane, S. (2010) 'Visibility and contamination on the Buenos Aires Waterfront: Under the bridges of Puerto Madero and La Boca', in Desfor, G., Laidley, J., Stevens, Q. and Schubert, D. (eds) *Transforming Urban Waterfronts: Fixity and Flow*, New York: Routledge, pp. 211–232.
Lee, R. (1992) 'London Docklands: The 'exceptional place'? An economic geography of inter-urban competition', in Ogden, P. (ed) *London Docklands: The challenge of development*, Cambridge and New York: Cambridge University Press.
Malone, P. (ed) (1996) *City, Capital and Water*, London: Routledge.
Moulaert, F., Martinelli, F., González, S. and Swyngedouw, E. (2007) 'Introduction: Social innovation and governance in European cities: Urban development between path dependency and radical innovation', *European Urban and Regional Studies*, 14(3), pp. 195–209.
Peck, J. and Tickell, A. (2002) 'Neoliberalizing space', *Antipode*, 34(3), pp. 380–404.
Prete, A., Sonenberg, B. and Hamersky, J. (2001) *Lavender Lake Brooklyn's Gowanus Canal*, New York: Filmakers Library.
Ramsey, K. (2010) 'Urban waterfront transformation as a politics of mobility: Lessons from Seattle's Alaskan Way Viaduct Debate', in Desfor, G., Laidley, J., Stevens, Q. and Schubert, D. (eds) *Transforming Urban Waterfronts: Fixity and Flow*, New York: Routledge, pp. 101–120.
Rubin, J. (2010), 'San Francisco's waterfront in the age of neoliberal urbanism', in Desfor, G., Laidley, J., Stevens, Q. and Schubert, D. (eds) *Transforming Urban Waterfronts: Fixity and Flow*, New York: Routledge, pp. 143–165.

Schaller, S. and Novy, J. (2010) 'New York city's waterfronts as strategic sites for analyzing neoliberalism and its contestations', in Desfor, G., Laidley, J., Stevens, Q. and Schubert, D. (eds) *Transforming Urban Waterfronts: Fixity and Flow*, New York: Routledge, pp. 166–187.

Schubert, D. (2010) 'Waterfront revitalizations: From a local to a regional perspective in London, Barcelona, Rotterdam, and Hamburg', in Desfor, G., Laidley, J., Stevens, Q. and Schubert, D. (eds) *Transforming Urban Waterfronts: Fixity and Flow*, New York: Routledge, pp. 74–97.

Swyngedouw, E., Moulaert, F. and Rodriguez, A. (2002) 'Neoliberal urbanization in Europe: Large-scale urban development projects and the new urban policy', *Antipode*, 34(3), pp. 547–582.

Taşan-Kok, T. and Sungu-Eryilmaz, Y. (2010) 'Exploring innovative instruments for socially sustainable waterfront regeneration in Antwerp and Rotterdam', in Desfor, G., Laidley, J., Stevens, Q. and Schubert, D. (eds) *Transforming Urban Waterfronts: Fixity and Flow*, New York: Routledge, pp. 257–273.

Thornley, A. (1991) *Urban planning under Thatcherism*, Oxford: Routledge.

Wonneberger, A. (2010) 'Dockland regeneration, community, and social organization in Dublin', in Desfor, G., Laidley, J., Stevens, Q. and Schubert, D. (eds) *Transforming Urban Waterfronts: Fixity and Flow*, New York: Routledge, pp. 54–73.

Chapter 4
Artificial Waterfronts

Quentin Stevens

Since the 1960s, urban waterfronts worldwide have been re-designed with a rich mixture of leisure, retail, offices, housing and cultural institutions. Revitalised waterfronts are among the most as archetypal elements of the post-industrial cityscape. These areas have also been re-engineered to provide new piers, esplanades, marinas, beaches and wetlands. Several studies have sought to comparatively catalogue postmodern waterfront landscapes, identifying different categories of forms and functions (Marshall 2001; Meyer 1999; Malone 1996; Breen and Rigby 1996), but in general these focus only on the built environment above and away from the water line. With the exception of Hudson (1996), surprisingly little academic attention has focused on the artificiality and superficiality of the waterfront geography itself. These sites are almost never natural shorelines. Many leisure waterfronts are built on the ruins of industrial port areas. First shaped by humans to enhance production, these places have now been reshaped to enhance consumption. They are almost entirely synthetic and carefully shaped to produce specific experiential effects. The landscaping of new waterfront precincts is just as spectacularised as their architecture and their land uses. These precincts tend to be poorly connected to the water and to their wider urban context. Many new waterfront redevelopments focus on visual quality while providing only limited stimulation of the other senses. They also tend to constrain people from having exciting, 'edgy' encounters with the physical landscape and with water.

This chapter examines the material landscape of a variety of contemporary urban waterfronts, including artificial beaches, lagoons, rivers and indoor waterscapes. It explores the relation between the physical geography and human geography of these waterfronts, focusing primarily on how these artificial landscapes are perceived and used by visitors. It analyses how people experience the physical conditions implied by the term 'waterfront', revealing how designers use engineering, landscaping and architecture to manufacture and control various geographic, climatological, and hydrological features of the waterscape and its interface with urban public space, so as to create idealised urban settings which optimise spectacular leisure and place promotion. the cases studied include 'typical' urban riverfront leisure precincts in Melbourne, Brisbane and London, as introduced in Chapter 1, and 'stereotypical' artificial lagoons on the tourist resort model in Australia's two largest tropical cities, Brisbane and Cairns (Dovey 2005; Macarthur 1999). A range of other more unusual case studies illustrate a great diversity of technical innovation and formal experimentation upon these basic models: two public fountains in London and Melbourne, a reconstructed urban stream in Seoul, floating swimming pools in Berlin, Vienna and Paris, and an indoor water theme park near Berlin. All the sites studied are major central destinations within post-industrial cities that are keen on place marketing to attract both tourists and inner-city residents. The case studies have been selected to explore the scope of four key aspects of people's experience of the artificiality of urban waterfronts:

1. Different cultural expectations in different places about waterfronts, leisure, the role of urban spaces, and bodily risks when using them, reflecting different visions of quality of life
2. Varying degrees of realism and artifice in the landscape designs, reflecting different aesthetic preferences and available technology
3. Different climates and different ways of physically containing water in different geographical contexts, including coastal, estuarine, riverine and land-locked settings
4. Different economic contexts, in particular the varied forms of ownership and funding of these landscapes

The chief sources of data are participant observation and photography of how these environments are used by the general public, and analysis of the physical organisation of the spaces themselves measured against the scale of human postures, movements and perceptions. The analysis includes examination of the specific architectural, engineering and landscape elements, materials, infrastructures and symbolism which are used to simulate and dissimulate nature, and comparisons between these built landscapes and the natural landscape systems which surround them. These physical and perceptual details are critical for moving beyond the popular 'spectacularisation' thesis, and, more significantly, to overcome scholars' own spectacular reception of these spectacular landscapes, so as to begin to understand users' richly-embodied perceptions of postmodern landscapes, the diversity of user behaviour, and how these are all shaped by material changes in the environment.

Inner-urban waterfront leisure precincts are very often built on former industrial sites, where natural landscapes have already been dramatically transformed to serve human needs. They are sites where nature is made to reappear in a sanitised and controlled form. These settings enable the cleaning up of the image of a city and (at least ostensibly) the cleaning up of its most polluted sites. They also engender a certain purification and control of the otherwise diverse informal social use of the waterfront, such that contemporary waterfront leisure is often carefully structured to optimise economic profitability and social segregation and to limit behavioural risks (Campo 2002; Boyer 1992, see Chapter 1). This chapter considers the elision of the social sanitisation and the physical cleansing of waterfronts, where scientific principles and criteria related to 'nature' provide a metaphor all-too-easily- applied to the social management of 'human nature'. A useful critical tool here is Lefebvre's (1991) concept of 'second nature', meaning an artificial landscape which gains the perception of being natural, where people become habituated to it and cease to recognise it as artifice, as something socially produced and managed. One proposition to be examined here through case study analysis is whether artificial waterfronts for leisure tend more to control social behaviour, rather than lending it freedom.

Waterfront leisure precincts tend to occupy the more low-lying bank of rivers, and tidal foreshores. These are soft, changing landscapes. They are often set apart from city centres which have been built on high, solid ground, and in their escapist functions they also contrast with the institutional and commercial activities which are concentrated in Central Business Districts. Waterfronts are by their nature loose and relatively uncontrolled spaces which offer many and shifting opportunities for experience (Franck and Stevens 2007). In a social sense too, urban leisure waterfronts are often sites of tensions, ongoing contestation and change (Schubert 2001). Behavioural control is not total, and these environments continue to evolve and, generally, to become more inclusive through changes in their use, their social significance, and through new and varied physical development. This chapter probes the relationship between shifting, malleable riparian geography and liminal, playful social experiences of leisure, to determine how the second nature of artificial waterfronts serves to reframe the possibilities of urban leisure.

This chapter explores four particular ways in which the design of artificial waterfronts makes them different to the 'natural' relation between water and land:

- The various natural conditions of the water and the edge of the land are tamed to reduce bodily risks and discomfort for users
- The natural conditions of water and landscape are augmented (intensified, and/or regulated) to optimise comfort and to enhance the escapism of the leisure experience
- The waterfront space is physically reconfigured or relocated to better fit in with nearby urban functions and spaces, or to make the setting more visible and accessible
- The waterfront changes over time in controlled, regular ways.

Taming the Waterfront

The most straightforward form of artifice in the design of urban leisure waterfronts is the control and refinement of the edge of the water itself. Dams, dikes, breakwaters, weirs, sluices and locks have long been used to control and reshape the large-scale form and flow of water in rivers, estuaries and coastlines for functionally productive reasons. Spatial manipulation of the water's edge in urban waterfront leisure environments ensures that users have a safe, predictable, and often distant encounter with the water's edge. Visitors to artificial urban waterfronts rarely if ever encounter open, 'wild' water, or experience its unpredictable natural forces or its diversity of living contents. Although visitors may be offered a variety of forms of close contact with water, the water they engage with is socially constructed to accord with human ideals of visual attractiveness, health, and ease and safety of movement. In typical urban waterfront precincts such as London's, Melbourne's and Brisbane's Southbanks, embankments and boardwalks regularise the edge condition between land and water vertically and horizontally, establishing a straight, smooth and level terrain for people to walk along next to rivers or shorelines. They allow people to be next to the water's edge without the risk of being touched by the water. Embankments are separated spaces ideal for looking at water. Continuous handrails, provided to ensure safety, also constrain human leisure impulses to cross the threshold. Steps leading down into the water, or down to exposed natural riverbanks, provide safe and controlled means of approaching the water.

Waterfront promenade spaces also have varied and complex profiles leading from the edge of the water back to the frontage of the adjacent buildings. In a recent focused study of Melbourne's Southbank Promenade (Wang and Stevens 2020), we observed that the section of the Promenade in front of the Casino complex was unique in having a mixture of three different cross-sectional profiles: flat, stepped and sloped. These varied surface topographies contributed to the diversity of informal seating and resting opportunities available in the space. The slope ensures that the artificial turf surface dries quickly after rain. This slope facing onto the Yarra River provides the most popular place for people to lie down along the Promenade. The artificial turf steps create small-scale settings where people like to sit alone or talk with friends. Our study found that the varied cross-sections added to the overall diversity of activity settings available in this part of the Promenade, and this diversity in turn contributed to this part of the Promenade having a higher utilisation than other parts.

The main waterfront areas of the two largest cities in Australia's tropical North, Brisbane and Cairns, are centred on parks with large swimming pools freely open to the public. At both sites, the pool and park are carefully integrated as a total landscape experience. Each pool is excavated into the ground to create a new waterfront close to the edge of the 'real' water. These water bodies are easily tamed because they are artificial and separated from natural hydrology.

Streets Beach and lagoon on Brisbane's South Bank was built in the early 1990s as part of the masterplanned redevelopment of a former industrial wharf area for leisure and cultural uses. This tropically-landscaped pool is divided into three sections: an evenly waist-deep pool with conventional concrete stepped entry and tiled bottom; a shallow flowing 'stream' with rock pools; and a large central lagoon. In Brisbane's sub-tropical climate, the pool requires no heating system. The lagoon has a sandy beach along one side; the sand slopes down and lines the sloping bottom of the pool. Further out, the sand peters out to reveal the smooth tiled concrete bottom surface: a direct material

Artificial Waterfronts

Figure 4.1 Artificial beach, Brisbane South Bank, Australia.

inversion of the Situationists' call for urban freedom and pleasure, 'underneath the pavement, the beach' (Dovey 2005, 24). On its far side, the pool is neck-deep and backs onto a wide riverfront promenade. Visitors sunbathing on the beach can view the lagoon superimposed in front of the Brisbane River, with promenaders crossing between the two water bodies, and the skyscrapers of the city skyline forming a fantastic backdrop (Figure 4.1). Careful grading of the entire site puts passers-by on the riverside promenade at eye level with bathers in the deep side of the pool – an arrangement seldom possible with natural waterways. These passers-by can also step up to a terrace to sit or lie on the wide concrete edge of the pool, dangle their feet in or dive in.

This lagoon offers many modulations of depth and edge condition, including bridges which cross over the pool. In cross-section, this waterfront manipulates the natural relation between beach and river and also the relation of both to a continuous waterfront pedestrian promenade. The artificial beach leads down into clear, still, purified water. The promenade is elevated and immediately adjacent to the real river, which is lined with a retaining wall; yet the elevated promenade does not block the view from the beach to the real river. Landscaping technology makes possible such precise ways of arranging various leisure surfaces, more advanced and more varied than the elevated Nineteenth-Century boardwalk, pier and oceanfront wave pool. The inclined cross-section of the beach, pool and river, and the complex interlacing of bridges and walkways around them, optimise views of water and also opportunities for people seeing each other and being seen. In plan, too, Brisbane's lagoon and waterfront boardwalk focus the gaze: they curve in an arc around the central beach, shaped like a lens that concentrates views onto the beach (Carter 1993).

In addition to the absence of current, the pool's separation from the river also means separation from the small sharks which are known to come upstream to clean themselves in fresh water. The lagoon provides for a variety of safe, tourist-oriented, camera-friendly forms of water-related leisure. However, its exclusions make it unsuitable for many other traditional forms of waterfront recreation, for example fishing and boating: active pursuits which are closely linked to the natural conditions of the river and to the necessities of human survival.

Cairns Esplanade Lagoon, opened in 2003, has much the same sectional form as Brisbane's. Triangular in plan, one side is an artificial beach sloping into the pool, one side has a conventional pool edge with concrete steps and timber decking, and the third side is a 1.5 metre vertical wall adjoining the oceanfront promenade, which itself then has an outer retaining wall facing the ocean (Figure 4.2). This promenade clearly reflects the functional origin of urban waterfront promenades as dikes. Designing two different water frontages into the lagoon heightens the artifice of the setting. Here the swimming pool is, unlike Brisbane's, salty; seawater is filtered and chlorinated.

Cairns, the largest city in Far North Queensland, does not have a natural sandy beach. Like many tropical coastal settlements, it is located at the mouth of a river, and is fronted by mangrove swamps and mudflats. The shoreline of the ocean shifts dramatically with the tides. It cannot be stabilised as easily as the embankments of Brisbane's river, and thus outside the artificial breakwater of Cairns's lagoon there is a six-meter-wide buffer strip of imported sand beach, beyond which stretches approximately 100m of often-exposed mangrove-rooted mudflats before the open water of the real ocean. People who try to walk across the saturated mud quickly sink and need to be rescued. Moving the water inland is the most feasible way to create a direct link between urban space and water, transforming the intertidal section of the waterfront, compressing it horizontally and clarifying it. The pool is not cut into solid ground: having been sited over deep mud, it stands on 240 tall concrete piles, and is effectively a basin standing on a large pier projecting into the mudflats. Both Cairns's and Brisbane's lagoons thus emphasise visual connection between lagoon and open water, whilst the concrete walls, boardwalks

Figure 4.2 Cairns esplanade, Australia.

Source: Bahnfrend - https://creativecommons.org/licenses/by-sa/4.0/deed.en

and sandbanks of both schemes actually create more rigid and uncrossable barriers between them. Close to the Cairns lagoon, a marina and jetty project a land connection out into the deeper ocean water; an arrangement suited to the scale and movement of boats for pleasure fishing and sightseeing. An older riverfront wharf in the deep river mouth is designed for the scale of bulk cargo ships. Artificial manipulation of the water's edge in urban areas varies tremendously in scale and form according to functional needs.

At 4800m^2, the Cairns pool has a capacity of 1000 people, and provides a wide variety of elements to add comfort and interest, with varying degrees of artifice, including its landmark fish sculptures, spraying fountains, boulders embedded into the pool which have re-sculpted surfaces, large fixed sunshades which stretch out over the water's edge, palm trees and lawns. However, its intense leisure activity and diverse furnishings seem simplistic when compared to the complex aquatic ecology of mangroves, which cope with the salinity of the ocean, stabilise silty estuaries, and provide breeding grounds for many fish, crustaceans and birds. The lagoon presents a comfortable tropical respite which excludes most of the wildlife which thrive in tropical conditions. Prominent signs facing Cairns's promenade warn against swimming in the ocean around the river mouth, as this is the prime habitat for saltwater crocodiles. Here, as in many other tropical resort areas in Far North Queensland, the beautiful-looking sandy ocean beaches are closed to swimming for eight months of the year because of the prevalence of small, transparent stinging jellyfish. Small areas of popular tourist beaches are made safe through the use of artificial barriers: large floating 'stinger nets' made of fine mesh, which extend out into the ocean.

These lagoons in Cairns and Brisbane highlight how much the management of appearances matters to the contemporary urban waterfront. Seeing, and its mechanical prosthesis, photography, are the main ways people consume these landscapes. Brisbane's beach was originally sponsored by the Kodak Corporation. Brisbane and Cairns present waterfront environments that meet the image that tourists – mostly foreigners – have of a tropical island resort, in both its natural and civilised elements (Macarthur 1999). Visitors often take photographs that highlight the improbable, dialectical juxtaposition of a resort-like waterfront against a city skyline (Figure 4.1). Careful masterplanning ensures visual linkage between the water, the wider waterfront precinct and the remainder of the city. Views of inner cities from their counterposed Southbanks dramatise the sense of escape and of being at leisure. Artificial urban leisure waterfronts are designed to unite a leisure area with a city centre and at the same time differentiate them.

Visibility is important to people's use of these artificial water bodies. The water in these pools is rendered transparent through filtration, a smooth, light-painted floor, and by restricting plant and animal life to the land around the water. Transparency enhances comfort and safety, eliminating the potential danger of unknowns in the environment. Visibility enhances the user's sense of control. Being able to see into the water in these pools contributes to the urban experience of seeing and being seen, as does the careful interweaving of spaces for swimming, sunbathing and promenading. Careful design of the edge between these lagoon pools and the river or ocean creates an almost seamless continuity between them, which creates an uncanny sense of being 'in' the river or ocean: an enlarged version of the ubiquitous hotel 'infinity pool'. These sunken public

Figure 4.3 Cheonggyecheon, Seoul, South Korea.

swimming pools provide swimmers with a good close view of the river or ocean surface, from a very low eye level. Artificially lighting these venues at night is another means of enhancing visibility that also extends the hours when water can be used safely for leisure.

In Seoul, South Korea, the inner-city stream regeneration project Cheonggyecheon (translated as 'clean stream' or 'open stream') presents an extremely complex riverfront landscape with rich potential for urban leisure (Figure 4.3). This artificial stream begins at a fountain pool in a plaza in the city's financial district, and then runs for 6km in the bottom of a heavily-landscaped concrete trench that varies from 4m to 8m in depth, until it enters the city's main Han River. The stream runs through densely-urbanised areas, and is crossed at street level by 10 road bridges and 12 pedestrian-only bridges. This waterscape does not appear highly controlled. The stream's path varies tremendously. There are numerous areas where the water splashes, spurts out of rocks, or descends small falls or rapids. The edges of the water vary greatly, from mown grass to reed beds, from seemingly-random rock formations to flat gravel to sharply-defined concrete channels and projections, and in many complex, fragmented combinations. Some crossing points are narrow, slippery, wet and apparently risky: people have to judge whether they are capable of crossing. Artifice involves creating obvious, measurable risks. Steps along the sides often lead down below the water's surface. A wide variety of plants grow in and along the stream, and it provides a home to fish and birds. What is particularly interesting about this stream and its embankments is that every variation has been carefully designed. Until its reconstruction in 2003–05, this stream was a nearly-dry concrete drain running below a six-lane elevated freeway viaduct. The streambed is still concrete underneath, but the designers have very artfully reconstituted a very naturalistic river setting, a kind of 'second nature' (Lefebvre 1991).

Artificial Waterfronts

The Cheonggyecheon project showcases the tremendous range of ways in which urban designers, landscape architects and engineers can shape the physical waterfront at a small scale to achieve effects suited to leisure and to bringing sensory pleasure to visitors. The immediate riverbanks are artificial, lined with concrete, stone, steel plates or timber planks. The stream's banks provided a tremendous variety of places to sit; although they appear natural, piled boulders have been artfully scaled and arranged to best suit human posture. The degree of artifice varies, ranging from large rough-hewn rocks to stones set flush in concrete to irregular concrete pavers to smooth granite blocks in complex geometric configurations. One feature is, however, remarkably constant: no matter how uneven the overall form of the elements, no matter how many changes in level, the top surface of every element is flat; the only exception being long, gentle ramps connecting between terraces. This is a naturalistic landscape where everything is consciously shaped to ensure human accessibility and stability. Some of the informal seating arrangements are culturally-specific, such as the flights of steps located underneath bridges, suited to the common Asian desire to stay out of the sunshine. This kind of specificity highlights that the landscape has been produced to meet particular objectives. The risks of approaching or crossing the water are all calculated, even when the stones placed for this purpose are widely or irregularly spaced, rounded or slippery. This aspect of Cheonggyecheon highlights that artificial waterfronts are carefully designed to suit human postures and human movement: ground surfaces and underwater surfaces are firm, visible and regular. The land and water always have either precise boundaries or very smoothly-graded interfaces, typified by the sandy sloping beach.

Conscious decisions have been made about every characteristic of the Cheonggyecheon stream's flow along every metre of its length. The water's volume depends on how much is pumped in at its artificial source in the financial district. Its speed is controlled through unnaturally frequent variations in the gradient and profile of the channel and variations in the smoothness of the concrete stream bed along its length. Hydraulic action is also modified to produce a variety of acoustic and visual effects with the water, which goes through innumerable contortions: quiet, meandering flow with eddies; gurgling brook; sucked rushing down through narrow sluices; shallow rippling and bouncing over small rocks. Water, the most malleable and plastic of landscaping materials, is choreographed into a cavalcade of forms. These features all remain constant over time. There are no dry spells and no floods. The stream's water is purified as it is pumped in from the upstream reaches of the Han River, to which this stream is also a tributary. Thus the watershed has been reorganised.

Around and within the naturalistic stream are a wide variety of rather more obviously artificial water features designed to allow close and safe encounters with water: veil-thin waterwalls for people to run their hands across and glazed water tunnels for them to walk under; spurting rows of water jets, lit at night, that form a barrel-vaulted ceiling over one section of the pedestrian path; fountains which spray high to make the stream visible from the surrounding city streets. The carefully-tuned music of the stream also works in combination with the acoustic properties of numerous bridge undercrofts and the high concrete walls of the trench in which the stream is sited, and the sounds of breezes in the trees and grasses along the banks. Even where plants grow in and close to the water, the soil is contained, usually in concealed pots. Riparian plants which die or grow too much can be removed and restocked from a nursery. There is no erosion; no silt is deposited or carried in this stream. Its course cannot change. There is no decay here, and not necessarily any growth either. It displays a static, idealised image of nature rather than the evidence of natural forces. The water has also been stocked with fish and plants.

Cheonggyecheon is a tremendously successful example of place marketing, remaking the image of downtown Seoul, drawing tourists, and encouraging gentrification of its surroundings and the further development of the city. It is also a focus for ongoing debates about the Seoul government's competence in managing the local ecology (Kim 2005; Ryu 2004). This project is an illustration of the extent to which the idea, form and role of nature in contemporary urban settings can be socially produced; the merits or damage of this waterway cannot be reduced only to scientific determinations of ecologists (Davison and Ridder 2006). This second nature is more important for the bodily and psychological comforts that it offers as for any role it might play in restoring actual ecological systems (Grenville 2007).

Another designed waterfront leisure space greatly accentuates attention to its artificiality. Adjacent to a dock in Berlin's Spree River, the 'Badeschiff' ('bath-ship' or 'swimming ship') is a floating swimming pool designed by local artist Susanne Lorenz and opened in 2004 (Figure 4.4) (Urban Catalyst 2007). In contrast to going swimming in natural waterways, which often requires that the body comes into contact with the natural riverbank or the river bottom, this pool involves very precise detailing of the sectional design of the physical edge between land and water to optimise human access

Figure 4.4 Badeschiff, Berlin, Germany.

Source: Ulrike Berlin/Flickr – https://creativecommons.org/licenses/by/2.0/

and comfort. The deck is firm and flat, not slippery or shifting. The gangway connecting the pool to the landing tilts, allowing smooth access to the pool even though it floats higher or lower on the changing river level. The effects of flooding are negated. The river surface always remains near eye level for people standing in the pool. There are handrails and ladders to facilitate measured, controlled descent into the water. A shallow ledge running around the edge of the pool is carefully scaled to the human body, allowing bathers to enjoy sitting in the water and either reclining in the sun or dangling their legs deeper. They can maintain a good view of their surroundings and also put themselves on display. It is possible to dive safely into the water's clear, visible, measured depth. This is very unlike untamed ocean and river frontages, where edge position, depth, and bottom surface all constantly change with tides and rainfall, often in unpredictable ways. There are also unfenced sections on the jetty where the pool is moored that allow people to be closer to the actual river.

The Badeschiff also optimises environmental comfort of the water in several ways, which makes the water itself rather artificial. Pollution is excluded. No-one need worry about the swimmability of the post-industrial eastern reaches of Berlin's Spree River. Human pollution is controlled through chlorination. The water temperature is controlled, so that the outdoor use of the Badeschiff can be extended in Berlin's cold climate. Its integral lighting allows safe evening swimming. A curving, translucent, cocoon-like roof also provides shelter from wind and rain, and allows winter-long use of the pool, complemented by the installation of an adjacent sauna room (Figure 4.5). Because the pool is self-contained, swimmers do not have to struggle against the river's current; nor can they enjoy swimming against it or floating with it.

Figure 4.5 Badeschiff in the frozen Spree River, Berlin, with insulated roofing and sauna on deck.

Source: Georg Slickers – https://creativecommons.org/licenses/by-sa/3.0/deed.en

This artificial aquatic environment requires less human effort to use, and offers more comfort and wider prospects for enjoyment, although at the expense of reducing prospects for encountering, comprehending and enjoying the mysteries of nature's complexity. This pool eliminates the physical properties of the river that made the riverfront a practical site for industry: its momentum, its thermal mass, its dilutive volume. It frames instead the artifice of feeling one is in the river because one can see the river up close at eye level; one can hear and smell the river and feel its breezes up close, without touching it.

Augmenting the Waterfront

Creating artificial leisure waterfronts often involves more than just constraining natural forces and reshaping natural space. Leisure waterfronts often include the introduction of completely new, artificial nature. Another artificial swimming environment, Tropical Islands (www.tropical-islands.de), tames the water and the land's edge in the same ways as Brisbane's and Cairns's riverfront lagoons. But it goes much further in creating a synthetic environment. Tropical Islands opened at the end of 2004. It was built inside a never-used zeppelin hangar 60km south of Berlin by a Malaysian conglomerate which specialises in building and operating cruise ships. This is a post-industrial setting within the very distinctive context of the ineffectual re-industrialisation of the East after German reunification. Built amidst open fields, the hangar's competitive advantages include a massive write-down of construction costs, ample free parking, and government receptivity toward creative entrepreneurial investment. 360m long and 100m high, Tropical Islands is claimed to be the world's biggest indoor water attraction (Figure 4.6). Covering

Figure 4.6 Tropical Islands, near Brand, Germany.

Source: Gerd Danigel, gerddanigel.de. – https://creativecommons.org/licenses/by-sa/4.0/deed.en

almost seven hectares, it has a capacity of 7000. The indoor air temperature is kept at 25°C year-round, and the venue is open 24 hours.

In this example, the 'tourist bubble' (Judd 1992) of waterfront enclaves like Southbank and the Badeschiff widens, to embrace not just the water's edge, but the whole beach context: the ground, the horizon, the weather and the native islander culture encountered at the site are all artificial. Tropical Islands is completely contained; there is no attempt at integration with the surrounding landscape. Inside the hangar is a 'South Sea' the size of four Olympic swimming pools, warmed to 31°C. The backdrop to the pool is a 150m-wide artificial azure skyline that shows a projected sunrise and sunset. Large windows above allow the real sun's rays in. The sea is indeed on the south side of the hangar, and facing toward it is a white sand beach with 900 sun lounges where people can work on their tans. There is also a Balinese lagoon for swimming, and several large waterslides. A separate sports area provides sand courts for beach volleyball, an 18-hole mini-golf course and helium balloons which lift harnessed visitors up into the air. A supervised children's area includes a track with pedal-powered go-karts, a pond with pedal boats, an adventure playground and trampolines. A separate 'beach' area contains tents that visitors can rent overnight. A 'wellness landscape' (beauty treatment spa) opened in mid-2007. The building also encompasses a rainforest walk featuring 600 species of tropical plants spread around an artificial hill and a mangrove swamp, a 'tropical village' where various architects have reconstructed huts from their own cultures, including Bali, Samoa, Kenya, Thailand, Malaysia and the Amazon, and numerous tropically-themed shops and restaurants. Sounds of tropical insects are broadcast through speakers shaped like rocks. Musicians from various parts of the Southern Hemisphere give concerts during the day. Every evening, performers put on a Las Vegas-style floor show to highlight the history and culture of a different tropical region (Brazil, the Caribbean, Polynesia), featuring authentic indigenous performers. The show changes every three months. Appropriately enough, the evening stage is an island in the middle of the 'South Sea', allowing the audience to remain in their sun lounges. Sometimes the concert spills over afterwards into an informal beach dance party with DJs, but the celebration itself is artificial: there is nothing in particular to celebrate; certainly not the seasonal cycles or coming-of-age rituals which typically defined the calendars of traditional cultures.

The Tropical Islands environment cleverly combines three different kinds of leisure experiences under one roof. The pools, artificial sun, mechanical heating and sand serve the need for residents of Berlin, a large inland city with a cool continental climate, to temporarily and cheaply escape the depression of a long winter of inclement weather, heavy snow and hard urban spaces, for their bodies to feel a different climate and landscape. Photographs cannot easily communicate how relaxing this setting feels. The various sports, activities and beauty pampering have no necessary relation to water. These activities have become a familiar part of beach tourism because they are among the things that tourists commonly do when they spend their free time near the beach, although these activities are also popular elsewhere. There is no need to integrate these behaviours with water, and they generally occupy a separate zone in the hangar, without a view of the water. The rainforest, its villages and their 'inhabitants', on the other hand, complement the material artifice of the waterfront, by framing the water in a very specific context of meanings which are intended to add to the escapism of the waterfront experience. More than just a big swimming pool, as in Brisbane and Cairns, this landscape is depicted as a Balinese lagoon. The outdoor lagoons in Queensland also use vegetation to help create an escapist atmosphere, but they do so within the climatic constraints of their locations. The entire Tropical Islands project is highly themed. The rainforest, which excludes poisonous and predatory animals, puts people in a relaxed mood. The emphasis on nature and exotic culture transports people away from their familiar urban lifestyle (Hannigan 1998; Cohen and Taylor 1976). The following visitor's comment highlights her positive view of the artificiality of this exotic waterfront:

> 'It is such a relief from the sad and gray winter weather', said Carmen Habermann, 38, a shopkeeper from Frankfurt. 'It has South Pacific flair, yet is only an hour's drive away and at a time of economic uncertainty, it's a good holiday "ersatz"'. (Connolly 2004)

What the artifice achieves is bringing the exotic within reach. The resort's main target audience is the large number of formerly-East-German retirees who have free time and some disposable income, but not necessarily the money, time or desire to travel to the real tropics. Because of the high ongoing cost of maintaining the artificial climate, here customers pay for admission by the hour, with off-peak discounts to encourage a more even spread of usage.

Positioning the Waterfront

Cities have historically been sited and planned in relation to natural water features such as ample sources of fresh water, narrow and shallow river crossings, and natural harbours. But the urban fabric today has become so extensive and so technologically developed that it now tends to dictate the terms of geography; like the site of Cheonggyecheon, many urban water bodies have been culvertised, diverted or buried under streets. After a century or more of being mostly closed off to the general public because of their association with industry and vice, waterfronts are being re-introduced into the wider urban realm with new forms and new functions (Schubert 2001; Pinder et al. 1988). These waterfronts require spatial, functional and conceptual reintegration, and this occurs according to both the structure and function of the wider urban artifice and the specific political, economic and social ambitions which give rise to these spectacular waterfront consumption settings. Artificial beaches, pools and streams built for leisure do not necessarily arise where natural hydrological forces would dictate.

The naming of each of Melbourne's, Brisbane's and London's inner-urban waterfront leisure precincts as 'Southbank' highlights a conscious effort to incorporate and situate these sites within citizens' mental images of the cities, so as to maximise these precincts' synergy with the serious world of work, while also maintaining a distinct identity. New pedestrian bridges have restructured the circulation networks of these inner cities, making the waterfront zones better connected to other pre-existing spaces and activities, particularly those on the opposite riverbank (see Chapter 1). Melbourne's and Brisbane's Southbanks have the virtue of superior solar exposure. London's South Bank suffers by comparison because in the Northern Hemisphere this embankment receives less of the sunshine which makes such precincts attractive for freely-chosen leisure time (Gehl and City of Melbourne 1994). Berlin's Badeschiff, moored on the south side of the Spree near the shadow of a large industrial building, manages good solar exposure because it is set forward from the 'real' edge of the river, occupying a zone of urban space usually only available to ships in motion.

In Cairns, a small city whose primary industry is tourism, the artificial waterfront has been carefully positioned to serve a wider logic of urban planning. A beach and a deep pool of water have been artfully placed at a convenient, highly visible and accessible point within Cairns's urban fabric, and these two elements have been drawn unnaturally close to each other. The lagoon has been sited to provide a terminating attraction on Shields Street, the city's main pedestrian axis, with the other end anchored by Cairns's main shopping mall. The lagoon sits adjacent to the city's marina and its largest waterfront hotels. Its elongated triangle is a most unnatural shape for a water body, but one which allows it to stretch from the nearest pedestrian intersection at Shields Street, where a forecourt of tall palm trees makes it visible along the axis, out to the waterfront edge of the existing land. Its shape lures people from the city streets deep into the waterfront setting.

Berlin's Badeschiff is also carefully positioned within the wider context of the expansive deindustrialised landscape around the Ostbahnhof railway terminus in the former East. This is a new creative milieu which includes temporary occupancies of vacant buildings, relocatable temporary buildings, start-up businesses, live-work spaces, illegal squatting, grassroots community projects, galleries, performance venues, and nightclubs. The Badeschiff does not function on its own, but operates as part of a broad system of enterprising spatial and social development: a post-industrial space of flows. Consumption of the artificial waterfront depends on new flexible forms of work and capital investment (Urban Catalyst 2007; SenStadt 2007). The Badeschiff's current position is in the stretch of the Spree which was in earlier times part of the 'death strip' between the city's East and West, across the river from the longest remaining section of the Berlin Wall. A pier running along the middle of the river is an historical monument where armed soldiers formerly patrolled for swimming escapees (Figure 4.4). This siting lends a subversive resonance to the pool's carefree leisure function, its conspicuous yet contained swimming. A place formerly hidden by a high wall and watched over by border guards has been reinvented as a place for seeing and being seen. The siting takes advantage of a gap in the city fabric where little is preordained and where the city government is keen to facilitate healing and redevelopment.

These various examples illustrate how municipal government investment and planning priorities have shifted from optimising the general public good to strategic place marketing. Such improvements in the accessibility and imageability of waterfronts for leisure use are not evenly distributed or value-neutral. They reflect the conscious reshaping of the markets for tourism and for private-sector investment in real estate development (Smith and Fagence 1995). One special property of the Badeschiff as a waterfront environment is that it can be repositioned as economic conditions require, or to take advantage of potential synergies with other sets of functions on different stretches of the riverbank; functions which are themselves relatively fixed. The Badeschiff can also be removed without leaving blighted ground for uses that follow. The artificiality and portability of this waterfront form – its commoditisation – is highlighted by its subsequent reproduction in Vienna, where it also provides year-round swimming in the inner-city, on a canalised arm of the Danube. In 2006, Paris also opened the Piscine Josephine Baker, adjacent to the artificial beach of Paris Plage (see Chapter 7). This pool extracts and purifies water from the Seine. The technology of this new waterfront landscape form continues to undergo refinement, marketing and distribution.

In the closing pages of *Delirious New York* (1994), Koolhaas tells the mythical story of a floating swimming pool built by Russian Constructivist architecture students in the 1920s, as a means to improve the world through architecture. The pool represents optimism. By swimming laps in unison, the architects discover they are able to make their pool move in the opposite direction, and they use it to escape Stalinism. Koolhaas writes of the 'shiftiness' and the submerged nature of the pool as being subversive. In the 1970s, these swimming architects reach Manhattan, where the post-modern New York architects criticise the pure Modernism of the pool, its lack of decoration. By contrast, the three real floating pools in these wealthy Western European capital cities seem thoroughly bourgeois, all about image and luxury and not at all about social transformation. The three floating swimming pools contrast with the two artificial lagoons in Australia in terms of their ownership and management. The lagoons are located in public parks and are free to enter. The pools all charge admission fees, starting from five Euros, and then hourly rates, despite the fact that the Badeschiff project was funded by an arts initiative of the state of Berlin. This is much more expensive than swimming in the river. The floating pool effectively has a moat around it, and a single controlled access point from the embankment. The controlled design of the waterfront space creates the potential for charging admission and for extracting financial profit. In an organised action in 2004, 12 'Spree-pirates' invaded the Badeschiff in rubber dinghies, protesting the increasing cost of all Berlin's swimming pools and the lack of concessional entry prices, which were turning such venues into elite enclaves. The pirates' attack took advantage of the public accessibility and the extent and flow of the real river. The playful but illegal nature of this action highlights the restricted and commercial conception of leisure shaping these new waterfronts. The positioning of artificial waterfronts is a matter of conflict between social access and market strategy.

The Changing Waterfront

Governments and private-sector developers can modulate the timing, movement and duration of these artificial urban waterscapes in unnatural ways to serve their economic and political goals. Natural water bodies are constantly in motion and constantly changing their volume, through gravitational flow, tides, precipitation, absorption, sedimentation and evaporation. The motion of water throughout the seasons and over time continually reshapes the landscape around it, eroding and depositing. In contrast, the artificiality of urban waterfronts often includes ways of controlling the water cycle and the land which fronts onto it, by making a water body more static, more dynamic or more ephemeral, or regulating how and when the water changes.

The clearest example of artificial control is those urban water features which are turned off in the evenings, such as the Lady Diana Memorial Fountain in London's Hyde Park. Water only flows here because and when there are tourists to see it, and not because natural forces cause it to. An unintended consequence is that for a short time after the water is turned off, and the gates are still open, this fountain becomes a very different landscape for visitors to explore. The great diversity of grooved, stepped and undulating surfaces in the fountain floor, designed only with a view to making the water move in interesting patterns, and still wet and slippery with runoff, become an obstacle course that visitors explore on foot. On Melbourne's Southbank, circles of fountain jets built flush into the pavement jump in randomly-programmed sequences that encourage tourists to play games: trying to run across the field of jets without getting wet, to run following their sequence, to catch the leaping shafts of apparently-solid water in their hands, standing right next to jets as they erupt to 6m in height, or placing hats over the jets to see how high the pressure will toss them (Stevens 2007). The pleasure lies in the mysterious and unpredictable forces. These actions are not what water does naturally; these are actions that water can be made to do. Just as the Diana Memorial and Cheonggyecheon compress an unnaturally large variety of water effects into a short length of stream, artificial water bodies that change a lot over time compress a lot of experiences of water into a brief visit. They highlight tourists' insatiable desire for the stimulus of novelty.

In many cases, entire urban waterfronts appear and disappear, or move, over time. Few of the projects described in this chapter existed more than 20 years ago. A freeway was constructed over the natural stream of Cheonggyecheon to serve economic development needs; when city marketing became a priority thirty years later, the stream was made to 'reappear'. The common observation that cities have turned to face back toward their waterfronts (Dovey 2005) usually neglects the fact that these waterfronts are new nature, not a return to a prior condition. Temporary waterfront landscapes which are cleared away when land is redeveloped for 'higher and better' (i.e. more profitable) uses serve a range of important social needs, particularly by providing open space amenity in areas where it is usually lacking. They also serve landowners' short-term economic needs, reducing costs (e.g. security, maintenance) and generating income. Spectacular artificial waterfronts help to draw the attention of future investors and customers to redeveloping waterfront areas (SenStadt 2007). The Badeschiff's popularity has led to it being redesigned and transformed for year-round use. This example highlights that fluid, temporary waterfront landscapes can be made more durable and more useful if that is what is desired.

Like Koolhaas's pool, artificial beaches on urban waterfronts provide a reminder of the utopian spirit of the 1960s and 1970s. Instead of following the Situationists' call to look underneath the pavement (representing functional urban planning) for the beach (epitomising environments for free play), today the sand is placed on top of the pavement. In many cases these beaches are private endeavours, and patrons are paying for the sand. These beaches can expand and contract as the market demands; they are customer-focused. New, naturalistic urban waterfronts are seldom the result of a rising ecological conscience. As Dovey (2005) notes, they usually owe their existence to global flows of financing, and political efforts to capture those flows in the local built environment. This newly-built second nature will itself most likely be re-exploited when economic needs change. However, the popularity, physical openness and naturalness of these artificial waterfronts means that social struggles will inevitably unfold over their use, meaning and form (Dodson and Kilian 1998). Although they are thoroughly manufactured products, artificial waterfronts also become places over t me; they take on a social reality, and they might not so easily be reduced to purely economic value and liquidated.

Unnatural Complexity, Unnatural Impacts

Artificial leisure waterfronts are among the most sophisticated examples of contemporary urban landscape design. Their scale is large, and they are of great importance to contemporary city function, city marketing, land development, and sometimes even locals' sense of place. This chapter has shown that detailed design of the physical edge where the urban landscape meets the water requires careful attention to many of the same key issues which Gordon (1996) identified with successful urban waterfront redevelopment more generally: improving image; adapting and re-using existing built form; improving public accessibility; integrating waterfronts with their urban surroundings and with the water; thinking small; and planning in increments. The cases presented here demonstrate that these elements of post-modern, post-industrial planning are also utilised at the smallest scale of landscape design. These schemes also pay great attention to the minutiae of human bodily and sensory comfort. Because these waterfronts are used during people's free time, when they have the most options about where to be, these spaces need to provide 'an adequate fulfilment of (users') fantasies about how to relax' (Carter 1993, 53). These spaces thus tell us a lot about what qualities people want from the urban public realm more generally: comfort, control, rich sensory stimulus, flexibility, novelty and escapism. The cases also suggest three refinements to Gordon's logic. Firstly, image and water are both socially produced, and are thus not limited by the natural context of sites. Secondly, success often depends on control, and that includes separating, distinguishing and protecting a waterfront leisure environment from the vagaries of water, weather and neighbouring sites – which runs counter to integration and accessibility. Thirdly, successful waterfront leisure settings specifically depend on careful attention to materiality and human scale, in terms of both comfort and sensory stimulation. There is more to waterfronts than spectacular views. The contemporary artificial waterfront is also felt underfoot and against the skin.

In addition to the diversity of artificial waterfronts worldwide, there is also tremendous variation of land use, behaviour, form and imagery within individual cities' waterfronts. Seoul's Cheonggyecheon, for example, consciously engages with the spectrum of artifice, framing a gradual transition from 'urban' to 'naturalistic' landscaping around the stream as it flows downhill to meet the Han River. Many cities' waterfronts now juxtapose a wide range of leisure facilities, which tends to emphasise the unnatural, constructed nature of the waterfront cityscape as a whole. Traditional urban uses and forms (historic docks, industrial districts, entertainment districts expelled to the 'far' side of the river, old office buildings dominating prime stretches of waterfront) are mixed together with a 'trophy collection' of stereotypical urban-renewal visitor attractions (hotels, convention centres, stadia, aquaria, casinos, museums and galleries (Frieden and Sagalyn 1989)) and a range of new landscape elements (floating and demountable spaces, hermetically-sealed zones, tropical motifs, swimming pools for exhibitionists). The introduction of cheap, temporary, changing and disposable landscape elements further complexifies the image, function and ecology of the urban waterfront, increasing the already-rapid pace at which these environments are changing, and undermining prospects for implementing any holistic strategic management approaches. These waterfronts are definitively postmodern, escapist environments where thematic, functional and spatial continuity and cohesion are seen as neither necessary nor desirable (cf Boyer 1992, 1994). Much recent literature on the redevelopment of urban spaces such as waterfronts critiques the production of idyllic and exclusive utopian enclaves which further gentrification and segregation (MacLeod and Ward 2002; Dovey 2005). The gathering together of various water-related activity spaces, often with quite clearly artificial and contrasting themes, serves consumers' appetite for novelty, and for the conceptual shallowness of escapist spectacle. These environments offer the pedestrian equivalent of channel-surfing. On a more positive note, the centralisation and co-location of waterfront facilities can attract a diverse public, and maximise repeat visits, by offering a range of experiences and recreational activities in one precinct (Carter 1993). The sensory, symbolic and physical richness of artificial waterfronts also tends to stimulate a wide range of fantasy and play by users.

As post-industrial, entrepreneurial landscapes, these waterfronts differ greatly from nature, although they often re-use natural elements and sensations (images, sounds and textures). The new artificial waterfronts escape from the rational, practical engineering constraints that determined waterfront spaces for industry, in terms of hydrology, energy use, transportation, location, scale, and control over land uses and access. Unlike earlier industries, contemporary urban waterfront uses often have no direct or obvious relation to natural water bodies, except views of them. The lack of a compelling natural or necessary connection to the physical potentials of rivers and oceans raises the question of what should count as a 'waterfront use' in the contemporary city (Malone 1996; Sairinen and Kumpulainen 2006). In spite of their naturalistic appearances, the ecologies of many of the waterfront projects described in this chapter are often radically unnatural and separated from their context. Their disregard for natural hydrological systems and their efforts to overcome natural variations of cold, wet and darkness may in fact lead to substantial negative impacts on the ecology of waterways. These new landscapes focus on serving the voraciously consumptive desires of urban leisure, maximising environmental comfort for users by synthesising the appearance of benign nature, eliminating unwanted sensations, and allowing light, temperature and water flow to be adjusted at will. These needs take precedence over limiting the landscapes' resource use or their external environmental effects, or addressing existing ecological problems. Visitors to Tropical Islands pay an hourly admission charge to cover the enormous ongoing energy costs of conditioning the water and air inside the dome. Delivering purified water to artificial lagoons and floating swimming pools requires large amounts of energy. Blanketing the tidal mudflats of Cairns with inert concrete and sand damages a distinctive habitat. The aesthetic pleasures of Seoul's rebuilt river mask the fact that the natural watershed has been drastically reshaped. The concrete paving and channelisation of urban river embankments worldwide contributes to the raising of flood levels and increasing runoff speeds. On a more positive note, the spread of Badeschiff projects to many German cities has in fact helped spur campaigns to make the rivers they float in safe and clean enough for swimming (BBU 2007). More research is needed to identify the short- and long-term environmental impacts of this new phase of waterfront development, as well as any potential environmental benefits, so that artificial leisure waterfronts do not produce a new legacy of degraded brownfield sites.

References

BBU (Freiburger Arbeitskreis Wasser im Bundesverband Bürgerinitiativen Umweltschutz e.V.) (2007) 'Freizeit/030: Frankfurt am Main – Badeschiff statt Flussbadeanstalt, Schattenblick', 18 Oct, http://www.schattenblick.de/infopool/umwelt/lebens/ulefr030.htm, accessed 1 October 2008.

Boyer, M. C. (1992) 'Cities for sale: Merchandising history at South Street Seaport', in Sorkin, M. (ed.) *Variations on a Theme Park*, New York: Hill and Wang.

Boyer, M. C. (1994) *The City of Collective Memory: Its Historical Imagery and Architectural Entertainments*, Cambridge MA: MIT Press.

Breen, A. and Rigby, D. (1996) *The New Waterfront: A Worldwide Urban Success Story*, London: Thames and Hudson.

Campo, D. (2002) 'Brooklyn's vernacular waterfront', *Journal of Urban Design*, 7(2), pp. 171–199.

Carter, L. (1993) *Sensual Southbank: The Power of the Body in the Transformation of Culture*, unpublished BArch thesis, Brisbane, Australia: University of Queensland.

Cohen, S. and Taylor, L. (1976) *Escape Attempts: The Theory and Practice of Resistance to Everyday Life*, London: Allen Lane.

Connolly, K. (2004) 'Germans get taste of tropics an hour's drive from Berlin', *Daily Telegraph (UK)*, 21 December, available from https://www.telegraph.co.uk/news/worldnews/europe/germany/1479454/Germans-get-taste-of-tropics-an-hours-drive-from-Berlin.html, accessed on 12 May 2020.

Davison, A. and Ridder, B. (2006) 'Turbulent times for urban nature: conserving and re-inventing nature in Australian cities', *Australian Zoologist*, 33(3), pp. 306–14.

Dodson, B. and Kilian, D. (1998) 'From Port to Playground: The Redevelopment of the Victoria and Albert Waterfront, Cape Town', in Tyler, D., Guerrier, Y. and Robertson, M. (eds), *Managing Tourism in Cities*, Chichester: John Wiley.

Dovey, K. (2005) *Fluid City: Transforming Melbourne's Urban Waterfront*, London: Routledge.

Franck, K. and Stevens, Q. (eds) (2007) *Loose Space: Possibility and Diversity in Urban Life*, London: Routledge.

Frieden, B. and Sagalyn, L. (1989) *Downtown, Inc.: How America Rebuilds Cities*, Cambridge MA: MIT Press.

Gehl, J. and City of Melbourne (1994) *Places for People*, Melbourne: City of Melbourne.

Gordon, D. (1996) 'Planning, design and managing change in urban waterfront redevelopment', *Town Planning Review*, 67(3), pp. 261–290.

Grenville, J. (2007) 'Conservation as psychology: Ontological security and the built environment', *International Journal of Heritage Studies*, 13(6), pp. 447–461.

Hannigan, J. (1998) *Fantasy City: Pleasure and Profit in the Postmodern Metropolis*, New York: Routledge.

Hudson, B. (1996) *Cities on the Shore: The Urban Littoral Frontier*, New York: Pinter.

Judd, D. (1992), 'Constructing the Tourist Bubble', in D. Judd and S. Fainstein (eds), *The Tourist City*, New Haven: Yale University Press, pp. 35–53.

Kim, N. (2005) 'Ecological restoration and revegetation works in Korea', *Landscape and Ecological Engineering*, 1, pp. 77–83.
Koolhaas, R. (1994) 'The Story of the Pool', in *Delirious New York*, New York: Monacelli Press.
Lefebvre, H. (1991) *The Production of Space*, trans. D. Nicholson-Smith, Oxford: Blackwell.
Macarthur, J. (1999) 'Tactile Simulations: Architecture and the Image of the Public at Brisbane's Kodak Beach', in Barcan, R. and Buchanan, I. (eds) *Imagining Australian Space: Cultural Studies and Spatial Inquiry*. Nedlands, Australia: University of Western Australia Press.
MacLeod, G. and Ward, K. (2002) 'Spaces of Utopia and Dystopia: Landscaping the Contemporary City', *Geographiska Annaler*, 84(3–4), pp. 153–170.
Malone, P. (ed) (1996b) *City, Capital and Water*, London: Routledge.
Marshall, R. (ed) (2001) *Waterfronts in Post-industrial Cities*, London: Spon.
Meyer, H. (1999) *City and Port: Urban Planning as a Cultural Venture in London, Barcelona, New York and Rotterdam*, Utrecht: International Books.
Pinder, D.A., Hoyle B.S. and Husain, M.S. (eds) (1988), *Revitalising the Waterfront: International Dimensions of Dockland Redevelopment*, London: Belhaven.
Ryu, J. (2004) 'Naturalizing landscapes and the politics of hybridity: Gwanghwamun to Cheonggyecheon', *Korea Journal*, Autumn, pp. 8–33.
Sairinen, R. and Kumpulainen, S. (2006) 'Assessing social impacts in urban waterfront regeneration', *Environmental Impact Assessment Review*, 26, pp. 120–135.
Schubert, D. (ed.) (2001) *Hafen- und Uferzonen im Wandel: Analysen und Planungen zur Revitalisierung der Waterfront in Hafenstaedten*, Berlin: Leue.
SenStadt = Senatsverwaltung für Stadtentwicklung Berlin (ed.) (2007) *Urban Pioneers: Temporary Use and Urban Development in Berlin*, Berlin: Jovis.
Smith, J. C. and Fagence, M. (eds) (1995) *Recreation and Tourism as a Catalyst for Urban Waterfront Redevelopment*, London: Praeger.
Stevens, Q. (2007) *The Ludic City: Exploring the Potential of Public Spaces*, London: Routledge.
Urban Catalyst (Philipp Oswalt, Philipp Misselwitz, Klaus Overmeyer) (2007) 'Patterns of the unplanned', in K. Franck and Q. Stevens (eds) *Loose Space: Possibility and Diversity in Urban Life*, London: Routledge, pp. 271–288.
Wang, Z. and Stevens, Q. (2020) 'How do open space characteristics influence open space use? A study of Melbourne's Southbank Promenade', *Urban Research and Planning*, 13(1), pp. 22–44.

Part II
Switching the Waterfront On

Chapter 5

Appropriating the Spectacle

Quentin Stevens and Kim Dovey

The urban riverfront of Melbourne, Australia has been transformed over the past 30 years, starting opposite the city centre with the popular leisure precinct known as 'Southbank'. This is a postmodern landscape of contrived spectacle, where playful urban life is simulated, choreographed and consumed. Yet it is also the site of many forms of unplanned and unstructured activity. This chapter explores the complex uses and meanings which can develop around such a waterfront, and outlines three dialectics which reveal how many new kinds of public life emerge within it. New tensions between global and local, politics and play, representation and embodied action lead to a rethinking of both formularized waterfronts and urban design theories.

Southbank is a kilometre-long cultural and leisure precinct located on the riverfront opposite Melbourne's central city grid, redeveloped during the 1980s and 1990s on former industrial land. This new urban landscape began with a publicly-funded arts centre (completed in 1983), followed by the shopping, dining and hotel complex called SouthGate (1992) and corporate office buildings (1991 and 1994). A giant gambling, cinema and nightclub complex known as Crown Casino followed (1997) together with an exhibition centre (1996), all linked by a rive-front pedestrian promenade (Figures 5.1 and 5.2) (Sandercock and Dovey 2002). Located on the south side of the Yarra River, the Southbank Promenade has the advantage of ample sun exposure, even in winter, and broad views of the city skyline. Southbank is physically set apart from the dense central city, although construction of a new pedestrian bridge and pathway network has put it within several minutes' walk.

In the decades since the construction of SouthGate and the Crown Casino, significant further re-zoning, property development and urban design investments have seen Melbourne's new leisure waterfront extend further east along the river, to the

Appropriating the Spectacle

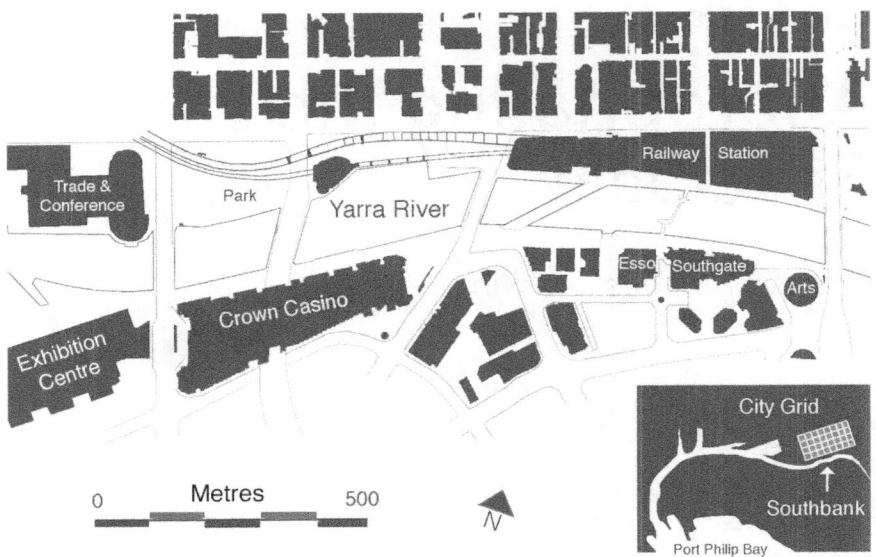

Figure 5.1 Southbank, Melbourne, circa 2002.

Figure 5.2 Southbank overview from the pedestrian bridge.

Docklands (Dovey 2005). The wider Southbank precinct covering 44 hectares 'inland' from SouthGate has also accommodated a tremendous amount of development, with four residential towers over 200m in height built since 2005, and a current gross density of more than 100 du/Ha (Dovey and Symons 2014). This chapter, written in 2004, draws on observations of the Southbank Promenade prior to this expansion, when the Promenade stood largely isolated on the riverside. There has been a lot of subsequent construction along and around the Southbank, which has done much to improve and extend its vitality and design quality. But this chapter's observations about the dialectical, constantly-unfolding relationships between a carefully-managed consumption landscape and the unstructured, unexpected nature of people's everyday uses of public spaces still remain true for the further-developed Melbourne waterfront, and for many other urban waterfront precincts in other cities.

Much of the waterfront development in Melbourne has followed the familiar patterns which have transformed disused waterfronts around the world (Breen and Rigby 1994, Breen and Rigby 1996; Marshall 2001; Malone 1996; Hannigan 1998, Kearns and Philo 1993; Hoyle et al. 1988; Boyer 1992). Southbank eschews any particular inspiration offered by the site or by local history, and largely ignores the interests of a wide range of prospective local patrons. The river's edge is lined with scheduled entertainment venues and saturated with choreographed street theatre, public artworks and illusory soundscapes, intended to attract a well-heeled clientele and to frame leisure within a context of consumption. The SouthGate and Crown Casino projects were launched with a spirit of festivity and carnival, filled with representations of excess and release. A row of giant pylons in front of the casino spurt forth exploding balls of fire on the hour (Figure 5.3). The urban design of the waterfront serves an instrumental function: feeding the escapist desires which the city awakens, channelling them into consumption and carefully managed forms of play. Only certain forms of escapist behaviour are tolerated. Opportunities for engagement with risk and danger are directed inside to the gaming tables.

One interpretation here is that the exploratory and liberatory possibilities of the city have been reduced to spectacle – stimulating the senses but passivising the body. The urban design of Southbank promenade appears to carefully manage social

Figure 5.3 Crown casino promenade.

experience, leaving no space for real urban life, with all its conflicts, risks, creativity, spontaneity and behavioural abandon. The theme park atmosphere suggests a reproduction of successful global formulae which have little to do with the complexities and particularities of Melbourne street life, the authenticities of the local. The theme of this chapter is that this riverscape is in reality much more complex and interesting than such a view would suggest. The chapter draws upon a detailed analysis of specific relations between urban structure, symbolism and behaviour. This case study shows that contemporary manipulations of place experience have their paradoxes; they can create conditions for a range of unexpected and resistant meanings and social activities.

In her study of inner-urban waterfront redevelopment in London and New York, Fainstein (2000, 204–11) assesses the many poststructuralist critiques of inner-urban leisure precincts which declaim their lack of diversity, authenticity and democracy. Fainstein's central argument is that spaces such as Southbank are an appropriate response to legitimate needs of 'middle class escapism', in their attention to such matters as visual aesthetics, artificiality, consumption, comfort and control. Our examination of Melbourne's waterfront focuses upon the contradictory and also rather indeterminate relations between these desired functions and meanings of 'leisure', and the complex reality of the behaviour that we have observed in this landscape.

Fainstein identifies several crucial issues through which to examine the relation between urban leisure precincts and social activity: the spatial and representational disconnection of the urban waterfront from the wider city; the question of whether such public spaces serve the needs of a diversity of social groups (including their needs for self-expression); and the many kinds of bodily pleasures which the physical environment facilitates (visual aesthetics being only one aspect of this). The commodification and globalisation of urban leisure precincts may jeopardise traditional forms of urbanity; what we argue is that these shifts themselves give rise to new and distinctive possibilities for social life. Fainstein argues that both passive and active forms of leisure, incorporating both aesthetic contemplation and bodily pleasure, can be engaging and satisfying; our analysis focuses on how the waterfront landscape frames these various pleasures in quite complex combinations, each helping to stimulate others (see also Lefebvre 1991a).

The discussion which follows opens up the contentious and difficult question of 'authenticity' with all its paradoxes and problems (Percy 1981, 46–63; Dovey 1985). While it would be easy to avoid such a term, our use of it here is crucial to the arguments – it is intended to evoke the idea of the creation (or 'authorship') of new forms of urban life and experience that can spring from the specificities of the local. This is not, however, a quest for 'authentic places' nor for the authentic in any absolute sense; indeed, the authenticities of urban life are linked to its ambiguities (Dovey 2002; Berger 1992, 216). Our quest is to understand the contradictory and ambiguous ways in which new urban life emerges within the frame of a global urban design formula. The chapter explores this landscape of desire through three dialectics where new and quite diverse forms of urban life emerge in the form of play and politics. There are cracks in the otherwise-saturated spectacle, where a more complex reality penetrates. Southbank's success in stimulating desires also gives rise to quite extreme, carnivalesque forms of abandon. And, to the extent that the riverscape is a regulated landscape, it also produces a dialectic tension between authority and resistance. The urban riverscape takes on a broader scope of meanings and uses for a wider range of citizens, as the spontaneity and creativity of play and politics cuts through the pre-packaged spectacle.

A Walk Along the Waterfront

To describe the everyday life of Southbank we will take a 'walk' from east to west, which is roughly the order in which the riverbank was developed. We begin at the historic Princes Bridge; adjacent to this stands the Arts Centre, whose Concert Hall provides the best evidence of the utter disdain with which the river was treated just a few decades ago. The Hall turns its back on the waterfront, and there is a massive, dark undercroft hard up against the river's edge (Figures 5.4 and 5.5). The task for the designers of the adjoining SouthGate project was to generate a pedestrian link between the busy arts precinct on St. Kilda Road, with its four major theatres and art gallery, and the vitality of the new riverbank below. With commercial imperatives in mind, the most direct connection was laid out with the aim of redirecting pedestrian traffic through the shopping mall on the way down to the river. Despite the attempted manipulation, the undercroft remains the most direct route between the arts precinct and the riverbank promenade. It is a site of constant flow and social exchange.

This undercroft is a gloomy and cavernous space which opens to the river on one side through a row of low arches. It is quite literally a 'backstage' area housing the stage door and loading dock. At first glance it seems like a major missed opportunity and a possible crime trap. To the outside observer, this does not seem to provide ideal

Figure 5.4 Concert hall undercroft.

Appropriating the Spectacle

Figure 5.5 Concert Hall (left) and SouthGate (right).

conditions for a vital urban space. Yet the social life observed in this clumsy interstitial zone is more interesting than on the terrace above. The undercroft has a dark and slightly menacing atmosphere; it is aesthetically, acoustically and thermally quite different to the typical urban waterfront. This space has a very long reverberation time, which attracts buskers, many of whom are talented music students from the nearby Victorian College of the Arts. A space of transition, it catches the passing leisure traffic moving between parkland, food and theatre. As one of the few large public spaces of the city which is protected from rain and summer heat, it has been appropriated on Sundays for a busy craft market. It is the very failure of this space to follow any sensible urban design principles which allows new opportunities to emerge. The undercroft provides a relief from the staged streetlife of the Arts Centre and SouthGate, attractions which are essential in making this site vital.

As our walk proceeds from the undercroft towards SouthGate, the gap available for temporary appropriations closes. The unregulated public space leads into the commodified, quasi-public: a zone of spectacle lined with alfresco restaurants, artworks and choreographed street theatre. A firm called 'Explosive Media' are employed to produce a range of 'events' here on Sundays. This is a voyeuristic zone which frames leisure through the seeing-and-being-seen activities of eating, shopping and promenading. Yet this quite carefully staged spectacle loosens as one approaches the water (Figure 5.5). The promenade is on two levels, with the less-trafficked lower level allowing for boat access and for occasional flooding. The additional privacy of the lower level creates a zone for somewhat marginal activities flowing over from the throng above: teenagers kissing, smoking, playing and wrestling. The bounded space of safety runs in parallel with a space of heightened risk.

The pedestrian bridge nearby has been through several cycles of use during the first decade of its existence (Figure 5.6). The boat-shaped artificial island surrounding the base of one of the bridge's supports combines physical isolation and high visual exposure. It

Figure 5.6 Pedestrian bridge looking towards SouthGate (left) and Esso (right).

has been subject to a good deal of graffiti over the years and its single tree has not exactly thrived. It has now gained a more vibrant life as the home of the city's smallest cafe, due to be submerged in the first flood. This is the place where urban life comes closest to the water, and like the undercroft, it has a touch of the sublime about it. The bridge itself is a site for a good deal of playful behaviour, from the harmless and incidental to the very risky. The flat upper surface of its structural steel arch frames the possibility that one might walk up and over it. This transgression was first suggested at the opening of SouthGate when a neon sculpture of a girl running across the arch was mounted here. The traces of use, frequently painted over, suggest it has been attempted many times, although this exceedingly dangerous undertaking has now been made more difficult, with barriers at both ends.

Where the pedestrian bridge intersects with the Southbank promenade is the corporate headquarters of Esso (Exxon). This building utilises the highly visible site for its 'billboard' potential, violating the planned vision of a public riverscape with a deadly dull security-controlled building, entirely bereft of public functions. However, as with the undercroft, we again see the paradox that poor quality urban design can nurture distinctive forms of leisure life. The creation of an inactive frontage at such a busy intersection of pathways renders the space in front of the Esso building useful and available for spontaneous performances (Figure 5.7). A low flight of steps leading up to a blank façade provides an ideal stage. On weekends this space is almost permanently occupied by street performers who often pull a larger crowd than that in front of SouthGate. Here there are no distractions, no compulsion to consume and the promenade has not been narrowed by alfresco dining. The private security guards' only role is to defend the Esso building itself; there's no choreographed spectacle here. This vacuum is filled with a genuine free-market in fire-eating, juggling, comedy and climbing through tennis racquets – anything that can pull a crowd. Gold and silver painted 'statues' line the walkway which pavement artists cover with chalk. Performers and their audiences often

Appropriating the Spectacle

Figure 5.7 Busking at the Esso entrance.

block much of the promenade. Passers-by are confronted by the action; drawn in to see what's going on. Some get into the act, helping jugglers mount unicycles, tossing them knives and flaming torches. In the absence of carefully regulated zones and roles, the safe, pre-packaged routine gives way to unplanned, active and risky involvement.

This zone of possibility diminishes as one approaches Queensbridge Square, a very poor pedestrian environment, large in scale, windswept and in the early 2000s, still awaiting redevelopment. One suspects that this site, too, will in time become overdetermined. In 1998 this became the site of a temporary sculpture formed of a series of white ceramic toilet pedestals stacked vertically to form a glistening white column (Figure 5.8). Located near the pedestrian crossing it seemed precariously balanced but was frequently climbed. This surreal and beautiful work with allusions to both Duchamp and the glistening casino across the street was unfortunately removed after its planned exhibition period.

Beyond the Queensbridge intersection stretches 500 metres of riverbank promenade in front of the casino and entertainment centre – the longest stretch of quasi-public space in the city. One side is lined by almost continuous restaurants and shops, with a row of pylons cascading water and exploding fireballs on the riverside (Figures 5.3). The landscape design here is a high-quality mix of concrete and grass, with steps and ramps to the water, generous seating and many changes of level. This is a landscape designed to encourage leisure and playful behaviour. One of the features is a fountain set flush into the pavement which squirts upward unexpectedly at people walking across. This is a somewhat formulaic design element, reproduced from such tourist attractions as CityWalk in Los Angeles. Yet the wetness is real, and so is the delight experienced by those who engage with it. A crowd often gathers to observe the spectacle of the dancing jets. The combination of the fountain's unpredictability and the expectant audience also encourages a lot of unprogrammed action: people often step out onto the stage and interact with the water. The public become actors and not just audience. Sometimes strangers also encounter each other in informal games framed around the jumping jets. The fountain

Quentin Stevens and Kim Dovey

Figure 5.8 Pedestals, Queensbridge Square, 1999.

is in several senses a representation of the games and machines inside the casino. The carefully orchestrated risks of engagement with this landscape of play are an illustration to potential gamblers that taking chances can be both fun and safe.

Whilst performing for money in front of the casino is prohibited, the passing crowd and the surfeit of unprogrammed open spaces adjoining the promenade here inevitably give rise to a variety of performances. On one featureless plaza, teenage cyclists do tricks against the backdrop of the city skyline across the river. The bending of the pathway frames them directly in the line of sight of strolling pleasure-seekers. Such acts thrive on the excitement and the crowds that the casino can muster. The casino management has responded by plugging this gap with planters which block the cyclists' run and new sculptures which recapture the tourist gaze for more profitable forms of escapism. Skateboarding is another unintended consequence of the sophisticated landscape treatment (Figure 5.9). The

Appropriating the Spectacle

Figure 5.9 Skating the lugs, casino promenade.

promenade's many ledges and edges lend themselves to the exploration of a wide range of skating moves. Anti-skating lugs have been fixed to many edges; this in turn heightens the challenge for the skaters, who then have to jump and weave to avoid the lugs. Attempts to deter skaters appear not only to have failed, but to have heightened the fun.

Three Dialectics

The brief descriptions above tend to cut across the notion that the meanings and spatial practices of this riverscape are in any way fixed or singular. Instead this waterfront frames a series of dialectic movements within which the complex realities of urban life cut through this fabricated landscape of desire and consumption.

Cracks in the Spectacle

The first is that this urban spectacle is neither integrated nor totalizing; there are cracks in the spatial field. This interpretation is linked to the work of de Certeau (1993) who argues that the production of urban spectacle and an overdetermined choreography of urban life produces a city with the qualities of a 'sieve'; despite the attempt to contain and order urban experience, meanings and actions consistently 'leak' through the cracks. Both the semantic field and the functional layout of the riverscape have gaps and margins, where new meanings and practices can insert themselves. The transgressive and the truly unexpected remain possible. Setbacks from the river have created a generous waterfront zone of publicly accessible yet privately controlled space which is at times underused – other uses and users fill the void. The Arts Centre undercroft and the Esso building both provide special kinds of public amenity which arise, paradoxically, from the very absence of conscious design intent. In the case of the Esso building – perhaps the worst piece of formal urban design on the waterfront – the pursuit of one kind of spectacle (the billboard building) creates a vacuum which is then filled by another. This setting is designed around a reductive sense of purpose – global representation – and this leaves it open to appropriation for new forms of social activity. The casino's ongoing efforts to mend gaps in the spectacular façade show that the struggle between careful scenography and free public play continues to evolve.

In this context, poor quality urban design and dormant, under-programmed spaces have their role in enabling authentic experiences of fantasy and release. They allow space for more marginal practices and identities to flourish. A seamless landscape of spectacular consumption would lack much of the diversity and vitality which we find here. It would be easy to conclude that a bit of bad design may be a good thing, yet urban spaces such as the undercroft and the Esso building are regularly produced in other locations where they have no positive effects. The positive effect of poor urban design is a dialectic phenomenon which operates in relation to an overdetermined landscape.

Poor urban design seems to have a certain value in overdetermined landscapes because they produce a certain 'looseness', and in the context of the 'tight' choreography of the spectacle they provide room for new forms of urban life to take place. Pockets of emptiness in a landscape full of predetermined meanings and behaviours contribute to the possibility of urban diversity. It is useful here to reflect upon the principles of urban diversity outlined by Jacobs (1961) six decades ago, particularly the need for the urban fabric to develop in a somewhat piecemeal manner at a relatively small grain size. This ensures a mix of building age and type, a mix of rental rates, and hence the integration of new, economically-marginal activities. Here, in a quite different context, we see a parallel principle operating. In this regard there is a significant distinction between the western and eastern zones of the riverscape. While the casino to the west is essentially one large-scale development framing a controlled diversity, the eastern zone of Southbank has developed as four separate riverfront sites, with two of them forming gaps in the spectacle as outlined above. The relatively smaller grain size here appears to enable this dialectic to operate in a manner that it does not along the casino riverscape. Jacobs also noted that small-scale secondary activities can best be sustained by a mix of primary uses to maintain a flow of people through a district at different times. In the case of Southbank, the variety of primary leisure attractions stretching from the Arts Centre to the Casino help sustain the many more fleeting and marginal forms of play which spring up in the cracks between them. Like the dumb-bell structure of a shopping mall, these spectacular, predictable 'magnets' draw the crowds of leisure-seekers along the riverfront promenade. But whereas a shopping mall is designed and managed as a totality, here piecemeal, incremental design has left gaps and failures through which the riverscape remains open to unstructured, unexpected forms of social life.

Overflowing Desire

The second dialectic is that in its attempts to create the spectacle of the carnival, the waterfront can stimulate a genuine sense of excess which spills over into spontaneous behaviour. The riverscape creates a place and a time set apart from serious, everyday urban society; it creates the illusion of a social world where rules are relaxed. Based on contradictory desires for fantasy and authenticity, this is a place where one comes close to large flows of water and explosions of fire, but in a safe context. Thus we get what Featherstone (1991) calls 'ordered disorder' – a packaged experience of urban diversity, to be consumed without danger, and with limited risk of contact with social difference. Hannigan (1998, 7) argues that this is a paradox: the desire for intense, 'authentic' experience is combined with the desire to avoid risk. It seems that the Southbank landscape is intended to facilitate only certain harmless forms of playful experience, mediating these through urban design and its spectacle. Bakhtin (1984) notes that the carnival traditionally operates as a social safety valve for letting off steam. In front of the casino the 'letting off steam' takes on a literal form, reduced to the spectacle of exploding gas balls.

But the spectacle also stimulates other desires which it cannot contain, leading to unbridled and spontaneous forms of escapism. People find ways to transcend its limits, explore, and create new identities. Whilst safety is clearly a desirable attribute of an urban space, so can be certain opportunities for taking risks. The eruptions of the fountain in front of the casino encourage a diversity of games and social encounters which can be difficult to control. Skating off ledges and climbing on the arch of the pedestrian bridge are risky engagements with the place, stimulated in part by the contradictory ways such transgressive behaviour both cuts through the audience expectation yet meets the market for 'authenticity' (Fainstein 2000, 206–10). These more transgressive, socially unacceptable and active forms of escapism are often hidden from the view of the general public. Turning aside from the spectacle, they are not a display for strangers so much as a part of the identity formation of teenagers, seeking to explore and extend their bodily potential, through direct engagements with each other and the material landscape (Borden 2001; Caillois 1961). The riskiness of activities like wrestling is heightened by proximity to the water's edge.

One way of understanding the urban spatial conditions through which these urban leisure experiences 'spill over' from one setting or activity to another is in light of Alexander's (1965) observation that 'a city is not a tree'. Alexander railed against the tree-like thinking which produced a modernist, instrumental city of hierarchically-defined functions and meanings. The deadening effects of such thinking were central to both his critique and that of Jacobs. The postmodern landscape of Southbank, with its mix of uses and blurring of boundaries, shows evidence of the desire to capture the fluidity and diversity of urbanity, yet to keep it contained within the imperatives of consumption. The multiplicity of activities along this waterfront shows how difficult it can be to contain and bring order to public behaviour.

This riverscape can also be interpreted through Deleuze and Guattari's depiction of space as being both 'striated' and 'smooth'. This setting frames the strictures of spatial control, but it is also a smooth space of flows, through which new potentials are explored and new identities formulated. The smooth and the striated are not different kinds of space, so much as a form of dialectic: '…smooth space allows itself to be striated, and striated space reimparts a smooth space… '. (Deleuze and Guattari 1987, 486). Here one could say that the highly 'striated' spaces of the casino and the upper promenade become 'smoother' as one approaches the water, the quintessentially 'smooth' space which stimulates the flows of desire which the casino seeks to capture.

Authority and Resistance

Pile (1997) has suggested that the politics of public space can be construed as a form of 'dance', a reciprocity between authority and resistance; this is our final dialectic. Playful uses of the physical terrain such as skating are not only dangerous, they challenge behavioural conventions. They thrive on confrontations with the spectacular scenography and with passive ways of consuming it. The raised steel lugs installed along the stone and concrete edges in the hope of deterring skating actually operate to stimulate the desire. Their locations can be read as a map of the frontiers of struggle between different modes of appreciating a seductive surface. The attempt to control desire encourages the invention of new forms of practice which slide over, weave between and sometimes damage the lugs. In some cases, skaters merely move to other parts of the landscape; a spatial 'dance' ensues between the nomadic and rhizomatic practices of the skaters and the proliferating lugs which both follow and attract them. The casino's introduction of new decorative landscaping to hinder the trick cyclists also illustrates how the dialectical struggle between authority and resistance constantly reworks the cracks in the spectacle. Yet such additions to the landscape, and the crowds they draw, continue to stimulate the desire for real transgression. The three dialectics continue to unfold through each other.

Each of the three dialectics we have outlined shows tensions behind the façade of a postmodern leisure landscape. These dialectics also suggest different ways in which the spectacularised urban space of the waterfront serves to propagate real social life. Authentic experience feeds off the very attempts to purify and rationalise social experience in place. Spectacular landscapes such as Southbank tend to organise social relations and social practices, by mediating them through a predetermined, generic and predictable palette of images, perceptions and opportunities for action. They tend to distance citizens from the diversity of the city, and to produce forms of passivity (Debord 1994, Lefebvre 1991b, 227). Yet as outlined above, the urban spectacle can also generate new forms of urban practice, stimulating desires and resistances which break out of the contrived spectacle and produce the real excitement of urban life.

Appropriating the Spectacle

Local Spaces/Global Politics

One event which occurred on Melbourne's Southbank in September 2000 shows how powerful actions can be in challenging and transforming the functional and representational brief around which such sites are designed. For one week, the entire riverscape precinct became engaged in a major inversion of use and meaning when it served as the host site of a major World Economic Forum (WEF) congress, the Davos group dedicated to the development of free trade agreements. Attracting global events of this kind was precisely the goal of the later waterfront strategy. In both its form and function, the casino complex served to draw together global decision-makers and raise the profile of the city through a celebration of the triumphs of international commerce. Demonstrations against the forum were organised by an internet-based coalition of environmental and social groups, encouraged by the success of Seattle and Washington demonstrations in broadening the agenda of the WEF and the World Trade Organisation. Expecting trouble, the Crown authorities sealed the entire complex with a concrete and steel barricade, forming a 17-hectare fortress encompassing the river and surrounding streets (Iveson and Scalmer 2000).

For three days the casino compound was cordoned off by more than 2000 police on the inside and encircled by tens of thousands of demonstrators outside, the largest political activity seen in Australia since the Vietnam War. This leisure landscape briefly became a space of genuine public engagement. Its manufactured atmosphere of playful abandon gave way to real social agendas, real conflict and violence (Figure 5.10).

The closure cost the casino more than five million dollars in revenue, as they sought to focus the world's media inside, on a spectacular celebration of capitalism (Iveson and Scalmer 2000, 8). The spectacle was turned inside-out: the casino and riverfront promenade became a serious operation of helicopters, boats and police, whilst an informal public carnival enveloped the perimeter barricade, a promenade of music, costumes and banners with 'clowns, ten-foot puppets and twenty-foot dragons' (Iveson and Scalmer 2000, 4). An instant 'tent city' headquarters was set up on the vacant Queensbridge Square. The casino's postmodern landscape of packaged festivity was temporarily replaced by a festival of protest. Iveson and Scalmer (2000, 10) note that '… the party-protest combination proved successful in helping to mobilise people for the protest, and in keeping them entertained during the long days of blockading'. These

Figure 5.10 The casino as fortress – as depicted in the media.

informal festivities thus took the place of the casino's normal instrumental functions: in attracting and entertaining demonstrators, they contested the casino's monopoly on the framing of leisure. In its attempt to provide a global stage for the WEF congress, the casino was effectively closed down and up-staged.

This carnival of protest was punctuated by occasional outbursts of violence as police were ordered to forge a passage through the cordon for delegates to the conference. The compound fence inscribed a temporary boundary between local and global space, as VIPs such as Bill Gates and the Australian Prime Minister were forced to enter and leave by helicopter and police launch. The image of the casino juxtaposed with graffiti covered barricades, the carnival of demonstrators and rows of police in riot gear produced powerful imagery which the mass media could not resist because of its capital value as media. The casino complex became a symbol of the wealth and intransigence of a globalised, privatised economy under siege.

While global demonstrations against the WEF focused primarily on the casino, they also spread up and down the Southbank promenade. Across the street to the west, the Exhibition Centre was draped in banners calling for 'global justice'. To the east, the entire Southbank promenade was covered with graffiti, with its global icons in particular being targeted: Esso/Exxon, Sheraton and IBM. Partly as a result of the violence, the struggle for media time was won by the demonstrators. The casino became a global spectacle of a very different kind to that envisioned in the place-marketing strategy. Iveson and Scalmer (2000, 11–12) highlight the demonstrators' success in exploiting the WEF and the media attention it generated to temporarily put both a face and a place to the problems of globalisation: 'Here, protesters tactically transformed Crown Casino into a place from which they could contest corporate capital's domination of global space'. The abstract forces of globalisation became temporarily grounded and territorialized in the casino compound, where they were confronted by local conditions and local sentiments. This event thus exemplifies the ways that seemingly totalizing and opaque mega-projects can become opportunities for new forms of transparency and agency. Global projects can attract global politics, creating a new contestation over both the use of public space and the meanings of the new urban imagery.

The events surrounding the WEF give reason to question the rigid designation of urban leisure precincts through the planning and urban design process, as the Southbank site is forced into the service of new and varied agendas for its private owners, wider commercial interests, the State, and the general public – agendas which aren't always playful. This case reveals the dynamics of appropriation, the continual spilling-over of uses and users which denies spatial clarity or stability to the 'precinct' or its choreography of 'leisure'. Urban functions constantly move and change; they can't easily be controlled or locked down by masterplanning.

The writings of Lefebvre (1991a, 1991b, 1996) are the best guide for understanding the political potential of spectacular urban space. A trenchant critic of the overprogramming of everyday life, he also saw everyday life in public space as the primary stage for political resistance. Lefebvre saw the festival as a time and place when everyday life becomes open to change and liberation, festivals 'tighten social links and at the same time give rein to all desires which have been pent up by collective discipline and

Appropriating the Spectacle

the necessities of everyday work' (Lefebvre 1991a, 202). For Lefebvre public space is the crucial zone of festivity and resistance, both disorderly and uncontrolled by institutions: 'Spontaneity acts like the elements: it occupies whatever empty space it can find…' (quoted in Merrifield 2002, 134). The events surrounding the Melbourne WEF show that desires for excitement, business and politics cannot easily be compartmentalised and regulated; contemporary public spaces such as Southbank need to be understood as the scene of their incessant interplay.

In the 15 years since this article was written, many of the gaps we have explored in Melbourne's Southbank have been filled up with commerce. The wide, sensuous, curving pedestrian ramps connecting the high-spanning Princes Bridge to the lower waterfront precinct have been supplanted by a large elevator (see also Chapter 1). The dark undercroft of the Arts Centre Concert Hall has been built out with an upmarket restaurant; its outdoor tables claim half the width of the promenade. The dead plazas where Southbank Promenade widens are now somewhat busier with foot traffic to and from the thousands of new apartments behind. The café on the boat-shaped island pier of the pedestrian bridge is now a jam-packed licensed bar. Queensbridge Square, once home to a toilet sculpture and a tent city, is now the frontage of Freshwater Place, one of the precinct's 200m-high apartment buildings, and a blank office tower housing global consulting firm PwC. The street cutting across it has been removed, and the casino's underground carpark entry masked by a massive, red, north-facing grandstand where people can sit to eat lunch and watch performers on the plaza below. A formerly-derelict heritage railway bridge has been renovated for pedestrian use, connecting the square to enhanced pedestrian pathways along the north riverbank. These provide access to a temporary restaurant squeezed into the gap between the river and the railway station tracks, and to several floating restaurants and bars moored again the north embankment. The casino's fountain is gone, covered with artificial grass that encourages people to sit and relax in all seasons (Wang and Stevens 2020). These changes have in some cases displaced free, creative, playful appropriation of the Southbank for non-commercial forms of social life. But they have not diminished them. Like the skateboarding lugs, they have stimulated people's discovery and invention of new spaces and new opportunities.

What kinds of lessons might one draw from the various narratives outlined above? One of the most troubling challenges facing urban designers and planners today is that the economic and cultural forces of globalisation so often lead to a proliferation of formularised placemaking: the sense that if you've seen one waterfront, you've seen them all. Attempts to ameliorate such placelessness with authentic local heritage, artworks and streetlife often result in the appropriation of local authenticity and its reproduction for a global market. Yet in some of the observations outlined here, we see a surprising paradox: a formulaic, spectacular, economically instrumental space gains new and authentic uses and meanings precisely because its presence becomes more global. Everyday urban life continues to evolve in response to the excesses of global spectacle. We are in no way suggesting that formulaic global mega-projects are somehow redeemed by the semantic and functional inversions which occur. This chapter doesn't offer ready prescriptions on how to make more inclusive, robust and locally significant leisure space. Indeed, what it shows is some of the limitations of even well-financed and well-managed masterplanning visions. In some ways these lessons are old ones: that the city is not a 'tree' (Alexander); that the real vitality of urban life lies in its diversity, its marginal activities, its tensions and its creativity (Jacobs). These have their spatial correlates: space stimulates, but it doesn't determine the patterns or changes in everyday life. These lessons need to be brought to bear on a new generation of themed, packaged, spectacular environments which attempt to circumscribe the spontaneity, excitement, risk and discord that make urban life truly vital and, perhaps, authentic.

References

Alexander, C. (1965) 'The City is not a Tree', *Architectural Forum*, 122 (1), pp. 58–62, and 122 (2), pp. 58–61.
Bakhtin, M. (1984) *Rabelais and His World*, Bloomington: Indiana University Press.
Berger, J. (1992) *Keeping a Rendezvous*, London: Penguin.
Borden, I. (2001) *Skateboarding, Space and the City: Architecture and the Body*, Oxford: Berg.
Boyer, M. C. (1992) 'Cities for sale: Merchandising history at South Street Seaport', in Sorkin, M. (ed.) *Variations on a Theme Park*, New York: Hill and Wang.
Breen, A. and Rigby, D. (1994) *Waterfronts: Cities Reclaim their Edge*, New York: McGraw Hill.
Breen, A. and Rigby, D. (1996) *The New Waterfront: A Worldwide Urban Success Story*, London: Thames and Hudson.
Caillois, R. (1961) *Man, Play and Games*, New York: Free Press of Glencoe.
de Certeau, M. (1993) 'Walking in the city', in: During, S. (Ed) *The Cultural Studies Reader*, London: Routledge.
Debord, G. (1994) *The Society of the Spectacle*, New York: Zone Books.
Deleuze, G. and Guattari, F. (1987) *A Thousand Plateaus*, Minneapolis: University of Minnesota Press.
Dovey, K. (1985) 'The quest for authenticity and the replication of environmental meaning', in Seamon, D. and Mugerauer, R. (eds) *Dwelling, Place and Environment*, The Hague: Martinus Nijhof, pp. 33–50.
Dovey, K. (2002) 'Dialectics of place: Authenticity, identity, difference', in Akkach, S. (ed) *De-Placing Difference*, CAMEA Conference Proceedings, University of Adelaide, pp. 45–52.
Dovey, K. (2005) *Fluid City: Transforming Melbourne's Urban Waterfront*, London: Routledge.
Dovey, K. and Symons, F. (2014) 'Density without intensity and what to do about it: reassembling public/private interfaces in Melbourne's Southbank hinterland', *Australian Planner*, 51 (1), pp. 34–46.
Fainstein, S. (2000) *The City Builders: Property Development in New York and London, 1980–2000*, 2nd ed., Lawrence: University Press of Kansas.
Featherstone, M. (1991) *Consumer Culture and Postmodernism*, London: Sage.
Hannigan, J. (1998) *Fantasy City: Pleasure and Profit in the Postmodern Metropolis*, New York: Routledge.
Hoyle, B., Pinder, D. and Husain, M. (eds) (1988) *Revitalising the Waterfront*, London: Belhaven.
Iveson, K. and Scalmer, S. (2000) 'Contesting the "Inevitable": Notes on S11', *Overland*, 161, pp. 4–12.
Jacobs, J. (1961) *The Death and Life of Great American Cities*, New York: Vintage.
Kearns, G. and Philo, C. (eds) (1993) *Selling Places*, Oxford: Pergamon.
Lefebvre, H. (1991a) *Critique of Everyday Life*, Vol. 1, 2nd. ed., London: Verso.
Lefebvre, H. (1991b) *The Production of Space*, trans. Nicholson-Smith, D. (ed) Oxford: Blackwell.
Lefebvre, H. (1996) *Writings on Cities*, Oxford: Blackwell.
Malone, P. (ed) (1996) *City, Capital and Water*, London: Routledge.
Marshall, R. (ed) (2001) *Waterfronts in Post-industrial Cities*, London: Spon.
Merrifield, A. (2002) 'Seattle, Quebec, Genoa: Après le Deluge… Henri Lefebvre?', *Environment and Planning D: Society and Space*, 20 (2), pp. 127–134.
Pile, S. (1997) 'Introduction', in: Pile, S. and Keith, M. (eds) *Geographies of Resistance*, London: Routledge.
Percy, W. (1981) *The Message in the Bottle*, New York: Farrar, Straus and Giroux.
Sandercock, L. and Dovey, K. (2002), 'Pleasure, politics and the public interest: Melbourne's waterfront revitalization', *Journal of the American Planning Association*, 68, 151–64
Wang, Z. and Stevens, Q. (2020) 'How do open space characteristics influence open space use? A study of Melbourne's Southbank Promenade', *Urban Research and Planning*, 13 (1), pp. 22–44.

Chapter 6

The 'City Beach' as a New Waterfront Development Model

Quentin Stevens

Formerly industrial waterfronts in many German cities are, as in other developed countries, being revitalised with the typical range of large-scale cultural institutions, office and housing complexes, public promenades and green spaces (Montag Stiftung and Regionale 2010 2008). A parallel and much more distinctive trend is the rapid emergence and diffusion throughout the country of hundreds of small, temporary artificial beaches on inner-urban waterfronts.

The expression 'city beach' is difficult to define comprehensively, as the characteristics of the many schemes that go by that name are varied and changing. The key physical attributes of a city beach are an urban location; a large volume of sand spread on an open space (a site cleared by demolition, a rail easement, a parking lot, or a public park); a view of the waterfront (sometimes with access to the water); and the inclusion of thematic objects commonly associated with beach environments, such as deckchairs, beach umbrellas, palm trees, thatched huts and tropical cocktails (Figure 6.1). The artifice of simply spreading these materials around on top of an existing urban site sets these schemes apart from beaches which are part of natural or renaturalised riverbanks and lakeshores. The informality of this material artifice is complemented by the relaxed use of these city beaches for informal socialising and play, sports, small-scale programmed cultural events, and casual drinking and dining. Another defining characteristic of city beach developments is that they are temporary and mobile. Most only operate in the warmer months, and many are removed from site and put in storage during the winter.

The first artificial city beach of contemporary times was not sited on a waterfront; it was created in 1996 on the main square of St. Quentin, a small provincial city in northern France. After the 2002 opening of a similar project adjacent to the Seine

Quentin Stevens

Figure 6.1 Strand Pauli, Hamburg.

river, *Paris Plage*, received worldwide media attention, the phenomenon of temporary artificial city beaches spread rapidly to major city-center waterfronts throughout Europe and in North America and Australia. Germany's first such project opened in Berlin in the summer of 2002. By 2010, there were well over 300 such beaches spread across more than 130 different German cities.

Germany provides a particularly fertile milieu for examining city beaches as a form of waterfront development. The majority of German city beaches are located on underutilised waterfront land which previously had industrial or port-related functions. These schemes illustrate that deindustrialised, 'unfixed' waterfronts provide spaces that a diverse range of new ideas, users and activities can flow into. But city beaches also show that urban waterfronts may have a distinctive and relatively fixed character, in terms of their physical landscape, meanings, and urbanised context, which can constrain and shape future development.

As a new and untypically fluid mode of urban development, city beaches illustrate several different kinds of flows and flexibilities which might change our thinking about how to plan and manage waterfront change: they are an example of how new spaces and new functions can be 'plugged into' brownfield waterfront sites; they involve a certain amount of 'unplanning' and deregulation to loosen up the existing waterfront landscape; they contain many loose elements; they include significant investments in changing services and event programs rather than relying only on major fixed physical investments; they react to seasonal flows of tides and customers; and the users and behaviours in these waterfront spaces are particularly relaxed, playful and diverse.

This chapter examines the spatial distribution of city beaches across Germany, and variations in the local development contexts where they have emerged, their ownership and management, and their design and programming. The findings highlight the tremendous variety, creativity and adaptability of a single temporary open-space use concept as a means of activating urban waterfront land.

The 'City Beach' as a New Waterfront Development Model

The chapter begins with an examination of the varied social, economic and land development conditions under which city beaches have emerged in Germany, providing an overview of where and why they have been created and of the flexible planning, financial and managerial processes through which they have been produced. The subsequent section considers the new user groups, playful behaviours, social relations and ambiences that city beaches introduce into urban waterfront areas, which lend the urban waterfront a new and fluid identity, enhancing its dynamism. The chapter then provides an empirical account of city beaches as built and used, focusing on the geographical diffusion of the concept, the diversity of sites, and how they have addressed the financial, management and regulatory challenges of re-using the industrial waterfront. The chapter concludes with an examination of the implications of city beaches for thinking about waterfront development more generally.

The chapter draws on a first-hand database and mapping of 327 existing and former city beach sites in Germany, assembled in 2010. This built on two early student dissertations on the topic (Otto 2007; Kahls 2009) and on early media reporting that had identified 130 such beaches (Stolz 2009), supplementing it with a systematic, snowballing web search in both German and English. Analysis of these many examples drew on local press reports, photographs posted online by visitors, 236 of the beaches' own websites, as well as websites of the hospitality industry and city marketing agencies, site analysis and participant observation during visits to 111 beaches, an online and telephone survey of 64 city beach operators, and more detailed interviews with 27 operators in 19 different cities. This detailed fieldwork was spread throughout Germany, and also between sites in major city centres, suburbs and small towns.

Spreading Sand Around

Since 2002, the city beach prototype has undergone extremely rapid geographical diffusion. The 327 city beaches identified across Germany were located on 312 unique sites in 130 different German cities and towns. Berlin, Germany's largest city and capital, had hosted 76 different beaches (Figure 6.2), and the next four largest German cities (Hamburg, Munich, Cologne and Frankfurt) had hosted 41 between them. Eighteen other cities had also hosted three or more beaches at some time, and these 23 cities together accounted for 60% of the total cases. Most of these cities were among Germany's 20 largest. Among the eight that weren't, most host major universities, and two of them, Mainz and Potsdam, are also state capitals. City beaches appear to be a quintessentially urban phenomenon: 80% of the beaches were located in the 81 German cities with populations over 100,000, where only 30% of the national population lives. Only six beaches were in towns of under 10,000. The extensive evolution and variegation of the city beach concept within Germany goes beyond simply reproducing a successful waterfront development model. The spread of the city beach concept throughout Germany highlights significant differences in their siting and design, underpinned by localised economic and political differences.

Quentin Stevens

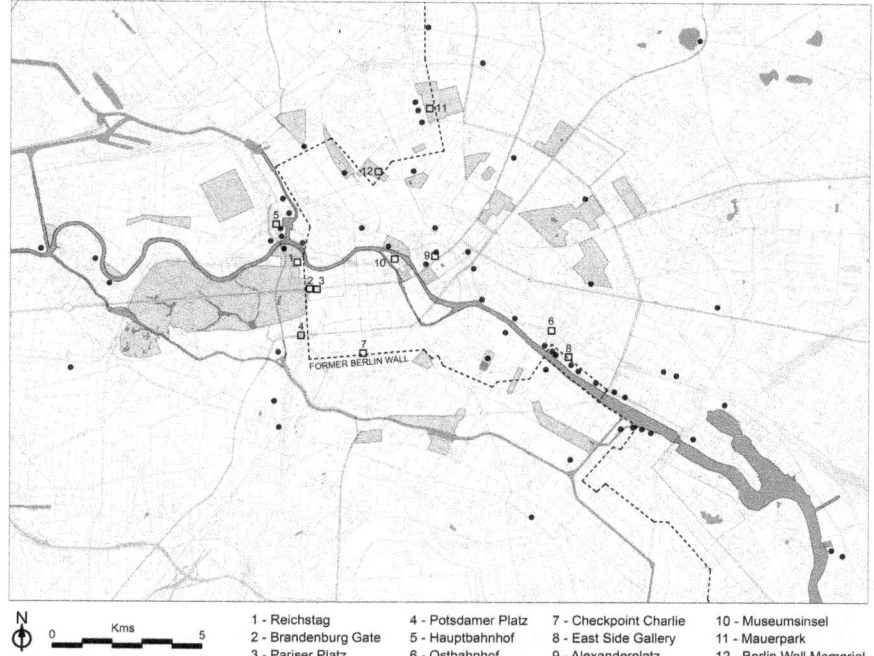

1 - Reichstag
2 - Brandenburg Gate
3 - Pariser Platz
4 - Potsdamer Platz
5 - Hauptbahnhof
6 - Ostbahnhof
7 - Checkpoint Charlie
8 - East Side Gallery
9 - Alexanderplatz
10 - Museumsinsel
11 - Mauerpark
12 - Berlin Wall Memorial

Figure 6.2 Map of Berlin's 'city beaches', 2010.

Source: Quentin Stevens and a Thai

Several of Germany's first city beaches were in Berlin's central district, Mitte. This area was part of the former border zone between Berlin's East and West; there were thus numerous underdeveloped sites adjacent to the Spree River in between the major new and rejuvenated governmental and cultural landmarks: the Reichstag and new parliamentary precinct, the 'Museum Island', and the new main train station. Berlin's very first city beach, *Strandbar Mitte* (Figure 6.3), occupied one corner of a public park that was awaiting large-scale renovation. The city beaches in these high-profile locations took advantage of existing flows of tourists, and provided a model for later developments elsewhere, many of which took shape under very different economic, spatial and tenure conditions.

Berlin has been a particularly popular location for city beach projects. The relatively recent large-scale collapse of state-owned enterprises following the city's reunification had left many sites idle. In Berlin, many of the city beach sites were not obtained through the conventional commercial property market. Instead, federal government agencies, who own a substantial amount of property, provide tenure at nominal rents. For example, there are numerous city beaches alongside the Spree in the former 'death strip' behind the Berlin Wall. The last remaining major section of the Wall, the East Side Gallery, encloses a strip of riverfront land only 50 meters wide. Because of this protected landmark, the land behind has very restricted access and poor visibility. This strip of land remained for a long time unviable for major development, but was a prime site for city beaches. City beaches also opened in Berlin on empty lots behind supermarkets and on the rooftops of multi-storey parking garages. The marked artificiality of these beaches

The 'City Beach' as a New Waterfront Development Model

Figure 6.3 Strandbar Mitte, Berlin.

illustrates that the creation of a pleasant waterfront atmosphere, through sand, palm trees, deckchairs and cocktails, is more important than the quality of water views and access. Waterfront-inspired landscape ideas could also flow to inland sites.

In Hamburg, a string of city beaches opened on the south bank of the Elbe River in St. Pauli, the historical port frontage which had long ago been superseded by larger-scale shipping operations elsewhere. Because it was subject to off-season flooding, this area had escaped redevelopment. These beaches benefited from their location close to Hamburg's dense city centre and to entertainment venues near the Reeperbahn, the city's well-known nightlife area. The next artificial beaches to appear in German cities were, similarly, in the now-deindustrialised, older port areas of other large cities including Cologne, Frankfurt and Bremen. These inner-city waterfront areas fall within 'the zone of transition' (Park et. al. 1925): they are cheaply-available, relatively marginal sites that lie outside the cities' established commercial districts, but are conveniently adjacent to them. Uses and land values in this urban zone are constantly in flux, and this favours temporary uses such as city beaches, which are typically seen by city officials, planners and landowners as an interim use of empty sites, useful until some more substantial investment in development materialises. Many of Germany's large cities are inland river ports, and city beaches are particularly numerous in the west of the country, along the Rhine (Figure 6.4) and its heavily industrialised tributaries, the Ruhr, Main and Neckar rivers. The large population in this area lives far away from the real beaches on the country's relatively short, cold northern coastlines (Stolz 2009).

The economic and spatial conditions for city beaches vary greatly between cities and between regions in Germany. The availability of relatively cheap waterfront sites in Berlin and the deindustrialised Ruhr can be contrasted with the much more prosperous southern state capitals, Stuttgart and Munich, where there are very few underdeveloped inner-urban sites. In Munich, there simply is no old industrial waterfront land near the

Figure 6.4 Kasteler strand on the Rhine River, Mainz.

centre; most of the Isar River is a protected green-space corridor. Stuttgart's only inner-city beach is on the roof of a parking garage. Haydn and Temel (2006) point out that under the highly competitive property market conditions in these southern cities, uses such as city beaches are not temporary by choice: they are frequently and rapidly displaced from their sites by larger-scale investments. This has also been the case on the deindustrialised waterfronts of Hamburg, Cologne and Berlin: city beach operators have had to find new sites to relocate their businesses once long-range development plans began construction. Some beach operators have had to relocate several times, although such relocations are invariably localised, to maintain links with existing clientele and with service providers.

Local Spatial and Developmental Contexts

The specific siting, land use and urban development context of various city beaches illustrates different ways that their local waterfront settings are 'plugged into' their surrounding cityscapes. In 135 cases the immediate spatial context of individual city beaches could be determined from first-hand observation, analysis of photographs, or the project's name. Only 40% of these beaches were on privately-owned riverfront sites, and only two-thirds of these were industrial. A further 22% were on public park-land, which in most cases had water frontage. But at least 60 city beaches (44%) were not on sites adjacent to water, which highlights that this specific temporary re-use of urban waterfront sites was also adapted and further developed in a range of other contexts. These included public plazas, inland industrial areas without river frontage, non-industrial inland sites (including adjacent to existing bars, theatres and universities), surface carparks and railway easements. Twenty-four city beaches were installed on rooftops of multi-storey carparks, and two were on roofs of other buildings. Twenty-four beaches were, like the Badeschiff discussed in Chapter 4, located on and around the former Berlin Wall 'death strip', only part of which runs alongside the Spree River. This spread of city beaches beyond the water's edge is unusual, especially considering most beach operators who were surveyed consider a view onto water (63%) or water frontage (53%) to be essential components of a city beach. Beach users rate water views as being significantly more important than the beaches' operators (Denzer et al. 2010).

The operators of city beaches also weigh up a range of other locational factors when deciding where and how to establish a project, including centrality, public transport access, car parking, solar exposure (especially toward the south and west), quietness, wind protection and greenery. Often water is reduced to a role as a distant backdrop. In London's gentrifying Shoreditch, a beach appeared temporarily in the courtyard of a disused former brewery. Here, the exclusion of the noise and pollution of cars was one of the most important prerequisites for efforts to create an escapist environment. For city beaches, a site with proximity to urban workplaces and to other leisure sites, and the creation of a contrasting style of environment, are more important than providing water for swimming, an activity which is in any case impractical for most urban leisure-seekers.

As small-scale interventions, Germany's city beaches are easily 'plugged in' amongst other flexible and innovative inner-city waterfront functions and populations. They demonstrate flexibility and innovation in terms of their spatial, behavioural and economic interrelations with the surrounding waterfront and the wider cityscape. Many city beaches include or adjoin commercial recreational facilities such as rock-climbing walls, volleyball and kayaking. City beaches also benefit from operational synergies with a surrounding creative milieu in the arts and creative industries, such as bars, nightclubs and theatres. There are beaches situated adjacent to large indoor performance venues in Berlin and Frankfurt, and next to Cologne's Messe (congress and exhibition center). Many other beaches are in former port areas where communities of artists occupy low-rent warehouses. Some city beaches are themselves constructed primarily as venues for cultural events (see Chapters 7 and 8). The concept of a 'creative milieu' emphasises two distinctive features of the development process where waterfronts in general can learn from city beaches in particular. First, the production and operation of city beaches is strongly based on the provision of a regular program of events and services, and not just on landscaping. This is the reverse of many waterfront developments, which are typically led by international signature architecture. Second, city beaches tend to have significant involvement from people working in small-scale creative businesses (Urban Catalyst 2007).

Although the small literature on city beaches highlights their role as temporary, inventive, catalytic uses of fallow waterfront urban land, city beach projects fit in a wide variety of ways into longer-term urban development cycles. Among the 135 analysed beach locations, only 28% sat on ex-industrial waterfronts, with another 7% occupying other kinds of industrial sites where large-scale redevelopment has not yet happened. These contexts offer plentiful space at low rents, and flexibility regarding construction and operation. There are few conflicts with existing users, and indeed, these beaches are often strongly integrated with other leisure and creative activities nearby, such as nightclubs, performance venues, restaurants and artists' studios. These beaches are low-cost interim uses of land awaiting major recapitalisation. Prospects and timeframes for the redevelopment of such brownfields vary greatly across Germany. A welter of government publications on the topic of temporary uses reflects the enthusiasm to facilitate and accelerate this process. Substantial long-term economic growth in Germany's Southwest contrasts with an arrested decline in the Ruhr and East. Only two of the ten beaches in Munich are on ex-industrial land, and none of Stuttgart's five, because these high-rent cities do not have much vacant land (Haydn and Temel 2006). The city-states Berlin, Hamburg and Bremen all have limited landholdings which are largely brownfields. One state distinctly over-represented in the sample is Saxony, with numerous beaches in Dresden, Leipzig and Chemnitz built on redundant industrial or railway land. There are less beaches in Germany's three main coastal states, relative to population, where artificial city beaches are in competition with the real thing.

Eighty-six percent of surveyed operators reported significant increases in local property values since they opened their city beach; all of these believed their beach had contributed to this increase. The few cases where property values had remained stable were largely beaches that were not in industrial areas. One potential indicator of development activity was that at least 68 temporary beaches had already closed down over the years 2002–2010. Among eight surveyed operators who provided reasons, four were yielding to new construction. The other main reasons for closure were economic (lack of financing, or unprofitability due to poor weather) or political (complaints from residents). Several beaches were only ever intended as very short-term events. The theme of development pressure was explored further through visits to eight now-abandoned beaches, and interviews with two former operators. In none of these cases had new development occupied the vacated site. Of eight beaches known to have moved to new sites, six were in the three largest cities, and five of these moved twice, highlighting perhaps that large cities have more potential sites. Düsseldorf's first beach operator relocated to Cologne when his original site was developed as the flagship international hotel within the 'Media Harbour' scheme. On Berlin's Spree, numerous beaches were displaced by the development of new public parklands.

Not all city beaches are harbingers of future large-scale redevelopment. At least eight beaches have been constructed on post-industrial waterfronts after such redevelopment happened, as upmarket themed outdoor cafés permanently integrated with an office park, shopping centre, or university campus. German beaches rarely appear to be strong catalysts to urban redevelopment on their own. Chapter 7 shows that this relationship between city beaches and waterfront redevelopment varies between cities and countries. As discussed below, not all city beaches are entrepreneurial projects which accompany gentrification. They are, however, complementary uses, and often serve as marketing tools. Münster's *Hafenweg* highlights beaches' varying roles throughout the development cycle: one beach still exists as an attraction at the far end of a formerly-industrial quayside promenade, while several earlier beaches have given way to new construction of restaurants, galleries and offices in this 'Media Harbour'.

The Design of City Beaches

When city beach operators were asked what physical elements were essential for a city beach, the components that they ranked most highly were, in order, deck chairs, beach umbrellas, a sandy surface, cocktails, palm trees (which are almost always in pots), and tents or roofing that provide weather protection for guests. This ranking correlates with analysis of the beaches' actual contents, and also with the priorities identified by 827 users who were interviewed on six beaches (Denzer et al. 2010), although users rated cocktails significantly lower. The core human comforts visitors are seeking on a city beach (to sit and relax, with shelter available) are more important than its aesthetic: surprisingly, seven surveyed 'beaches' actually had no sand. Rain protection is clearly a practical and business necessity in the German climate; 47% of surveyed operators noted weather was a key operational difficulty. Almost 40% of operators felt water access was unnecessary – which correlates with the 44% of beaches that do not have waterfront locations. About one quarter of beaches provide access to swimming, usually in self-contained above-ground pools; many others provide outdoor showers.

An additional element present in more than half of city beaches surveyed was a dance floor, which supported one of the key kinds of programming of these spaces, discussed below. Physical elements valued by a minority of beach operators included beach baskets, volleyball pitches, performance stages and heat-lamps; although all of these elements were actually provided on a majority of beaches. Specific aesthetic elements, such as rowboats, pirate ships and public art, were recommended by relatively few beach operators.

In terms of overall design approaches used for city beach sites, four broad aspects differentiate among them: their relationships to their surroundings, sand, aesthetics, and practical aspects of internal layout. The typical city beach is stretched along a riverfront, sloping, and has a low wire or rope fence – all to maximise views in and out. Tall elements are generally kept to the rear (non-waterfront) side of the site, except some palms. Internal layouts seek to maximise sun exposure and orientation. The typical beach's buildings are stretched along the rear boundary to form a visual and acoustic barrier to the surroundings and to screen back-of-house functions. A land-side fence of 3m-high cyclone mesh, covered with ubiquitous, cheap reed matting and sponsor banners, contributes to security, exclusivity and escapism. The blank walls of adjoining industrial buildings are often decorated with large murals of beach landscapes, graffiti art, the beaches' logos, or advertising. A controlled, highly-decorated entry gate from the land side may include a booth for ticketing and guests' bags. Several beaches have ornamental ponds at the entry. Even beaches with few palm trees invariably have two flanking the gateway and one ahead as an axial landmark.

Beach sites' connections to water vary; many have none, or just a view. On very few city beaches does the sand extend down into the water; there is almost always a substantial horizontal and vertical separation, across public waterfront pathways, downslopes, embankments, or floodplains, often overgrown with plants obscuring the view. Several city beaches have rows of canopy beds along their water frontage; these tend to block views to the water for other guests who are seated on the beach further into the site. Steps down to the water are also rare.

The city beach aesthetic is defined by its most essential physical elements – deck chairs, beach umbrellas, sand and palm trees, although the extent and quality of all these components, including sand, varies greatly. Only 84% of surveyed beaches actually had sand, which provided on average only 56% site coverage. Several beaches had at least 2500 m² of sand cover, but nine had less than 20% site coverage, three only had 100 m² sand (enough for a volleyball pitch) and three were smaller still. The sand varies considerably in cost and quality; one operator explained that the best combination of appearance and comfort without clinging is a proprietary mix of two grain sizes. Ground surface without sand was sometimes the underlying grass or paving of the waterfront site, but was often areas of timber decking in dining areas (for tables and chairs) and forming circulation paths over the sand for the benefit of prams, high-heeled shoes, and waiting staff, leading from the entry through the site and to the bar, toilets and back-of-house areas, which are also sand-free. Sometimes small sand patches are surrounded by decking, more for show than to be used. Often sand is very dense with furniture, and there is little space to sit on or even touch the sand, except underfoot when seated. Germany's few small non-commercial beaches have more emphasis on an open sand landscape and equipment for sand play, and less deck chairs and purely decorative elements like palm trees. One commercial beach in the city of Plauen optimised serving both interests. It was built on a divided riverfront site underneath a bridge; one side was a typical beer-garden on gravel and decking, the other side was a typical German children's playground with sand and a few beach baskets added for atmosphere.

Palm trees are a key scenographic element that transforms waterfronts into an escapist leisure environment. These vary greatly in number, size, quality and authenticity. They are often short (being cheaper and easier to transport) and provide little shade. There are companies that provide synthetic ones. They are typically rented, in pots masked by reed matting, and are often spaced out in regular rows. Other potted plants and flowers provide colour accents and screening, including fast-growing bamboo. Some sites contain existing large trees, which generally produce too much shade, which compromises a German city beach's attractiveness for sunbathing. Lighting is generally subdued: up-lighting under palms and umbrellas, flaming torches, retro table lamps, Chinese lanterns, footlights, and string lights on railings and steps.

Most beach operators curate an overall image. Four broad thematisations relate to desired clienteles: the white-plank chic of a cruise ship; Mediterranean resort town; laid-back 'castaway' with driftwood and corrugated iron; and South Pacific 'indigenous' with bamboo and thatch, including thatched umbrellas. Many beach names reinforce these main themes. Several names evoke the Mediterranean (del mar, sol, plage, playa), exotic deserts (oasis, dune, Sahara, Casablanca, Zanzibar) or tropicality (cabana, coco, Copa, 'Baykiki'). Eight beaches used the name 'Island', although none of their sites actually are. This label reflects an aspiration that a visit to the waterfront is an escape from the everyday city. The beaches' escapism overlaps with decorations celebrating the surrounding industrial waterfront aesthetic, including shipping containers,

44-gallon drums, industrial ruins such as dock cranes, and graffiti. Many beaches have custom-made buildings in a shipping-container aesthetic.

Image management also means controlling the amount and variety of commercial logos, particularly to prevent a hodgepodge of colours of deckchairs, which are usually provided free as sponsorship by beverage and cigarette companies. Drink, food and cigarette vendors offer beach operators a wide range of pre-branded furnishings. Most beaches provide diverse seating options, including tables and chairs, beach baskets, beds, sofas, hammocks, sunlounges and beanbags, in various configurations. Deckchairs are moveable, but often crammed in tight rows facing the water, the sun, or large-screen TVs. Numerous smaller 'props' evoke specific beach themes, places and cultures: surfboards, life preservers, paddles, ship's anchors, helms and bells, lighthouses, cargo chests, pirate flags, fishing nets and shells. Some beaches have no exotic theming.

In terms of site layout, commercial city beaches invariably have a main, centrally-located bar and/or restaurant, for service and surveillance, which is of relatively substantial construction, often has more than one openable facade, and is elaborately decorated with props. As the largest building and main visitor contact point, this building carries a great semantic burden. It may have a dancefloor close by. There are frequently other small, temporary buildings spread to the site peripheries: timber-framed huts, modified shipping containers, or mobile vending trailers. This dispersal optimises selling of drinks, and isolates smelly food-preparation areas. Other buildings include undercover seating (especially for dining), ice-cream booths, DJ booths, lockable storage and toilets. Only about half of beaches make use of existing permanent buildings on their site: adjoining industrial buildings provide weather-protected facilities, and existing toilets avoid the expense of having portable units emptied.

City beaches' internal layouts generally seek to maximise exposure and orientation to the sun. Some structures (including sail roofs, tents with transparent or openable sides, and large umbrellas) can be relocated, dissembled, or their sides opened, to suit different seasons, weather, and times of day. Beaches thus provide modest demonstration of how flexibility in the design and management of waterfront spaces might address some of the challenges of climate extremes and climate change that were raised in Chapters 2 and 3. Another practical planning consideration is creating different, closable sub-areas internally, for different activities, for different user groups (including children's areas with playground and sandcastle equipment), or to allow scaling of service to changing demand.

Programming

From most entrepreneurial beach operators' perspectives, drinking and eating are the key visitor activities, and to this end, programmed activities on site seek to attract a wide clientele at varied times, and to prolong their visits. Yoga classes bring early, mostly female patrons, as does providing children's play areas. Some operators suggested female patrons also attract more male patrons. Free wireless internet attracts students and creative workers throughout the day. Dance floors, and free dance lessons, attract couples and singles. Beaches benefit from the contemporary craze in Germany for Latin dancing, especially Salsa; several interviewees admitted the link between dancing and sandy beaches is very oblique. Some dancefloors are packed away when not used for lessons, although dancing to music played by DJs is also common. One distinctive and extremely popular activity on Germany's city beaches is 'public viewing' – a German-language term coined to describe watching football games or films on large outdoor screens, which often have purpose-built shelters protecting them from weather. For several entrepreneurs with event-management backgrounds, hosting live music, poetry readings, debates, and similar performances is the prime reason for creating a beach; the creation of a temporary venue in a waterfront location is a means to this end. Many beaches have permission to host several major events per season; nearby residents' complaints typically restrict their number, scale and amplification. Exhibitions of art and theatre were important to those few beach operators who already ran such businesses.

Sport is another major function for city beaches. Almost 40% of sites provide beach volleyball courts, and in many cases, it is the beach's main raison d'être. Other less common active sport opportunities include beach soccer, boules, minigolf and canoeing.

For entrepreneurs, 'events' also has an additional connotation: renting the beach site (often partly) for company promotions or family celebrations. Several beaches have hosted religious services. Germany's few non-profit city beaches aim to provide a space that brings people of different ages together, and particularly to create a space for local children and youth, which hosts social, educational and play activities. The average number of employees for each city beach is 26, although one quarter of them have five or less staff. These are mostly bar, security and cleaning staff. Events and catering are typically run independently.

Having described where and what city beaches are, we now move on to a critical examination of how they differ from traditional forms and modes of waterfront redevelopment. After outlining the city beach's fundamental contrasts with the 'mainstream' of waterfront masterplanning, the discussion has two main thematic foci. Firstly, it views (and feels) the city beach from the perspective of consumers, by examining the distinctive experiential dimensions of this specific type of artificial waterfront environment. The focus then turns to the processes that produce city beaches, by highlighting the various actors, roles and relationships involved, the commercial entrepreneurship that has driven most city beaches in Germany (which distinguishes them from their French counterparts), and the ways that this particular flexible model relates to, and can inform, the approaches that are used to redevelop waterfronts and other urban areas elsewhere.

Outside the Mainstream of Waterfront Masterplanning

As a reflection of wider economic and political forces, German city beaches provide a contrast to the internationally-famous examples of inner-urban waterfront regeneration (see Marshall 2001; Breen and Rigby 1996). City beaches illustrate very different processes of development and operation with different aims; as outcomes they also have a very different appearance and include different contents. The most well-known cases of waterfront development, such as London Docklands, Hamburg HafenCity, and New York's Battery Park City, are generally undertaken at a relatively large-scale and over a long time frame. Their master planning and physical development are often driven by private-public partnerships such as those found in urban development corporations, and they feature signature buildings designed by international 'starchitects'. The primary aim of such regeneration is to attract international investment capital and highly-mobile international knowledge workers and tourists. The public sector often provides infrastructure and subsidies to encourage flows of private capital into development (Dovey 2005; Desfor and Jørgensen 2004; Malone 1996).

City beaches tend to arise on waterfronts precisely when and where these major flows of power, finance and attention are lacking. They thus illustrate a distinctive and important alternative mode of reusing and redeveloping urban waterfronts. In comparison with internationally famous landmark projects, and with many of the development schemes discussed in Part I of this book, city beaches are relatively unfixed: they involve short-term investments in temporary, mobile facilities, and frequent changes in locations and uses. Most of these projects are initiated and run at low cost by individual entrepreneurs with a small amount of private capital. Rather than fixing a new development pattern, city beaches depend upon temporary loosening-up of land-use regulations, construction standards and licensing requirements. In physical terms, they are loose, informal arrangements of mass-produced objects and scrounged materials. City beaches generally do not require major political commitments, new planning schemes and governance arrangements, major financial underwriting, engineering or infrastructure works, or environmental cleanups. City beaches are also not deeply embedded in the existing cultural and historical context of a waterfront area. Rather than attempting to draw upon a local sense of place, these places consciously set themselves apart as exotic and escapist. What city beaches exemplify is new, very small-scale flexibility and creativity in all these respects. These city beaches are thus part of the flow of ongoing urban waterfront change. As temporary uses, they figure as part of the development process, rather than as a definitive and enduring outcome. All these aspects of city beaches illustrate a 'post-industrial' approach to managing and transforming urban waterfronts. This will be further elucidated and explored in Chapter 7.

As noted in Chapter 5, the transition of urban waterfronts from large-scale industrial uses to mixture of consumption uses is not tidy, complete or permanently fixed. At all stages of development, the waterfront landscape remains fragmentary, with 'gaps' and marginal spaces that are ill-defined, underdeveloped, and less regulated. With the breaking-up of the rationalised landscape of production, the inner city has become increasingly heterotopic, providing spatial opportunities for different, non-conforming groups and activities (Franck and Stevens 2007; Shields 1991). Campo (2002, 188–9) describes the informal, unplanned uses of areas along

Brooklyn's deindustrialised waterfront which had not yet been designated for public leisure use:

> The spaces and uses in these areas are under-utilized; they lack unity and permanence, support economically marginal uses and are subject to relatively rapid changes in use and form. The vernacular and non-intensive use of these sites (many of which were once bustling centres of modern industrial production and commerce) often defies conventional conceptions of urban land use, with its pre-occupation of single-function spaces and permanence.

City beaches also often involve the appropriation and reconfiguration of derelict, unused or underutilised pieces of urban waterfronts, whether industrial brownfields, other sites undergoing regeneration, vacant public land, or unnoticed, ill-defined, intermediate spaces.

Increases in the spatial flexibility and diversity of urban waterfront areas have been accompanied by a shift in the temporal flows of their use. This shift is linked to the explosive growth in outdoor dining and hospitality venues and the 'night time economy' (Bianchini 1995), and also reflects the increasing importance of planned special events for city development and marketing. The complexity of political, financial, environmental and managerial factors shaping post-industrial waterfronts tend to break up the temporal flow of their physical development, such that there are spurts of growth, periods of stagnation, and difficulties of phasing and coordination (Carmona 2009; Gordon 1996). City beaches are just one among a wide range of temporary urban uses that occupy land in the time between abandonment and new formal development projects (Urban Catalyst 2007; Haydn and Temel 2006; Misselwitz et al. 2003).

Enjoying the Looseness of the Urban Waterfront

From the perspective of consumers, city beaches exemplify many of the general characteristics of post-industrial urban waterfronts which have made them popular sites for public leisure. Because of their former function, deindustrialised waterfronts tend to be marginal zones physically segregated from the remainder of the cityscape, often with restricted access points. They are places of isolation in the midst of the city's density; places where rules and enforcement are relaxed (Campo 2002). They thus offer a respite from the regular built form and activity patterns of the working city, where people can escape from and forget the fixed roles and the tensions and responsibilities of work and the domestic sphere (Stevens 2007a, 2007b). The sense of freedom and possibility that the urban waterfront presents is linked to its physical 'between' condition, the 'edginess' of its mediation between the fixities of the cityscape and the constant flows of the water (Dovey 2005). This liminal spatial condition helps stimulate escapist, exploratory, playful and transgressive behaviours (Stevens 2007b; Shields 1991). Dovey (2005, 17) suggests that 'many of the pleasures of the city are linked to different forms of spatial practice and experience that are possible in marginal and interstitial spaces such as the beach and waterfront which, to some degree, escape the instrumentalisation of the

The 'City Beach' as a New Waterfront Development Model

market'. Many of the playful uses of waterfront public spaces are not captured by the commercial forms of consumption that are designed into large-scale, long-term waterfront developments. As noted in Chapter 5, such unsanctioned activities often find their place in the underdesigned, underdetermined 'cracks' within the consumption spectacle of the wider waterfront, such as artificial beaches.

Chapter 1 pointed out that the popularity of the urban waterfront for informal, playful uses depends on its separation and difference as well as on its visual and functional links to other existing nearby attractions. Large-scale demolition and views across the water lend deindustrialised waterfronts an openness and visibility unrivalled in the inner city. These features make waterfronts excellent settings for contemporary leisure activities centred on seeing and being seen. Waterfront open spaces are secondary uses; they are not major attractions in themselves. Like many other kinds of informal social settings, they need to be tightly linked into existing circuits of urban activity, and in particular to other inner-urban leisure uses. Many informal uses of the waterfront for public play depend on flows of people to and from the waterfront, which lead to the intermingling of a diversity of actors and activities (Franck and Stevens 2007). Thus connectivity to public transport is important, as are connections along the waterfront.

The water's edge offers particular environmental comforts for users which cannot easily be found in other inner-urban sites, such as excellent solar exposure, especially on the north embankment of rivers, which is where the majority of German beaches are located. The water brings relatively cool, moist breezes into the site and moderates the ambient temperature. Waterfronts are relatively quiet locations because there is often no adjacent development or road traffic on the waterfront side (Figure 6.5). Campo (2002, 171) foregrounds the specific looseness and lack of regulation of 'unkempt' waterfronts, which have been abandoned but not

Figure 6.5 Sandburg Cologne.

yet been redeveloped, contrasting them with the typical plans for 'waterfront as tourist destination... as extension of financial district... as new residential district... [which] are expensive, time consuming, often difficult to implement... and not always in keeping with the needs or desires of local residents'. He draws attention to the broad and unique scope of uses and users on 'vernacular' waterfronts such as Brooklyn's, including many beach-related activities on an 'informal' beach formed there through the erosion of the industrial landscape.

The specific design characteristics of city beaches provide additional stimuli that make people feel different and encourage them to behave differently. These stimuli allow visitors a sense of escape both from the everyday city and from the choreographed spectacle of the contemporary global waterfront development model. Most obvious is the stark contrast to earlier generations of large-scale urban waterfront redevelopment schemes (Marshall 2001; Dovey 2005) in terms of physical materials and forms. City beaches gather together a range of physical and representational elements that promote escapist experience.

It is the sandy beach, even more than water, which has become the primary metonym for escapism and for leisure on these kinds of waterfront sites; and this is as much because of sand's physical properties as its representational ones. Sand can, like water, be moved and reshaped. It also keeps it shape when moulded into sandcastles and sand sculptures or when people write their names in it. People can reshape it to suit the human body, to create makeshift headrests or to change the body's orientation to the sun and to views. Sand is very soft underfoot, comfortable to play sport on, for children to fall down on, to dance, sit or lie on. Comfort is improved by the potential that a soft sandy surface offers for play without risk. People's first response when approaching sand is to take their shoes off and play with the sand with their feet, to have a close, stimulating and active engagement with the landscape. Sand is cheap, not worth stealing, easy to replace and easy to clean and maintain; it is unbreakable and fireproof; it stays dry, even after rain, and can easily be brushed off clothes and hair. Sand and water are both ideal raw materials for artificial landscapes, as discussed in Chapter 4. Sand is an unfixed, disorderly material, which encourages initiative and creativity in its use (Franck and Stevens 2007). Sand epitomises the city beach as an unfixed waterfront; its surface cannot easily be tightened up through planning or management. Children's playful use with buckets and spades demonstrates that the city beach is a 'do it yourself' landscape, always being transformed.

Sand is just one of the myriad of small elements of the city beach landscape that evoke an escapist atmosphere and add comfort. Palm trees, bars that look like thatched huts, wooden decks and deckchairs (a reminder of ocean liners), volleyball and shuffleboard courts, decorative surfboards, Polynesian music, and tropical cocktails all provide representational links to other kinds of waterfront leisure environments. Like the many other kinds of artificial waterfronts discussed in Chapter 4, the escapist atmosphere of city beaches is greatly enhanced by their deliberate artificiality and exoticism. These small elements all also add comfort and pleasure to a space, and are loose and adaptable to different tastes and activities. Users of city beaches freely relocate deckchairs, umbrellas and towels according to desired social arrangements, views, and the angle and intensity of the sun. All elements can be readily relocated according to changing needs, or even removed entirely. People are encouraged to be active; not simply passively observers of these waterfront landscapes. The waterfront's sun, water and breezes, combined with city beaches' sand and shade, provide multi-sensory triggers which stimulate playful, carefree actions such as lying down, running, digging and idly dragging fingers or toes through the sand. These beaches are also loose spaces in the sense that their openness, their softness and their furnishings allow and encourage unconstrained bodily movements and postures, so that people can physically 'stretch out' and relax (Franck and Stevens 2007). Dovey (2005) argues that as a landscape type, the beach exemplifies leisure. It is a metonym of conditions of free accessibility, physical openness and publicness; its 'uninterrupted prospect and exposure to the elements' make it 'a "smooth" space where the strictures of urban life are escaped to some degree' (Dovey 2005, 230, 241). In social terms, the beach is permissive, a setting 'where everyday taboos regarding modes of dress or the justification for interacting with strangers are generously relaxed' (Franck and Stevens 2007, 25).

Producing the Beach

Understanding the city beach as a development approach requires more than looking at the built form as a finished product; it also necessitates examining the various actors, roles and development processes involved. It is astonishing that the city beach concept spread in Germany with such rapidity, even though there is almost no formal coordination of knowledge or production. These schemes generally bypass the much-lauded but rarely followed 'rational planning process' for long-range public sector investments and waterfront development. They illustrate a new approach that is relevant to marginal spaces and contemporary economic conditions.

City beaches demonstrate low-cost solutions for the construction and maintenance of waterfront open space, using minimal amounts of start-up and operational capital. In contrast to the waterfront development literature's frequent mentions of the impact of big multi-national corporations and architecture firms (Marshall 2001; Breen and Rigby 1996), city beaches are almost always designed, built and run by small-scale local entrepreneurs, with little involvement from design professionals. Rather than employing the latest high-technology materials and sophisticated construction techniques and equipment, they use simple materials and tools which are often borrowed, self-built or obtained second-hand, such as ordinary concrete-making sand from construction firms, or donated sand left over after the world beach volleyball championships (SenStadt 2007). City beaches require significant investments of 'sweat equity': labour from the operators themselves and their friends. Websites for city beaches in Berlin, Magdeburg, Mainz, and Trier proudly illustrate this construction process. The self-build approach is facilitated by their small scale, their temporary nature and the need for flexibility of arrangement, which requires that most of the beach's elements are easily demountable and transportable. The sand, potted plants, deck chairs and portable cabins which constitute city beaches are low cost but high impact, in terms of both appearance and use. These elements can also later be rearranged and re-used in other kinds of projects on other sites.

The cost of sites is also minimal. Land is sometimes provided at nominal rent because there is an agreement between owner and tenant to allow use of a site until a viable investor is found for it, or the operators agree to undertake necessary site repairs or remediation, or to accept public indemnity costs (SenStadt 2007). City beaches illustrate entrepreneurial forms of risk-sharing among parties, rather than one party assuming fixed long-term ownership of all property rights and responsibilities. Under normal local planning guidelines in Germany, city beaches usually require many permits, because they involve complex arrangements for land rental, public access, waterways, land use changes, construction of buildings, liquor licensing and insurance liabilities (Herold 2007). However, the senate of the state of Berlin eventually published a new planning policy (SenStadt 2007) in which they proposed to waive some permit requirements, and to create a 'one-stop shop' for all necessary licensing arrangements, as well as facilitating the issuance of more temporary permits. This new permissive regime reflects a pragmatic shift toward encouraging and coordinating private enterprise. Such temporary uses also provide investment, employment and amenities for local residents, in contrast to large, planned projects that may never materialise.

The production relationships among the various private- and public-sector actors in city beaches are generally short-term and project-centred, rather than permanent. They nonetheless help the various participants to develop the working relationships, knowledge and skills to pursue new and durable strategies for open space financing, construction, operation and programming. Chapters 7 and 8 will explore some of the rich variety within these relationships.

Beach as Business Opportunity

The vast majority of German beaches are entrepreneurial ventures. 78% of surveyed operators considered gastronomy (cafés, restaurants, bars) and events (concerts, dancing and movies) as their beach's main functions. The temporary nature of these schemes means they typically have to turn a profit within the timeframe of their initial use permit and rental contract, often just one summer season. Their initial investments are thus generally very small. While surveyed operators often mentioned idealistic motivations (for example, 'creating a holiday atmosphere'), their typical commercial objective is to attract new clientele, and to create a balanced income throughout the year, because people shun indoor venues in the summer. Seventy percent of surveyed beach operators identified with the proffered ambition of 'creating a public space', but few articulated this social ideal in detail. Only a small number of city beach operators are financed as an integral part of large-scale, long-range development of waterfront areas, as with *Sommerwelt*, a beach-like boardwalk installed next to an existing pond within Berlin's mixed-use Potsdamer Platz complex. Here a private sector landowner had a beach installed as a means of promoting their wider business. Only ten of Germany's 327 city beaches are clearly *not* private-sector businesses, but instead developed by public or non-profit agencies – alternative models which are discussed further in Chapters 7 and 8. Few of these non-commercial city beaches occupied waterfront sites.

The 'City Beach' as a New Waterfront Development Model

Figure 6.6 Traumstrand, Berlin, on temporarily-vacant land adjacent to the city's new central railway station.

A permanent artificial beach in Duisburg constitutes only one percent of a new 55-hectare public open space on a former riverfront industrial site. One beach was run on a waterfront university campus by its student association.

Germany's entrepreneurial city beaches take advantage of the low rents, attractive views and distinctive atmosphere offered by former waterfront industrial sites during the years preceding the decontamination of these sites and their large-scale, planned mixed-use development for apartments, offices and retailing (Figure 6.6). Their fluid, small-scale, bottom-up mode of economic development is often at odds with large-scale long-term fixing of waterfronts through plans, regulations and investments. Many entrepreneurial city beaches in Germany receive some kind of local government support, whether through grants, loans, rent-free land, free services, streamlined licensing approvals or tax reductions. Although most privately-run city beaches are not technically public spaces, local governments are generally supportive, and often provide publicly-owned sites at low rents because, through their system of free entry, these ventures provide public access to sites that would otherwise not be available for use, diversifying the forms and amenities of open space that the general public is able to enjoy. City beaches also create economic and social activity precisely where cities are lacking it.

The operational overheads and cash-flow needs of city beaches are generally very low. Operators cover their costs through the sale of drinks and through corporate sponsorships. They largely forego charging admission, so using the 'beach' is often free. But most beaches ban people bringing their own food and drinks, many have a minimum-purchase scheme (Weindl 2004), on weekends and evenings there is often a cover charge, and beaches are sometimes closed to the public for promotional events.

Figure 6.7 Oststrand, Berlin, 2009. Remaining section of Berlin Wall is visible top left.

The simplicity, low initial overheads and flexibility of the city beach model allows entrepreneurs ready expansion, duplication or modification of their businesses as spaces and resources allow. The spread and success of the city beach phenomenon has led to a high level of professionalisation and systematisation in their operation, and the emergence of 11 chain operators who each manage several beaches. The operator of Berlin's very first city beach, *Strandbar Mitte*, opened a second larger beach the following year, *Oststrand*, further East along the Spree River, behind the remaining stretch of the Berlin Wall (Figure 6.7). 'Freiluftrebellen' ('open air rebels') ran four beaches in Berlin. Their website notes that they are constantly looking to enter into potential partnerships on new sites and concepts (Freiluftrebellen, n.d.). Five companies in Berlin run a total of 14 beaches between them; operators in Hamburg and Magdeburg run two each. Two regional operators are based near the Rhine River industrial port of Mannheim, including 'LeschinEvent', who operate four beaches (Leschin Event 2019), and one near Düsseldorf. Another operator in Stuttgart copyrighted his concept 'Skybeach', a beach on the roof of a parking garage, opened further branches in Cologne and Dortmund, sold a branch in Hannover, and later licensed his brand name to franchisees (Stadtengel GmbH, n.d.). Two of these chains specialise in beaches on parking garages because the site and management factors are highly standardised. In ten cities, sites that had already been made into beaches were taken over by different operators in later years. These changes do not create beaches; they centre on rebranding and new management and activation approaches.

Learning from the Beachmaking Process

Waterfront redevelopment in post-industrial cities often continues to use old-fashioned, 'rational' managerial approaches to land development and use, albeit through partial privatisation. These approaches engender new fixities of form, programme, ownership and control. Solutions focus too tightly on long-range master planning, durable landscaping solutions, and maximising private investment (Dovey 2005). Germany's city beaches suggest other ways forward which may seem more outlandish and frivolous, yet which are actually more modest and commercially more viable because they are dynamic, accepting the inevitability of flow and change.

The conclusions from German city beach experiences relate more to planning and decision-making processes for waterfronts than they do to design outcomes. While the form of city beaches is unique but not everywhere useful, the thinking and practice underpinning them provide options for waterfront development which can have much wider application. Indeed, city beaches have an analogue in the physically more substantial 'Entertainment Zones' examined by Campo and Ryan (2008). In sharp contrast to the urban 'megaproject' approach, which is often used for waterfronts and which 'is characterised by substantial outlays and blending of public and private capital, long and sometimes contested public review processes, long build out periods and the need for large plots of land and standardised development formats', Campo and Ryan (2008, 305) observe that small-scale leisure precincts develop incrementally and without a coordinated, unifying plan, through a myriad of individual actions. These 'everyday spaces' focus on improving the vitality and use of existing built contexts, and on messy, continual evolution rather than fixed formal design solutions (Chase et al. 1999). Similarly, Germany's city beaches are post-industrial landscapes, not just in terms of their land uses and their user groups, but also in terms of the ways in which their development occurs. This theme will be explored further in Chapter 7. The wide variety of beach examples demonstrates the flexibility of this approach to adapt to local circumstances, and to make adjustments to particular built spaces over time so as to better suit user needs, sites, and changing market conditions. The flexibility of city beaches rests on loose physical elements, and is underpinned by careful events programming: 'software' that is itself diverse and variable.

Whether urban waterfront sites are focused on industrial production or newer, more entrepreneurial uses, the State is one of the main fixities that can hinder flows of new ideas, materials, forms and activities into them. City beaches, as collaborative, fluid projects, present an argument against continued centralised control of urban waterfronts by special-purpose port authorities, which lack flexibility in both goals and means, and in favour of government acting as a coordinator and creative facilitator of a wider range of small, new and flexible solutions, pursued by combinations of actors from the private and non-profit sectors and from a range of government agencies. Indeed, the city beach may be a harbinger of a more deregulated waterfront. The public approval and support processes for city beach projects test out at a small scale a different kind of planning regime, one which is more proactive, responsive and dynamic. Rather than merely regulating private development to ensure minimum standards, it suggests the need for government to help discover, market and exploit opportunities (SenStadt 2007).

Campo and Ryan (2008, 311–12) suggest two general strategies for urban development that can nurture the continuous informal evolution of urban social space: first, to 'reconceptualize and reduce the scale of new urban development', which will 'permit local entrepreneurs to have a stake in new development, adding to [its] variety… and to… creativity and uniqueness'; and second, to 'consider designating "free zones" or "free moments" within the city' that can 'spur local entrepreneurship, generate a sense of place and add to, rather than subtract from local character'. As an approach to urban waterfront development, city beaches exemplify such an approach. Campo's (2002) examination of waterfront sites that are relatively unplanned, undeveloped and 'unfixed' suggests that such opportunities 'occur in so few places throughout the more rationalised spaces of the city as to warrant more formalised recognition, legitimacy and perhaps a mechanism to protect these spaces from conventional development' (Campo 2002, 173). He argues that something will be lost if every section of a city's waterfront is developed in conventional, fixed ways.

But this does not mean that city beaches themselves must be preserved as new permanent features of the waterfront. It is in part the temporariness of city beaches that overcomes the resistance to change and novelty that can hinder more permanent proposals; risks are reduced because the built consequences of city beaches can easily be changed or removed. The influence of city beaches on waterfront design and development can be carefully played out over the longer term, rather than being fixed in advance into permanent plans and contracts. City beaches are by their nature an interim solution, even though in Berlin, thirty years after the fall of the Wall, it is clear such an interregnum can itself last a long time. To fix artificial beaches to waterfront sites and make them completely official is to lose some of their qualities. We need to also turn our attention to what might come next; where these beach settings themselves can flow to, and what might arrive on the waterfront after them.

References

Bianchini, F. (1995) 'Night cultures, night economies', *Planning Practice and Research*, 10 (2), pp. 121–126.
Breen, A. and Rigby, D. (1996) *The New Waterfront: A Worldwide Urban Success Story*, London: Thames and Hudson.
Campo, D. (2002) 'Brooklyn's vernacular waterfront', *Journal of Urban Design*, 7 (2), pp. 171–199.
Campo, D. and Ryan, B. (2008) 'The entertainment zone: Unplanned nightlife and the revitalization of the American downtown'. *Journal of Urban Design* 13 (3): 291–315.
Carmona, M. (2009) 'The Isle of Dogs: Four development waves, five planning models, twelve plans, thirty-five years, and a renaissance... of sorts', *Progress in Planning*, 71 (3), pp. 87–151.
Chase, J., Crawford, M. and Kaliski, J. (eds) (1999). *Everyday Urbanism*. New York: Monacelli Press.
Denzer, V., Köppe, H., Sachs, K. and Kühne, O. (2010) 'Stadtstrände – Urlaubsoasen im urbanen Raum? Erste empirische Annäherungen – ein Werkstattbericht' in Wöhler, K., Pott, A. and Denzer V. (Eds.) *Tourismusräume: Zur soziokulturellen Konstruktion eines globalen Phänomens*, Bielefeld: Transcript, pp. 191–206.
Desfor, G. and Jørgensen, J. (2004) 'Flexible urban governance: The case of Copenhagen's recent waterfront development. *European Planning Studies* 12 (4): 479–496.
Dovey, K. (2005) *Fluid City: Transforming Melbourne's Urban Waterfront*, London: Routledge.
Franck, K. and Stevens, Q. (eds) (2007) *Loose Space: Possibility and Diversity in Urban Life*, London: Routledge.
Freiluftrebellen. (n.d.) http://www.freiluftrebellen.de, accessed 1 December 2009.
Gordon, D. (1996) 'Planning, design and managing change in urban waterfront redevelopment', *Town Planning Review*, 67 (3), pp. 261–290.
Haydn, F. and Temel, R. (eds.) (2006) *Temporary Urban Spaces: Concepts for the Use of City Spaces*, Basel: Birkhäuser.
Herold, M. (2007) 'Mit Leidenschaft für den Sommer in Berlin', *Mittendrin*, (4): 5.
Kahls, S. (2009) *Stadtstrände: Südseefeeling in deutschen Großstädten*, Hamburg: Diplomica.
Leschin Event (2019) *Aktuelle Projekte in Eigenregie*, http://leschinevent.de, accessed 9 August 2020.
Malone, P. (ed) (1996) *City, Capital and Water*, London: Routledge.
Marshall, R. (ed) (2001) *Waterfronts in Post-industrial Cities*, London: Spon.
Misselwitz, P., Oswalt, P. and Overmeyer, K. (eds) (2003) *Urban Catalysts: Strategies for Temporary Uses*, Berlin: Urban Catalyst, available from http://www.templace.com/think-pool/one786f.html?think_id=4272

The 'City Beach' as a New Waterfront Development Model

Montag Stiftung and Regionale 2010 (eds) (2008) *Riverscapes: Designing Urban Embankments*, Birkhäuser: Basel.

Otto, M. (2007) *Beach Clubs: Zwischennutzung auf innerstädtischen Brachflächen mit Standortempfehlungen für Hamburg*, unpublished Diploma thesis, University of Hamburg.

Park, R., Burgess, E. and McKenzie, R. (1925) *The City*. Chicago: University of Chicago Press.

SenStadt = Senatsverwaltung für Stadtentwicklung Berlin (ed.) (2007) *Urban Pioneers: Temporary Use and Urban Development in Berlin*, Berlin: Jovis.

Shields, R. (1991) *Places on the Margin: Alternative Geographies of Modernity*, London: Routledge.

Stadtengel GmbH (n.d.) available from http://www.skybeach.de, accessed 1 December 2009.

Stevens, Q. (2007a) *The Ludic City: Exploring the Potential of Public Spaces*, London: Routledge.

Stevens, Q. (2007b) 'Betwixt and between: Building thresholds, liminality and public space' in Franck, K. and Stevens, Q. (eds) *Loose Space: Diversity and Possibility in Urban Life*, New York: Routledge, pp. 73–92.

Stolz, M. (2009) 'Deutchlandkarte: Stadtstraende', *ZEITMagazin*, 10 June, p. 8.

Urban Catalyst (Philipp Oswalt, Philipp Misselwitz, and Klaus Overmeyer) (2007) 'Patterns of the unplanned', in Franck, K. and Stevens, Q. (Eds.) *Loose Space: Possibility and Diversity in Urban Life*, London: Routledge, pp. 271–288.

Weindl, F. (2004) 'Rimini ist überall', *Süddeutsche Zeitung*, 3 August.

Chapter 7
Post-Fordist Placemaking

Quentin Stevens and Mhairi Ambler

The first artificial city beach of contemporary times was created in France in 1996 in the main square of the provincial capital St. Quentin. After worldwide media reporting of *Paris Plage* in 2002 brought the phenomenon of 'city beaches' to popular consciousness, the idea of temporary, artificial beaches on inner-urban sites spread rapidly throughout Europe. Most major European cities now have at least one city beach. Germany's first such project, Berlin's *Strandbar Mitte*, also opened in summer 2002, and in the eight years since more than 300 such beaches have appeared in over 100 German cities, with more than 60 in Berlin alone. Although there are also isolated examples in North America and Australia, to date city beaches have been a quintessentially European trend.

The expression 'city beach' is difficult to define comprehensively; the characteristics of the many schemes vary significantly. The key physical attributes are an urban location; a large volume of sand spread on an open space; a view of the waterfront (sometimes including water access); and the inclusion of thematic objects associated with beaches, such as deckchairs, beach umbrellas, palm trees and thatched huts. It is the artifice of simply spreading these materials around on top of empty urban sites that sets these schemes apart from beaches that are part of natural or renaturalised riverbanks and lakeshores. The types of sites used for city beaches include derelict factories, sites cleared through demolition, new landfill sites, rail easements, road rights-of-way, parking lots, roofs of parking garages, public plazas and parklands. Most of these locations are marginal and are not conventionally thought of, or accessible as, public open space. By utilising such sites, city beaches thus supplement the range and variety of urban open space provision. The informality of the material artifice of these beaches is complemented by their use by a very wide demographic for informal social sing and play, sports, programmed cultural events, and casual drinking and dining. Another defining characteristic of city beach developments is that they are temporary and mobile. They often change location. Most only operate in the warmer months, and are removed and stored during winter.

We argue that Europe's new city beaches illustrate processes, forms and flexibilities which might change how planners, designers and managers think about the production of urban open space more generally. City beaches demonstrate how new spaces and new functions can be 'plugged into' urban brownfield sites. They involve a certain amount of 'unplanning' and deregulation to loosen up the urban landscape. They contain many loose elements. They make significant investments in services and event programs instead of major fixed physical investments. They adjust to seasonal changes in weather and patronage. These beaches are temporary, often appearing for only one or two summers, until they are displaced by longer-term development of their sites. The users and behaviours in these beach spaces are particularly playful and extremely diverse. Unlike traditional forms of urban open space, city beaches are generally created and operated by small-scale entrepreneurs using small amounts of private capital, or by non-profit organisations. Public sector agencies generally encourage these projects, but they are rarely an active partner in their design and management. Rather than attempting to draw upon a local sense of place, these places consciously set themselves apart as exotic and escapist. In most of these respects, city beaches contrast with conventional open space planning and development in city centres and on regenerated waterfronts. City beaches tend to arise when or where major flows of urban development finance are lacking. They thus illustrate a distinctive and important alternative mode of reusing and redeveloping urban open space which exemplifies very small-scale flexibility and creativity.

This chapter examines the creative and varied approaches to design, planning, financing, construction and management that have produced four key 'city beach' projects in four different European countries: in chronological order of their creation, *Paris Plage*, Berlin's *Strandbar Mitte*, Amsterdam's *Blijburg aan Zee* and *Bristol Urban Beach*. The Paris and Berlin examples are amongst the oldest, whereas Bristol's beach lasted only six weeks. These cases illuminate four very different models for delivering such schemes, led by different actors: a city mayor's office, a private entrepreneur, the consortium of a municipal land development department and its private developers, and a non-profit think-tank.

Our case study material was primarily obtained from semi-structured interviews and correspondence with the sites' initiators and managers, investigating the production process for the city beach and their role within it. Interviews were also conducted with other formal stakeholders, such as local government officers, to understand the political and administrative context. The interviews explored the motivations for constructing each city beach, whether the project was conceived primarily as a short-term event or as part of a longer-term place-making initiative, and to identify its impacts and legacy for its surrounding area. Urban design representatives from Bristol's city council were also interviewed regarding the significance of city beaches for the long-term development of Bristol's public realm. Where not otherwise cited, our analysis is based upon this set of interviews. Information about the location, design and management of the city beaches was also collated from secondary sources including the city beaches' websites, their promotional literature, websites of city marketing agencies and the hospitality industry, from media reportage, and from the limited existing academic research examining *Paris Plage* (Gale 2009; Webster 2007; La Pradelle and Lallement 2004).

The following sections of the chapter introduce each beach in turn, identifying the vision and objectives behind it, the main actors, processes and financing shaping its development, and its physical setting, atmosphere and programming. Analysis then looks across the case studies to consider four novel aspects of open space production illustrated by these beaches: the introduction of a new sense of place, the relation between temporary open spaces and long-term property development, the continual, performative co-production of place by managers and users, and the flexibility in reconfiguring production resources and processes according to dynamic demand and supply factors. This final theme links our case study material to a broader theorisation of 'post-Fordist' landscape development.

Four Pioneering City Beaches

Paris Plage

Paris Plage (Figure 7.1) became a possibility after Socialist Bertrand Delanoë was elected mayor of Paris in March 2001 on a platform of reducing automobile use and making the city more liveable for its residents. One of his first initiatives was to close the Pompidou Expressway alongside the Seine for one month in summer 2001. In 2002, set designer Jean-Christophe Choblet, assisted by sociologists, was invited by Delanoë to develop a beach-themed transformation of the same expressway space. The focus was

Figure 7.1 Paris Plage, 2007.

Source: Peter Haas – https://creativecommons.org/licenses/by-sa/3.0/deed.en

on social inclusivity and engagement, aiming to 'to give the riverside back to Parisians', and to provide 'a nice hangout [where] people, with their differences, will mingle', especially poor suburbanites 'who never leave [Paris] on vacation' (Delanoë quoted in La Pradelle and Lallement 2004, 135). This city beach thus originates in a strategy tied to place: in contrast to real beaches that seasonally draw wealthier Parisians to the French coast, this landscape is brought to the consumers. The area reclaimed for *Paris Plage* was chosen for its superb views of the UNESCO-listed historical cityscape, previously only enjoyed by motorists speeding along the expressway. The central location also guaranteed significant media attention. *Paris Plage* attracted 600,000 visitors on its opening day, and two million during the month it remained open in 2002. It has free admission; two thirds of its original €2 million cost was covered by sponsors, the remainder came from the mayor's office.

Choblet highlights three aspects crucial to his vision of an artificial city beach: populism, scenography and the temporal dimension of public space. He depicted *Paris Plage* as a traditional French seaside resort in the centre of the city, utilising stereotypical beach imagery: striped bathing cabins, sea-blue parasols, palm trees, deckchairs and three tonnes of sand. Basic amenities lacking in many of Paris's public spaces were installed, such as toilets, changing cabins and baby changing facilities. The site was designed as fully accessible. Free wireless internet access expanded the range of activities available. Visitors to the initial *Paris Plage* were disappointed that the Seine itself was not available for swimming; that the representation fell well short of a real beach (La Pradelle and Lallement 2004). In 2003, Europe's hottest summer for 100 years, there was an upsurge in visitor numbers, and vaporisers, water fountains and a swimming pool were added.

The diversity of activity possibilities presented on Paris's beach are designed 'to mimic those that occur on a natural beach' (personal communication), so that users themselves contribute to the overall impression. The programmed events encourage interaction with the setting. The 'sensory immersion' of the design allows users to engage in the spectacle and become producers of the space themselves, redefining the project as a lived event, rather than merely a physical installation (La Pradelle and Lallement 2004).

A wide range of free activities, including performances, art and environmental exhibitions, libraries, educational workshops, dance lessons, climbing, art classes and book clubs, make the beach an attractive and popular alternative to conventional public spaces. The scope of activities caters to a wide variety of ages and tastes, to enhance the 'social equity' of the space and create opportunities for engagement and interaction (Choblet 2008, personal communication). The activities are arranged along the riverbank in a spatial sequence which accords with the position and intensity of the sun, so as to replicate a day at the beach: early morning tai-chi, sunbathing and beach games, refreshments and picnics, a nap, and an evening drink at an open-air café (La Pradelle and Lallement 2004).

The city has expanded *Paris Plage* over time. In 2005, a beach volleyball area was installed in front of the Hotel de Ville. In 2006, a second large beach site was opened 1km upstream at le Port de la Gare, a regeneration area that incorporates the national library and the entertainment complex Paris Bercy. This proximity stimulated that site's focus on cultural facilities: a lending library, a café and wi-fi hotspot, art classes and nightlife venues (Mairie de Paris 2007b). The Seine River is wider at this point, and the beach here includes moored boats that provide evening musical shows, as well as the Joséphine Baker floating swimming pool, which extracts and purifies its water from the Seine. In 2007, another beach site on a canal at La Bassin de La Villette added water sports including kayaking, pedal boats and a pool with aquagym classes. At the earlier sites, river currents and tourist boat traffic had precluded such activities. La Villette is an economically-deprived former industrial area, named for its former abattoirs which closed in 1974, and best known for its Parc, designed by Bernard Tschumi, which is home to many cultural institutions. The installation in this area of *Paris Plages* (now plural) in this area serves dual purposes: providing water-based leisure activities to residents of a less-affluent quarter, and raising the profile of the area to attract more tourists. For both aims it has been important to use this network of waterfront projects to 'symbolically reconnect' La Villette into the city (Choblet 2008). All sites are linked by ferry.

Paris Plages is open only one month each year. The municipality officially defines and promotes it as an event. As with other events, the beach offers Parisians and visitors the chance to perceive the city in a new way, and to visualise one possible alternative future. Choblet (2008) sees the ephemerality and 'reversibility' of *Paris Plages* as one of its most important qualities: it is not only a spatial rupture in the city, but also a temporal and behavioural rupture, breaking into people's daily routines, and inviting them to immerse themselves temporarily in an alternate experience, to break away from urban norms, intensities and rhythms and interact with the unexpected and unusual elements offered by the beach (personal communication). In his professional practice Choblet (2008) emphasises the importance and the potential of such approaches to 'the sequential planning of public spaces in time'.

Despite its ephemerality, *Paris Plages* has had long-term impacts. The beach is now a regular part of the annual event calendar. It contributes to the collective memory of the city's inhabitants and has quickly become part of the city's cultural heritage. Criticism of its high cost is countered by its incredible popularity; well over half the visitors are Parisians (Mairie de Paris 2007a). Its role in igniting debate within Paris about the use, value and expenditure for urban open space is also part of its legacy (Choblet 2008). In terms of the production of urban spaces and events, the *Paris Plages* project has encouraged holistic, co-ordinated working among the municipality's 12 different departments, all of which have their objectives represented on the beach, and with external organisations (Choblet 2008). The use of private sponsorship has also encouraged the formation of new working relationships between the municipality and businesses. The worldwide media exposure of *Paris Plages*' spectacular imagery, along with the city's other events, guarantees Paris's ability to attract interest from multinational companies eager to share its success, while the site's world heritage status means that no on-site advertising is permitted. As a long-term event, *Paris Plages* offers the city an innovative way to raise funds and improve the range and quality of public realm amenities they can offer.

Post-Fordist Placemaking

Figure 7.2 Strandbar Mitte, Berlin, 2005.

Source: Mikko Lahti/Flickr – https://creativecommons.org/licenses/by/2.0/

Strandbar Mitte, Berlin

Opening just one month after *Paris Plage*, Berlin's first beach (Figure 7.2) was very different in terms of siting, financing, design, clientele and operation. Its founder Christian Schulz, a 32-year-old entrepreneur from Munich, was part of the squatter scene in the Prenzlauer Berg neighbourhood and had run a theatre there since 1994. In 1999, he relocated and started a small temporary summer open-air theatre in Monbijou Park in nearby Mitte, opposite the happening bar scene on Oranienburgerstrasse (Aulich and Janovsky 2008). Major improvements to the park were already planned. In a relatively unused corner of the park was a sandy area from the ruins of a demolished building. Schulz wanted to provide food and drink on the site, rather than losing this potential income to surrounding venues, but his theatre structure was too small. He obtained a liquor licence, brought in 70 tonnes of additional fine sand from a lake outside Berlin, and opened a bar with deckchairs and potted palm trees (Weindl 2004). Unlike many other outdoor bars and cafés, this site is not fenced off from its surroundings. Visitors are able to enter the beach and occupy its chairs without having to purchase anything from the bar, which is set well back within the site. Although the site itself was somewhat isolated, the theatre brought prospective customers, and the location was very close to existing flows of tourists on Oranienburgerstrasse and nearby Hackescher Markt. The site, facing onto the Spree River, also offered excellent views of the Bodemuseum on the UNESCO-listed 'Museum Island' directly opposite and of other landmarks. This temporary, informal beach was thus complementary to existing leisure offerings nearby.

This city beach project has grown and changed significantly over its years of operation. Within six months of opening, Schulz had already applied for permission to double the beach's size. With profits from 2002, in 2003 he purchased 1000 tonnes of sand from the Baltic coast and opened an additional, larger beach, *Oststrand,* behind the remaining stretch of the Berlin Wall near Ostbahnhof. By 2004, *Strandbar Mitte* was largely financing the theatre's operations (Rolff 2004). The summer of 2004 was much cooler, so Schulz installed heat lamps and marquees to improve comfort. He spread 350 tonnes of sand on the Monbijou park site, at a cost of €7/tonne. Despite poor weather, the beach still attracted 1500 visitors per day, and a total of 100,000 over the summer. In 2006, the entire landscape of *Strandbar Mitte* had to be re-installed 20 metres further east, to allow room for reconstruction of a pedestrian bridge linking Monbijou Park and the Museumsinsel across the river. By 2008, €3.3million had been spent on renovating the surrounding park, including reinstatement of a paved public waterfront promenade where *Strandbar* had previously stood. The bar continued operating, with deckchairs and beach umbrellas, but without sand. In 2009, the city government tendered for operation of a 'cultural and gastronomic offering' on the site. Schulz defeated six other applicants and continued his operations. *Strandbar Mitte* has gone from a temporary appropriation of a neglected and inaccessible waterfront space to a permanent – albeit seasonal – feature of the park and the neighbourhood. Schulz's company now operates two theatres, two beaches, two restaurants, and a ballroom dancing venue in Berlin. He employs 200 people. One employee's job is solely to obtain the dozen separate annual permits that are necessary for each of these temporary schemes.

As a pioneering use, *Strandbar Mitte* revealed the potential of its waterfront site and attracted new users. It stimulated and acted as a prototype to later developments in the park and elsewhere in Berlin (Urban Catalyst 2007). This privately-run beach has not been without opposition. Complaints have been brought at the local political level against the granting of temporary variances to local by-laws, excessive noise and garbage, bad behaviour of departing patrons, the use of public green space for a commercial bar and nightclub, and Schulz's increasing physical transformation of the site (BV SpV 2002; BI PRO SpV 2007). A local councillor from the Green Party, chairman of the district's Committee for Environment, Nature, Transport and Local Affairs, has suggested that as a 'pioneer', Schulz should not remain on parkland now it has been redeveloped, but move onto new, still underused sites:

> ... we ask ourselves whether the District Office will apply the relevant laws... The area in Monbijoupark is much too small for this hype, it's not suitable and it will become overused. At other locations Mr. Schulz can spread his beach, theatre (etc.) without any problems, for example on Heidestrasse [a large-scale new inner-urban neighbourhood]. That site should be developed. Cultural uses will be sought for that. Here is everything Schulz and Co. need: access to the Spree, land for spreading sand for beach bars ... those who play so 'innovative' with (non-)licensing, administration and the District Assembly, they can come up with a groundbreaking approach on Heidestrasse.

Mr. Schulz, who proudly carries the label of 'mother of all beach bars', could here again prove himself as an 'event culture' pioneer. That would really be something. (Jaath 2008, our translation)

Blijburg aan Zee, Amsterdam

Blijburg aan Zee (Figure 7.3) translates roughly as 'happyland at the sea'; it plays on the name of IJburg, the new residential district where it is situated. Planned for 45,000 owner-occupiers, IJburg is being built in eastern Amsterdam on seven artificial islands of dredged sand. Although *Blijburg*, like *Strandbar Mitte*, has been designed and run by an entrepreneur from the entertainment sector, the idea for this beach scheme originated with the public-private consortium responsible for the residential development. The first housing was built in IJburg in 2001, and while strong housing demand in the 1990s had generated a waiting list of 30,000, according to Igor Roovers, Project Director for IJburg, after the 9/11 attacks interest from property investors evaporated. The municipality and property developers, joint partners in the scheme, held an emergency meeting, and discussed how they could creating an urban atmosphere on the empty site, to attract investors. One civil servant noted people were swimming in the local dyke and sunbathing. This inspired a public relations initiative, designed to attract people to come see the islands for themselves, because the local media had reported very critically on the scheme. In 2003, a press release invited proposals to create a temporary beach for two years on the development's outer edge, to draw people through and raise IJburg's profile. After this time the beach was expected to close, as the site would be needed for construction. A successful beach was also seen

Figure 7.3 Blijburg aan Zee, Amsterdam.

Source: Bas Leenders/Flickr – https://creativecommons.org/licenses/by-sa/2.0/

as something that could significantly increase the value of its site. Three proposals were submitted: a bus selling ice cream and French fries, a stall selling pancakes, and the winner, a beach club proposed by 35-year-old Stanja van Mierlo, an entrepreneur, former radio station DJ and manager, and communications consultant, who had previously organised several festivals and music events. Van Mierlo had for years been seeking a site to create a freshwater beach club, as an alternative to the saltwater beaches elsewhere in Holland. She had already approached the city with a similar proposal for Ijburg in 2002 but was rejected.

The one-hectare *Blijburg* site is entirely fabricated from dredged sand. It has 250m of beach frontage onto a freshwater lake, which means people can swim, and *Blijburg* could avoid the high costs that completely artificial city beaches face of providing water-related amenities. The development consortium provided the site free of charge and installed electricity and sewage. A new tram line was also built connecting the island to the city centre. Van Mierlo funded the development and operation of the site through sponsorship. First opened later in summer 2003, the beach club includes a bar, bookshop and restaurant. Unostentatious in design and simply constructed, it utilises many second-hand components. Van Mierlo argues: 'It's not finished and it's not chic, so this element of imperfection creates a certain relaxed feeling' (personal communication). The municipality had decreed that the beach had to be constructed and commence operation within three weeks. Van Mierlo had a professional background in organising festivals and music events, and she used her personal networks to help with construction and operation. The creation of *Blijburg* was an opportunity for her to demonstrate and develop her organisational skills.

Van Mierlo wanted to recreate the beach bars she had seen in Ibiza and the music festivals she had witnessed on South Africa's beaches. Music is therefore a key element that defines the atmosphere of *Blijburg*. The scheme incorporates several indoor and outdoor spaces that allow performances in all weather conditions. *Blijburg* is a permanent installation operating throughout the year. Van Mierlo reinvests some of the project's profits into subsidising musical events there. She places more importance on the music and its audiences than on the physical environment where it occurs. The varied music performances offer something for all ages and tastes. The combination of the music and the open playful setting of the beach is intended to attract all residents to visit and use *Blijburg*. Both the municipality and van Mierlo recognise the importance of using culture to define the urban environment. Although she had little formal involvement in the municipality's cultural policy for IJburg, Van Mierlo feels these 'soft values' are her main contribution to IJburg's development.

There has always been tension between the municipality and van Mierlo regarding the temporary nature of *Blijburg*. Project Director Igor Rocvers argues, 'the ground is very valuable, so to let a temporary project like *Blijburg* stay on IJburg is costing the community a lot of money' (personal communication). For the development consortium, '*Blijburg* was apparently nothing more than a marketing trick to attract buyers to houses in IJburg. Now that was successful, the idea is to remove this hippie beach' (van Mierlo in Cohen 2008, our translation). After the initial two-year period, *Blijburg* was asked to close. The site was needed for a lock for the harbour which was a key feature of the masterplan. Van Mierlo fought the city for the right to stay on the site a third year. A loyal following of *Blijburg*'s users helped campaign to save the beach. After several months van Mierlo was successful, although she lost all financial aid from the municipality when she returned in 2005. *Blijburg* then vacated its original location in September 2005 so that construction could proceed. After much negotiation, van Mierlo was granted another location 400m south-east, and reopened in May 2006. In June 2008 *Blijburg* again came under review. The new site was needed for IJburg's second phase, construction of a bridge to four new islands further east. This construction was delayed, so *Blijburg* was granted another year on the current site in 2009. In 2010 the beach has had to move 400m further south-east. *Blijburg* has now existed for eight years, despite the municipality's opposition.

A permanent beach has always been part of the IJburg masterplan, at its south-eastern edge on Strandeiland (Beach Island), where construction of houses is planned to commence in 2010. That beach was originally proposed to run the island's full length, but EU legislation protecting an adjacent nature reserve reduced it significantly. To compensate, a more urban beach is now under consideration for the inner side of Strandeiland. Igor Roovers is elusive on the question of whether *Blijburg* could become one of these two permanent beaches. His vision for the *Blijburg* site had always been to help create an 'urban atmosphere' on IJburg (personal communication). However, as a low-budget, temporary project, very few constraints were imposed upon the development of *Blijburg*, meaning its character was entirely determined by van Mierlo. She too sought 'to set the tone' for IJburg, but her principal objective was to create a fun and vibrant place within the city that could be enjoyed by everyone (personal communication). This vision of urban space is far removed from Roovers' commercial perspective. Van Mierlo argues that the local community has played a significant role in *Blijburg*'s formation, and that her project could not simply be moved to another location in Amsterdam: 'I'm not *Cirque de Soleil*, you can't move me around. *Blijburg* is made for the people here. In another area I would make something else' (personal communication). She is dismayed at the municipality's failure to acknowledge that *Blijburg* is a place that has grown up with the local neighbourhood, and at its reluctance to incorporate *Blijburg* into the overall development.

Despite its short time frame and small budget, *Blijburg* has clearly been a success, in terms of creating a social atmosphere, attracting interest from house buyers, changing the municipality's views on what a city beach can be, and shaping the overall image of Amsterdam. When asked what he had learnt from the entire process, Roovers notes that 'with something small you can reach something big. The people in Amsterdam really want a beach here, they don't want to travel' (personal communication). He maintains, however, that *Blijburg* was not solely responsible for IJburg's success; it worked in combination with the new tram and boulevards. Van Mierlo believes that by helping to attract people from all over Amsterdam, she contributed to the quality of customers purchasing houses in IJburg. Those who moved here because of *Blijburg* might be disappointed if it subsequently disappears. The municipality has realised the importance of an urban beach in the long-term future of IJburg, witnessing that *Blijburg* helped to solidify the relationship between urban dwellers and the lake, in particular by providing access to the water. In addition to increasing awareness of IJburg locally, *Blijburg* has also become synonymous with Amsterdam in the global travel media.

The constraints of continuing business on a temporary basis are increasingly problematic for van Mierlo. She finds it difficult to obtain support from financial institutions. Banks need assurances that a business will be in operation long enough to repay loans; with the future of *Blijburg* always under threat, this cannot be guaranteed.

Bristol Urban Beach

Bristol's beach (Figure 7.4) was installed on an underutilised carpark facing a canalised section of the River Avon. The site is adjacent to Bristol's historic Redcliffe Wharf, the new office district Temple Quay, and also some of Bristol's most deprived neighbourhoods (Mean et al. 2008). The idea for a beach on this site came from two city council staff: urban designer Julie Witham, and Emily Price, a community liaison officer in Redcliffe. As a temporary and accessible project, they felt a city beach would increase public awareness about the area and demonstrate the importance of

Figure 7.4 Bristol Urban Beach 2007

Source: Matt Gibson/Flickr – https://creativecommons.org/licenses/by/2.0/

public space within its long-term development. For months they sought unsuccessfully to convince local councillors to fund the project. During a community barbeque in Redcliffe, Price met Melissa Mean, head of the Cities Programme at UK think-tank DEMOS. Mean had just moved to Redcliffe, and was inspired by city beaches she had seen in Amsterdam and others in Berlin and Paris. With the derelict space on Redcliffe Wharf within view, she put forward a proposal to run a city beach there the following summer. The beach project took nine months from conception to realisation and opened in July 2007.

At DEMOS, Mean had undertaken research about the public realm and local people's role in the production of public space. She was keen to use this prominent, central site to experiment with and to illustrate DEMOS's ethos of public placemaking. Bristol's beach thus explicitly espoused the following principles: providing open spaces for performances and classes led by the local community; programming diverse participatory activities at different times to encourage broad community involvement; stimulating practical engagement with the setting; encouraging people to envisage future possibilities for the space; stimulating awareness of environmental issues by presenting this 'beach within reach' as an alternative to low-cost flights to southern Europe, using sustainable materials, and contracting eco-friendly local entrepreneurs; developing and testing new practices of public participation in urban regeneration projects; and exploring how cultural institutions can help people develop their own cultural activities in local everyday spaces (DEMOS 2007; Mean et al. 2008). Bristol council was keen to work with DEMOS to realise both organisations' objectives. After considering the feasibility of the council managing the project or undertaking it in partnership, the council and DEMOS's board of directors determined that the project could only be delivered if the liability rested uniquely with DEMOS.

As a charity, DEMOS could contribute little funding. The £120,000 budget was mostly provided by sponsors, including the South West of England Regional Development Agency, Bristol City Council, Hewlett Packard, and major Swedish construction firm Skanska. Two local companies supplied construction assistance and materials; one donated 800 tonnes of sand (Faircliff 2007). As with *Paris Plage*, Bristol's sponsors were acknowledged in promotional material but not on site. Like our other case studies, Bristol's beach was free to use; visitors were not obliged to purchase anything, although there was a café on site and deckchairs were for hire. Much of the beach's budget was for full-time security staff. This requirement was imposed by the local police, concerned that such an inclusive public event might generate many incidents, and it also helped to reassure Council officials about their numerous health, safety and public liability concerns.

Three types of programming initiatives were used to encourage an engaged, playful atmosphere on the beach. One was provision of simple props such as palm trees and deck chairs, and free-to-use beach equipment such as buckets, spades, volleyballs and boules. The sand was deep enough to support games such as building sandcastles that were typical of real beaches. Swimming in the adjacent river was ruled out on health and safety grounds, but a hosepipe was provided on hot days. Mean believes these props heightened people's mental

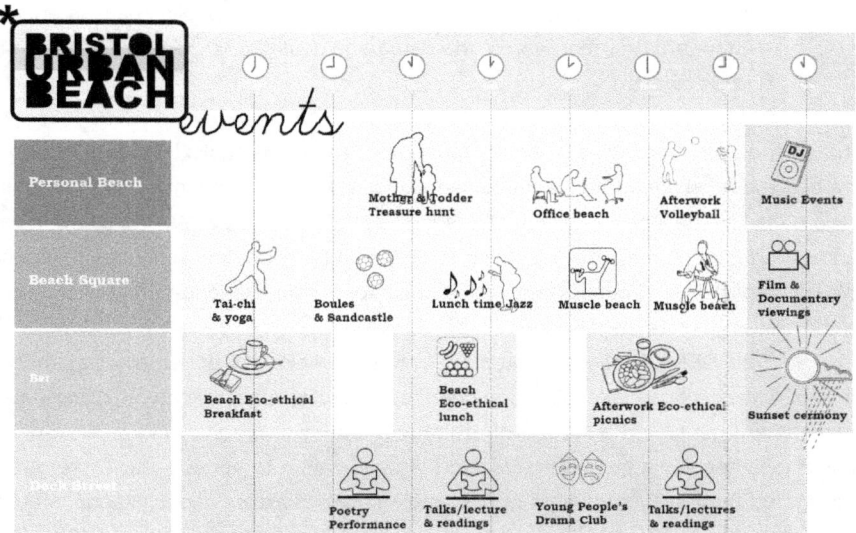

Figure 7.5 Bristol Urban Beach. Conceptual illustration of a hypothetical set of programmed events for different sections of the beach, across the course of the day.

Source: Mean et al. 2008

recognition of a beach, and this encouraged typical beach behaviours (personal communication). Secondly, the council employed a resident artist to develop a public arts programme for the beach, to explore the cultural heritage and social character of the area, and to seek to bridge some of its social and economic divides. This included involving children from a socially-disadvantaged housing estate nearby in a poetry competition linked to the beach. Thirdly, the beach's managers sought to develop an activity program that provided a diversity of events at different times throughout the day, which would attract and involve different user groups (Figure 7.5): an informal crèche organised by local mothers, life-drawing classes, lessons in tai-chi, yoga and kung-fu, areas for building sandcastles and for poetry performances, space for office workers to have lunch, after-work volleyball, music workshops, jazz performances, film screenings, lectures, and a drama club. These programmed events encouraged high levels of participatory behaviour and interaction. Over half the 130 people interviewed about their experience of visiting the beach said they interacted with strangers there (Mean et al. 2008). One of the beach's key social achievements was providing a relaxing environment where visitors could learn to be comfortable with extremely high user density, and thus with close proximity to strangers, and overcome their fear of difference. The organisers felt the design and management of this beach demonstrated the potential of a well-designed space to host a multitude of opportunities, both over time and at any one time. As Mean et al. (2008, 19) argue:

> Approaches to public space design and management tend to focus on cleanliness and maintenance and aesthetic design. What the Beach shows

is that the emotional and programmatic content of public space is equally important. In other words, the range and quality of experiences a space is able to host.

The 'DIY' ethos of providing diverse opportunities for active public involvement within the beach demonstrated the general potential for public engagement in urban regeneration projects. The local citizens' own planned performances, events and informal participation illustrated their role in helping to define and produce the space, emphasising the key importance of publicly-accessible open spaces for the long-term development of the area and for its identity.

The DEMOS beach existed for only six weeks. Its ephemeral nature had several distinct consequences. Its sudden, spectacular appearance within the urban environment generated a high level of interest and involvement, with a broad diversity of local residents being attracted to the space. As a temporary place, the beach highlighted the benefits to users of suspending everyday rules of social engagement. Its impermanence helped alleviate the opposition that more permanent projects often attract, particularly considering its unusual character. However, the cost and timeline increased, because all events in the UK lasting over 28 days must go through a major planning application process, including preparing a flood risk assessment. Bristol's beach also showed that short-term projects can be used to develop and illustrate possibilities for the future of open spaces, suggesting the potential for similar occurrences elsewhere in the city.

The development of Bristol's beach required inputs of skills from every department of the council; thus the city administration has benefitted from enhanced inter-departmental working relationships. The culture and leisure department and the events department are now involved with Emily Price's general cultural strategy for Redcliffe. The council's urban designer, Julie Witham, says the beach has given her department a new vocabulary. Terms like 'animation' of space are now commonplace, where previously they had been lacking. She noted the beach offered a new space for children in the city centre, and was keen to extend this legacy. In contrast to the mostly commercially-driven development of the city centre, the beach had shown both the desire and the potential for increased quality in the design of Bristol's public realm, and for offering socially diverse and inclusive places which encourage sensory engagement, active participation and interaction. As a test project for the council, the beach demonstrated the need for public space to be incorporated into the overall development of Redcliffe Wharf.

The success of the DEMOS beach project enhanced general civic pride in Bristol and encouraged entrepreneurial spirit. It helped local businesses showcase their goods and services. It also inspired city council staff: their ambition has grown to have beaches spread throughout the city, with Berlin as their explicit inspiration. They began to identify other potential sites, prepared SWOT analyses, and identified potential partners for funding, development and programming. One suggested location links to another forthcoming initiative to make Bristol the UK's first 'biking city'. The proposed site for this beach is a city-centre carpark in a prime waterfront location.

What would make this project contentious for the council is that the city owns the carpark and thus would lose its revenues. For Julie Witham and Emily Price, this highlights the city beach's potency: to reimagine and reevaluate public land so as to maximise its social benefits. Despite the council's efforts and enthusiasm, the project has not been repeated. Although it was well received by the public, the project has not gone entirely without criticism:

> It is certainly puzzling that a city like Berlin has for years had dozens of urban beaches, all seemingly set up by entrepreneurial types at ro cost to the public purse, and Bristol needs £200k, a think tank, a blog, and a philosophy to produce just one. ('Greengage' on thebristolblogger 2007)

Novel Aspects of Placemaking

Adding a New Sense of Place

The four city beaches presented here illustrate novel ways that new open spaces can engage with their physical, representational, functional and historic contexts. They sit lightly on the existing landscape and can be removed to reinstate it. While present, they radically reframe residents' and visitors' perceptions and use of the surroundings.

Our cases are sited in two distinct contexts: high-profile central-city tourist areas, and areas where new development aims to attract residents and visitors. Berlin's and Paris's riverfronts are UNESCO World Heritage sites. This designation constrains new real estate development. Entrepreneurs and local governments are seeking new modes of investing capital productively into these built environments; this has precipitated the introduction of a new landscape type which is temporary, which is thus permitted, and which complements the heritage by presenting many diametrical contrasts: built-up vs. open; hard vs. soft; institutionalised vs. informal; timeless vs. ephemeral. The open beach landscapes offer excellent views onto surrounding museums, palaces and churches.

In Bristol, changing perceptions of the site is part of a longer-term regeneration strategy. In Amsterdam's IJburg, we see character being created from scratch: the venue operator and land developer have conflicting views on how *Bijburg* fits into that production process. The sand underlying the site has helped the formation of a significant and distinctive community identity, shaping the relationship between new residents and the water. Future development may well bury this. Both sites use spectacle to attract new users, to put a place on the map and bring people through it, hoping to change perceptions and thereby increase value. From a production perspective, the constant flow of themed events, their often participatory nature, and annual changes in the theming of entire beaches all provide novelty, which keeps visitors interested in returning to the location (Gale 2009).

City beaches also help produce sense of place in a broader sense, by presenting a new vision of public space which redefines wider urban identity. Bristol's beach enhanced civic pride and raised ambition. It has changed the way the council thinks and speaks about public space, sharpening the focus on content and social inclusion. *Paris Plages* has added another dimension to Paris's city image, being a public setting accessible to, and used by, a diverse spectrum of people, without commercialisation (La Pradelle and Lallement 2004). *Paris Plages* also has a legacy as a vision and a general physical model for many subsequent city beaches elsewhere. The beaches in Bristol and Paris are more than just public spaces; they are political statements, to both residents and the world, about the city governments' social, ecological and developmental achievements and ambitions.

Blijburg has changed the Amsterdam authorities' perception: they have recognised the importance of an urban beach within the permanent plans for IJburg. *Strandbar Mitte* is often referred to as the 'mother' of Berlin's 60-odd beaches, which are now a key part of Berlin's attraction and lifestyle. Many people clearly learn about Europe's city beaches through first-hand visits. However, as temporary, stimulating, different and extremely photogenic settings, these projects also become widely known and experienced through their own websites, through internet forums, photo-hosting websites, news stories and word of mouth (see Mean et al. 2008, 20–21). They exemplify the use of media to promote space. More than just spectacles, they are a kind of open space that effectively advertises itself. Mediatised depictions precede and prefigure users' interest in and experience of the actual place.

The relocation of Berlin's and Amsterdam's beaches showed that meaningful, memorable and well-patronised places need not actually be fixed to particular geographical spaces. An alternative grounding for these places lies in their synergies with other activity patterns, which also shift. The city beaches' success shows that sense of place can come from flows of 'soft' content, harnessing intangible resources, including the users' own imaginations.

Temporary Open Space within the Long-Range Development Process

City beaches such as the ones in Bristol contribute to the incremental and variegated redevelopment of deindustrialised inner-urban areas, particularly waterfronts, which were formerly large, integrated, mono-functional Fordist production zones. In many older Western cities, including our four cases, government economic policy has shifted away from industrial growth, to focus instead on marketing general quality of life and leisure opportunities for potential residents and tourists (Judd and Fainstein 1999). To this end, contemporary urban development emphasises public investment in new infrastructure and cultural *grand projets*, as a form of city marketing and as incentives to private investment in new housing, retail and entertainment facilities (Dovey 1999; Ward 1998; Sorkin 1992; Zukin 1991). The obsolescence of inner-city industrial areas, their distinctive natural and heritage assets, and their high visibility within the cityscape have made them prime targets for such reinvention (Dovey 2005). Areas that were previously dominated by large-scale, integrated, 'Fordist' industrial production have been broken up and replaced by consumption facilities and activities (Norcliffe et al. 1996; Schubert 2001; Meyer 1999). This transition is not tidy, complete or permanently fixed. The post-industrial urban landscape is fragmentary, with 'gaps' and marginal spaces that are ill-defined, underdeveloped, and less regulated. With the breaking-up of the rationalised production landscape, the inner city has become increasingly heterotopic, providing spatial opportunities for different, non-conforming groups and activities (Franck and Stevens 2007; Shields 1991; Foucault 1997). Europe's city beaches often involve the appropriation and reconfiguration of derelict, unused or underutilised pieces of urban waterfronts, whether industrial brownfields, vacant public land, or unnoticed, ill-defined, intermediate spaces. These city beaches show that small and marginal 'gaps' are places too, and can be particularly crucial to local environmental quality, diversity and distinctiveness. Increases in the spatial flexibility and diversity of urban industrial areas have been accompanied by a shift in the temporal flows of their use. This shift is linked to the explosive growth in outdoor dining and hospitality venues, the '24-hour city' and the 'night time economy' (Bianchini 1995), and also reflects the increasing importance of planned special events and event spaces for city development and marketing.

Our four cases highlight that open space developments of brief duration can nonetheless be extremely well-utilised. Indeed, their ephemerality can heighten their attraction and impact and their legacy. The temporariness and relative intangibility of city beaches do not mean that they are completely disconnected from the conventional land development process. Indeed, they serve important niche roles within this process. In their study of temporary uses in five European cities – Helsinki, Amsterdam, Berlin, Vienna and Naples – Urban Catalyst identified eight distinct ways that temporary uses relate to longer-term development of sites (Misselwitz et al. 2003). Table 7.1 illustrates how our case studies reflect these possibilities. *Paris Plage* was only ever intended to sit lightly on top of a functioning expressway and then be cleaned away a month later. It has become institutionalised and has given impulse to similar developments on other sites in Paris and beyond. As a form of open space that is light, flexible, quick to assemble and to adjust, the initial prototype has developed quickly over time, and has been readily adapted to other sites. Bristol's beach has not had any later impacts, although the city has tried to replicate the prototype's success. Berlin's *Strandbar Mitte* began as a parasitic use dependent on, and in synergy with, the adjoining theatre. Its success in creating a sense of place convinced the city government to later incorporate it into the permanent plans for the park, with which it now coexists, albeit in a reduced, more controlled form. The diminution of this city beach highlights that it was only ever provisional, and must adjust to changes in surrounding development and activity. *Strandbar Mitte's* influence on its surroundings played out over many years, rather than being fixed in advance into permanent plans and contracts, as with Fordist production. *Blijburg aan Zee* was a pioneering use which helped define place, and which even reshaped the long-range plans for IJburg. This example shows how even a very rapidly-designed and -assembled open space can consolidate and become relatively permanent, although it has had to change location.

Table 7.1 Typologies of temporary uses in a long-term perspective, in the context of three city beach case studies. (Typologies in left column are taken from Misselwitz et al. 2003, 14–15)

Typology	Case study	Key characteristic
a **Stand in:** Temporary uses do not have any lasting effect on the location, but only use the vacant space for the time available.	Paris Plage	Prototypical
b **Impulse:** Temporary use gives an impulse for the future development of the site by establishing new programs/new programs cluster at a certain location.		
c **Consolidation:** Temporary use establishes itself at a location and is transformed to a permanent use. The consolidation can also take place at a different location.		
d **Coexistence:** Temporary use continues to exist (in a smaller size) even after establishment of a formal permanent use at the location.	Strandbar Mitte, Berlin	Provisional
e **Parasite:** Temporary use is developed in dependence of existing permanent uses and takes advantage of existing potentials and availability of space.		
f **Subversion:** Temporary use is interrupting an existing permanent use (institution) by squatting as a political action. Even so this occupation is normally of a very limited time-period, it effects the squatted institution and results in change of the institution. In the situation of the squatting different uses than normal are established at the location.		
g **Pioneer:** The temporary use is the first 'urban' use of the site, establishing a way of settlement, which might become permanent.	Blijburg aan Zee, Amsterdam	Portable
h **Displacement:** A permanent institution is displaced for a limited period of time and during this time established in an improvised way as a temporary use.		

Place as a Performance Involving Many Actors

Although all four city beaches received wide-ranging support from local government, each was essentially conceived and driven by one or two individuals. In Paris, Amsterdam and Bristol, a public champion imagined the beach as a suitable initiative for a specific location, and an outside entrepreneur (a scenographer, an event organiser, a non-profit researcher) had the technical and organisational capacities and autonomy to carry it out. For all three sites, private capital, sponsorship and public subsidies were combined to facilitate open space projects that provided public amenity for locals while also promoting inward urban investment in tourism and real estate. The financing model for these projects prompted development of new working relationships between municipalities and businesses. Both Paris and Bristol employed an innovative approach of 'off-site' sponsorship, to safeguard accessibility, inclusivity and environmental quality. Both municipalities also reported that because these projects required skills from many different government departments, they promoted more holistic working practices. Within the complexity of internal and external collaborations and contracts, it was clear that city beaches serve different purposes, require different inputs and yield different benefits for the various players involved. For example, Amsterdam's planners saw *Blijburg* as a successful PR tool, no longer needed; for visitors it is simply a fun place to be; for its manager and local residents it has become the heart of the neighbourhood.

Two main difficulties remain with such networks of production relations. One is the complexities of determining, sharing and managing the risks associated with such innovative open space projects. In Bristol, legal and health and safety requirements, and planning regulations that underpin them, inflated project costs and made the project challenging for decision-makers. The other problem is that relationships that are project-centred do not necessarily become permanent. On both grounds, the transaction costs of running such projects can be high (Mean et al. 2008).

Strandbar Mitte was, exceptionally, the brainchild of one man, who raised the capital, coordinated the permissions and inputs, bore most of the risks, and struggled with neighbours over negative externalities, but who accordingly pocketed much of the benefit. This private entrepreneurial model is in fact the most common one for city beaches, particularly in Germany.

The beach users also have important roles in the production of place. In all four projects, sense of place is shaped more by visitors' sensory engagements and the diversity of activities than by the unusual physical landscape alone. Instead of the passivisation which is a core critique of contemporary, spectacular urban open spaces, the design and programming of city beaches stimulates high levels of participation by a wide range of users, both scripted and unscripted; 'it becomes a theatrical production acted out by its visitors… in front of an audience of spectators' (Gale 2009, 126–7). Residents are encouraged to think differently about neighbourhoods and urban spaces by acting differently in them. These themed environments are encountered up close. Sensory elements such as music and tropical cocktails add to the beaches' direct stimulus on visitors, relaxing their minds and bodies and prompting actions such as dancing. In combination with other themed elements such as palm trees, thatched 'island' huts, artworks, and performances by 'exotic' dancers, these props stimulate escapist moods and memories that help people forget the everyday, make them open to new experiences, and stimulate their imagination. These deliberately artificial and exotic beaches add a dimension of playfulness to the sense of places. The city beach is also an experience that constantly changes, through the introduction and reorganisation of temporary physical elements, intangible elements such as music, sounds, and food smells, and through users' actions. Its temporariness heightens interest.

The beaches facilitate social gathering and interaction. They stimulate and display the local community's capacity to run cultural events. Their physical openness and free admission help dissolve physical and socio-economic boundaries. The beach setting appears to allow people to feel comfortable to be in very close bodily proximity to each other, in the middle of the city, even when they are exposed in their swimwear. This proximity increases informal encounters. All four projects stress that they appeal to people of all ages and from all social backgrounds. The findings suggest that events are perhaps better than fixed infrastructure in ensuring the social and cultural diversity of users, and thereby ensuring the broadening and deepening of a public sense of place.

These spaces are enlivened by a rich, robust human infrastructure. While some staff serve food and drink, many others are engaged in the post-Fordist production of content, providing changing schedules of entertainment: music and films, 'public viewing' of live sporting events, live theatre, readings, dance and exercise classes, and sand castle competitions. Other staff provide security and maintenance that enhance the robustness of these temporary places. Van Mierlo noted that *Blijburg* contributed 'soft values' to the development of IJburg. Such labor accounts for much more of the budget than does the landscaping. The process for delivery is more that of a service than of a product.

The constant flow of themed events, their often participatory nature, and annual changes in the theming of entire beaches all provide novelty, which keeps visitors interested in coming back to the location (Gale 2009). The temporariness of any given event or aesthetic theme, the general temporariness of a city beach environment, and the forced relocation of some city beach projects from one site to another, all intensify its fantastic, liminal nature as an escapist environment where people want to behave differently (Cohen and Taylor 1976). From a management perspective, themes and events also help to differentiate one city beach from the increasing number of competing sites that are in purely physical terms quite similar.

Post-Fordist Placemaking

Our case study findings about how city beaches are created, managed and used can also be linked to a broader theorisation of 'post-Fordist' placemaking. In response to new economic demands and opportunities, the development process for these spaces is much more flexible and dynamic than the Fordist approaches to open space production usually employed.

The complexity of political, financial, environmental and managerial factors shaping post-industrial urban landscapes have tended to break up the temporal flow of their development: there are spurts of growth, periods of stagnation, and difficulties of phasing and coordination (Desfor et al. 2010, Carmona 2009, Gordon 1996). Throughout Europe, city beaches and many other uses temporarily occupy urban land in the time between abandonment and new formal development projects – if indeed such projects ever materialise (Misselwitz et al. 2003; Groth and Corijn 2005; Haydn and Temel 2006). City beaches illustrate an approach that is particularly relevant to an unpredictable economic future. The cost-recovery timeframe for investment in these open space schemes extended only as long as their initial permits – usually about one month. Any return on physical investments beyond that time means profit for both private investors and users. The beaches' short time horizon encourages design which is highly responsive to the needs of various potential users, making the most of low-value materials and optimising flexibility in service provision and in the provision of the space itself. Little capital is tied up in large-scale, inflexible construction.

The distinctive production processes of city beaches fit well to the description presented in the emerging literature on post-Fordist tourist development. Gertler (1988) defines post-Fordist production generally through the high flexibility and continuous innovation with which groups of producers bring labour, capital and ideas together to meet diverse, rapidly-changing market demands. Ioannides and Debbage (1997) argue post-Fordism also describes a way of producing the landscape itself, so that it can be consumed. They examine the tourist industry's efforts to overcome the structural rigidities of mass-produced 'package' tourism. The post-Fordist tourist industry uses outsourcing to bypass traditional, vertically-integrated production processes. A myriad of small entrepreneurial businesses engage in highly specialised, small-scale, short-term production. Integration of production occurs horizontally, through temporary, flexible networks of people, skills, resources, and processes. These arrangements require complex logistics: the formation of short-term strategic alliances (including those with government), through contracts, incentives and waivers. Traditional open-space procurement processes are rigidly vertical. For three of the four city beach schemes we studied, the development procedures were managed outside the respective councils, and in Berlin the initiative lay entirely outside the public sector. The facilitation and decision-making roles for producing these open spaces were not filled by professional designers, but rather by entrepreneurs from the hospitality sector and/or their public-sector equivalents in cultural and recreational planning or non-profit organisations. Nevertheless, all these schemes required inputs, support and scrutiny from many different areas of government. These examples should encourage all those interested in urban open space provision to consider various potential working arrangements. Although the production relationships driving city beaches appear to generally be project-centred rather than permanent, they nonetheless help the various participants to develop relationships, knowledge and skills to pursue new strategies for the financing, construction, operation and programming of open space. As an example, the senate of the state of Berlin recently published a planning policy proposing to waive some permit requirements for temporary uses, and to create a 'one-stop shop' for all necessary licensing arrangements, as well as facilitating the issuance of more temporary permits (SenStadt 2007). This new permissive regime reflects a pragmatic shift toward encouraging and coordinating the role of private enterprise.

Flexible, post-Fordist approaches to the production of tourist landscapes arise to meet the diverse and volatile demands of the market, with its insatiable demand for novelty. These production arrangements facilitate the differentiation of goods and services, rapid innovation, customisation to user needs, and 'just-in-time' production in small volume (Ioannides and Debbage 1997). Relative to most public realm investments, which are designed to last many decades, the eight years during which city beaches have occupied urban spaces is a very short-term investment, a 'just-in-time' model of open space provision which optimises the use of a distinctive spatial resource before the next cycle of large-scale reinvestment. City beaches offer a new model of fluidity in the 'development' of urban space: they develop patronage, activity and ideas, without needing major physical development. They temporarily provide investment, employment and amenities for local residents. In contrast to the long-term fixity of 'traditional' urban redevelopment schemes, city beaches are extremely flexible in location, scale, and duration. They are a landscaping solution that can be spread over a site at short notice. City beaches illustrate landscape design and innovation as continuous processes; this should give encouragement to designers and managers of urban open spaces to test new ideas and to increase variation in both form and programming over time, and to build-in flexibility through the use of loose materials and equipment which can easily be reconfigured, or expanded, or re-used on a different site according to changes in demand, financing and land availability throughout investment cycles.

Post-Fordist production methods also change the nature of goods and services and the way they are supplied. The post-Fordist tourist industry facilitates the transportation of light and portable products to the consumer; a 'mediatisation' of the product, which Gale (2009) argues curbs the need for consumer travel. In this context, the escapism of artificial city beaches can be seen as a substitute for 'real' tourism: the local water-themed environment 're-places' more exotic waterfronts further away. In the context of the global economic downturn, this substitute is more affordable and accessible to both the urban poor and 'those urbanites who are cash-rich but time-poor' (Gale 2009, 125; see also Connolly 2004). In their quest to differentiate their products, the producers of post-Fordist tourism focus largely on investment in and management of specialised *content* (the labour-intensive, 'soft' infrastructure of services, events, experiences and branding) rather than on more durable *form* (long-term capital-intensive investments in large, inflexible buildings, expensive landscaping, and physical infrastructure). The mediatisation of content includes 'theming', which lends 'atmosphere' to the tourist landscape. Intangible differentiation is also pursued by linking beach projects into the local arts and creative industries. Additionally, post-Fordist tourism seeks to harness the creativity of consumers, by providing them with active roles in their experience of place. Through participatory events, production and consumption are blurred in the 'co-production' of individualised experiences (Richards and Wilson 2006). In this context, Gale (2009, 126) notes that a city beach 'would be nothing without the presence and actions of its visitors… whether soaking up the sun or playing pétanque… those who participate in this spectacle are performing the beach'. City beaches highlight that quality of life in public spaces is partly about users' potential for action, and especially for playing an active role in shaping the landscape, a hands-on, 'DIY' form of place-making (Mean et al. 2008). Temporariness, lightweight construction and portability all facilitate sharing this role around to different actors, down to the scale of repositioning deckchairs and umbrellas and digging in the sand.

Although the post-Fordist tourist industry appears to offer useful insights as to how distinctive place experience can be produced, and highlights scope for innovative alignments of public and private interests, the public benefits of urban open space can only be equitably secured through governmental foresight, involvement and oversight. Two critical questions about the private sector's role in the production of city beaches require further study of a wider range of examples (see Chapter 6). The first is the extent to which such city beaches are actually public spaces. Our four case studies all have free entry and allow people to bring their own food and drinks. Yet the partitioning of such beach environments from the wider public realm, the prominence of their gastronomical offerings, and their high-quality, luxurious furnishing can suggest private ownership and control, potentially discouraging access and use. *Strandbar Mitte* remains a point of contention because it has been allowed to occupy a designated 'public green space'. A second, related question is whether city beaches may be signs or tools of gentrification, as suggested by the after-hours popularity of many sites with an up-market clientele of young adults drinking cocktails, and their high-profile contribution to marketing and reinvestment in former industrial areas.

On both questions it is important to recognise that very few city beaches occupy existing public open spaces. The few public-sector schemes generally supplement existing open space offerings. Most beaches are privately-financed developments on underutilised privately-owned spaces, most importantly urban waterfronts, which offer new kinds of accessibility and amenity to the general public, without admission fees. Even the most profit-oriented city beaches with the most exclusive clientele only charge admission in the evenings and for special events. Importantly, city beaches only receive temporary approvals, which can thus be revoked or amended according to public needs. In terms of gentrification, entrepreneurs have been able to construct and operate beaches in former industrial areas precisely because no existing residents or higher-and-better users are displaced or disadvantaged. Our case studies suggest that even privately-run city beaches can help provide amenity and sense of place for a very broad public.

A third challenge with city beaches, and with many of the varieties of post-industrial leisure waterfronts discussed in this book, is that they are merely a more recent and more fluid version of the earlier generation of thematised, consumption-oriented urban waterfront leisure spaces that were created in earlier decades (Dovey 1999; Hannigan 1998; Gottdiener 1997; Harvey 1989). If city beaches do not link the experiences they offer to local characteristics of place, which are specific, unique, and relatively fixed, they may not retain the loyalty of the local residents and local governments on which their financial and regulatory security ultimately depend. The very fluidity and temporariness that makes city beaches such exciting places also puts them at risk of rapid obsolescence in a fast-moving competition for tourist attention:

in subverting the rule of spatial fixity in tourism, whereby the supply of tourist experiences tends to be fixed to particular places and slow to respond to changing economic and socio-cultural conditions, installations such as *Paris Plage* that have only weak, if any, ties to a physical place are even more vulnerable to reproduction in the short- to medium-term, compared to the places they mimic. It seems, judging by the number of places that now boast an urban beach, that what began as an innovative experiment in setting Paris apart from other world cities in terms of its tourist product is now, potentially, yet another example of the 'serial reproduction of culture' in tourism. (Gale 2009; 127–8, citing Richards and Wilson 2006).

References

Aulich, U. and Janovsky, S. (2008) 'So ein Theater', *Berliner Zeitung*, 14 August.

BI PRO SpV (= Betroffenenvertretung Spandauer Vorstadt) (2007) *Monbijoupark: Der Park und das Kinderbad, der Platz und die Torhäuser, Parkbesetzer and Bebauungsabsichten*, available from http://www.bvspv.de/monbijou.html, accessed 30 April 2009.

Bianchini, F. (1995) 'Night cultures, night economies', *Planning Practice and Research*, 10(2), pp. 121–126.

BV SpV (= Betroffenenvertretung Spandauer Vorstadt) (2002) *Stellungnahme zum Genehmigungsverfahren 'Strandbar' im Monbijou Park*, available from http://www.bvspv.de/st-021219strandbar.html, accessed 30 April 2009.

Carmona, M. (2009) 'The Isle of Dogs: Four development waves, five planning models, twelve plans, thirty-five years, and a renaissance… of sorts', *Progress in Planning*, 71(3), pp. 87–151.

Carmona, M. (2010) 'Contemporary public space: Critique and classification, part one: Critique', *Journal of Urban Design*, 15(1), pp. 123–148.

Choblet, C. (unaccredited interview with) (2008) *One of the fundamental ideas behind Paris Plage is social equity*, available from http://www.eukn.org/urbanmatrix/news/2008/08/interview-jean-christophe-choblet_1004.html, accessed 11 January 2010.

Cohen, M. (2008) *Stanja van Mierlo (interview on blog Vrij Nederland from July 2006)*, available from http://kinderenrevolutie.ning.com/profiles/blog/show?id=2142360%3ABlogPost%3A130, accessed 12 May 2009.

Cohen, S. and Taylor, L. (1976) *Escape Attempts: The Theory and Practice of Resistance to Everyday Life*, London: Allen Lane.

Connolly, K. (2004) 'Germans get taste of tropics an hour's drive from Berlin', *Daily Telegraph (UK)*, 21 December, available from https://www.telegraph.co.uk/news/worldnews/europe/germany/1479454/Germans-get-taste-of-tropics-an-hours-drive-from-Berlin.html, accessed on 12 May 2020.

DEMOS (2007) *Bristol Urban Beach*, available from http://www.demos.co.uk/projects/bristolurbanbeach/overview, accessed 30 Sept 2008.

Desfor, G., Laidley, J., Stevens, Q. and Schubert, D. (eds) (2010) *Transforming Urban Waterfronts: Fixity and Flow*, New York: Routledge.

Dovey, K. (1999) *Framing Places*, London: Routledge.

Dovey, K. (2005) *Fluid City: Transforming Melbourne's Urban Waterfront*, London: Routledge.

Faircliff, R. (2007) *Sun, sand and salsa. Forget Barbados, welcome to Bristol Beach!*, DEMOS press release, available from http://bristol.indymedia.org/article/26592, accessed 22 May 2009.

Foucault, M. (1997) 'Of other spaces', in Leach N. (eds.), *Re-Thinking Architecture*, London: Routledge, pp. 350–356.

Franck, K. and Stevens, Q. (eds) (2007) *Loose Space: Possibility and Diversity in Urban Life*, London: Routledge.

Gale, T. (2009) 'Urban beaches, virtual worlds and 'The end of tourism'', *Mobilities*, 4(1), pp. 119–138.

Gertler, M. (1988) 'The limits of flexibility: Comments on the post-fordist vision of production and Its geography', *Transactions of the Institute of British Geographers*, 13(4), pp. 419–432.

Gordon, D. (1996) 'Planning, design and managing change in urban waterfront redevelopment', *Town Planning Review*, 67(3), pp. 261–290.

Gottdiener, M. (1997) *The Theming of America: Dreams, Visions and Commercial Spaces*, Boulder: Westview.

Groth, J. and Corijn, E. (2005) 'Reclaiming urbanity: Indeterminate spaces, informal actors and urban agenda setting', *Urban Studies*, 42(3), pp. 503–526.

Hannigan, J. (1998) *Fantasy City: Pleasure and Profit in the Postmodern Metropolis*, New York: Routledge.

Harvey, D. (1989) *The Condition of Postmodernity*, London: Blackwell.
Haydn, F. and Temel, R. (eds) (2006) *Temporary Urban Spaces: Concepts for the Use of City Spaces*, Basel: Birkhäuser.
Ioannides, D. and Debbage, K. (1997) 'Post-fordism and flexibility: The travel industry polyglot', *Tourism Management*, 18(4), pp. 229–241.
Jaath, J. (2008) 'And the winner is …', *Grüne Aussichten* (Magazine of the Green Party faction in the Berlin-Mitte district council) Summer, p. 5, accessed 30 April 2009.
Judd, D. and Fainstein, S. (eds) (1999) *The Tourist City*, New Haven: Yale University Press.
La Pradelle, M. and Lallement, E. (2004) Paris Plage: 'The city is ours', *The ANNALS of the America Academy of Political and Social Science*, 595(1), pp. 134–145.
Mairie de Paris (2007a) *Paris Plages: Evenement*, Paris: Mairie de Paris.
Mairie de Paris (2007b) *Paris Plages: Guide Pratique*, Paris: Mairie de Paris.
Mean, M., Johar, I. and Gale, T. (2008) *Bristol Beach: An Experiment in Place-making*, London: DEMOS.
Meyer, H. (1999) *City and Port: Urban Planning as a Cultural Venture in London, Barcelona, New York and Rotterdam*, Utrecht: International Books.
Misselwitz, P., Oswalt, P. and Overmeyer, K. (eds) (2003) *Urban Catalysts: Strategies for Temporary Uses*, Berlin: Urban Catalyst, available from http://www.templace.com/think-pool/one786f.html?think_id=4272
Norcliffe, G., Bassett, K. and Hoare, T. (1996) 'The emergence of postmodernism on the urban waterfront: Geographical perspectives on changing relationships', *Journal of Transport Geography*, 4(2), pp. 123–134.
Richards, G. and Wilson, J. (2006) 'Developing creativity in tourist experiences: A solution to the serial reproduction of culture?', *Tourism Management*, 27(6), pp. 1209–1223.
Rolff, M. (2004) 'Sonne, Sand, Caipi – nur in München nicht', *Süddeutsche Zeitung*, 18 August.
Schubert, D. (ed.) (2001) *Hafen- und Uferzonen im Wandel: Analysen und Planungen zur Revitalisierung der Waterfront in Hafenstaedten*, Berlin: Leue.
SenStadt = Senatsverwaltung für Stadtentwicklung Berlin (ed.) (2007) *Urban Pioneers: Temporary Use and Urban Development in Berlin*, Berlin: Jovis.
Shields, R. (1991) *Places on the Margin: Alternative Geographies of Modernity*, London: Routledge.
Sorkin, M. (ed.) (1992) *Variations on a Theme Park*, New York: Hill and Wang.
thebristolblogger (2007) 'How our beach has been turned into a desert…', available from http://thebristolblogger.wordpress.com/2007/06/12/how-our-beach-has-been-turned-into-a-desert/, accessed 18 May 2009.
Urban Catalyst (Philipp Oswalt, Philipp Misselwitz, Klaus Overmeyer) (2007) 'Patterns of the Unplanned', in K. Franck and Q. Stevens (eds) *Loose Space: Possibility and Diversity in Urban Life*, London: Routledge, pp. 271–288.
Ward, S. (1998) *Selling Places: The Marketing and Promotion of Towns and Cities 1850–2000*, London: Spon.
Webster, C. (2007) 'Property rights, public space and urban design', *Town Planning Review*, 78(1), pp. 81–101.
Weindl, F. (2004) 'Rimini ist überall', *Süddeutsche Zeitung*, 3 August.
Zukin, S. (1991) *Landscapes of Power: From Detroit to Disney World*, Berkeley: University of California Press.

Chapter 8
Sandpit Urbanism

Quentin Stevens

Chapter 6 noted that over 350 city beaches have been installed on vacant sites in over 100 different German cities, and that most of them have been developed as profit-oriented hospitality ventures by private entrepreneurs, as discussed in Chapter 7. Even for experienced commercial operators, creating these novel environments requires new engagements with public bureaucracy, neighbours and clientele, because these projects are open to a very broad public for a very wide range of uses. This chapter's focus is on the small number of city beaches which have been initiated, designed, produced and operated by local citizens. While these projects look similar to commercial beach bars, their social functions and meanings are rather different, and the processes through which they are produced require even more initiative, learning, and improvisation. Citizen-initiated beaches are a fun and low-budget way to temporarily transform city-centre open spaces for residents, and in particular to give local children something to do in the summer. Local citizens are very involved in determining, and participating in, a wide range of social activities within these settings. But city beaches' capacities to facilitate creative social action go well beyond the distinctive openness, looseness and escapism of the completed settings. Most importantly, these informal landscaping projects provides opportunities for citizens to become actively engaged in imagining future forms and uses for urban spaces, and to be 'hands-on' in physically making, inhabiting and managing these environments. Citizen-led city beaches generally draw upon formal models that were pioneered by artists and businesspeople. Citizens' enterprising initiatives centre on learning how to modulate and re-perform these received approaches to meet focused social objectives. In doing so, they explore ideas about landscape design, construction, use programming, financing, government regulation and management.

Conceptualising Citizen Engagement in Placemaking

To understand the potentials that temporary urban space projects such as city beaches offer ordinary citizens to engage in the making and experiencing of urban social space, it is useful to understand several linked concepts that describe the processes and organisational milieux through which these environments develop.

Performance

City beaches do not have a fixed physical form. These are temporary landscapes that appear virtually overnight. A city beach landscape is in itself a performance, a flexible assemblage of sand, props and scenography staged *on top of* an urban site. They can be quickly rearranged by different operators and users according to different tastes and activities, or redeployed in different locations. Many of the pioneering and most successful commercial beaches were developed by entrepreneurs with backgrounds in theatre, music promotion, media or advertising, and much of the atmosphere of city beaches is performed rather than physically built: through lighting and recorded music, through diverse and changing programs of music, dance, plastic arts, literature, film, circus and live theatre, and also through participatory events including beach sports, yoga, children's art, treasure hunts, and dancing. This flexible provision of labour-intensive 'soft' infrastructure opens up opportunities for a diversity of community actors to co-create the beach, and bestow it with local identity and value. Users also have a continuous dramaturgical role in performing a city beach's meanings and functions, by bringing towels and swimwear and sunbathing, playing beach volleyball, building sandcastles, or simply taking off their shoes (La Pradelle and Lallement 2004; Gale 2010). City beaches are thus escapist in the sense of involving users' bodily and multi-sensory immersion and active participation (Pine and Gilmore 1998).

The production of city beach landscapes involves constant transformations. These include cyclical changes over the course of a day and changing seasons, involving unpacking, rearranging and repacking, and over historical time, through the development and testing of new material forms, meanings, uses and user groups. Changing user preferences, weather, budgets, regulations and space availability all stimulate the ongoing rearrangement and reinvention of these spaces. This continual production draws upon the desires and skills of a wide variety of actors: legislators and bureaucrats, artists and designers, financiers and sponsors, managers, suppliers and employees, patrons and objectors, security staff, thieves and vandals.

The nature of city beaches as experienced events, rather than durable material forms, brings a governance emphasis on performance-based regulations, related to levels of inebriation, noise, light and waste, which focus on optimising the usability of these urban open spaces. This is in contrast to urban planning's typical focus on built form controls. German building code provisions for so-called 'flying buildings' exempt these kinds of simple, temporary, self-built projects from many stringent, time-consuming and expensive requirements and approval processes which would otherwise thwart the efforts and interests of low-budget citizen initiatives.

Urban Pioneers and 'Culturepreneurs'

City beaches exemplify significant recent shifts in the scale, settings, modes and actors through which changes in urban land use, physical form and economy now occur. In Germany, deindustrialisation has left many large vacant inner-city sites. An absence of adequate financing and market demand for their large-scale redevelopment has created opportunities for a wide range of new users to experiment with occupying and transforming such sites, usually with very little investment and small economic turnover, but often serving surprisingly broad and previously-neglected clienteles. Such users include a broad scope of 'creative industries', small-scale entrepreneurs and start-up companies, non-profit organisations, and local community groups supporting culture, sport and gardening. Many of these actors are new to engaging with the processes of urban development. As well as developing their own practices and discovering the potentials of new physical settings, these actors must also move creatively within the bureaucratic, regulatory and financial terrains that condition their capacities to shape the urban realm (SenStadt 2007; Oswalt et al. 2013).

These provisional, 'pioneering' uses of sites broaden the scope of skills, ideas, and values involved in urban development and its decision-making. They engage a range of actors who had previously been excluded, because they lacked the necessary economic or social capital, or their ideas for using space did not fit within existing paradigms. These actors bring new knowledge and unconventional understandings of sites, aesthetics, local needs and history. The scope of their entrepreneurship extends beyond innovative products and services, to their creative engagement with urban development processes themselves. The non-profit city beaches discussed here highlight the reimagining and re-enchantment of a range of marginal urban spaces that lack use and investment, including semi-public courtyards, shopping streets, fringe areas and parks.

The term 'culturepreneur' applies to a range of pioneering roles in shaping how urban space is produced and consumed. One definition is creative entrepreneurs who themselves develop and manage new products, services and experiences, such as city beaches, which span traditional industries, professions and artistic media (Lange 2011). Another is a newly-emerged category of actors who mediate between these innovative users of open space, government regulations and strategies, and property owners with vacant sites (Jorg 2008; Kruse and Steglich 2006). Both kinds of agents drive innovation and flexibility in the rules, processes and investments that shape the use and redevelopment of urban land, exploring alternatives to long-range, large-scale, top-down, sectoralised approaches to urban development.

The general history of city beaches, as pioneering projects, illustrates ongoing transfers of knowledge and skills in different directions between artists, entrepreneurs, local residents and local governments. It also shows transfers of imagination and initiative, willingness to change, and enthusiasm for action.

Temporary Use

City beaches are one of many current creative uses of vacant land in German cities that are only approved to occupy their sites temporarily. Such temporary use is seen as a strategy to maximise both the income and the social benefit of such land prior to presumed larger, longer-term investment in redevelopment. Creative and not-for-profit actors are valued for their capacity, flexibility and readiness to discover, develop and occupy disinvested spaces in interesting ways on a temporary basis (SenStadt 2007; Bishop and Williams 2012). Allowing such temporary uses is often a conscious planning strategy for testing possible future uses for sites, and incubating new urban activities, by making space available to new users with lower capitalisation (Bürgin and Cabane 1999; Angst et al. 2009; Oswalt et al. 2013). Because their temporal and financial horizons are limited, temporary uses of urban sites can be more experimental than permanent projects that require larger budgets and face larger risks. They can cater to smaller, more specialised audiences. External impacts of unconventional uses are also more easily tolerated when they are only occupying marginal spaces that were previously unused, and are only short-term. The development, regulatory and management processes for novel temporary uses such as beaches offer opportunities for both their producers and various local government agencies to test out and develop new roles, skills and relationships, by loosening up the conditions under which such projects develop.

Sandpit

The metaphor of a sandpit (for Americans, sandbox) gathers the various concepts outlined above together around a specific landscape form. The sandpit metaphor is used in contemporary management, organisational psychology, game theory and pedagogy to describe social and physical milieux that are open and unstructured, that contain a diversity of peer actors and objects that can take on a variety of roles, and which are thus conducive to child-like, playful learning, and the value-free, creative exploration of functional and collaborative possibilities (Phipps 2010; Twaroch and Frank 2005). Such sandpits help to foster new, interdisciplinary business and research approaches.

The following case studies of non-commercial city beaches draw upon archival histories, site analysis, and interviews with producers and managers to illustrate how 'loose' urban spaces, temporary uses, entrepreneurial drive and the 'experience economy' come together to reshape the urban environment and social interactions within it. Five of these beach projects were developed by local community organisations to enhance the range and attractiveness of urban spaces available for local residents, including children and youth, so that they could play and meet. Four other beaches were developed as public art projects, with similar goals.

'Grassroots' Beaches

Four small German cities have hosted community-based beaches. Although three of these beaches occupied pedestrianised town squares or public parklands that were separated from the cities' riverfronts, in one case, the parkland in question was a waterfront site. In Esslingen near Stuttgart, population 92,000, a beach was established in 2009 by a group of youth work associations and the city youth council. They felt local adolescents lacked outdoor activity options, and wanted to motivate youths to exercise. They knew of commercial beaches in Stuttgart and other large cities (though not another community-led beach in Vaihingen an der Enz, on the other side of Stuttgart), and decided to adapt the idea. This beach was installed rent-free on city-owned waterfront parkland, and supported by a community fund and sponsorships, including discounted sand. It was supervised by paid and volunteer educators, and offered a frequent program of participatory activities. The beach's popularity grew. When it was repeated in 2010, adolescents who had not gained an apprenticeship were trained and supervised to rebuild and decorate a second-hand Christmas market stall as a beach cabin, which gave them a sense of pride and encouraged them to visit the beach regularly.

One beach project in Berlin bears strong similarities to Esslingen's socially-oriented example. YAAM (Young and African Art Market) is a non-profit organisation focused on arts and supporting the social integration of problem youth and multicultural migrants. YAAM operated on several sites since 1994, but gained a beach when it moved in 2004 close to Ostbahnhof, within a narrow strip of land wedged between the former Wall and the River Spree which has also been occupied by numerous temporary commercial city beaches (Figure 8.1) (SenStadt 2007). The venue covers 20,000m², half of it sand. It provides a stage for music, cultural performances, youth activities, sports, and art exhibitions, and a children's play area. It also houses several small Caribbean and African food and clothing vendors in pre-existing industrial buildings and temporary kiosks. YAAM claim to have always operated without government support, and to be regarded critically by the local government (SenStadt 2007; YAAM n.d.). Much of their staffing has involved volunteers, young people doing their civil service, job-creation schemes, job support funding, and apprenticeships for event technicians (Hesping 2006).

Figure 8.1 YAAM (Young and African Art Market), Berlin.

Avant-Garde Beaches

Four further open, public beach projects were the product of artistic inspiration. One of these, in historic Weimar, population 65,000, occurred in 2009. Galerie Eigenheim, a local private contemporary art gallery, had helped the city win the *Entente Florale*, a Europe-wide landscaping award seeking to bring together citizen associations and art institutions to make cities more liveable and attractive. Their proposal centred on IlmArkadien, a beach aiming to bring children, families and artists together. For the *Entente Florale*, the project ostensibly served three linked goals: to develop a community network for a healthier river, to establish an inner-city natural pool, and to sustainably improve playspace for children. It was proposed to forge longstanding links to Weimar's university to develop a local waterway rehabilitation concept (IlmArkadien 2009). The beach was also a sculpture park, with site-specific works created by local and guest artists. The city provided the site next to the Ilm River for free; state and private sponsors covered construction costs. The city's building office assisted with meeting construction regulations. The organisers dealt with their lack of a hot-food vending license by selling disposable barbecues to visitors, with the lack of potable water supply by only selling bottled water, and with the unfortunate lack of safe river access by installing a fence and providing paddling pools.

A second avant-garde beach project, Munich's Kulturstrand (Figure 8.2), also sprang from idealist social and artistic origins. It was created by the Urbanauten, a debating society involving university students from various city-related disciplines, discussing how to encourage residents to see and use public spaces differently, and seeking to modify left-over spaces into venues for performances, cultural events, public debates and social engagement. Some individuals had experience in running public events: their first beach in 2004 lasted only two days during a street festival they helped manage. In 2005, they considered applying for arts funding to create a public beach, where people could bring their own refreshments. They applied for planning permission and unexpectedly received a month-long permit at short notice. Lacking

Figure 8.2 Kulturstrand, Munich, 2010, on a bridge bastion, with its performance stage.

any funding, they contacted a restaurateur they knew through the street festival, who helped with financing and operated a bar on the beach. A significant portion of their financial turnover is re-invested in their daily program of live music, film, theatre, and children's activities, which they invite local organisations to contribute to. The Urbanauten had originally intended to relocate the beach each year, to enliven new spaces. Having occupied six different locations, and discovered the effort required to obtain new permissions and develop new sites, by 2008 they were exclusively using a bridge bastion in the Isar River. This site's small size (500m^2) limited their options for cultural and participatory events. After residents' complaints, they agreed with the city in 2011 to rotate annually between four different sites.

Kulturstrand's contribution to local social and cultural life and its enlivening of numerous uncared-for spaces is recognised by Munich's mayor (their official patron), the city departments for economy and sport and leisure which endorse its applications, and by its thousands of visitors, although the neighbourhood councils where it is sited are generally against it. This beach is run by a joint-venture private company, with no public subsidies or community participation. It is, like other commercial beach bars, a private landscape financed by selling drinks. In this respect, Kulturstrand differs from the beaches in Esslingen and Weimar, where drinks were sold, but which were always available for public use without purchasing anything. Kulturstrand's manager admits that the Urbanauten mostly live out their artistic and cultural ideals through other projects. Through three such projects they have striven to bring new ideas and physical enhancements to Munich's riverfront, marshalling technical and political support and utilising open design competitions to encourage debate. An unrealised 2010 initiative sought to temporarily retrofit an abandoned railway bridge as a pedestrian river crossing to reconnect inner-city neighbourhoods. In connection with their relocation in 2012, they organised a public ideas competition for revitalising the inner-Munich waterfront, and funded a competition to fit out their new location, won by a student's proposal for a continuous red tubular beanbag winding several hundred metres across the site.

A third art-related beach was created on the waterfront side of Arena, a large bus garage in Berlin's Treptow district converted for cultural uses in 1995. The beach accompanied the 2004 introduction of the Badeschiff, a floating swimming pool constructed from a barge, which is anchored adjacent in the Spree River. The Badeschiff was initially designed as a temporary art installation for a competition hosted by a non-profit association aiming to raise public consciousness about the Spree River and its qualities. Part of the original concept was the potential mobility of both the pool and the beach area. The project was realised through funding from the city cultural foundation and a city magazine, and through an €8 admission charge (Wikipedia.de 2012; SenStadt 2007).

Spaces for Action

Keep It Simple

City beaches initiated by citizen groups are generally quite small, around 100m^2, whereas commercial beaches are typically over 1000m^2. The main reasons are the limited dimensions of their central sites and smaller budgets. Most community beaches are thus physically more simply equipped than commercial beaches. The small scale and simplicity of these landscapes and their key props makes them relatively cheap and easy to install, manage and transform. As Esslingen illustrates, even relatively untrained youth can contribute to this. City technical staff and sponsors often provide significant advice, assistance and resources for these socially-oriented projects, especially the most laborious task: spreading and removing sand. These relatively simple settings create a very engaging atmosphere which offers residents opportunities to escape their everyday social settings and roles, relax, mingle with other residents, and thereby expand their social experience. This is particularly the case for teenagers and children, the main target group for all of the community-focused beaches.

Looseness

These beaches are very open to use. Weimar's beach included a ten-metre-long boat designed for multi-functionality for different groups: for children's play during the daytime, and as a stage for evening events such as readings, music festivals, and a children's film workshop. Physical looseness provides a high level of control and comfort to users. It also means the beaches' creators can experiment, modify and extend the setting and its use, depending on their developing experience, knowledge, technical skill, finances and labour resources. Germany's longest-running community-led beach, Strandleben in Vaihingen an der Enz (Figure 8.3), illustrates best the incremental, cumulative learning and physical development of such projects, even though it is completely demounted and reconstructed every year. After the first, artist-initiated year, the Mayor said the beach would never happen again, but fortuitously the sandpit's wooden border was not

Figure 8.3 Local gym class on Strandleben, Vaihingen an der Enz, near Stuttgart, 2010.

thrown away and could be re-used. The sand itself has never been purchased; it is rented cheaply as sponsorship from a construction supplies company, the organisers pay for delivery, and afterwards the company collects the sand and sells it. Additional elements have been introduced in various years, including a free lending library in a portable bookcase. Deckchairs printed with the associations' logo were purchased, after experience with cheaper chairs that broke quickly. A mini-lighthouse was created by a local organisation in 2010, as an advertising pillar to display the beach program, other community notices, and the rules for use.

Because all the cafes surrounding Strandleben were already closed by 6pm, a vending trailer was donated by the local football club, decorated with raffia mats. The operator has volunteer staff; they pack away the deckchairs at night and when it rains, provide informal site supervision, and serve as a contact point. The beach's organisers told the council that having the vendor there would help their project, and the city agreed not to charge vending fees. As the organisers noted, 'It's not worth charging a fee… (she makes) less than security staff would earn'. Unlike commercial city beaches, residents are perfectly welcome to bring their own drinks and food to Strandleben, but they are aware that buying drinks there helps make such an arrangement possible.

Security problems result from the physical looseness of city beaches' components. Supplies and electrical equipment have to be locked away somewhere and furnishings must be chained down. Weimar's portable toilet cabin was once thrown into the river. Someone broke open Esslingen's cabin to steal beer. Such problems are rare, indicating the strong sense of ownership and the informal surveillance that city beaches generate. City governments tend to favour community-focused beaches over other kinds of 'public' events that sometimes occupy the same spaces, not just because of their public benefit and their inclusiveness, but because compared to externally-organised events such as 'public viewing' of football games, festivals, or concerts, the beaches' events are usually smaller, quieter, and finish earlier, and their managers are relatively permanent and reliable; thus city beaches cause less damage and generate less residents' complaints. By making a space welcoming and busy, city beaches help to displace unwanted and illegal activities. At Esslingen's youth beach, mothers with children arrived each day before the beach was even staffed, teenagers arrived late afternoon, and adults in the evening. The organiser notes, 'We were surprised that such a broad spectrum (of visitors) developed, but we were surprised in a good way… because there aren't many venues where many different generations really meet, in a very peaceful way'. In Weimar, people held private birthday parties, and a nearby church used the site for early-morning services. Looseness means a certain toleration of unexpected users and uses.

Performance

These community beach landscapes are physically less sophisticated and luxurious than their commercial cousins. However, in terms of social atmosphere, activities, and meaning, they are very rich. This is even though – or perhaps, because – the organisers typically have no budget for organising and carrying out events. The performers are primarily local and amateur. In their first year, Esslingen did not allow recorded music to be played, to encourage live performances. These included student bands, slam poetry, fashion shows, and juggling. Weimar's planned events drew upon the local arts scene. Performances on other beaches ranged from fire eaters and clowns to local choirs and school groups practicing acrobatics. In contrast to passive consumption of professional shows, city beaches emphasise roles and benefits for participants as much as for audiences. Many scheduled events were entirely about local resident participation and personal development, including, in Vaihingen, 'Karate, Yoga, Tai-chi, Qi-Gong, Aikido, Indiaca (and) Samba', as well as Parkour and a treasure hunt. Esslingen's beach provided sports opportunities for youth, including slacklining, beach volleyball, and football tournaments focusing on fair play. Weimar's beach offered rental of equipment for unprogrammed engagement in sports such as cricket, golf and bacminton. Local businesses and community groups in Vaihingen organised many different events, including a 'healthy' public breakfast for school students, hosted by the local organic food store, trampolining sponsored by a local physiotherapist, a weight-throwing competition sponsored by the local newspaper, student tutoring, and a candlelight vigil remembering the Hiroshima bombing. Performances on community city beaches are mostly about doing, in groups, rather than watching.

Action and Actors

Community Entrepreneurship

Community-driven and artist-driven city beach projects show that innovation and risk-taking in urban development are not just the purview of profit-motivated agents. Esslingen's beach pursued social development for youth and demonstrated physical improvement of a rundown riverfront site. For these reasons, it was supported by the city and received community funding. It also prompted a lot of incremental learning on the part of the organisers:

> In the first year, I was in charge. It was my project. I managed it. I handled the accounting. I handled the discussions and meetings. I was also there every day, together with other educators and volunteers – the volunteers are very important for this project… this (second) year, I have hired an employee to take care of this project who is on site every day. (All quotes are the author's translations)

In the first year of Esslingen's beach, everything was run out of shipping containers. With its success, and the longer operating season in the second year, they improved the infrastructure considerably, including getting the local youth to repair and decorate a kiosk. The adolescents were not just consumers of the setting and services, but also contributed to the production of both, and developed skills, self-worth and attachment through the process. Community engagement also included the local, in-kind basis of much of the sponsorship: 'most sponsors have provided services or products to us. We had sponsors who helped us spread out the sand,... or who delivered the sand at a very reasonable price... I wouldn't know how else I could distribute the sand'. Although there were no carry-over profits from the Esslingen beach's first year, its second year of operation was easier because all the logistics and contacts were already known.

The external cultural and artistic initiative that had established Vaihingen's beach in 2001 had been strongly supported by the mayor. Such a daring proposal would otherwise have probably been quite difficult to realise in a conservative town. The mayor had never expected the scheme to re-occur. The town centre residents' association appealed to the council to repeat the beach, but when that didn't happen in 2002, they decided they would attempt it themselves. As Vaihingen's council has become increasingly in favour of the beach and recognise its benefits, they have reduced their charges for assembling and dissembling the beach, and they have begun to ask the organisers to run the event every year; 'It is appreciated and desired. It's not just tolerated'. Since 2010 Strandleben has occurred annually. The citizens describe their experience in this way:

> We take care of everything. The city prefers this... We are always there. We are there at the weekend. We communicate to each other by telephone quickly. If there is an issue, well, we would have to call the cultural office and the public order office and whatever, and it would go back and forth... it is too complicated. During the preparation phase, we meet about three times in a big circle where the city is also represented... someone from the marketing bureau, there's someone there from the newspaper. We meet in advance and talk about everything.

Support and responsibility are exchanged between the council, the community association, and organisers of individual events; the association has effectively been deputised to perform council administrative responsibilities. For example, when someone proposes to hold an event on the beach:

> We talk (to the applicant) about the conditions so that they are actually responsible for this themselves... They have to tidy up... We have the key for the electricity... We pass the program on to the city so that they know what takes place... The *Ordnungsamt* (Public Order Office) trust us with this. They told us that they don't want to take care of every individual event. The basic conditions are set: (closure) at 11pm at the latest... alcohol sales are limited. We talk to them about this and it works very well... We take care of everything.

The Vaihingen association has close relationships with local businesses and other companies who run promotional events on the beach, 'But the condition is that it's public, nothing exclusive where one has to pay an admission fee... it has to be something where everybody can participate easily'.

Across the various city beach cases, the expansion of social participation differs in both scope and form. The non-profit beaches in Esslingen and Vaihingen illustrate community organisations and residents actively advocating and producing such public spaces for children. A small community beach project in the town of Kevelaer, population 28,000, was coordinated by local government and targeted at enhancing social space for children and youth. In the town of Schwedt, population 36,000, the idea of a city beach motivated the town's youth to create the beach for themselves. These are community spaces that emphasise that children and teenagers are part of the general public. This includes young people having opportunities as actors (negotiators, builders, musicians and acrobats), and not just consumers of an adult-determined environment. Berlin's YAAM has a broader agenda, also promoting and celebrating the social integration of minorities and the unemployed into urban beach culture. The Esslingen, Vaihingen and YAAM beaches are elements within wider projects seeking to enhance the general social prospects for their target demographics. Thus these beaches also provide their public with mentoring, training, work and creative, expressive and commercial opportunities. The focus of these small cities' community-run beaches on bringing people together is underscored by their choice of very central locations, in pedestrian shopping areas, and in Esslingen's case, near the train station. This contrasts with the artist projects' more edgy, didactic and aesthetically dramatic focus on abandoned, often ex-industrial waterfronts.

Weimar's beach illustrates well the entrepreneurial and improvisatory contributions that artists can make to re-imagining urban space and its use. Although Weimar is small, 'there are so many creative people in such a small place', so they can achieve a lot. Resources were limited: the gallery notes, 'we had to produce something out of nothing'. For rain protection, sailcloth roofs were sewn by a local artist, held up by large trees taken with permission from the surrounding forest. Chairs were cut from other tree trunks with a chainsaw, and a cluster of white umbrellas was used as a projection screen. In addition to material transformation, as 'culturepreneurs' (Lange 2011), the artists and their temporary performance of a beach also helped the council to change local residents' and tourists' thinking about the uses of Weimar's open spaces:

> Because of (Weimar's history and image of) high culture... there used to be a law... forbidding picnics or playing football in the city's waterfront park. So it was something special that there was suddenly a site where such things were allowed.... It is the city's long-term aim to turn the Ilm embankment into a recreational area. The beach was a very welcome pioneering project to make people more aware... that there are no buildings there anymore... Something to let people know what would come.

Temporary Use

These 'non-profit' city beaches were mostly intended as short-term, one-off events, partly because of limited, uncertain funding and permissions. But the two main purposes of these beaches are for their creators "to try it out" (Esslingen), thereby developing knowledge and skills in making and managing places, and to change citizens' and governments' use and thinking about urban space and their interactions within it, by offering a very novel spatial experience. These aims of learning and re-enchantment seem to be well served by the projects' transience. Vaihingen's beach's timeframe is constrained to seven weeks between the city's summer and autumn festivals, reinforcing the fact that the beach itself is more like an event than a fixed physical change.

The beaches' temporariness conditions the attitudes of both their supporters and their opponents. The temporariness makes potential objectors more tolerant of noise and other disruptions. However, the intentionally unconventional, contested sites and functions of Kulturstrand made it unlikely it would endure, at least not on one fixed site. The longstanding Kulturstrand project maintains a certain novelty for the public, because it gets reinstalled each summer, and has been reconfigured on several sites. Its rotation among several sites extends the historical precedent of itinerant markets and circuses, as a social setting which is assembled and lived, rather than fixed to place. Vaihingen is the only truly citizen-run beach that has been installed for more than two summers. Vaihingen's organisers had felt their beach's biennial infrequency helps to maintain the enthusiasm of the organisers and users, that 'maybe the idea wouldn't be so new anymore if one did it every year'.

But temporariness is not necessarily the unanimous preference of city beaches' organisers, patrons and host cities. Vaihingen's Strandleben was only planned to happen once, but found new promoters. Esslingen's beach wanted to continue operating, but had to wait until 2012 to find a new location. Organisers wish to make Schwedt's beach permanent, but lack a suitable site. Weimar's beach might have continued longer, but they were required to expend their grant within two months, and six months later nothing remained on site. Some necessary expenditures, including electricity connection, were much higher than a temporary use could realistically afford. Those who have installed city beaches more than once recognise that because many inputs are donated, and sand once spread is difficult to re-gather, it can actually be more expensive to remove a beach than install it. Nevertheless, these operators have developed a distinctive set of skills in sourcing, installing and demounting the various elements of these whimsical landscapes. Esslingen's beach organisers report, 'it takes us about a week to set it up, including the sand dumping, distributing the sand, having the containers delivered, equipping the containers... The disassembly is a bit faster. About half a week." In Vaihingen, the city council staff with their heavy equipment can now assemble their beach in half a day.

Sandpits and Players

In keeping with the spatial and operational constraints implied by the sandpit metaphor, city beaches organised by public and non-profit actors typically arise in small cities. The four big-city beaches in Munich and Berlin were all driven by artists and intellectuals. The five other non-profit cases all arose in cities with populations between 30,000 and 90,000. Commercial city beaches, in contrast, are predominantly located in Germany's larger cities. In small cities, the economics of commercial gastronomy seem to rarely support lavish speculative ventures. Local governments in three small cities resorted to actively courting private-sector beach operators. Cities of 30,000 to 90,000 are big enough for substantial citizen initiatives to develop, yet small enough that such initiatives have personal contacts and influence with the city administration. Small-city beaches have a distinctive advantage that they often obtain very central locations, sometimes even the main city square, because their non-profit organisers are more likely to have the support of local councils and civic associations. Such sites encourage broad, informal citizen engagement.

Interviews with community-based organisers in these smaller cities emphasise the open communication, engagement, and trust that exist there between local government, other actors and the general public, which helped make their beaches possible:

> What I think is very important is a good cooperation with the respective authorities and the city administration. For the most part we already had this, but *in certain respects it has improved because of this event*. I am not just talking about the city administration, but also various institutions that are involved. I think it is important to distribute this on as many shoulders as possible. In this way, one achieves a broad acceptance. The more people are involved, the more the project is accepted. (Esslingen, emphasis added)
>
> What was good was that a lot of people were involved. Either in the planning process or simply by making them think about whether they want it…and if yes, what can I do for this? We have flyers 'What can I do for the Vaihingen beach?' There's donations and accepting cleaning shifts and organizing events, etcetera. We told them that if they want to have it, they will have to become active and do certain things… I think the good thing is that the people of Vaihingen consider this to be their beach… I think that this is the secret to success. No one simply set it up. One had to fight for it and one had to do something for this beach every day. They identify with this beach. (Vaihingen)

The grassroots beaches demonstrate the importance of a range of pre-existing, robust, small-scale non-profit organisations that could manage the projects and negotiate responsibilities with the respective city councils and other actors: Esslingen's *Stadtjugendring* (a network of city youth agencies), Schwedt's local youth club, Vaihingen's inner-city residents association, the diocese responsible for Kevelaer, and for YAAM, the non-profit association 'Kult'. The organisers of Vaihingen's Strandleben emphasised the pervasiveness of such social infrastructure as a resource for grassroots placemaking: 'The association *Vaihinger Aktion Innenstadt* is a totally normal German… non-profit association… according to statistics every German is a member of three associations on average. I would say that's typically German'. The variety of community sector organisations leading these projects highlights that there is not one set model structure for how such initiatives develop and how the various costs and responsibilities for assembling, operating and maintaining a community-oriented city beach will be met. For example, to cover the risks of such an experiment, Esslingen's *Stadtjugendring* was able to take out insurance that covers youth work events. In Vaihingen, the beach's liabilities are covered by the council, and that is why they also do the construction work. In Weimar, the gallery had to take out liability insurance. In all cases, it is clear that small, single-purpose community organisations cannot easily carry out such urban development projects entirely on their own.

Weimar's was the only small-city beach driven by a close group of artists rather than a wider community organisation. For Galerie Eigenheim, the beach project was 'the start of the relationship' with local authorities, one that developed significantly as the two groups negotiated their respective objectives. The city provided them a site for free, helped them meet construction regulations, and licensed their events. Nevertheless, in contrast to the community organisations, Galerie Eigenheim emphasise their avant-garde stance in relation to the government: 'to confront the authorities… I think this is something that one experiences as an artist in general'. In all five beach projects instigated by artists, including Vaihingen's, the artists' vanguard role is not in form-making, but in engage strategically and creatively with existing funding and regulatory processes to address a perceived lack in the quality and variety of local public spaces and their social potential, and to enliven underused sites that the authorities had not necessarily conceived of as public and worthy (in Kulturstrand's case, for six separate sites). These projects are conscious, performative critiques of local government bureaucracy, and this they share with several of their community-driven cousins. Badeschiff illustrates the substantial shortfall of public amenity in the former East Berlin, being located in a de-industrialised area where the Spree River formed the internal border wall. Badeschiff and Weimar's IlmArkadien both use art to advance consciousness and action on improving urban water quality, by promoting public engagement with the water, although neither ultimately allowed direct river access.

Most of the beach-creating artists had limited prior expertise in public approvals processes, landscape design, construction, or event management. Through these small, temporary sandpit projects, what these artists demonstrated and developed was entrepreneurship in coordinating the actions of other parties to make things happen, rather than superior aesthetic judgment and craft skill. Low budgets, bargaining over resources, sweat equity, donations, and in-kind sponsorship of goods and services are all key to bringing these beaches to life. Badeschiff and the Weimar and Vaihingen beaches managed to leverage arts funding to develop their sites, which gave the projects a measure of independence from the limits of consumer market demand. The artists also brought creativity to seemingly prosaic issues around the governance and management of open space, for example by negotiating accountabilities and carefully defining the anticipated uses of the setting.

The artistic and intellectual projects Nigihaven na der Zen in Vaihingen (2001), Badeschiff (2004) and Kulturstrand (2004) are all among the earliest city beach schemes in Germany, which affirms their avant-gardism. The citizen-initiated city beaches all started several years later, in 2009 and 2011, after the huge wave of private-sector beaches established by hospitality-sector entrepreneurs in 2006 when Germany hosted the Football World Cup. This history suggests that for these kinds of innovative public space projects, the chain of copying and adapting creativity generally leads from artists, who explore ideas with public funding, to entrepreneurs, who develop them as profitable and explore potential clientele, to residents, who pursue them for their social benefits. These different actors have all taken steps in enterprising placemaking. learning about, re-performing and hybridising a new open space type.

One should not overstate the originality of the individual artists who happened to propose the earliest German schemes. City councils had already developed artificial city beaches in France in 1996 and 2002. Furthermore, neither ideas nor enterprise develop in a vacuum; milieux for creative actions are also important (Florida 2005; Landry 2006). Artistic, cultural and intellectual creativity in city making go hand-in-hand with organisational creativity in terms of how cities are managed, particularly in terms of how the public and civil sectors foster entrepreneurship (Hall 1998; Jorg 2008). With Badeschiff and Weimar's and Vaihingen's beaches, the original impetus for spatial intervention came from larger, longstanding non-profit organisations with wider remits to enhance urban space: Berlin's *Stadtkunstprojekte* and their programme 'Constructed Connections', the *Entente Florale*, and the Stuttgart region's local government cultural initiative, 'Open Spaces: Empty, Limit, Landscape'.

As the manager of Esslingen's beach noted, getting local government and other institutions to be open and engaged in these projects is key to success and a sense of ownership. The nurturing of flexibility and commitment among diverse actors is in fact a core outcome of such projects, teaching the players to think and act differently, to cooperate and facilitate rather than just regulate (SenStadt 2007). Enterprising urban placemaking begins with open discourse. The community-initiated beaches all illustrate ongoing collaborative learning among various actors, many of them assuming new and unfamiliar roles: teenager as project manager, youth educator as tradesman, customer as cook, resident as liquor license administrator, artist as swimming pool attendant.

The openness, escapism and whimsy of these artificial beach landscapes have parallels in the relaxed, flexible, exploratory means that have been used to achieve them. Even for commercial operators, city beaches seem to often offer a way to 'drop out' of the pressures and strictures of the hospitality industry, to be their own boss and create an atmospheric space in their own way, at their own pace, with their own hands; and to be able to personally enjoy both the process and the outcome. Such casual milieux also suit artists exploring governments' regulatory regimes and civic actors with limited experience and resources. City beaches show that novel urban spaces can be spectacular without being alienating. Perhaps they even suggest a modest contemporary re-enchantment of the rich varieties of citizen engagement that were imagined into existence in a diversity of loose, communal environments in the 1960s and 1970s (Sadler 1998), when citizens first discovered the beach under the pavement.

References

Angst, M., Klaus, P., Michaelis, T., Müller, R. and Wolff, R. (2009) *Zone*Imaginaire: Zwischennutzungen in Industriearealen*, Zürich: Vdf Hochschulverlag.
Bishop, P. and Williams, L. (2012) *The Temporary City*, London: Routledge.
Bürgin, M. and Cabane, P. (1999) *Akupunktur für Basel: Zwischennutzung als Standortentwicklung auf dem Areal des DB-Güterbahnhofs in Basel*, available from http://www.areal.org/areal_alt/download/zn_mb.pdf, accessed 11 April 2012.

Florida, R. (2005) *Cities and the Creative Class*, New York: Routledge.
Gale, T. (2010) 'Urban Beaches as Social Tourism Installations: Case studies of Paris Plage and Bristol Urban Beach', in S. Cole and N. Morgan (eds) *Tourism and Inequality: Problems and Prospects*, Wallingford: CABI Publishing, pp. 183–193.
Hall, P. (1998) *Cities in Civilization: Culture, Technology and Urban Order*, London: Weidenfeld and Nicolson.
Hesping, C. (2006) 'Stadt-Strand statt Strand: Naherholung an der Spree', available from http://www.friedrichshainer-chronik.de/spip.php?article32, accessed 27 July 2012.
IlmArkadien (2009) 'Einladung', *Ilm-Zeitung, March*, 1.
Jorg, J. (2008) *Make Use: A comparison between temporary-use strategies of intermediary organizations with the goal of using vacant buildings as workplaces for social and creative entrepreneurs*, unpublished masters thesis, POLIS MA in European Urban Cultures, Amsterdam/Brussels.
Kruse, S. and Steglich, A. (2006) *Temporäre Nutzungen: Stadtgestalt Zwischen Selbstorganisation und Steuerung*, Fakultät III – Umwelt und Technik: Universität Lüneburg.
La Pradelle, M. and Lallement, E. (2004) 'Paris Plage: 'The city is ours'', *The ANNALS of the America Academy of Political and Social Science*, 595(1), pp. 134–145.
Landry, C. (2006) *The Art of City Making*, New York: Routledge.
Lange, B. (2011) 'Professionalization in space: Social-spatial strategies of culturepreneurs in Berlin', *Entrepreneurship and Regional Development: An International Journal*, 23(3-4), pp. 259–279.
Oswalt, P., Overmeyer, K. and Misselwitz, P. (2013) *Urban Catalyst: The Power of Temporary Use*, Berlin: DOM publishers.
Phipps, A. (2010) 'Drawing Breath: Creative elements and their exile from higher education', *Arts and Humanities in Higher Education*, 9(1), pp. 42–53.
Pine, J. and Gilmour, J. (1998) 'Welcome to the experience economy', *Harvard Business Review*, July/August, pp. 97–105.
Sadler, S. (1998) *The Situationist City*, Cambridge MA: MIT Press.
SenStadt = Senatsverwaltung für Stadtentwicklung Berlin (ed.) (2007) *Urban Pioneers: Temporary Use and Urban Development in Berlin*, Berlin: Jovis.
Twaroch, F. and Frank, A. (2005) 'Sandbox Geography: To Learn from Children the form of Spatial Concepts', in Fisher, P (ed.) *Developments in Spatial Data Handling: 11th International Symposium on Spatial Data Handling*, Berlin: Springer, pp. 421–433.
Wikipedia.de (2012), 'Badeschiff (Berlin)', available from http://de.wikipedia.org/wiki/Badeschiff_(Berlin), accessed 31 July 2012.
YAAM (n.d.) *YAAM (Young and African Art Market)*, available from http://www.jugendhilfeportal.de/db4/projekte/eintrag/yaam-young-and-african-art-market/, accessed 4 April 2012.

Chapter 9

A Temporary Waterfront

Prompting Public Engagement

Jacob Bjerre Mikkelsen, Quentin Stevens, Catherine Hills and Florian 'Floyd' Mueller

This chapter reports on a design research project that explores the possibilities for people to engage with water within the public spaces of contemporary waterfront projects. Building on the insights developed in earlier chapters, especially Chapter 4, the project entails attention to the materialities and affordances of the boundary conditions between land and water; a focus which is often lacking in literature on waterfront urban design (Gibson 1979, Hudson 1996). The project investigates underused and monofunctional waterfront spaces as potential sites for physical engagement and play with water (Dodson and Kilian 1998, Montag Stiftung and Regionale 2010, 2008, Lamm and Brandt 2012). As this book has shown, studying engagements with water also requires investigation of the appropriations and interactions of users of public spaces on water edges. This chapter breaks with the notion of the waterfront user as a passive observer of water, and explores opportunities for facilitating active play through bodily engagement with the water environment as a unique spatial condition. Using a small, temporary design installation as a tool to translate between idea and implementation, the study connects design scenarios with users' desires and behaviours in public spaces on waterfronts. The temporary installation provides a method for testing hypotheses about urban design, for deriving and qualifying knowledge and direct multi-sensory spatial experience that can be implemented in future waterfront projects (al-Ibrashy and Gaber 2010).

The first section of the chapter reviews recent literature on user interaction and public spaces in contemporary waterfront precincts, and relates these discussions to a specific precinct of interest, the Docklands in Melbourne, Australia. This review identifies three key research questions and a set of related aims that guide our subsequent design research intervention in the Docklands: how users of the waterfront engage with the water's surface and depth, the multiple behavioural affordances of the water, and how users might adapt waterfront public spaces after they are built. The conception, site and form of the authors' temporary waterfront installation are then described. Our analysis and evaluation of the installation's use by members of the public show that users of urban waterfronts are keen to engage actively with the water, and our intervention demonstrates some of the potentials and limitations of enabling this engagement through design.

Public Spaces for Water Engagements

Waterfront regeneration projects worldwide have transformed cities' edges into new public spaces. The water is often noted to be a crucial element for these sites that presents a space of escape from busy and congested inner cities (Fainstein 2000). This escapism is described as the experience of openness in contrast to dense city centres, providing a sense of freedom, ease and inspiration amongst waterfront users (Völker and Kistemann 2013). One critique of these newly-formed urban spaces is that design regulates and limits the complex desires of users, and directs activities towards consumption and risk-free activities in a collective 'spectacle', which stimulates the senses but pacifies the body (see Chapter 5). Furthermore, the designs of urban waterfronts do not often accommodate diversity, authenticity and democracy (Fainstein 2000). Chang and Huang (2011) argue that the planning of urban waterfront precincts follows global formulaic approaches (see also Chapter 2). Such planning is at risk of over-determining the use of public spaces. Instead, Chang and Huang suggest that allowing indeterminate spaces for spontaneity and diverse uses and users affords experimental approaches that might question existing uses and perceptions of public spaces on the waterfront. A unilateral focus on the physical aspects of the waterfront entails generic design. Instead, development must be content-oriented, through integrated strategies that continuously involve the users of the site (Sepe 2013).

Following this line of thought, this chapter explores the urban waterfront for indeterminate, under-used spaces that can be sites for temporary interventions which might uncover diverse user desires and new potentials for the future design of waterfront public spaces. The role and meaning of water and its relation to the city has shifted significantly over the past 100 years, from being a practical, material necessity for industrial activities, to much more indirect uses of water in the context of leisure. As noted in Chapter 1, Gordon (1996) defines five key criteria for successful waterfront transformation, and one of these is the importance of connecting to the water. Yet much analysis of urban waterfront regeneration focuses on how the projects are carried out, and the role that the new buildings and uses have in economic development. In this context, improved access is usually explored only in terms of access to the waterfront development, through new promenades, bridges, and river taxis, rather than to the water itself, and visitors' experience of water is expressed in terms of views and the ambiance of the built form, rather than activities that involve close contact with water (Jones 1998, Sepe 2013). It is relatively rare in the existing design literature that waterfront regeneration projects are criticised for having a vague relation to, and use of, the water, for focusing mainly on visual sensory experiences, for neglecting other sensory impressions and for preventing direct bodily engagements with water (Macarthur 1999; Rahman and Imon 2017). In their documentation of user well-being in leisure experiences of waterfronts, Völker and Kistemann (2013) stress the importance of allowing users to get as close to the water as possible. The experience of water is predominantly visual, through movements and light effects on the surface, but water also affects other senses through its smell, the sounds of waves and boats, the sensation of winds coming across water, its moderating effect on microclimate, and opportunities for paddling and swimming. Furthermore, water spaces hold significant potential as therapeutic landscapes for the well-being of urban dwellers (Foley and Kistemann 2015). However, most urban waterfront designs appear not to support active engagement with the water, and instead constrain people to a role as passive observers (see Chapters 4 and 5).

The Public Spaces of Melbourne Docklands

The Docklands precinct is a much-debated part of Melbourne. It lies directly to the west, downstream, from the Southbank precinct discussed in Chapters 1 and 5, which was developed earlier. Planning and infrastructure investments sought to develop it as a mixed residential and commercial extension of Melbourne's Central District. The planning process of Melbourne's Docklands has been criticised for a lack of public involvement, its discrete, partly privatised governance arrangements, and its generic outcomes (Dovey 2005), which conforms to the critiques of many other cities' contemporary waterfront regeneration projects (White 2016; Oakley 2014; Desfor et al. 2010; Gordon 1996). While visions of integrating water into the Docklands precinct through canals and programming were presented through plans and visualisations, these master plans were not legally binding, and construction followed loosely-defined plans largely driven by private investment (Dovey 2005). The outcome contains built spaces and functions such as shopping malls and stadiums that are only vaguely connected to the water, and privately-owned promenades. The project has failed to develop the Victoria Harbour waterfront as the centrepiece of the precinct, and has created large building plots with little accommodation of diverse places and users (Dovey 2005). Recent analyses have criticised the precinct for lacking small scale spaces, water access and engagement with water, and possibilities for users to interact with, alter and appropriate urban spaces in order to create a sense of community and place in Docklands (Gehl 2010; Douglas and Monacella 2012).

Our own first-hand analysis of the waterfront public spaces in Melbourne Docklands was based on theoretical literature, previous analyses and recent planning documents, which provided a list of key critiques. The area of study was limited to the quays and connected public spaces surrounding Victoria Harbour. A map annotated with key points of interest guided the on-site observational studies. With the prepared documents and preliminary formulated research questions, the researchers performed a walk-through analysis around the edge of Victoria Harbour, starting at the newly constructed public library and ending at the most recent developments on the harbour's opposite side. Several specific sites were revisited to undertake additional studies of user behaviour at different times of the day and under different weather conditions. The initial walk was repeated as a walk-along interview with a local researcher who had done in-depth study of the Docklands area, to further gain understandings and reflections on the area.

The design of public spaces in Docklands was explored in terms of the relation between users' desires and spatial affordances. The analyses showed that the public spaces along the quays in Docklands are appropriated in different ways, which reveal diverse understandings, readings and desires. One example is the use of the benches in the waterfront public spaces, and how these are appropriated in multiple ways, including ways they were not designed for (Whyte 1988). The following examples illustrate the complexity in the uses of these spaces. As a bench was orientated away from water, a man was observed turning around to face the water using a curb as a footrest (Figure 9.1). Another bench lacked a backrest, resulting in a couple sitting on the ground, using the bench as backrest, instead of sitting on the bench seat (Figure 9.2). Some street furnishings in Docklands comfortably afforded sleeping (Figure 9.3); others were not comfortable to sleep on but were used for this purpose anyway.

Another prevailing critique of the area is the lack of smaller, intimate and diverse spaces (Gehl 2010). The Docklands is said to lack 'fine grain' and atmosphere, being dominated by buildings with large footprints (Gehl 2010; Lynch 1981). Some small-scale enclosures exist; for example, a small-scale, intimate space on the Victoria Harbour Promenade, along the south quay of Victoria Harbour (Figure 9.4). This space is near the water and defined by columns and an overarching pergola. The enclosure provides space for self-expression in public space through people's markings on walls and benches – traces not seen in the open parts of the promenade. Hence, the enclosure creates space for private emotions to be expressed in public settings. Another relevant space was found on the Harbour Esplanade on the eastern side of Victoria Harbour (Figure 9.5). The wooden structure found here provides a space for self-expression through the privacy provided by the small enclosure. The wooden material affords writing, tagging and carving (Figure 9.6). The writings on these walls reflect social diversity, through the use of different languages, alphabets and modes of expression, as well as the content. Though this is a minor space with in the larger urban landscape, it supports social interaction in the Docklands area. It also reflects some of the critiques of the lack of social diversity of users in Docklands, and recommendations for its urban spaces to afford more human interaction, as discussed above. Several notes that people have left here express discontent with the area – the space functions as a forum for public debate in the city. The space provides a possibility for expressing feelings about the Docklands, a precinct which was also criticised for a lack of public involvement in its construction phases. This space deviates from the general critique of the area as lacking social identity and sense of place (Douglas and Monacella 2012). As discussed in Chapter 5, these kinds of spaces can also be perceived as having a potential for nurturing urban diversity in the fringes and interstices of formal urban spaces (Stevens 2007).

Jacob Bjerre Mikkelsen, Quentin Stevens, Catherine Hills and Florian 'Floyd' Mueller

Figures 9.1–9.3 Users appropriating benches in Docklands.

Figure 9.4 Intimate space on Victoria Harbour Promenade.

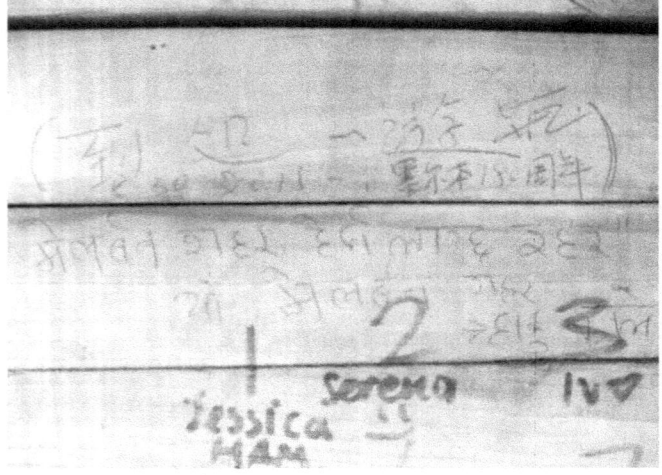

Figures 9.5 and 9.6 Wooden structure on Harbour Esplanade.

Jacob Bjerre Mikkelsen, Quentin Stevens, Catherine Hills and Florian 'Floyd' Mueller

Site Analysis of Existing Water Accessibility in Docklands

Analysis conducted through studies of maps and on-site observations revealed that the Docklands promenades are separated from the water by a series of different boundaries (Figure 9.7). Several of these boundaries are formed by berthing pontoons used for mooring sailboats. As these berthing areas are organised through private clubs, most of them are sealed off from the public, resulting in very limited public access to the water. Our count found that over eighty percent of the more than 200 berthing points in the Harbour are sealed off, only accessible with a membership card. Other boundaries are formed by pavilions placed on the edge of the promenade, blocking views and access to water, which was evident at street level along the promenade and along adjacent streets leading to the promenade. These pavilions are used by upmarket restaurants, which increase social stratification on the water edge.

The water access at Docklands is therefore delimited in various ways, even though recent planning documents for the area note that water should be an essential feature of its public space designs (Hassell Ltd. 2015, 28). Because the Docklands area has poor connections to the waterfront, Gehl (2010) has recommended designing ways of getting closer to the water and supporting a wider spectrum of water activities. This aligns to the discussion in Chapters 1 and 4 about the importance, and difficulty, of getting close to the edge on urban waterfronts, and the need for careful consideration of the nature of the edge condition. Figures 9.8–9.10 show examples of users' desires to get close to Docklands' water and study its marine life. Users sitting, lying and kneeling on the flat, hard quays and pontoons highlight that people will pursue these interests even when the physical environment is very uncomfortable and unsupportive.

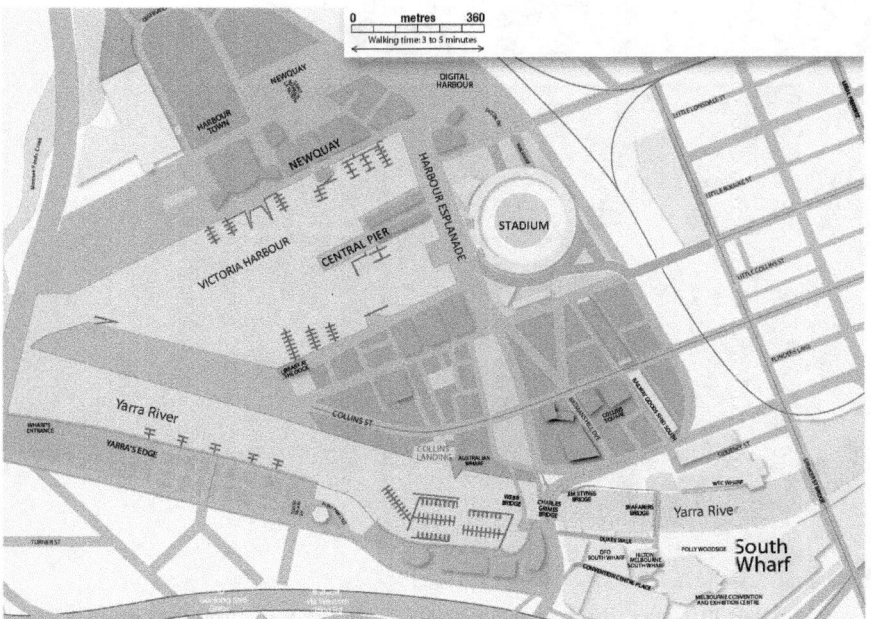

Figure 9.7 Map of Docklands.

A Temporary Waterfront

Figures 9.8–9.10 Users appropriating berth pontoons and showing interest in the harbour's marine life.

Jacob Bjerre Mikkelsen, Quentin Stevens, Catherine Hills and Florian 'Floyd' Mueller

Creating a Temporary Waterfront Installation

On the basis of the analysis of Docklands outlined above, the design phase of our research employed a temporary installation to investigate the boundaries between urban land and water. The installation process followed an action research method to investigate the Docklands area and the connections between its public spaces, users and water.

The temporary installation focuses specifically on edge materialities and the affordances these could provide for engagement with water. The aim of the installation was to investigate design potentials and user desires for water engagement in public spaces along the water edge, to inform the design of future urban spaces. This included the installation and evaluation of objects and devices on-site to test proximity and engagement with water. It also involved documentation and assessment of user experiences to improve understandings of the problems and potentials of the site and the Docklands precinct as a whole. The installation was therefore designed to produce data on how people engage or desire to engage with water, and to obtain their feedback on the installation, so as to contribute to the development of parameters and criteria for the future design of more engaging urban water spaces at various scales. While the research project's core focus was within the field of urban design, the research team also include researchers with expertise in user experience and game design research, who introduced a further range of ideas and technologies for active water engagement.

The installation had an experimental approach, to pose a set of questions instead of providing specific answers. Three research questions were investigated through the installation. The first question relates to users' desires to engage with the natural properties and biological contents of water, and the current constraints on such possibilities in the Docklands. The second question considers the multiple user desires in the area and how these can relate to water. Hence, it concerns the investigation of the affordances of water and potentials for water interaction in public spaces on the waterfront. The third question concerns the overall installation approach, and addresses the lack of public involvement and the limited possibilities for interaction n the area, as outlined in the site analysis. This question thus investigates the potential of users appropriating and adapting public spaces in the area, and the use of ephemeral installations as a methodology for testing and informing design.

Research Questions

1. How can the installation enhance experience of the water at the Docklands, as one of the city's largest natural environments? In particular, how can it enhance the waterfront precinct's vertical connection with the water's surface and the depth below it?
2. How can the installation investigate and nurture the various experiential and behavioural affordances of water?
3. How can we create adaptable public spaces that engage users in ways that allow them to inform the design of future waterfront spaces?

A Temporary Waterfront

Within our temporary installation, research question one is investigated through prototypes that let participants focus on specific elements of marine life in its natural setting, thereby enhancing experience of the nature qualities of the water. The second question is investigated through the installation of interactive play objects that operate in the water, as a tool to prompt interaction among users and between users and water. The third question is investigated through the overall installation approach, and its introduction of a range of moveable and adaptable objects. The activities of visitors in this installation were documented through users' written and drawn feedback, supplemented by participant observation and semi-structured interviews. The results are presented in relation to future design possibilities for urban waterfront precincts. The following section outlines the installation elements in detail.

The Temporary Installation

A set of small wooden crates that offered varied interactive experiences were developed and installed on a waterfront site in the Docklands for one day in May 2016 so that participants' reactions and responses could be observed and recorded. The crates were distributed across a carpet of synthetic turf, and participants were invited to interact with them. The crates were designed to prompt people to feel or do things with water and explore their own relation to water, so that the research team could learn more about their experiences of and reactions to water in urban spaces. As design research, this installation should not be considered as providing definitive answers about waterfront public space, but rather as an experimental tool to explore a set of questions. The installation used wood and a soft carpet of artificial turf to contrast with the hard concrete and steel of the existing waterfront space and to draw attention to the intervention. The use of wood was inspired by our observations about user behaviour in the existing waterfront wooden structure outlined in the site analysis above. The introduction of artificial turf responded to our observation of users' desires to sit and lie down on the mostly-concrete surfaces in Docklands; a softer material was therefore investigated to explore ways of accommodating these desires. Figure 9.11 provides an overview of the developed prototypes and devices employed in the installation. The different parts of the installation were all developed from the discussions of theory, critiques and analyses above and the three key research questions derived from these insights. Extended reflections on the relation between our site analysis, research questions and the various physical elements of the installation are provided at the end of the chapter. The installation consisted of the following elements:

- A 'water telescope' and a 'water periscope', enabling visitors to see marine life under the water surface, related to research question one.
- A water robot remotely controlled by a waterproofed tablet computer floating in a crate filled with water, related to research question two. The water robot could be manoeuvred through a custom-made track floating on the water.
- A miniature diorama of the waterfront installation made from interlocking plastic bricks, enabling visitors to alter the design of the waterfront, related to research question three.
- A feedback crate for collecting feedback on the installation through survey sheets and drawings on the sides of the crate.

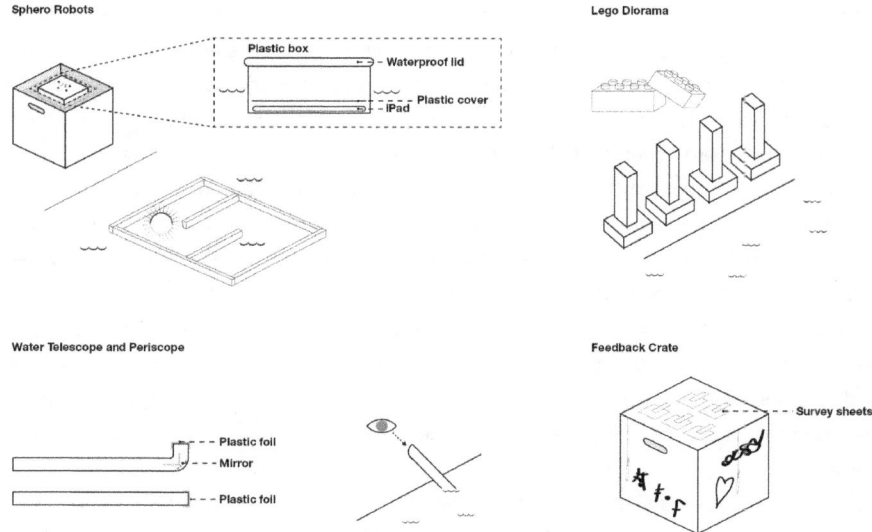

Figure 9.11 Diagrammatic overview of installation elements.

The Use of Interactive Robot Play Objects

The interactive play objects used in the installation were two water-resistant self-propelled 'Sphero' robots. These spherical robots were given removable, colourful, rubbery silicon covers that looked like jellyfish or sea urchins. The covers had textured surfaces that allowed the robots to gain traction in the water when movement was invoked by a controller, giving them a fish-like locomotion. The robots were remotely controlled through an application on a touchscreen tablet computer. The tablets were sealed inside plastic boxes to make them water resistant. The tablet application allowed participants to control the robots' direction and velocity remotely from the harbour pier, by tilting the tablet to engage the tablet's built-in accelerometer. The robots were immersed in water where the participants could see them, either in the water next to the pier or in one of the installation's crates. The intention was to enable participants to touch the robot in the crate and play with it, and to experience the tactility of the object in the water, which appeared to be a kind of artificial sea creature. Additionally, an interactive game was framed by the placement of the water robots within a winding course that was marked out by a tethered timber frame floating on the harbour surface adjacent to the installation.

The Selected Site

We selected the site for our installation (Figures 9.12 and 9.13) for the following reasons. We wanted low-level access to the water in order to maximise possibilities for water engagement and test interactive play with water objects. Therefore, the site needed to be on a publicly-accessible mooring berth, as the wharves at other locations within this tidal harbour are more than two metres above the water. Only two sites met this key criterion. Secondly, the site should provide space for the investigation to unfold with minimal impact on other uses. Thirdly, the site needed to be connected to a significant flow of people to engage potential participants. We therefore selected one of the few accessible berth pontoons. Our previous studies of this area showed that empty berths hold potential for other uses beyond merely mooring boats (see Figures 9.8–9.10). In these studies, users were observed to have a clear interest in what is under the water surface, and through their actions they were testing multiple affordances of the berthing site. This site represented a rare opportunity in Docklands for getting close to the water, and for rethinking a space that was designed merely as a transit zone between the waterfront promenade and boat transport. But, as our observations showed, the site is already used for activities other than boarding and unboarding. It was therefore interesting to explore the berth as something more than a transit zone, where one moors a boat and walks straight up onto the promenade. This also presents a challenge, as it could take more than one day for people to imagine the berth as a place for a range of other activities.

The selected site for the installation was challenging in terms of accessibility and visibility. Key problems with the design of the berthing area and the adjacent waterfront related to how people approach it along a convoluted zig-zag of stairs and ramps, and the positioning of restaurants and cafés blocking visual and pedestrian connections from the promenade down to the water. Another consideration was the amount of water movement, which affected the ease of controlling the water robots in the harbour as part of the installation. The range of activities and visual stimulations available on the Harbour's upper promenade also prevent people from seeking out the empty berths or the water. These challenges of the site reflected the broader issues identified with water access within the Docklands.

The specific site chosen on the berth pontoon was approximately 3 meters wide and 5 meters long, has water on three sides, and is visible from several points along the Harbour's main pedestrian promenade. The site was suitable for the installation because it is close to water, the pontoons enclose a small basin for the robots and other interactive objects to be placed in, and the pontoon's anchoring poles and framing are inhabited by easily-visible marine life. We also note that the installation could not impede the main function of the berth, namely allowing people to move freely between the promenade and the moored boats.

Recruiting Participants

In total 43 individuals visited the installation between 11.30 am and 4:30 pm on a Sunday in late Autumn, in 10 groups. This sample appeared to represent common users of the promenade in terms of age and gender, with a majority being families with young children. The participants included 17 children between the ages of 1 and 6 years and 17 adults in the range of 30 to 40 years. Other groups included young adults (2 couples and one individual aged 20–30 years) and elderly people (4 individuals aged 70–80 years). The fact that only small groups visited allowed the researchers optimal opportunities to engage in conversation with participants. It also allowed participants to spend more time at the site, because there was not a line of people waiting to access it. The fact that there were pauses between visits also allowed the research team time to reset the

Figures 9.12 and 9.13 The site at the end of the west berth pontoon on New Quay, Docklands.

installation and discuss what was learned from the previous visit. For example, technical problems with the water robot were resolved during these off-times.

Most participants came down to get close to the water without solicitation, and therefore it was easy to engage them in the installation, as they already had interest in the water. Some participants also came down while the research team was setting up the installation, and some noted that they had seen the installation being constructed earlier in the day and became curious and wanted to explore it. Hence, the act of setting up the installation generated attention and curiosity among potential participants. Participants were particularly attracted by the opportunities for play offered by the installation, including the use of the water robots, the ability to look under the sea with a mirror and pipe construction and the population of jellyfish in the adjacent water.

The role of the construction phase in raising public attention confirms findings from an earlier temporary intervention project in Melbourne's Docklands by Douglas and Monacella (2012). On several occasions our researchers went up to the adjacent harbour promenade to promote the installation, in order to recruit additional participants. This was regarded by some potential participants on the promenade as a marketing activity, despite the researchers explaining that this was a research study. Additionally, the researchers were not able to easily point to the installation from the promenade, as the installation was obscured by buildings from the part of the promenade closest to the berth. Recruitment of participants was positively affected by a coincidental birthday party in the adjacent restaurant. The birthday party was attended by families with children, and as the research site was visible from the room where the party occurred, children at the party became curious, and many participants came from this source, which assisted the researchers with snowball recruiting of further participants. The party room was separated from the water by glazing, walls and level changes, and the installation therefore provided the children with a focus point, an attraction on the waterfront that presented a space in contact with water.

Data Collection Methods

Data was collected through photographing, video recording and audio recording of participants, written and drawn comments produced by participants on provided paper sheets, and written and drawn observations by the researchers. A video camera recorded the participants for the duration of the project. This was done to document situations unfolding over a longer time span, to document which crates were used most, and to document changes to the installation throughout the day, for example when participants moved crates to create seating arrangements. Semi-structured interviews were conducted during and after the participants' visits to the installation. The questions elaborated on the key research questions above. The first research question, concerning the water as a natural environment, was transformed into the prompting question: *'Did you learn anything new about the urban water as a natural environment in Melbourne?'* The second question on the affordances of water generated the prompting question *'Did the installation reveal potentials of water and diverse uses of the water that you didn't know about and hadn't thought about before?'* The third research question on adaptable spaces was transformed into the question: *'Did you change the setting of the installation, for example by moving the crates?'* Additionally, the participants were prompted with several sub-questions about preferences and wishes regarding the design of waterfront public spaces. The interviews also explored the positive and negative aspects of living in Melbourne Docklands, as well as asking participants about their preferences by describing their favourite waterfront urban spaces elsewhere in the world, and what specific qualities those spaces have.

A feedback crate was placed at the entry/exit point of the site, near an existing bridge that connects the pontoon to the pedestrian waterfront promenade on land. This crate was designed as a combination of a mailbox and a drawing board. Participants could write or draw their impressions either on the side of the crate or on paper sheets to be put inside the crate. These sheets contained simple printed questions based on the research questions above, accompanied by a picture of one of the crates, to evoke responses to the installation:

- Water Telescopes and Periscopes: what did you see and did you learn something new? *(Research Question 1)*
- Water Robots: what was your experience of playing with water and the robots? *(Research Question 2)*
- Plastic Brick Diorama: did you change the diorama? What did you do and why? *(Research Question 3a)*
- Did the installation make you aware of your preferences for the design of public spaces in Docklands? *(Research Question 3b)*

The participants remained anonymous, but were asked to provide their gender, age and residential postcode on the sheet.

Observing Public Engagement with the Installation

The following analysis of the installation is organised according to the three research questions outlined above. It draws together the various data obtained to formulate themes for conceptualising water engagements on urban waterfronts.

Scoping Underwater Environments

The first research question, about how vertical connections can enhance people's experience of the water as one of the largest natural environments in the city, was investigated through the installation's location on a low pontoon and through the water telescopes and periscopes (Figures 9.14 and 9.15). These devices were mainly used around an anchoring pole on the site, as researchers encouraged participants to look at the poles to investigate the marine life around them. Several participants also found interest in the numerous jellyfish swimming freely in the shallows of the water, though these were harder to observe through the telescope because of distance. One practice often observed was an adult locating an animal or plant with the telescope and then letting a child look while the adult held the telescope still. Other participants simply held the telescope while their children used it to freely look around. Some children also ventured by themselves along the edge of the pontoon. This indicated their studies of the underwater environment, which on several occasions resulted in the discovery of something exciting. One boy who was looking for an extended period suddenly made a discovery, causing him to jump and yell: 'I saw a jellyfish! I saw a jellyfish!'. Another boy had a similar reaction after seeing a fish. These outbursts would draw the attention of other participants, and on several occasions they gathered around the discovered creatures, forming small groups with shared interests in what was under the surface. The participants would crouch on the pontoon or even lie prone to get a closer look. One boy was also observed borrowing from the installation the fishing net intended for retrieving the water robots and trying to catch the living animals he was observing, thereby appropriating the provided equipment to interact further with

A Temporary Waterfront

the water environment. Interviews with the participants revealed their desires to get closer to the water and to explore the marine life of the harbour. One man reflected on his diving experiences elsewhere, and how these kinds of experiences could be brought into the urban space and make the underwater 'world' visible:

> 'I just want to look down and see how it looks, because I have been to Cairns [in tropical northern Australia], where I did a scuba dive and saw a different world altogether. You can see the mullets, different fish and plants – it's a different world altogether. Above the surface we can't see that...' (Man, 30 years old, living in Docklands for 4 years)

The water telescopes made participants aware of the water as a natural environment in the city, and gave them a tool for investigating and further examining a variety of plants and

Figures 9.14 and 9.15 Participants using water telescopes and periscopes alone and in groups.

animals in the water. The installation provided some printed learning material on the different animals that could be seen in Melbourne's aquatic environments, so that visitors could compare what they saw to what was on the provided material to enhance their learning about marine life, biology and nature. This part of the installation also engendered interaction among visitors, and some level of competition to find animals and plants. Furthermore, participants who did not use the telescopes still tried to look down and observe the marine life with the naked eye. Thus the telescopes seem to have brought more attention to the water in general, and evoked discussions and interaction between participants about water as a natural resource and its characteristic marine life. The installation indicated the broad potential for making what is under the surface more visible and more engaging.

The water telescopes and periscopes seem to have 'scoped' certain aspects of the underwater environment, and enabled users to focus and more closely study specific kinds of marine life in their natural setting. In this way, the devices augmented the edge of the waterfront and enhanced visibility and proximity between users and the water environment, helping to reveal it as a place rich with distinctive contents and qualities. Together with the learning materials on marine life, this generated in-depth understandings about the underwater environments that exist adjacent to waterfront urban developments.

Prompting Surface Interaction

The second research question, on the affordances and multiple uses of water, was mainly investigated through the introduction of water-based robots as a playful mediator between users and water. The game setup, based on two 'Sphero' robots with jellyfish-like silicon covers, involved participants remotely steering the robots through a marked course that we had set out on the water surface next to the berth (Figures 9.16 and 9.17). This challenge was undertaken by the first group of visitors, a father and his 5-year-old son. Firstly, they were invited to touch the water robot and get a sense of its soft 'skin'. After they initially tested the water robot in the water crate by tilting a tablet controller held directly in their hands, the tablet device was packed inside a watertight box and placed on the water surface inside the water crate. The screen of the tablet device was covered over so that the users would focus on moving the box by touch and observing the water robot, which was then placed in the winding course floating on the harbour surface. The tablet control box was mainly operated by the father, because the child initially found it difficult to control. At first the father kept the box on the water surface inside the crate full of water, but as the box required a lot of tilting to move the water robot, he eventually lifted the box above the surface to get a better grip. This disrupted the research aim of using the remote control game to bring participants into direct bodily contact with water. The configuration of this installation could probably be improved through further studies of the sensitivity settings for the control tablet, so that less tilting is required to move the water robot. Several other participants also operated the water robot with the tablet box in their hands instead of in the water crate. One man was observed moving his entire upper body to tilt the tablet in the right direction. His determination to make the water robot move in the right direction seemed to make him unaware of his extreme bodily movements, which were not actually necessary to tilt the tablet. By setting his entire body in motion, the participant also showed his intense engagement with the game.

A Temporary Waterfront

Practice was necessary to steer the water robot through the course, and it would usually take participants several tilts to each side and several unintended detours before they developed adequate control of the water robot. After they had gained control, they generally showed more satisfaction and enjoyment in the experience. One participant reacted by shouting 'Woo-hoo, go for it!' as he figured out how to make the water robot move in the right direction.

The research team experienced numerous technical issues with the water robot, including signals from other devices on the harbour interfering with the connection

Figures 9.16 and 9.17 The water robot in its custom-built course. To the right of Figure 9.17, a young man is controlling the water robot through a floating box with a tablet controller inside, which he cannot see.

to the tablet and the robot's very short battery life. However, during the periods of dysfunction and recharging, participants were still observed having a range of interactions with the non-active water robot, as well as engaging with the removed jellyfish 'skin' of the robot while it was out of the water being recharged (Figure 9.18). The water robot could be interacted with in water within the safe and confined environment of the water crates, which seemed to ease parents' protective concerns for their children's safety. The water robot helped draw participants' attention to the water, and it triggered immediate curiosity and a desire for engagement from participants, especially children. The important role of this animated object was evident where users would only interact with the water crate with a water robot in it, and not with a crate that only contained water. The water robot evoked curiosity and facilitated water engagement. Rather than visitors just putting their hand in the water, the water robot object enabled enhanced experiences of water, where the sensation of water on skin was an inherent part.

The animal-like appearance and tactility of the water robot skin, when removed from the Sphero during charging, seemed to enhance its attractiveness for play. It appeared to be frightening to some participants, who thought it was a real animal. Before operating the water robot, participants were invited to hold it in their hand. The water robot vibrates when it is switched on, which makes it livelier. Explorations of the water robot gathered several participants around the water crates at the same time. Several participants lifted the water robot by one of its 'tentacles' to test their elasticity. One boy was observed approaching the water robot in a crate three times and touching it briefly, getting his hand wet in the process. With help from one of the researchers, he then dared to pick it up to investigate it further. On other occasions, children played with one water robot in each crate and discussed with each other how the robot felt. The characteristics of the water environment inside the crate were also explored through the water robot. One boy was observed taking the water robot skin out of the water and

Figure 9.18 Child interacting with water robot skin in water crate.

throwing it back in to make the water splash. One girl squeezed water out of the water robot skin, and when asked how it felt, she replied 'Squishy!'.

The water robots, as tangible objects immersed in water, were observed to have prompted a range of both direct and indirect interactions with the water's surface and substance. These objects presented tactile and 'animal'-like qualities and appeal, which sparked curiosity and prompted participants to further investigate both the robots and the water they moved through. The water robots' mobility facilitated new types of interactions between the participants and the water. The water robots were 'in-between' objects, in between the live fish and jellyfish that participants could observe using the periscope (but could not touch) and the inanimate physical objects sitting on the berth, such as the crates. The water robots were 'alive' in the water, yet were controllable to some extent and could also be touched by the participants. In essence, the water robots facilitated vicarious contact with water and presented new ways of exploring the water's various properties. This activity evoked emotions and thereby overcame visitors' indifference about water. These emotional responses to the design installation raise challenges and opportunities to conventional urban design solutions which are typically static and leave visitors passive, and where water is kept at a distance.

Unfolding Waterfront Multiplicities

The third research question, regarding appropriable and adaptable spaces on waterfronts, was investigated through several elements of the installation. The manipulable diorama model of the installation made from plastic bricks was part of this investigation, although it was a less prominent element and was not emphasised in the introduction that researchers gave to participants. Several participants were observed interacting with the diorama and sitting on the artificial turf next to it (Figure 9.19), but they did not seem to be aware of the research intention that they should use these materials

Figure 9.19 Children using the plastic brick diorama.

to imagine alterations to the design of the waterfront. The diorama did however provide a space for free, unchoreographed playful activities on the site. This was facilitated by the simple expression of the diorama and the provided box of loose plastic bricks. Participants were observed building from their own imagination, without any introduction or guidance from researchers, and forming informal groups around the practice of building with plastic bricks – an unusual activity in a waterfront context.

Another broader way to explore this question was through the open invitation for visitors to interact with any part of the installation. This proved to be hard to realise under the practical circumstances on the day of the installation. Each different part of the installation required its own introduction, and therefore the researchers had to direct participants to one specific part of the installation at a time. Larger groups were easier to divide, especially in the case of one group, which became increasingly familiar with the installation and was then observed taking the water telescope to the eastern edge of the site and searching in the water by themselves. Another larger group showed similar behaviour: two parts of the group were occupied with the water robots and with the water telescopes, and a third part wandered through the installation on their own. One girl lost interest in the water robot and started playing with the plastic brick diorama, and another boy periodically joined her.

The artificial turf laid onto the surface of the pontoon was another element that seems to have afforded playful uses. Several children were observed sitting on the turf and playing with the plastic brick diorama. A boy ran towards the diorama and slid on his knees to reach it – an act that would have been very painful on the bare concrete surface of the pontoon. Other practices include kneeling or lying on the turf to see into the water, both with and without the water telescope (Figure 9.20). This practice is also possible on concrete, but is more pleasant on a soft artificial turf. The several un-programmed crates provided as informal, moveable seating were also rearranged by participants to support their activities – for example by placing them in front of the water robot for a more comfortable interaction.

Figure 9.20 Installation overview.

A Temporary Waterfront

The feedback crate was a key element for documenting the participants' activities; it was mainly used by children, serving as a small drawing table for them to gather around (Figure 9.21). The returned survey sheets mainly consisted of drawings on blank sheets depicting animals that the children had discovered (mostly jellyfish). The research team observed that the serendipitous presence of jellyfish around the installation elicited expressions of fascination and joy from many participants. Some feedback concerned the water robots and the experience of playing with them. A mother stated her interest in using the water telescope to observe and study sea creatures up close. The prototype provided her with close contact to the marine life, and made her aware of her own interest in life under the water's surface. One father commented on the intuitiveness of the water robot game; another commented on the innovativeness of presenting a participatory game in this waterfront context.

The researchers had not predicted the observed activity of participants drawing directly onto the side of the feedback crate. This crate was presented as a table where survey sheets could be filled out on top when sitting or crouching. If participants have been able to spend more time at the site, we imagine that more participants might have

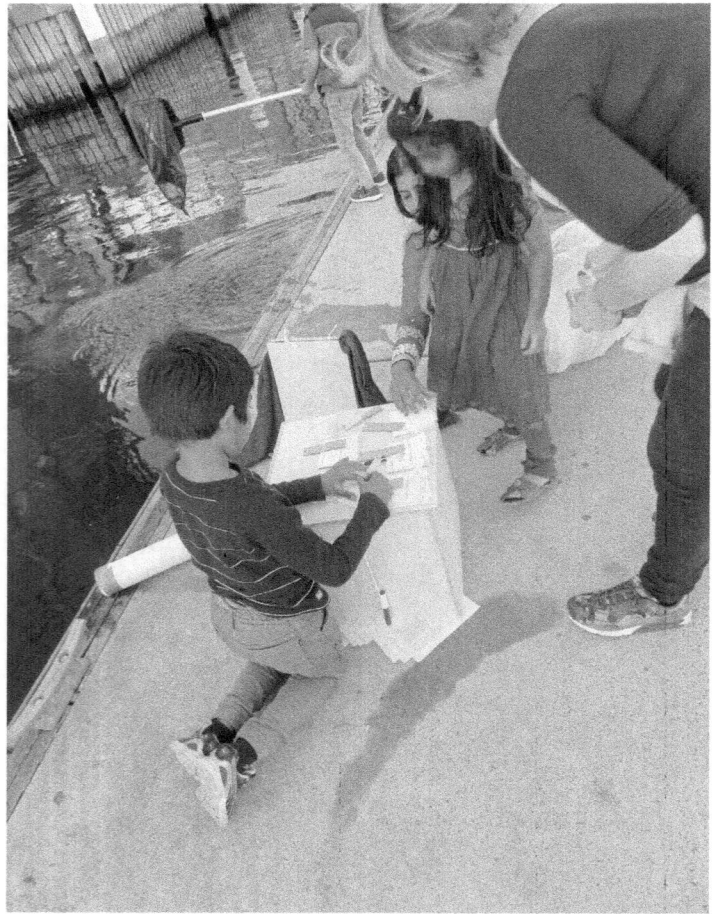

Figure 9.21 Children gather around feedback crate to draw.

been aware of opportunities for drawing on the box itself, as we had observed in site analysis of the larger existing wooden enclosure on the other side of the harbour.

Future Design Perspectives for Urban Waterfronts

This design installation at the Melbourne Docklands employed a variety of physical elements, devices, and opportunities for action to investigate the potential enrichment of the interactions between open space users and water, in relation to three key themes.

Firstly, the water telescopes and periscopes expanded the visual scope of users' engagement with the water's edge. They allowed participants to 'scope out' marine life, revealing what is under the reflective surface through a range of investigative and interactive practices. These devices broke through the boundary that conventional urban design often establishes between urban waterfront visitors and water, and investigated closer proximities between them. These small prototype devices revealed users' desires to investigate marine life. Such ideas could be translated and tested in the design of larger constructions, for example the kinds of semi-submerged, glass-walled spaces that are generally only used in paid-entry aquarium and zoo exhibits.

Secondly, the water robot objects prompted interaction with the water's surface, evoking both curiosity and emotional responses. They enable an indirect, vicarious form of sensory contact between users and this natural element, thereby affording opportunities to explore water's properties of texture, depth and motion. In this study, placing curious objects into water, both motorised and floating, prompted users to get their hands wet. This too might be translated into other, larger interventions. The robots overcame people's typical indifference to, and lack of contact with, water as a material, and challenged the constraints of conventional, distancing urban design solutions. Further waterfront design research could probe full-body immersions that position visitors even further down, closer to, and more richly immersed in the element of water.

Thirdly, the varied materials and forms of the installation 'unfolded' the potential multiplicities of the waterfront, and of users' desires, by providing a wide range of surfaces and objects that offered multiple options for appropriation and adaptation. Through interviews and surveys conducted within this setting, and participants' use and reorganisation of the various devices, the design installation provided space for users to perform and express their opinions and feelings about the presented experiences and ideas, and about waterfront design in general, as a means to inform future urban design solutions. In this way, the installation showed the potential of engaging and involving the public on-site with the materials at hand, instead of constraining them to reviewing abstract planning documents in a location far removed from the actual spatial context.

In these three ways, this study contributes methodologically to how urban design practice and research might translate between ideas and concepts and their implementation in built form. Drawings and other visualisations present hypotheses about urban life and user engagements in public space that typically have to be accepted or rejected at face value. Engaging users in temporary installations that physically manifest these ideas can test their potentials and their probability of success. While the duration and number of participants in this study was limited, the intervention discussed here demonstrated that ways of engaging users with water can be quickly and cheaply trialled in the context of an existing waterfront space. The project confirms other recent research (Bishop and Williams 2012; Hou 2010) indicating that such installations can yield useful insights into design concepts and user desires that can inform future large-scale urban design projects, and their implementation processes.

References

al-Ibrashy, M. and Gaber, T. (2010) 'Design with the Senses and for the Senses: An alternative teaching model for design studio', *Archnet-IJAR: International Journal of Architectural Research*, 4 (2-3), pp. 359–75.
Bishop, P. and Williams, L. (2012) *The Temporary City*, London: Routledge.
Chang, T. C. and Huang, S. (2011) 'Reclaiming the city: Waterfront development in Singapore', *Urban Studies*, 48 (10), pp. 2085–2100.
Desfor, G., Laidley, J., Stevens, Q. and Schubert, D. (eds) (2010) *Transforming Urban Waterfronts: Fixity and Flow*, New York: Routledge.
Dodson, B. and Kilian, D. (1998) 'From Port to Playground: The redevelopment of the Victoria and Albert Waterfront, Cape Town', in Tyler, D., Guerrier, Y. and Robertson, M. (eds), *Managing Tourism in Cities*, Chichester: John Wiley.
Douglas, C. and Monacella, R. (eds) (2012) *Urban Realities: Temporary Urban Catalysts for Change*, Melbourne Books: Melbourne.
Dovey, K. (2005) *Fluid City: Transforming Melbourne's Urban Waterfront*, London: Routledge.
Fainstein, S. (2000) *The City Builders: Property Development in New York and London, 1980–2000*, 2nd ed., Lawrence: University Press of Kansas.
Foley, R. and Kistemann, T. (2015) 'Blue space geographies: Enabling health in place', *Health and Place*, 35, pp. 157–165.
Gehl, J. (2010) *Places for People: Docklands 2010 report (preliminary findings)*, Melbourne: VicUrban, available from http://www.melbourne.vic.gov.au/about-council/committees-meetings/meetingarchive/MeetingAgendaItemAttachments/510/8555/5.6.pdf
Gibson J. (1979) *The Ecological Approach to Visual Perception*, Boston: Houghton Mifflin.
Gordon, D. (1996) 'Planning, design and managing change in urban waterfront redevelopment', *Town Planning Review*, 67 (3), pp. 261–290.
Hassell Ltd. (2015) *Harbour Esplanade Master Plan Report*, Melbourne: Places Victoria, link: http://www.places.vic.gov.au/__data/assets/pdf_file/0007/18664/Harbour-Esplanade-Master-Plan.pdf, accessed 16 February 2016.
Hou, J. (ed.) (2010) *Insurgent Public Space: Guerrilla Urbanism and the Remaking of Contemporary Cities*, Routledge: New York.
Hudson, B. (1996) *Cities on the Shore: The Urban Littoral Frontier*, New York: Pinter.
Jones, A. (1998) 'Issues in waterfront regeneration: More sobering thoughts – A UK Perspective', *Planning Practice and Research*, 13 (4), pp. 433–442.
Lamm, B. and Brandt, C. B. (2012) 'Urban play', *Landskab*, 3, pp. 84–87.
Lynch, K. (1981) *Good City Form*, Cambridge MA: MIT Press.
Macarthur, J. (1999) 'Tactile simulations: Architecture and the image of the public at Brisbane's Kodak Beach', in Barcan, R. and Buchanan, I. (eds) *Imagining Australian Space: Cultural Studies and Spatial Inquiry*. Nedlands, Australia: University of Western Australia Press.
Montag Stiftung Urban Räume and Regionale 2010 (eds) (2008) *Riverscapes: Designing Urban Embankments*, Birkhäuser: Basel.
Oakley, S. (2014) 'Understanding the planning and practice of redeveloping disused docklands using critical urban assemblage as a lens: A Case Study of Port Adelaide, Australia', *Planning Practice and Research*, 29 (2), pp. 171–186.
Rahman, M. and Imon, S. (2017) 'Conservation of historic waterfront to improve the quality of Life in Old Dhaka', *Archnet-IJAR: International Journal of Architectural Research*, 11 (2), pp. 83–100.
Sepe, M. (2013) 'Urban history and cultural resources in urban regeneration: A case of creative waterfront renewal', *Planning Perspectives*, 28 (4), pp. 595–613.
Stevens, Q. (2007) *The Ludic City: Exploring the Potential of Public Spaces*, London: Routledge.
Völker S. and Kistemann T. (2013) '"I'm always entirely happy when I'm here!" Urban blue enhancing human health and well-being in Cologne and Düsseldorf, Germany', *Social Science and Medicine*, 78, pp. 113–124.
White, J. T. (2016) 'Pursuing design excellence: Urban design governance on Toronto's waterfront', *Progress in Planning*, 110, 1–41.
Whyte, W. H. (1988) *City: Rediscovering the Center*, New York: Doubleday.

Conclusion

This concluding chapter explores four inter-related aspects of access to urban waterfronts that influence the vitality of their redevelopment, through two overarching concerns which have been focussed upon in the two sections of this book. The first concern, plugging waterfronts into cities, addresses firstly the physical aspects of visibility and movement between waterfront precincts and other urban activity areas, and secondly the fine-scaled design of the interface between the land and water, so that people can actually have close engagement with the water. The second major concern, how to switch waterfronts on, examines the activation of waterfront spaces. This also examines two aspects: increasing the demand for waterfront access, by attracting a diversity of public use, and the empowerment of a range of new actors who can engage with the production and operation of waterfront areas.

This work draws together a range of my research into large-scale redevelopment of urban waterfront industrial sites for leisure uses, which has examined their morphology and landscape design, the actors and processes that have shaped them, and users' appropriations of the public spaces within these precincts. The research methods I have employed have involved studying waterfronts across different scales and timeframes, through spatial analysis, discourse analysis, analysis of landscape materials, study of waterfront development processes, and analysis of projects' wider economic and political contexts. Chapter 3 summarised an even wider range of methods that other scholars have used for examining waterfronts and the ways they develop over time. Most importantly, I have undertaken participant observation. Relatively little research into waterfront precincts has involved going down to these sites and observing how various groups of people actually use them. Similarly, little attempt has been made to understand how design characteristics of the waterfront leisure landscape shape and support perceptions and behaviour.

Waterfront Visibility and Access

Urban waterfronts are places of high mobility, where vehicles, people, goods, money and water flowing in multiple directions. Waterfronts are always being 'opened up'; new

Conclusion

spaces and connections are constantly being produced, albeit unevenly, and so are new blockages. In Chapter 1, I noted Gordon's (1996) recommendation to improve public accessibility and connectivity to waterfronts, to better integrate them with their urban surroundings and with the water; alongside four other key stratagems: improving their image and imageability; learning from what exists and adaptively re-using existing built form; thinking small and planning in increments; and coordinating public and private investments to create a coherent urban environment. The first three of these stratagems all emphasise the importance of plugging the waterfront into the surrounding city's life, in spatial and functional terms.

In London, Melbourne and Brisbane, formerly-industrial waterfront areas on the opposite side of the river to their cities' central business districts could only be redeveloped into successful leisure precincts called 'Southbank' by overcoming a dearth of transport infrastructure connecting them to their respective north riverbanks. In Chapter 1, I identified two distinct spatial aspects of user experience that contributed to the success of these leisure settings. Firstly, their separation across the river frames an escape from the everyday city of work. The physical juxtaposition of work and leisure enliven the waterfront's leisure experience. Although they are now 'mixed use', these Southbanks all retain a sense of difference to their city centres, through different architectural and open space forms, their primary leisure focus, and their accessible, mostly-sunlit water frontage. Secondly, the sites were re-connected into the myriad flows of people moving through the city, which makes them sites to experience a lively mixing of strangers. I noted six distinct important elements of connectivity: building bridges to connect the Southbank to the city centre; the design of those bridges; designing public spaces for changing water levels; the continuity of riverfront paths through the precincts; connecting the Southbank to its surrounding neighbourhood; and managing pedestrian networks at a scale where many people will actually be willing to walk them.

I emphasised that while new bridges are crucial for enhancing urban permeability, their design also matters, because it can make them visible, memorable and well-connected to waterfront pathways and to nearby city streets. Waterfront promenades are typically many metres lower than the bridges that pass over them and the city streets around them. I argued that small-scale blocks and a fine-grained mixing of primary and secondary uses are just as important to the vitality of waterfront areas as they are to other urban neighbourhoods (Jacobs 1961); flows of people and pools of uses mutually underpin each other. I also stressed the importance of designers and policymakers turning their gaze away from the water, to ensure that waterfront development's scale, permeability, views and transport infrastructure all also contribute to the vitality of their urban hinterlands and enable synergies with them.

All six of the dimensions of flow that I have identified with successful urban waterfronts illustrate that the experience of arriving at and moving through such precincts can itself be a fundamental part of their magic. In particular, bridges that pedestrians will use should be understood as more than just transport investments, and should be budgeted and programmed as key pieces of open space infrastructure, and planned in combination with adjacent land parcels to ensure the creation of nodal points that are lively, public and cohesive in character.

Conclusion

Positioning the Waterfront

I illustrated a different way of optimising the accessibility of urban waterfront leisure settings in Chapters 4 and 6. Artificial beaches in Cairns, Australia, and in Germany show how entire new waterfront settings can be artfully, strategically positioned at convenient, highly visible and accessible points within a city, in order to maximise economic synergy with their wider urban milieux. With Seoul's Cheonggyecheon, the river itself was re-created so that the city's commercial core could once again have a waterfront environment. I noted that a large proportion of Germany's 'city beaches' are actually not adjacent to waterways. They bring typical leisure waterfront models and atmospheres to a range of other vacant urban sites that offer centrality, good public transport access and carparking, good solar exposure, quietness and wind protection. 'Waterfront' environments can be placed on public plazas, on inland industrial sites, adjacent to existing bars, theatres, or universities, on railway easements and the roofs of parking garages, even inside former zeppelin hangars, if the necessary connections and the demand exist.

Shaping Encounter with the Water's Edge

While economic development objectives often mean that waterfront connectivity is primarily thought of in terms of physical access between the city and the waterfront, through new promenades, bridges, and river taxis, Chapters 1, 4 and 9 highlighted the importance of the small-scaled design of the immediate physical interface between the land and the water. Activating waterfronts requires enabling and encouraging people to have close bodily engagement with water's distinctive material, sensory and functional attributes. Visitors' experience of water on contemporary waterfronts is too often limited to passive, distant views, rather than activities that involve close contact with water (Jones 1998; Sepe 2013). Too many contemporary urban waterfront uses have no direct relation to water. Planners and policymakers need to think carefully about what should count as a 'waterfront use' in the contemporary city (Malone 1996; Sairinen and Kumpulainen 2006). In this book, I have sought to follow Gordon's (1996) recommendation to give attention to the link between waterfronts and water, in terms of connectivity to water at the very close scale of the human body's senses and movements; and how the material, spatial and sensory affordances of the boundary conditions between land and water can facilitate active playful engagement with water's unique spatial and sensory conditions. This focus is too often lacking in the literature on waterfront urban design (Hudson 1996; Jones 2014). In my discussion of the landscape designs of the Southbanks of Melbourne, Brisbane and London in Chapter 1, I noted that pedestrian bridges, embankment walls, river stairs and beaches can provide a rich range of bodily experiences of open space and water near the rivers' edge.

Artificial Waterfronts

Chapter 4 illustrated other ways that urban waterfront redevelopment can provide engaging access to water, by examining the material landscapes of various recently-built artificial beaches, lagoons, and rivers in urban tourist precincts, and how they are

Conclusion

perceived and used by visitors. Such projects use engineering and landscaping elements, materials, infrastructures and symbolism to manufacture and control various geographic, climatological and hydrological features of waterbodies, and also to shape their interfaces with urban public space. To attract and enable people to approach the water, its edge is designed and managed to maximise visual attractiveness, safety, and ease of movement, and to reduce bodily risks and discomfort. This is the case both for waterfronts that simulate natural settings and those that create highly artificial ones.

The large, free-access swimming pools in Brisbane and Cairns create new waterfront edge conditions that are adjacent to, but separated from, real rivers. The complex edge conditions between these artificial water bodies and the adjacent land also enable a rich range of views and interactions between bathers, passing pedestrians and the surrounding cityscape. Seoul's Cheonggyecheon presents an even more complex riverfront landscape, transitioning from obvious artifice to apparent naturalness along its six kilometre length. These waterfronts are clean, safe and camera-friendly. They highlight how much the management of both appearances and bodily comfort matters in the design of contemporary urban waterfront landscapes. Every detail is carefully designed and regulated, including the volume, speed, temperature, cleanliness and sound of the water.

Testing the Waters Through Design Research

In Chapter 9, we described a short-term design research installation in Melbourne's Docklands, led by Danish researcher Jacob Mikkelsen, which explored how small-scale open space interventions could encourage and enable people to have close, active engagement with the water on an urban waterfront. This sought to overcome the many waterfront design elements that, consciously or otherwise, impede views and access from the Docklands' public promenade to the water in its harbour, such as the promenade's high level, the pavilion buildings spaced along its waterside edge, and the limited amount of publicly-accessible moorings.

We identified and developed several small design elements that heightened people's interaction with the water. These included a 'telescope' and 'periscope' that provided views of marine life under the water's reflective surface, water robots that gave people a vicarious means of floating on the water and moving across it, and a malleable diorama that enabled people to explore their own ideas about re-designing the waterfront. These tools broke through the spatial barriers between urban space and water space. The tools also broke the barrier that constrains most visitors to waterfronts as passive receivers of experiences that are designed and controlled by others. These achievements were best illustrated by the robot control device being immersed in water, so that operators were required to get their hands wet. This design intervention brings together this book's two core themes: plugging the waterfront more tightly into the city (connecting people and water), and switching the waterfront on, by empowering people to actively engage with waterfront space.

We noted that both the small, short-term approach and the specific design concepts developed in Chapter 9 could be translated into the design of larger and more permanent constructions on waterfronts. This kind of design research into the immediate city-water interface could also be extended. The submersed robot control device, and the diverse city beaches discussed in Chapters 4 and 6, suggest that further waterfront design research could discover a rich variety of ways that visitors might immerse themselves sensorily and bodily into water. Most importantly, the materials and forms of both the Docklands installation and the city beaches offer multiple opportunities for appropriation and adaptation by users. This allows users to perform and express their opinions and feelings about how waterfronts should be designed, on site. The artifice of waterfront experience can be placed in the hands of waterfront users, not just designers.

Waterfront Uses That Attract and Stimulate Diverse Users

While Chapters 1 to 4 focused on the importance of increasing public accessibility to waterfronts and to the water itself, they also introduced the idea that this goes hand-in-hand with increasing the flows of people and the range of activities that are brought to these areas. That became the focus of Part II of this book. Activating, managing and maintaining the demand for waterfront access involves managing land uses and providing public amenities and programming that can attract and support broad, diverse public use. Lively waterfront spaces are not just well-connected; they are constantly crossed by people with many different interests and trajectories.

Overlapping Pools of Uses

In my Introduction and Chapter 1, I noted that this book seeks to move beyond the common critique of redeveloped waterfronts as spectacularised theme parks (Harvey 1989; Sorkin 1992), by focussing on their actual users and uses. Visitors to urban waterfronts are actively involved in the ongoing production of the meaning and value of these places. They bring with them different identities, values, perceptions and practices. In spite of earlier research which showed that a diversity and mixing of people and activities contributes to the attraction and success of waterfront leisure precincts (Gordon 1996; Dodson and Kilian 1998), surprisingly little subsequent research has involved analysing how people actually use waterfront spaces, particularly during the times when there are no scheduled events to stimulate activity. This book has aimed to expand the focused studies of Campo (2013) and Jones (2014) to present a wider analysis of how people enjoy a range of waterfront spaces.

As noted in Chapter 5, one key solution lies in allowing under-designed 'gaps' or 'loose spaces' (Franck and Stevens 2007) within waterfront precincts, so that these places are not over-determined and exclusionary, but allow users to appropriate and transform them and augment their uses. On both Melbourne's and London's Southbanks, early brutalist architecture and site-by-site planning that ignored neighbours were in some ways blessings, creating leftover, marginal spaces, including loading docks, closed entrances, bridge superstructures and perpendicular laneways, which allowed opportunities for a range of short-term interventions and actions, including protests,

Conclusion

skateboarding, street art, temporary markets and street performers. Such leftover spaces have supported a wide range of uses that are unofficial and not commercially profitable. Many of these informal appropriations have subsequently guided later phases of official planning, which typically incorporated ongoing support and infrastructure for a range of temporary installations that encourage active participation; a shift away from old-fashioned masterplanning of waterfront leisure precincts.

In Chapter 1, I highlighted that on the east end of Melbourne's Southbank, built first and in small phases, building footprints are small in scale, similar to the Melbourne CBD's fine-grained block structure with its network of pedestrian laneways. This area's building tenancies are also small-scale. This indicates the merits of a waterfront urban design framework which optimises mixing of land uses, tenancies and development forms along the high-value river frontage, as well as permeability to and from the water's edge, of creating narrow and deep development parcels aligned perpendicular to the waterfront and having staged site release. Such an approach can enliven a waterfront promenade by accommodating a richer mix of activity. I contrasted this with the later-developed western end of Melbourne's Southbank, which reveals the flaws of large-scale plans and site ownership. At a smaller scale of open space design, Melbourne's Southbank Promenade succeeds in attracting and mixing users and leisure activities partly because it offers a large number of both formal and informal places to sit (Gehl and City of Melbourne 1994). Recent analysis of Melbourne's Southbank has shown that those lengths of the waterfront promenade that have the most users are the ones with the greatest number and variety of informal 'secondary' seating opportunities, including various configurations of ledges, steps, walls, lampposts and flat and sloping areas of grass (Wang and Stevens 2020).

Programming Uses

Chapters 6 to 8 used Germany's city beaches to illustrate entrepreneurial approaches to maximising the activity and social mixing on waterfront spaces by attracting and supporting a diversity of users and uses. Returning to a key conceptual distinction mapped out in Chapter 3, this focus on (flexible) use, rather than (fixed) built form, suggests adjusting how planners, designers and managers approach the production and management of waterfronts more generally. Beach operators program activities ranging from children's play to 'public viewing' of football matches, and from live theatre to kung-fu classes to religious services, to attract a wide clientele at varied times and prolong their visits. The community-led city beach in the small city of Esslingen did not allow pre-recorded music, to encourage live performances. Like many community-run beaches, it hosted a wide range of participatory events. My examination of the activation of these waterfronts drew attention to their highly-flexible provision of relatively-cheap but labour-intensive 'soft' infrastructure, which opens up opportunities for a diversity of community actors to co-create the waterfront. This includes every visitor who brings a towel and swimwear and sunbathes, or simply puts their bare feet in the sand, 'acting out' the beach. In contrast to spectacular waterfront arts complexes where visitors passively consume professional entertainment, city beaches attract local people by providing roles, benefits and social interaction for participants.

I noted that city beaches, like our temporary design intervention presented in Chapter 9, are more like events than durable material places. Paris's and Berlin's first city beaches were created by a scenographer and a theatre director (see Chapter 7). The focus on programming necessitates a shift in the governance of urban waterfront leisure precincts, from design controls to performance regulation. Local governments need to manage levels of light, noise and waste on waterfronts, and not just their built form. In contrast to the emphasis on expensive, large-scale signature architecture identified in Chapters 1, 2 and 5, these modest waterfronts show how the provision of small and simple physical props such as sand, spades, palm trees and volleyball nets can be crucial in encouraging and supporting a range of behaviours. Nevertheless, the first section of this book showed that formal waterfront precincts can also provide infrastructure that attracts and supports a wide variety of local users and activities: in Chapter 1 through the provision of free amenities like pools, lockers and barbecues, in Chapter 2 through spaces that suit local social customs and climate, and in Chapter 4 through the use of materials and forms that optimise bodily comfort and enjoyment.

New Actors and Relationships

The fourth and final major theme addressed in this book was who is involved in activating waterfront areas. This included questions of which social groups access to the waterfront is actually being improved for (in Chapters 2, 3 and 5), what roles various actors have in waterfront change, beyond being passive consumers, and what kinds of processes and networks engage them with developing and accessing waterfront areas. The new roles of entrepreneurs, 'culturepreneurs' and local residents in facilitating the creation and activation of waterfronts were contrasted in Chapters 7 and 8. I also identified two other ways that the non-expert public are engage in shaping the use of urban waterfronts: firstly through resistant, subversive, dialectical opposition to received, controlled, spectacular waterfront landscape designs (in Chapter 5), and secondly through hands-on, exploratory co-production by visitors (in Chapters 7, 8 and 9). Chapters 1 and 4 also examined how visitors discover opportunities for 'edgy' excitement and risk, and push their experience beyond design and management controls such as railings, skate lugs, steps and signs – for example by sliding or jumping where they are expected to walk. These observations provide a focused application to waterfront leisure zones of my earlier insights into how people appropriate the public realm for creative play (Stevens 2007; Franck and Stevens 2007).

Substantial, creative and lasting activation and transformation of waterfronts requires coordinated action by multiple individuals. A wide range of actors are engaged in a wide range of roles in leading, facilitating, shaping and experiencing the production of contemporary urban waterfront projects. Waterfront development involves alliances of varying durability at different scales, organised around varied and changing waterfront problems and ambitions. Chapter 3 emphasised that policies, the power to act, and development outcomes are always products of cooperation and conflicts among a great multiplicity of parties and forces. Three key aspects of actor engagement are significant

Conclusion

for switching waterfronts on (Stevens and Dovey 2019). The first is, as discussed above, the engagement of new actors, many of whom have little prior experience of the development and management of urban open spaces. The second feature is that these varied actors bring with them new ideas, entrepreneurial skills, social networks and resources, and thereby bring new activities and values to waterfronts. Government and non-government intermediaries may facilitate the involvement and empowerment of such actors and projects, which can lead to new working relations, site users, developers, artists and designers, and new institutional structures. A third important feature is that engagement can change the relationship between production and consumption.

These factors all converge around what we characterised in Chapter 7 as 'Post-Fordist placemaking'. City beaches show how activating a waterfront space and creating a sense of place is just as much about the richness of visitors' bodily engagements, the diversity of potential activities, and the 'soft' infrastructure that supports them, as it is about creating a distinctive, durable physical landscape. Much investment, management and innovation is directed to 'mediatised' content. These post-Fordist waterfront spaces harness the creativity of consumers, or more correctly 'prosumers' (Toffler 1980), who have active roles in their experience of place, both scripted and unscripted. Below I discuss some of the distinctive roles and contexts that activate contemporary waterfronts.

'Culturepreneurs'

Our study in Chapter 7 of four city beaches in different European cities showed that although they all received wide-ranging support from their municipalities, the development procedures for these waterfront projects were managed outside the respective local governments. The key conception, facilitation and decision-making roles were not filled by professional designers, but rather by one or two individual entrepreneurs – or rather, 'culturepreneurs' – from the arts and hospitality sectors or non-profit organisations. These projects illustrate well the many potential working arrangements that can be used to guide the activation of waterfront sites. Although the production relationships driving these city beaches were generally project-centred and thus temporary, they helped the various participants to develop new working relationships, knowledge and skills and to pursue new strategies for the financing, construction, operation and programming of waterfront spaces.

Grassroots Waterfronts

While most of Germany's city beach projects are commercial entrepreneurial ventures, Chapter 8 drew attention to the small number of beaches that have been developed by community groups, local governments, and other non-profit agencies. These generally focused on serving local residents, including children. These waterfront projects, which have been initiated, designed, produced and operated by local citizens, student or artists, may look physically similar to commercial beach bars, but their social functions and meanings and the processes through which they are produced are rather different. They involve incremental learning and significant local in-kind support, for example from local businesses who provide materials and local unemployed youths who provide labour and develop new skills and new social attachments. Significantly, these waterfronts are community spaces that emphasise that children and teenagers are part of the general public; not just consumers of an adult-determined environment (or, worse, nuisances to be excluded), but initiators, negotiators, builders, musicians and acrobats. Berlin's *YAAM* and Esslingen's *Stadtstrand* make the waterfront into a place that integrates minorities and the unemployed into the city.

I noted that not-for-profit city beach projects in Germany typically occurred in small cities, with populations under 100,000. Within these milieux, beaches' instigators can develop and deploy personal contacts, engage effectively with experts and decision-makers in the local government, and garner support from existing local civic associations and businesses. Open communication and trust and high levels of social engagement within these cities enable waterfront projects that are very lively, even though patronage and resources are usually very modest. These projects strengthen a virtuous circle, by further enhancing mutual trust.

Most of the artists who initiated city beach projects had little prior expertise in developing and managing urban spaces. They were able to create new waterfront spaces and bring them to life by keeping budgets small, bargaining over resources, soliciting donations and sponsorship, and providing hands-on physical labour. In several cases, they leveraged arts funding to develop waterfront projects. The artists also applied creativity to waterfront governance processes, by negotiating risks and accountabilities.

I pointed out in Chapter 6 that the role of artists in relation to these local, non-profit beach projects is in marked contrast to the role of the international 'starchitects' who provide spectacular shapes for the typical 'trophy collection' of spectacular waterfront tourist attractions discussed in Chapter 1, and for the waterfront corporate headquarters critiqued in Chapter 5. These artists' creativity does not go into form-making, but instead, into creative ways of engaging with mundane funding and regulatory processes and of coordinating the actions of a diverse range of other actors, with the aim of enriching the social value of local waterfront spaces.

An Holistic Understanding of Waterfront Activation

The range of analytical approaches and conceptual frames that I have used across this research emphasise various scales and characteristics of accessing and activating urban waterfronts. Putting the flat landscape of the water edge on the map, making it part of people's mental image of the city and part of their circuits of activity, requires enhancing the waterfront's visibility (its vertical height and visual distinctiveness, and views along axes to and from the waterfront), and connecting it to its urban hinterland, to other attractions, and to the water itself. Sometimes this involves strategic decisions about where within the city a new waterfront space should be created. Attention to changes in level, materials and furnishings greatly affect how comfortable waterfront users are, how long they might stay, and what they can do there.

In framing this book, I have sought to show that the accessibility of urban waterfronts needs to be thought of in close relation to who these landscapes attract,

Conclusion

and that this in turn also requires thinking through what experiences, roles, postures and activities various users might engage in within those settings. My observations indicate the benefits of maximising the variety of landscapes, activities and price brackets that a waterfront offers, and mixing users and uses together, to optimise diversity and surprise as well as economic and social sustainability. The studies in this book show that the management, soft infrastructure and programming of waterfront spaces is just as important as their architecture. They highlight the importance of increasing opportunities for user input and user control in making waterfronts into meaningful, attractive places, for example by allowing time and space on the waterfront for 'urban sandpits' that allows creative exploration of possibilities, as illustrated in Chapter 9. Chapter 5 showed that appropriation of waterfront spaces and creative uses of them will occur even when waterfront designers and managers try to prevent this. These observations on process point towards the wider issue of getting more actors involved in the development, resourcing and management processes that shape urban waterfronts, which can also enhance identity, attachment and resilience.

In all these respects, the ongoing and inevitably fragmentary (re)development of all cities' waterfronts suggests that their design and management should strive to remain inclusive, incremental and flexible; not to overdesign, but to remain open to new forms of access, new actors, and new opportunities.

References

Campo, D. (2013) *The Accidental Playground: Brooklyn Waterfront Narratives of the Undersigned and Unplanned*, New York: Fordham University Press.
Dodson, B. and Kilian, D. (1998) 'From Port to Playground: The Redevelopment of the Victoria and Albert Waterfront, Cape Town', in Tyler, D., Guerrier, Y. and Robertson, M. (eds) *Managing Tourism in Cities*, Chichester: John Wiley.
Franck, K. and Stevens, Q. (2007) 'Tying Down Loose Space', in K. Franck and Q. Stevens (eds) *Loose Space: Possibility and Diversity in Urban Life*, Abingdon: Routledge.
Gehl, J. and City of Melbourne (1994) *Places for People*, Melbourne: City of Melbourne.
Gordon, D. (1996) 'Planning, design and managing change in urban waterfront redevelopment', *Town Planning Review*, 67(3), pp. 261–290.
Harvey, D. (1989) *The Condition of Postmodernity*, London: Blackwell.
Hudson, B. (1996) *Cities on the Shore: The Urban Littoral Frontier*, New York: Pinter.
Jacobs, J. (1961) *The Death and Life of Great American Cities*, New York: Vintage.
Jones, A. (1998) 'Issues in waterfront regeneration: More sobering thoughts –a UK perspective', *Planning Practice and Research*, 13(4), pp. 433–442.
Jones, A. (2014) *On South Bank: The Production of Public Space*, Ashgate: Farnham.
Malone, P. (ed) (1996) *City, Capital and Water*, London: Routledge.
Sairinen, R. and Kumpulainen, S. (2006) 'Assessing social impacts in urban waterfront regeneration', *Environmental Impact Assessment Review*, 26, pp. 120–135.
Sepe, M. (2013) 'Urban history and cultural resources in urban regeneration: a case of creative waterfront renewal', *Planning Perspectives*, 28(4), pp. 595–613.
Sorkin, M. (ed) (1992) *Variations on a Theme Park*, New York: Hill and Wang.
Stevens, Q. (2007) *The Ludic City: Exploring the Potential of Public Spaces*, London: Routledge.
Stevens, Q. and Dovey, K. (2019) 'Pop-ups and Public Interests: Agile Public Space in the Neoliberal City', in Arefi, M. and Kickert, C. (eds) *The Palgrave Handbook on Bottom-up Urbanism*, New York: Palgrave, pp. 323–337.
Toffler, A. (1980) *The third wave*, New York: Bantam Books.
Wang, Z. and Stevens, Q. (2020) 'How do open space characteristics influence open space use? A study of Melbourne's Southbank Promenade', *Urban Research and Planning*, 13(1), pp. 22–44.

Bibliography

Abdul Latip, N.S., Heath, T., and Liew, M.S. (2009) 'A Morphological Analysis of the Waterfront in City Centre', Kuala Lumpur INTA-SEGA Bridging Innovation, Technology and Tradition Conference Proceedings.
AECOM (2013a) *Master Plan Report for the River of Life (ROL) Project*, Kuala Lumpur: AECOM.
AECOM (2013b) *Technical Report for the River of Life Project: Environmental Study*, Kuala Lumpur: AECOM.
AECOM (2013c) *Technical Report for the River of Life Project: Economic Report*, Kuala Lumpur: AECOM.
Alexander, C. (1965) 'The City is not a Tree', *Architectural Forum*, 122(1), pp. 58–62, and 122 (2), pp. 58–61.
Alexander, C., Ishikawa, S. and Silverstein, M. (1977) *A Pattern Language: Towns, Buildings, Construction*, New York: Oxford University Press.
al-Ibrashy, M. and Gaber, T. (2010) 'Design with the senses and for the senses: An alternative teaching model for design studio', *Archnet-IJAR: International Journal of Architectural Research*, 4(2–3), pp. 359–75.
Altmann, B. (1999) 'Freibad auf dem Hinterhof: Zutritt nur für Anwohner', *Die Welt*, 4 August.
Angst, M., Klaus, P., Michaelis, T., Müller, R. and Wolff, R. (2009) *Zone*Imaginaire: Zwischennutzungen in Industriearealen*, Zürich: Vdf Hochschulverlag.
Arlt, P. (n.d.) 'Aktionen + Temporäre Bauten', http://www.peterarlt.at/index.php?kat=1, accessed 31 July 2012.
Aulich, U. and Janovsky, S. (2008) 'So ein Theater', *Berliner Zeitung*, 14 August.
Babulal, V. (2019) 'River of Life project has fallen short of objectives', *New Straits Times*, 7 October, available from https://www.nst.com.my/news/nation/2019/10/527674/river-life-project-has-fallen-short-objectives, accessed 15 April 2020.
Bahr, R. (2005) *Die Stadt entwickeln mit Zwischennutzungen: Voraussetzungen und politische Begründungen – Eine Untersuchung in Berlin*, Unpublished Diploma thesis, Humboldt University Berlin, available from https://zope.sowi.hu-berlin.de/lehrbereiche/stadtsoz/abschlussarbeiten/diplarbeit_raiko_bahr.pdf, accessed 30 April 2009.
Bakhtin, M. (1984) *Rabelais and His World*, Bloomington: Indiana University Press.
Ball, M. and Sutherland, D. (2001) *An Economic History of London 1800–1914*, London: Routledge
Barnes, J., Colenutt, B. and Malone, P. (1996) 'London Docklands and the State', in Malone, P. (ed), *City, Capital and Water*, London: Routledge.
Bavani, M. (2019) 'KL's Venetian dream collapses', *The Star*, 22 May. https://www.thestar.com.my/metro/metro-news/2019/05/22/kls-venetian-dream-collapses/. Accessed 15 April 2020.
BBR (Bundesamt für Bauwesen und Raumordnung) (2004) *Zwischennutzung und neue Freiflächen – städtische Lebensräume der Zukunft (Transitional uses and reclamation of urban land)*. Berlin: H. Heenemann GmbH and Co, available from https://www.bbsr.bund.de/BBSR/DE/veroeffentlichungen/sonderveroeffentlichungen/2005undaelter/zwischennutzung.html, accessed 9 August 2020.
BBU (Freiburger Arbeitskreis Wasser im Bundesverband Bürgerinitiativen Umweltschutz e.V.) (2007) 'Freizeit/030: Frankfurt am Main – Badeschiff statt Flussbadeanstalt, Schattenblick', 18 Oct, http://www.schattenblick.de/infopool/umwelt/lebens/ulefr030.htm, accessed 1 Oct 2008.
Becker, C. (2010) 'Kreativwirtschaft als Chance der Brachflächenreaktivierung', in Dosch F. and Glöckner, S. (eds), *Neue Zugänge zum Flächenrecycling (Informationen zur Raumplanung 1/2010)*, Bonn: BBR, pp. 71–82, Available from http://www.bbsr.bund.de/cln_016/nn_23470/BBSR/DE/Veroeffentlichungen/IzR/2010/1/Inhalt/DL__Becker,templateId=raw,property=publicationFile.pdf/DL_Becker.pdf, accessed 30 March 2011.
Bengs, C., Hentilä, H. and Nagy, D. (2002) *Urban Catalysts: Strategies for Temporary Uses – Potential for Development of Urban Residual Areas in European Metropolises*, Espoo: Centre for Urban and Regional Studies, Helsinki University of Technology, available from http://www.hut.fi/Yksikot/YTK/julkaisu/E2Urbancat_wp3.pdf

Bibliography

Berger, J. (1992) *Keeping a Rendezvous*, London: Penguin.
BI PRO SpV (= Betroffenenvertretung Spandauer Vorstadt) (2007) *Monbijoupark: Der Park and das Kinderbad, der Platz and die Torhäuser, Parkbesetzer and Bebauungsabsichten*, available from http://www.bvspv.de/monbijou.html, accessed 30 April 2009.
Bianchini, F. (1995) 'Night cultures, night economies', *Planning Practice and Research*, 10(2), pp. 121–126.
Bishop, P. and Williams, L. (2012) *The Temporary City*, London: Routledge.
Bistum Hildesheim (2009) 'Singen und beten am 'Strand' von Kevelaer', available from http://www.bistum-hildesheim.de/bho/dcms/sites/bistum/nachrichten/nachrichten.html?f_action=showandf_newsitem_id=9994, accessed 9 March 2010.
Blumner, N. (2006) *Planning for the Unplanned: Tools and Techniques for Interim Use in Germany and the United States*, Berlin: Deutsches Institut für Urbanistik, available from http://www.difu.de/english/occasional/06-blumner_planning.shtml
BMVBS (Bundesministerium für Verkehr, Bau und Stadtentwicklung) and BBR (Bundesamt für Bauwesen und Raumordnung) (2008) *Zwischennutzungen und Nischen im Städtebau als Beitrag für eine nachhaltige Stadtentwicklung*, Bonn: BBR, available from http://www.bbsr.bund.de/cln_016/nn_21890/BBSR/DE/Veroeffentlichungen/BMVBS/WP/2008/heft57__DL,templateId=raw,property=publicationFile.pdf/heft57_DL.pdf
Böhme, C., Henckel, D. and Besecke, A. (2006) *Brachflächen in der Flächenkreislaufwirtschaft (Expertise)*, Berlin: BBR, available from http://www.flaeche-im-kreis.de/veroeffentlichungen/expertisen/flik-expertise-brachflaechen-national.pdf
Borden, I. (2001) *Skateboarding, Space and the City: Architecture and the Body*, Oxford: Berg.
Bornmann, F., Erbelding, D. and Froessler D. (2008) *Zwischennutzungen: Temporäre Nutzungen als Instrument der Stadtentwicklung*, Düsseldorf: Innovationsagentur Stadtumbau NRW, available from http://urbano.de/pdf/2008/zwischennutzungen.pdf
Bosetti, N. and Colthorpe, T. (2018) *Meanwhile, in London: Making use of London's Empty Spaces*, London: Centre for London, available from https://www.centreforlondon.org/publication/meanwhile-use-london/, accessed 20 May 2019.
Boyer, M. C. (1992) 'Cities for Sale: Merchandising History at South Street Seaport', in Sorkin, M. (ed.) *Variations on a Theme Park*, New York: Hill and Wang.
Boyer, M. C. (1994) *The City of Collective Memory: Its Historical Imagery and Architectural Entertainments*, Cambridge MA: MIT Press.
Breen, A. and Rigby, D. (1994) *Waterfronts: Cities Reclaim their Edge*, New York: McGraw Hill.
Breen, A. and Rigby, D. (1996) *The New Waterfront: A Worldwide Urban Success Story*, London: Thames and Hudson.
Brenner, N. and Theodore, N. (2002) *Spaces of Neoliberalism: Urban Restructuring in North America and Western Europe*, Oxford: Blackwell.
Brownhill, S. (2010) 'London Docklands Revisited: The Dynamics of Waterfront Development', in Desfor, G., Laidley, J., Stevens, Q. and Schubert, D. (eds) *Transforming Urban Waterfronts: Fixity and Flow*, New York, Routledge, pp. 121–142.
Bruttomesso, R. (ed) (1993) *Waterfronts: A New Frontier for Cities on Water*, Venice: International Centre 'Cities on Water'.
Bryce, P. H. (1892) 'Letter to John Hendry, The Globe, 3 September', in *The River Don and Ashbridge's Bay*, Toronto Port Authority Archives: SC 26, box 4, folder 4.
Buck-Morss, S. (1991) *The Dialectics of Seeing: Walter Benjamin and the Arcades Project*, Cambridge MA: MIT Press.
Bunce, S. (2009) 'Developing sustainability: Sustainability policy and gentrification on Toronto's waterfront', *Local Environment*, 14(7), pp 651–667.
Bunnell, T. (1999) 'Views from above and below: The Petronas Twin Towers and/in contesting visions of development in contemporary Malaysia', *Singapore Journal of Tropical Geography*, 20(1), pp 1–23.
Bürgin, M. and Cabane, P. (1999) *Akupunktur für Basel: Zwischennutzung als Standortentwicklung auf dem Areal des DB-Güterbahnhofs in Basel*, available from http://www.areal.org/areal_alt/download/zn_mb.pdf, accessed 11 April 2012.
BV SpV (= Betroffenenvertretung Spandauer Vorstadt) (2002) *Stellungnahme zum Genehmigungsverfahren 'Strandbar' im Monbijou Park*, available from http://www.bvspv.de/st-021219strandbar.html, accessed 30 April 2009.
Caillois, R. (1961) *Man, Play and Games*, New York: Free Press of Glencoe.
Calthorpe, P. (1993) *The Next American Metropolis: Ecology, Community, and the American Dream*, Princeton: Princeton Architectural Press.
Campo, D. (2002) 'Brooklyn's Vernacular Waterfront', *Journal of Urban Design*, 7(2), pp. 171–199.
Campo, D. (2013) *The Accidental Playground: Brooklyn Waterfront Narratives of the Undersigned and Unplanned*, New York: Fordham University Press.
Campo, D. and Ryan, B. (2008) 'The entertainment zone: Unplanned nightlife and the revitalization of the American downtown'. *Journal of Urban Design* 13(3): 291–315.
Carmona, M. (2010) 'Contemporary public space: Critique and classification, part one: Critique', *Journal of Urban Design*, 15(1), pp. 123–148.

Bibliography

Carmona, M. (2009) 'The Isle of Dogs: Four development waves, five planning models, twelve plans, thirty-five years, and a renaissance… of sorts', *Progress in Planning*, 71(3), pp. 87–151.

Carta, M. and Ronsivalle, D. (eds) (2016) *The Fluid City Paradigm: Waterfront Regeneration as an Urban Renewal Strategy*, Cham, Switzerland: Springer.

Carter, L. (1993) *Sensual Southbank: The power of the body in the transformation of culture*, unpublished BArch thesis, University of Queensland, Brisbane, Australia.

Chang, T. C. and Huang, S. (2011) 'Reclaiming the city: Waterfront development in Singapore', *Urban Studies*, 48(10), pp. 2085–2100.

Chang, T. C., Huang, S., and Savage, V. (2004) 'On the waterfront: Globalization and Urbanization in Singapore', *Urban Geography*, 25(5), pp. 413–436.

Chase, J., Crawford, M. and Kaliski, J. (eds) (1999). *Everyday Urbanism*. New York: Monacelli Press.

Choblet, C. (unaccredited interview with) (2008) *One of the fundamental ideas behind Paris Plage is social equity*, available from http://www.eukn.org/urbanmatrix/news/2008/08/interview-jean-christophe-choblet_1004.html, accessed 11 January 2010.

City of Melbourne (1997) *Grids and Greenery Case Studies*, Melbourne: City of Melbourne.

Cohen, M. (2008) *Stanja van Mierlo (interview on blog Vrij Nederland from July 2006)*, available from http://kinderenrevolutie.ning.com/profiles/blog/show?id=2142360%3ABlogPost%3A130, accessed 12 May 2009.

Cohen, S. and Taylor, L. (1976) *Escape Attempts: The Theory and Practice of Resistance to Everyday Life*, London: Allen Lane.

Colomb, C. (2012) 'Pushing the urban frontier: Temporary uses of space, city marketing, and the creative city discourse in 2000s Berlin', *Journal of Urban Affairs*, 34(2), pp. 131–52.

Connolly, K. (2004) 'Germans get taste of tropics an hour's drive from Berlin', *Daily Telegraph (UK)*, 21 December, available from https://www.telegraph.co.uk/news/worldnews/europe/germany/1479454/Germans-get-taste-of-tropics-an-hours-drive-from-Berlin.html, accessed on 12 May 2020.

Cox, K. (1998) 'Spaces of dependence, spaces of engagement and the politics of scale, or Looking for local politics', *Political Geography*, 17(1), pp. 1–23.

Craik, J. (1992) 'Expo 88: Fashions of Sight and Politics of Site', in T. Bennett, P. Buckridge, D. Carter and C. Mercer (eds) *Celebrating the Nation: A Critical Study of Australia's Bicentenary*, St Leonards (Australia): Allen and Unwin.

Crawford, M. (1992) 'The World in a Shopping Mall', in Sorkin, M. (eds) *Varations on a Theme Park: The New American City and the End of Public Space*, New York: Hill and Wang, pp. 3–30.

Cresswell, T. (2006) *On the Move: Mobility in the Modern Western World*, New York and London: Routledge.

Davison, A. and Ridder, B. (2006) 'Turbulent times for urban nature: Conserving and re-inventing nature in Australian cities', *Australian Zoologist*, 33(3), pp. 306–14.

DBKL = Dewan Bandaraya Kuala Lumpur (2014) *Personal interview with staff from the city planning department*, 16 April.

DBKL = Dewan Bandaraya Kuala Lumpur (Kuala Lumpur City Hall) (2012) *Kuala Lumpur City Plan 2020*.

de Certeau, M. (1993) 'Walking in the City', in: S. During (ed) *The Cultural Studies Reader*, London: Routledge.

Debord, G. (1994) *The Society of the Spectacle*, New York: Zone Books.

Deleuze, G. and Guattari, F. (1987) *A Thousand Plateaus*, Minneapolis: University of Minnesota Press.

DEMOS (2007) *Bristol Urban Beach*, available from http://www.demos.co.uk/projects/bristolurbanbeach/overview, accessed 30 Sept 2008.

Denzer, V., Köppe, H., Sachs, K. and Kühne, O. (2010) 'Stadtstrände – Urlaubsoasen im urbanen Raum? Erste empirische Annäherungen – ein Werkstattbericht' in K. Wöhler, A. Pott and V. Denzer (Eds.) *Tourismusräume: Zur soziokulturellen Konstruktion eines globalen Phänomens*, Bielefeld: Transcript, pp. 191–206.

Department of Public Works (Queensland, Australia) (2005) *State Budget 05–06: Budget Highlights*, available from http://www.publicworks.qld.gov.au/about/publications.cfm

Desfor, G. (2010) 'Deep Water and Good Land: Socio-nature and Toronto's Changing Industrial Waterfront', in Desfor, G., Laidley, J., Stevens, Q. and Schubert, D. (eds) *Transforming Urban Waterfronts: Fixity and Flow*, New York: Routledge, pp. 191–210.

Desfor, G. and Jørgensen, J. (2004) 'Flexible urban governance: The case of Copenhagen's recent waterfront development. *European Planning Studies* 12(4): 479–496.

Desfor, G. and Laidley, J. (2010) 'Introduction: Fixity and Flow of Urban Waterfront Change', in Desfor, G., Laidley, J., Stevens, Q. and Schubert, D. (eds) *Transforming Urban Waterfronts: Fixity and Flow*, New York: Routledge, pp. 1–13.

Desfor, G. and Laidley, J. (eds) (2011) *Reshaping Toronto's Waterfront*, Toronto: University of Toronto Press.

Desfor, G., Laidley, J., Stevens, Q. and Schubert, D. (eds) (2010) *Transforming Urban Waterfronts: Fixity and Flow*, New York: Routledge.

Desse, M. (1996) 'L'inégale Maritimité des Villes des Départments d'outre-mer Insulaires', in Péron F. and Rieucau J. (eds.) *La Maritimé Aujourd'hui*, Paris: L'Harmattan, pp. 241–249.

Dodman, D. (2007) 'Post-independence optimism and the legacy of waterfront redevelopment in Kingston, Jamaica', *Cities*, 24(4), pp. 273–284.

Bibliography

Dodson, B. and Kilian, D. (1998) 'From Port to Playground: The Redevelopment of the Victoria and Albert Waterfront, Cape Town', in Tyler, D., Guerrier, Y. and Robertson, M. (eds), *Managing Tourism in Cities*, Chichester: John Wiley.
Douglas, C. and Monacella, R. (Eds.) (2012) *Urban Realities: Temporary Urban Catalysts for Change*, Melbourne Books: Melbourne.
Dovey, K. (1985) 'The Quest for Authenticity and the Replication of Environmental Meaning', in Seamon D. and Mugerauer R. (eds) *Dwelling, Place and Environment*, The Hague: Martinus Nijhof, pp. 33–50.
Dovey, K. (1999) *Framing Places*, London: Routledge.
Dovey, K. (2002) 'Dialectics of Place: Authenticity, Identity, Difference', in S. Akkach (ed) *De-Placing Difference*, CAMEA Conference Proceedings, University of Adelaide, pp. 45–52.
Dovey, K. (2005) *Fluid City: Transforming Melbourne's Urban Waterfront*, London: Routledge.
Dovey, K. and Symons, F. (2014) 'Density without intensity and what to do about it: Reassembling public/private interfaces in Melbourne's Southbank hinterland', *Australian Planner*, 51(1), pp. 34–46.
Dransfeld, E. and Lehmann, D. (2008) *Temporäre Nutzungen als Bestandteil des Modernen Baulandmanagements*, Dortmund: Forum Baulandmanagement NRW, available from www.forum-bauland.nrw.de/downloads/temporaere_nutzungen.pdf
Eckstut, S. (1986) 'Solving Complex Urban Design Problems', in A. R. Fitzgerald (ed), *Waterfront Planning and Development*, New York: American Society of Civil Engineers, pp. 54–57.
Fagence, M. (1995a) 'City waterfront redevelopment for leisure, recreation, and tourism: Some common themes', in J. C. Smith and M. Fagence (eds), *Recreation and Tourism as a Catalyst for Urban Waterfront Redevelopment*, London: Praeger, pp. 135–156.
Fagence, M. (1995b), 'Episodic progress toward a grand design: Waterside redevelopment of Brisbane's South Bank', in J. C. Smith and M. Fagence (eds), *Recreation and Tourism as a Catalyst for Urban Waterfront Redevelopment*, London: Praeger, pp. 71–87.
Fainstein, S. (2000) *The City Builders: Property Development in New York and London, 1980–2000*, 2nd ed., Lawrence: University Press of Kansas.
Fainstein, Susan. (2005) 'The return of urban renewal: Dan Doctoroff's grand plans for New York City', *Harvard Design Magazine*, 22, pp. 1–5.
Faircliff, R. (2007) *Sun, Sand and Salsa. Forget Barbados, Welcome to Bristol Beach!*, DEMOS press release, available from http://bristol.indymedia.org/article/26592, accessed 22 May 2009.
Fang, C. (2012) *Waterfront Landscapes*, Shenyang, China: Liaoning Science and Technology Publishing House.
Featherstone, M. (1991) *Consumer Culture and Postmodernism*, London: Sage.
Florida, R. (2005) *Cities and the Creative Class*, New York: Routledge.
Flyvbjerg, B. (1998) *Rationality and Power: Democracy in Practice*, Chicago: University of Chicago Press.
Foley, R. and Kistemann, T. (2015) 'Blue space geographies: Enabling health in place', *Health and Place*, 35, pp. 157–165.
Foucault, M. (1997) 'Of other spaces', in Leach N. (eds), *Re-thinking Architecture*, London: Routledge, pp. 350–356.
Franck, K. and Stevens, Q. (eds) (2007) *Loose Space: Possibility and Diversity in Urban Life*, London: Routledge.
Franck, K. and Stevens, Q. (2007) 'Tying down loose space', in K. Franck and Q. Stevens (eds) *Loose Space: Possibility and Diversity in Urban Life*, London: Routledge.
Freiluftrebellen. (n.d.) http://www.freiluftrebellen.de, accessed 1 December 2009.
Frieden, B. and Sagalyn, L. (1989) *Downtown, Inc.: How America rebuilds cities*, Cambridge MA: MIT Press.
Gale, T. (2009) 'Urban beaches, virtual worlds and 'the end of tourism'', *Mobilities*, 4(1), pp. 119–138.
Gale, T. (2010) 'Urban beaches as social tourism installations: Case studies of Paris Plage and Bristol Urban Beach', in S. Cole and N. Morgan (eds) *Tourism and Inequality: Problems and Prospects*, Wallingford: CABI Publishing, pp. 183–193.
Ganis, M., Minnery, J. and Mateo-Babiano, D. (2014) 'The evolution of a masterplan: Brisbane's South Bank, 1991–2012', *Urban Policy and Research*, 32(4), pp. 499–518.
Garreau, J. (1992) *Edge city: life on the New Frontier*, New York: Anchor Books.
Gassner, O. (2001) 'Die Gesichter von Nigihaven', available from http://oliver-gassner.de/presse/presse_nigihaven_gesichter.html, accessed 7 April 2012.
Gastil, R. (2002) *Beyond the Edge: New York's New Waterfront*. New York: Van Alen Institute & Princeton Architectural Press.
Gehl, J. (2010) *Places for People: Docklands 2010 Report (Preliminary Findings)*, Melbourne: VicUrban, available from http://www.melbourne.vic.gov.au/about-council/committees-meetings/meetingarchive/MeetingAgendaItemAttachments/510/8555/5.6.pdf
Gehl, J. (1987) *Life Between Buildings*, New York: Van Nostrand Reinhold.
Gehl, J. and City of Melbourne (1994) *Places for People*, Melbourne: City of Melbourne.
Gertler, M. (1988) 'The limits of flexibility: Comments on the Post-fordist Vision of Production and Its Geography', *Transactions of the Institute of British Geographers*, 13(4), pp. 419–432.
Gibson J. (1979) *The Ecological Approach to Visual Perception*, Boston: Houghton Mifflin.

Bibliography

Gidel, M. (2010) 'Fragmentation on the Waterfront: Coastal Squatting Settlements and Urban Renewal Projects in the Caribbean', in G. Desfor, J. Laidley, Q. Stevens, and D. Schubert (eds) *Transforming Urban Waterfronts: Fixity and Flow*, New York: Routledge, pp 35–53.

Gilloch, G. (1996) *Myth and Metropolis*, Cambridge: Polity Press.

Goffman, E. (1963) *Behaviour in Public Places*, Westport CT: Greenwood.

Goodale, T. and Godbey, G. (1988) *The Evolution of Leisure: Historical and Philosophical Perspectives*, State College PA: Venture.

Gordon, D. (1996) 'Planning, design and managing change in urban waterfront redevelopment', *Town Planning Review*, 67(3), pp. 261–290.

Gordon, D. (1997) *Battery Park City: Politics and Planning on the New York Waterfront*, Amsterdam: Gordon and Breach Publishers.

Gottdiener, M. (1997) *The Theming of America: Dreams, Visions and Commercial Spaces*, Boulder: Westview.

Graf, A. and Beng-Huat C. (eds) (2007) *Port cities: Asian and European Transformations*, Oxford: Routledge.

Green Building Index (2014) www.greenbuildingindex.org, accessed 14 November 2014.

Grenville, J. (2007) 'Conservation as psychology: Ontological security and the built environment', *International Journal of Heritage Studies*, 13(6), pp. 447–461.

Groth, J. and Corijn, E. (2005) 'Reclaiming urbanity: Indeterminate spaces, informal actors and urban agenda setting', *Urban Studies*, 42(3), pp. 503–526.

Gstach, D. (2006) *Freiräume auf Zeit: Zwischennutzung von urbanen Brachen als Gegenstand der kommunalen Freiraumentwicklung*, Unpublished Diploma thesis, University of Kassel, available from http://kobra.bibliothek.uni-kassel.de/bitstream/urn:nbn:de:hebis:34-2006082214468/3/gstach_diss.pdf

Hagerman, C. (2012) 'Shaping neighborhoods and nature: Urban political ecologies of urban waterfront transformations in Portland, Oregon', *Cities*, 24(4), pp 285–297.

Hall, P. (1998) *Cities in Civilization: Culture, Technology and Urban Order*, London: Weidenfeld and Nicolson.

Hall, P. and Clark, A. (2010) 'Maritime Ports and the Politics of Reconnection', in Desfor, G., Laidley, J., Stevens, Q. and Schubert, D. (eds) *Transforming Urban Waterfronts: Fixity and Flow*, New York: Routledge, pp. 17–34.

Hannigan, J. (1998) *Fantasy City: Pleasure and Profit in the Postmodern Metropolis*, New York: Routledge.

Harvey, D. (1989a) *The Condition of Postmodernity*, London: Blackwell.

Harvey, D. (1989b) 'From managerialism to entrepreneurialism: The transformation in urban governance in late capitalism', *Geografiska Annaler*, 71(1), pp. 3–17.

Hassan, N. and Hanif, N.R. (2012) 'Privatization of urban space: "The Kuala Lumpur City Centre" City Innovation case Study Brief', available from https://pdfs.semanticscholar.org/5bc1/c909a35ace8de994f375207949b39f1be989.pdf, accessed 9 August 2020.

Hassell Ltd. (2015) *Harbour Esplanade Master Plan Report*, Melbourne: Places Victoria, available from: http://www.places.vic.gov.au/__data/assets/pdf_file/0007/18664/Harbour-Esplanade-Master-Plan.pdf, accessed 16 February 2016.

Haydn, F. and Temel, R. (eds.) (2006) *Temporary Urban Spaces: Concepts for the Use of City Spaces*, Basel: Birkhäuser.

Hazel, G. and Parry, R. (2004) *Making Cities Work*, Chichester: John Wiley.

Heeg, S. (2010) 'Flows of capital and fixity of bricks in the built environment of Boston: Property-led development in urban planning?', in Desfor, G., Laidley, J., Stevens, Q. and Schubert, D. (eds) *Transforming Urban Waterfronts: Fixity and Flow*, New York: Routledge, pp. 274–294.

Hentilä, H. and Lindborg, T. (2003) 'Central Micro-Peripheries: Temporary uses of Central Residual Spaces as Urban Development Catalysts', Conference paper at ERSA 2003 Congress, Jyväskylä, Finland, available from http://www-sre.wu-wien.ac.at/ersa/ersaconfs/ersa03/cdrom/papers/242.pdf, accessed 9 August 2020.

Heriot-Watt University (2014) 'Our Campus', available from http://www.hw.ac.uk/malaysia/about/campus.htm, accessed 14 November 2014.

Herold, M. (2007) 'Mit Leidenschaft für den Sommer in Berlin', *Mittendrin*, 4, p. 5.

Hesping, C. (2006) 'Stadt-Strand statt Strand: Naherholung an der Spree', available from http://www.friedrichshainer-chronik.de/spip.php?article32, accessed 27 July 2012.

Ho C. S., Azeez A. and Adeyemi, J. (2013) 'Low carbon cities – the way forward in real estate development in Malaysia', *International Journal of Real Estate Studies*, 8(1), pp 50–59.

Hou, J. (ed.) (2010) *Insurgent Public Space: Guerrilla Urbanism and the Remaking of Contemporary Cities*, Routledge: New York.

Hoyle, B., Pinder, D. and Husain, M. (Eds) (1988) *Revitalising the Waterfront*, London: Belhaven.

Hudson, B. (1996) *Cities on the Shore: The Urban Littoral Frontier*, New York: Pinter.

Huizinga, J. (1970) *Homo Ludens: A Study of the Play Element in Culture*, London: Temple Smith.

IlmArkadien (2009) 'Einladung', *Ilm-Zeitung*, March, 1.

Ioannides, D. and Debbage, K. (1997) 'Post-fordism and flexibility: The travel industry polyglot', *Tourism Management*, 18(4), pp. 229–241.

Iveson, K. and Scalmer, S. (2000) 'Contesting the 'inevitable': Notes on S11', *Overland*, 161, pp. 4–12.

Bibliography

Jaath, J. (2008) 'And the Winner is ...', *Grüne Aussichten* (Magazine of the Green Party faction in the Berlin-Mitte district council) Summer, p. 5, accessed 30 April 2009.
Jacobs, J. (1961) *The Death and Life of Great American Cities*, New York: Vintage.
Jacobs, J. (1970) *The Economy of Cities*, London: Cape.
Jameson, F. (1984) 'Postmodernism, or the cultural logic of late capitalism', *New Left Review*, 46, 53–92.
Jinnai, H. (1995) *Tokyo: A Spatial Anthropology*, Berkeley: University of California Press.
Jones, A. (1998) 'Issues in waterfront regeneration: More sobering thoughts – a UK perspective', *Planning Practice and Research*, 13(4), pp. 433–442.
Jones, A. (2014) *On South Bank: The Production of Public Space*, Ashgate: Farnham.
Jorg, J. (2008) *Make Use: A comparison between temporary-use strategies of intermediary organizations with the goal of using vacant buildings as workplaces for social and creative entrepreneurs*, unpublished masters thesis, POLIS MA in European Urban Cultures, Amsterdam/Brussels.
JUBM and Langdon Seah (2014) *Construction Cost Handbook*, available from www.langdonseah.com.
Judd, D. (1992) 'Constructing the Tourist Bubble', in D. Judd and S. Fainstein (eds) *The Tourist City*, New Haven: Yale University Press, pp. 35–53.
Judd, D. and Fainstein, S. (eds) (1992) *The Tourist City*, New Haven: Yale University Press.
Kahls, S. (2009) *Stadtstrände: Südseefeeling in deutschen Großstädten*, Hamburg: Diplomica.
Kane, S. (2010) 'Visibility and Contamination on the Buenos Aires Waterfront: Under the Bridges of Puerto Madero and La Boca', in Desfor, G., Laidley, J., Stevens, Q. and Schubert, D. (eds) *Transforming Urban Waterfronts: Fixity and Flow*, New York: Routledge, pp. 211–232.
Kearns, G. and Philo, C. (Eds) (1993) *Selling Places*, Oxford: Pergamon.
Kim, N. (2005) 'Ecological restoration and revegetation works in Korea', *Landscape and Ecological Engineering*, 1, pp. 77–83.
King, R. (2007) 'Re-writing the city: Putrajaya as representation', *Journal of Urban Design*, 12(1), pp 117–138.
King, R. (2008) *Kuala Lumpur and Putrajaya: Negotiating Urban Space in Malaysia*, NIAS Press, Copenhagen.
Kloos, M., Knüvener, T. and Wachten, K. (2007) *Freiräume auf Zeit: Neue Konzepte für Grünflächen in Stadterneuerungsgebieten*, Aachen: Internationales Institut für Gartenkunst und Landschaftskultur Schloss Dyck – available from http://docplayer.org/7669419-Freiraeume-auf-zeit-neue-konzepte-fuer-gruenflaechen-in-stadterneuerungsgebieten-michael-kloos-thomas-knuevener-kunibert-wachten.html, accessed 9 August 2020.
Koolhaas, R. (1994) 'The Story of the Pool', in *Delirious New York*, New York: Monacelli Press.
Kostof, S. (1992) *The City Assembled: The Elements of Urban Form Through History*, London: Thames and Hudson.
Kozlowski, M (2014) 'Revisiting Putrajaya', *Architecture Malaysia*, 26(3), pp. 72–75.
Krauzick, M. (2007) *Zwischennutzung als Initiator einer neuen Berliner Identität?*, Berlin: Universitätsverlag der TU Berlin (Graue Reihe, TU Berlin, Institut für Stadt- und Regionalplanung, No. 7), available from https://depositonce.tu-berlin.de/bitstream/11303/2091/1/Dokument_2.pdf, accessed 9 August 2020.
Kreuzer, S. (2001) 'Temporäre freiräume: Szenarischer replik zum vortrag des soziologen Peter Arlt', *Zolltexte*, 38, pp. 18–19.
Kröniger, B. (2005) *Der Freiraum als Bühne: Zur Transformation von Orten*, doctoral thesis, Technical University Munich, available from https://www.baufachinformation.de/der-freiraum-als-buehne/dis/2007079021967, accessed 9 August 2020.
Kruse, S. and Steglich, A. (2006) *Temporäre Nutzungen: Stadtgestalt zwischen Selbstorganisation und Steuerung*, Fakultät III – Umwelt und Technik, Universität Lüneburg.
Kulturamt der Stadt Vaihingen an der Enz (ed.) (2002) *Nigihaven na der Zen*, Vaihingen: Printmedien Karl Heinz Sprenger.
Kum, T. L. and Ujang, N. (2012) 'The application of mental mapping technique in Identifying the legible elements within historical district of Kuala Lumpur city centre', *Alam Cipta*, 5(1), pp. 55–62.
La Pradelle, M. and Lallement, E. (2004) Paris Plage: 'the city is ours', *The ANNALS of the America Academy of Political and Social Science*, 595(1), pp. 134–145.
Lamm, B. and Brandt, C. B. (2012) 'Urban play', *Landskab*, 3, pp. 84–87.
Landry, C. (2006) *The Art of City Making*, New York: Routledge.
Lange, B. (2011) 'Professionalization in space: Social-spatial strategies of culturepreneurs in Berlin', *Entrepreneurship and Regional Development: An International Journal*, 23(3–4), pp. 259–279.
Law, L. (2002) 'Defying disappearance: Cosmopolitan public spaces in Hong Kong', *Urban Studies*, 39(9), pp 1625–1645.
Lee, R. (1992) 'London docklands: The 'exceptional place'? An economic geography of inter-urban competition', in Ogden, P. (ed) *London Docklands: The challenge of development*, Cambridge and New York: Cambridge University Press.
Lefebvre, H. (1991a) *Critique of Everyday Life*, Vol. 1, 2nd. ed., London: Verso.
Lefebvre, H. (1991b) *The Production of Space*, trans. D. Nicholson-Smith, Oxford: Blackwell.
Lefebvre, H. (1996) *Writings on Cities*, Oxford: Blackwell.
Leschin Event (2019) *Aktuelle Projekte in Eigenregie*, http://leschinevent.de, accessed 9 August 2020.
Ley, D. and Olds, K. (1988) 'Landscape as spectacle: world's fairs and the culture of heroic consumption', *Environment and Planning D: Society and Space*, 6, pp. 191–212.

Bibliography

Lofland, L. (1998) *The Public Realm: Exploring the City's Quintessential Social Territory*, Hawthorne NY: Aldine de Gruyter.

Longhurst, R. (1992) *South Bank: An Historical Perspective from then Until Now*, Brisbane: State Library of Queensland and South Bank Corporation.

Loukaitou-Sideris, A. and Banerjee, T. (1998) *Urban Design Downtown: Poetics and Politics of Form*, Berkeley: University of California Press.

Lyman, S. and Scott, M. (1975) *The Drama of Social Reality*, New York: Oxford University Press.

Lynch, K. (1961) *The Image of the City*, Cambridge MA: MIT Press.

Lynch, K. (1981) *Good City Form*, Cambridge MA: MIT Press.

Lynch, K. and Hack, G. (1985) *Site Planning*, 3rd Ed, Cambridge MA: MIT Press.

Macarthur, J. (1999) 'Tactile Simulations: Architecture and the Image of the Public at Brisbane's Kodak Beach', in Barcan, R. and Buchanan, I. (eds) *Imagining Australian Space: Cultural Studies and Spatial Inquiry*. Nedlands, Australia: University of Western Australia Press.

Macdonald, E. (2018) *Urban Waterfront Promenades*, London: Routledge.

MacLeod, G. and Ward, K. (2002) 'Spaces of Utopia and Dystopia: Landscaping the Contemporary City', *Geographiska Annaler*, 84(3-4), pp. 153–170.

Mairie de Paris (2007a) *Paris Plages: Evenement*, Paris: Mairie de Paris.

Mairie de Paris (2007b) *Paris Plages: Guide Pratique*, Paris: Mairie de Paris.

Malone, P. (1996a) 'Introduction', in Malone, P. (ed.) *City, Capital and Water*, London: Routledge.

Malone, P. (ed) (1996b) *City, Capital and Water*, London: Routledge.

Marshall, R. (ed) (2001) *Waterfronts in Post-industrial Cities*, London: Spon.

Mean, M., Johar, I. and Gale, T. (2008) *Bristol Beach: An Experiment in Place-making*, London: DEMOS.

Merrifield, A. (2002) 'Seattle, quebec, genoa: Après le deluge… Henri Lefebvre?', *Environment and Planning D: Society and Space*, 20(2), pp. 127–134.

Meyer, H. (1999) *City and Port: Urban Planning as a Cultural Venture in London, Barcelona, New York and Rotterdam*, Utrecht: International Books.

MFT = Ministry of Federal Territories (2014) *EPP5: River of Life*, Putrajaya: Ministry of Federal Territories, available from http://app.kwpkb.gov.my/greaterklkv/entrypoint- project-river, accessed 20 May 2014.

Misselwitz, P., Oswalt, P. and Overmeyer, K. (eds) (2003) *Urban Catalysts: Strategies for Temporary Uses*, Berlin: Urban Catalyst, available from http://www.templace.com/think-pool/one786f.html?think_id=4272

Montag Stiftung Urban Räume and Regionale 2010 (eds.) (2008) *Riverscapes: Designing Urban Embankments*, Birkhäuser: Basel.

Moser, S. (2010) 'Putrajaya: Malaysia's new federal administrative capital', *Cities*, 27(4), pp 285–297.

Moulaert, F., Martinelli, F., González, S. and Swyngedouw, E. (2007) 'Introduction: Social innovation and governance in European cities: Urban development between path dependency and radical innovation', *European Urban and Regional Studies*, 14(3), pp. 195–209.

Mules, T. (1998), 'Events tourism and economic development in Australia', in Tyler, D., Guerrier, Y. and Robertson, M. (eds) *Managing Tourism in Cities*, Chichester: John Wiley, pp. 195–214.

Mullins, P., Natalier, K., Smith, P. and Smeaton, B. (1999), 'Cities and consumption spaces', *Urban Affairs Review*, 35(1), pp. 44–71.

Musgrave, E. (2002), 'Goodwill overture', *Architecture Australia*, 91.

Nita Jay, B. (2017) 'Najib launches River of Life, Blue Pool projects', *New Straits Times*, 28 August, available from https://www.nst.com.my/news/nation/2017/08/273894/najib-launches-river-life-blue-pool-projects, accessed 15 April 2020.

Noble, L. (2001) 'South bank dreaming', *Architecture Australia*, 90, pp. 86–93.

Norcliffe, G., Bassett, K. and Hoare, T. (1996) 'The emergence of postmodernism on the urban waterfront: Geographical perspectives on changing relationships', *Journal of Transport Geography*, 4 (2), pp. 123–134.

Oakley, S. (2014) 'Understanding the planning and practice of redeveloping disused Docklands using critical urban assemblage as a lens: A case study of port adelaide, Australia', *Planning Practice and Research*, 29(2), pp. 171–186.

O'Brien, C. (1997), 'Form, function and sign: Signifying the past in urban waterfront regeneration', *Journal of Urban Design*, 2(2), pp. 163–78.

Oswalt, P., Overmeyer, K. and Misselwitz, P. (2013) *Urban Catalyst: The Power of Temporary Use*, Berlin: DOM publishers.

Otto, M. (2007) *Beach Clubs: Zwischennutzung auf innerstädtischen Brachflächen mit Standortempfehlungen für Hamburg*, unpublished Diploma thesis, University of Hamburg.

Park, R., Burgess, E. and McKenzie, R. (1925) *The City*. Chicago: University of Chicago Press.

Peck, J. and Tickell, A. (2002) 'Neoliberalizing space', *Antipode*, 34(3), pp. 380–404.

Percy, W. (1981) *The Message in the Bottle*, New York: Farrar, Straus and Giroux.

Phipps, A. (2012) 'Drawing breath: Creative elements and their exile from higher education', *Arts and Humanities in Higher Education*, 9(1), pp. 42–53.

Pile, S. (1997) 'Introduction', in Pile, S. and Keith, M. (eds) *Geographies of Resistance*, London: Routledge.

Pinder, D.A., Hoyle B.S. and Husain, M.S. (eds) (1988), *Revitalising the Waterfront: International Dimensions of Dockland Redevelopment*, London: Belhaven.

Bibliography

Pine, J. and Gilmour, J. (1998) 'Welcome to the experience economy', *Harvard Business Review*, July/August, pp. 97–105.

PP = Perbadanan Putrajaya (1997) 'Master Plan for Putrajaya'.

PP = Perbadanan Putrajaya (2012) 'Putrajaya Draft Structure Plan: Sustainable Putrajaya 2025: From Garden to Green'.

PP = Perbadanan Putrajaya (2014), *personal interview with staff from the Lake Management department*, 14 April.

Prete, A., Sonenberg, B. and Hamersky, J. (2001) *Lavender Lake Brooklyn's Gowanus Canal*, New York: Filmakers Library.

Putrajaya Holdings (2014) *Putrajaya Facts and Figures*, available from http://www.pjh.com.my/corporate/putrajaya-facts/

Queensland Government (1990) *Queensland Government Gazette*, 28 April 1990, Vol CCXCIII, No 111.

Queensland Government (2004) *Preferred North Bank Strategic Plan*, available from http://www.northbankbrisbane.com.au, accessed 20 September 2005.

Rahman, M. and Imon, S. (2017) 'Conservation of historic waterfront to improve the quality of life in old Dhaka', *Archnet-IJAR: International Journal of Architectural Research*, 11(2), pp. 83–100.

Ramsey, K. (2010) 'Urban waterfront transformation as a politics of mobility: Lessons from seattle's alaskan way viaduct debate', in Desfor, G., Laidley, J., Stevens, Q. and Schubert, D. (eds) *Transforming Urban Waterfronts: Fixity and Flow*, New York: Routledge, pp. 101–120.

Richards, G. and Wilson, J. (2006) 'Developing creativity in tourist experiences: A solution to the serial reproduction of culture?', *Tourism Management*, 27(6), pp. 1209–1223.

Richert, W. (2005) 'Den Strand unterm Pflaster entdeckt, die Sterne aufs Parkdeck geholt... 'Nigihaven na der Zen' – ein Sommerprojekt mit offenem Ausgang', in B. Mandel (ed) *Kulturvermittlung-zwischen kultureller Bildung und Kulturmarketing: Eine Profession mit Zukunft*, Bielefeld: Transcript, pp. 239–243.

Rojek, C. (1995) *Decentering Leisure: Rethinking Leisure Theory*, London: Sage.

Rolff, M. (2004) 'Sonne, Sand, Caipi – nur in München nicht', *Süddeutsche Zeitung*, 18 August.

Rubin, J. (2010), 'San Francisco's Waterfront in the Age of Neoliberal Urbanism', in Desfor, G., Laidley, J., Stevens, Q. and Schubert, D. (eds) *Transforming Urban Waterfronts: Fixity and Flow*, New York: Routledge, pp. 143–165.

Rubin, J. (2016) *A Negotiated Landscape: The Transformation of San Francisco's Waterfront Since 1950*, 2 Edn. Pittsburgh: The University of Pittsburgh Press.

Ryu, J. (2004) 'Naturalizing landscapes and the politics of Hybridity: Gwanghwamun to Cheonggyecheon', *Korea Journal*, Autumn, pp. 8–33.

Sadler, S. (1998) *The Situationist City*, Cambridge MA: MIT Press.

Sairinen, R. and Kumpulainen, S. (2006) 'Assessing social impacts in urban waterfront regeneration', *Environmental Impact Assessment Review*, 26, pp. 120–135.

Sandercock, L. and Dovey, K. (2002), 'Pleasure, politics and the public interest: Melbourne's waterfront revitalization', *Journal of the American Planning Association*, 68, 151–64

Savage, V., Huang, S. and Chang, T. (2004) 'The singapore river thematic zone: Sustainable tourism in an urban context', *The Geographical Journal*, 170(3), 212–225.

Schaller, S. and Novy, J. (2010) 'New York City's waterfronts as strategic sites for analyzing neoliberalism and its contestations', in Desfor, G., Laidley, J., Stevens, Q. and Schubert, D. (eds) *Transforming Urban Waterfronts: Fixity and Flow*, New York: Routledge, pp. 166–187.

Schubert, D. (ed.) (2001) *Hafen- und Uferzonen im Wandel: Analysen und Planungen zur Revitalisierung der Waterfront in Hafenstaedten*, Berlin: Leue.

Schubert, D. (2010) 'Waterfront revitalizations: From a local to a regional perspective in London, Barcelona, Rotterdam, and Hamburg', in Desfor, G., Laidley, J., Stevens, Q. and Schubert, D. (eds) *Transforming Urban Waterfronts: Fixity and Flow*, New York: Routledge, pp. 74–97.

Schwarting, H. and Overmeyer, K. (2008) *Suboptimale Nutzungen lieben lernen: Eine Schlüsselstrategie der integrierten Stadtentwicklung*, Wiesbaden: Hessischen Ministeriums für Wirtschaft, Verkehr und Landesentwicklung, available from https://nachhaltige-stadtentwicklung-hessen.de/media/pub_suboptimale_nutzungen.pdf, accessed 9 August 2020.

Sennett, R. (1971) *The Uses of Disorder: Personal Identity and City Life*, Harmondsworth: Penguin.

Sennett, R. (1974) *The Fall of Public Man*, Cambridge: Cambridge University Press.

SenStadt = Senatsverwaltung für Stadtentwicklung Berlin (ed) (2007) *Urban Pioneers: Temporary Use and Urban Development in Berlin*, Berlin: Jovis.

Sepe, M. (2013) 'Urban history and cultural resources in urban regeneration: a case of creative waterfront renewal', *Planning Perspectives*, 28(4), pp. 595–613.

Shamsuddin, S, Abdul Latip, N.S, Ujang, N., Sulaiman, A.B., and Alias, N.A. (2012) 'How the city lost its waterfront: Tracing the effects of policies on the sustainability of the Kuala Lumpur waterfront as a public place', *Journal of Environmental Planning and Management*, 56(3), pp. 378–397.

Shamsuddin, S., Abdul Latip, N., and Sulaiman, A.B. (2013) *Regeneration of the Historic Waterfront: An Urban Design Compendium for Malaysian Waterfront Cities*, Kuala Lumpur: ITBM.

Bibliography

Shields, R. (1991) *Places on the Margin: Alternative Geographies of Modernity*, London: Routledge.
Siksna, A. (1998) 'City centre blocks and their evolution: A comparative study of eight American and Australian CBDs', *Journal of Urban Design*, 3(3), pp. 253–283.
Simões Aelbrecht, P. (2017) 'The complex regeneration of post-war modernism: London's southbank centre's masterplan', *Urban Design International*, 22(4), pp. 331–348.
Siong, H. C., Abdul-Azeez, I. A. and Adeyemi, I. (2013) 'Low carbon cities – the way forward in real estate development in Malaysia', *International Journal of Real Estate Studies*, 8(1), pp. 50–59.
Smith, H. and Ferrari, M. (eds) (2012) *Waterfront Revitalization: Experience in Citybuilding*, London: Routledge.
Smith, J. C. and Fagence, M. (eds) (1995) *Recreation and Tourism as a Catalyst for Urban Waterfront Redevelopment*, London: Praeger.
Sorkin, M. (ed.) (1992) *Variations on a Theme Park*, New York: Hill and Wang.
Southbank Development Corporation (Brisbane) (2002), *Southbank Development '97 Plan (amended)*.
Stadt Kevelaer (2009) 'Ministranten erholen sich am Mini-Strand', available from http://www.kevelaer.de, accessed 9 March 2010.
Stadt Schwedt/Oder (2011) 'Klettergarten-Einweihung mit Strandbar', available from http://www.schwedt.eu/sixcms/detail.php/bb3.c.266061.de?_lang=nirzrbkinbjand_nid=, accessed 16 April 2012.
Stadtengel GmbH (n.d.) available from http://www.skybeach.de, accessed 1 December 2009.
Stevens, Q. (2007a) *The Ludic City: Exploring the Potential of Public Spaces*, London: Routledge.
Stevens, Q. (2007b) 'Betwixt and Between: Building Thresholds, Liminality and Public Space' in Franck, K. and Stevens, Q. (eds) *Loose Space: Diversity and Possibility in Urban Life*, New York: Routledge, pp. 73–92.
Stevens, Q. and Dovey, K. (2019) 'Pop-ups and public interests: Agile public space in the neoliberal city', in Arefi, M. and Kickert, C. (eds) *The Palgrave Handbook on Bottom-up Urbanism*, New York: Palgrave, pp. 323–337.
Stolz, M. (2009) 'Deutschlandkarte: Stadtstraende', *ZEITMagazin*, 10 June, p. 8.
Swyngedouw, E., Moulaert, F. and Rodriguez, A. (2002) 'Neoliberal urbanization in Europe: Large-scale urban development projects and the new urban policy', *Antipode*, 34(3), pp. 547–582.
Taşan-Kok, T. and Sungu-Eryilmaz, Y. (2010) 'Exploring innovative instruments for socially sustainable waterfront regeneration in Antwerp and Rotterdam', in Desfor, G., Laidley, J., Stevens, Q. and Schubert, D. (eds) *Transforming Urban Waterfronts: Fixity and Flow*, New York: Routledge, pp. 257–273.
thebristolblogger (2007) 'How our beach has been turned into a desert...', available from http://thebristolblogger.wordpress.com/2007/06/12/how-our-beach-has-been-turned-into-a-desert/, accessed 18 May 2009.
Thornley, A. (1991) *Urban Planning Under Thatcherism*, Oxford: Routledge.
Toffler, A. (1980) *The Third Wave*, New York: Bantam Books.
Twaroch, F. and Frank, A. (2005) 'Sandbox Geography: To learn from children the form of spatial concepts', in Fisher, P (ed.) *Developments in Spatial Data Handling: 11th International Symposium on Spatial Data Handling*, Berlin: Springer, pp. 421–433.
Urban Catalyst (Philipp Oswalt, Philipp Misselwitz, Klaus Overmeyer) (2007) 'Patterns of the Unplanned', in K. Franck and Q. Stevens (eds) *Loose Space: Possibility and Diversity in Urban Life*, London: Routledge, pp. 271–288.
Vale, L. (2008) *Architecture, Power and National Identity*, 2nd ed., London: Routledge.
Voesgen, H. (n.d.) *Kunst als Faktor der lokalen Entwicklung*, available from forge.fh-potsdam.de/~kultur/Festschrift_IRS_2609.pdf, accessed 3 April 2012.
Völker S. and Kistemann T. (2013) "I'm always entirely happy when I'm here!' urban blue enhancing human health and well-being in Cologne and Düsseldorf, Germany', *Social Science and Medicine*, 78, pp. 113–124.
Waldis, S. (2009) *Zwischennutzung urbaner Brachflächen und Nachhaltigkeit: Theoretisches Konzept zur Verbindung von Zwischennutzungen und Nachhaltigkeit*. Unpublished Masters Thesis, University of Basel, available from http://www.zwischennutzung.net/downloads/Zwischennutzungen_Nachhaltigkeit_Samuel_Waldis.pdf, accessed 9 August 2020.
Wang, Z. and Stevens, Q. (2020) 'How do open space characteristics influence open space use? A study of Melbourne's Southbank Promenade', *Urban Research and Planning*, 13(1), pp. 22–44.
Wanna, J. (2001), 'Political chronicles: Queensland', *Australian Journal of Politics and History*, 48(2), pp. 259–267.
Ward, S. (1998) *Selling Places: The Marketing and Promotion of Towns and Cities 1850–2000*, London: Spon.
Webster, C. (2007) 'Property rights, public space and urban design', *Town Planning Review*, 78(1), pp. 81–101.
Weindl, F. (2004) 'Rimini ist überall', *Süddeutsche Zeitung*, 3 August.
White, J. T. (2016) 'Pursuing design excellence: Urban design governance on Toronto's waterfront', *Progress in Planning*, 110, 1–41.
Whyte, W. H. (1988) *City: Rediscovering the Center*, New York: Doubleday.

Bibliography

Wikipedia.de (2012), 'Badeschiff (Berlin)', available from http://de.wikipedia.org/wiki/Badeschiff_(Berlin), accessed 31 July 2012.

Wonneberger, A. (2010) 'Dockland Regeneration, Community, and Social Organization in Dublin', in Desfor, G., Laidley, J., Stevens, Q. and Schubert, D. (eds) *Transforming Urban Waterfronts: Fixity and Flow*, New York: Routledge, pp. 54–73.

YAAM (n.d.) *YAAM (Young and African Art Market)*, available from http://www.jugendhilfeportal.de/db4/projekte/eintrag/yaam-young-and-african-art-market/, accessed 4 April 2012.

Zukin, S. (1991) *Landscapes of Power: From Detroit to Disney World*, Berkeley: University of California Press.

Index

Note: Page numbers in *italics* and **bold** refer to figures and tables respectively.

accessibility 31–34, 106–107, 222–223
The Accidental Playground: Brooklyn Waterfront Narratives of the Undersigned and Unplanned (Campo) 4
action *see also* actors 189–195
active leisure experience: on urban waterfronts 23–24
actors 189–195, 227–229
Albert Embankment, London 20
Alexander, C. 126
Andersson, Thorbjorn 6–7
artificial city beach 132–133
artificial waterfronts 223–224; augmenting waterfront 103–105; changing waterfront 107–109; Cheonggyecheon, Seoul, South Korea *99*, 99–101; overview 92–94; positioning waterfront 105–107; taming waterfront 94–103; unnatural complexity 109–111; unnatural impacts 109–111
artist-driven city beach projects 189
augmenting, waterfronts 103–105
Australia: bicentennial celebrations 21; 'post-industrial' cities in 17
'authenticity' 126
avant-garde beaches 185–186

Badeschiff, Berlin, Germany *101*, 101–103, *102*, 186, 194–195
Battery Park City: Politics and Planning on the New York Waterfront (Gordon) 3
beaches: avant-garde 185–186; as business opportunity 149–151; citizen-initiated 180, 194; 'grassroots' 183–184; producing 148–149; *see also* specific entries
Berlin, Germany 93; Badeschiff *101*, 101–103, *102*, 186, 194–195; map of, 135; Spree River 76, 101–102, *102*, 139; *Strandbar Mitte* 151, 155–156, *160*, 160–162
Berlin Wall 'death strip' 138
Beyond the Edge (Gastil) 4
Blair, Tony 20
Blijburg aan Zee, Amsterdam 156, *162*, 162–165
Boston Redevelopment Authority (BRA) 79
Breen, A. 6
Brenner, N. 86
bridges 20–21, 29–36, 39–42; pedestrian bridges / footbridges 19–21, 31–37, 43, 46, 115, *116*, 120–121, *121*, 126, 130, 223
Brisbane, Australia *44*, 93; as host of 1988 World Expo 21; Kurilpa Bridge 32, 34, *34*; non-white population of 25; pedestrian Goodwill Bridge 35; poor visibility and obstructed access to *33*; popular tourist image of 26
Brisbane South Bank, Australia 26; artificial beach *96*; Energex Arbour *36*; family using barbecue shelter adjacent to swimming pool *28*; Grey Street and residential neighbourhoods *38*; interface between riverfront promenade and swimming pool *27*; public investments at 27; Queensland Performing Arts Centre *38*
Bristol City Council 166
Bristol Urban Beach 156, *165*, 165–169, *167*
Britain 17
Brownhill, S. 78, 80, 81, 83, 86–87
Bruttomesso, R. 6, 8
business opportunity, beach as 149–151

Cairns, Australia 93, 106
Cairns Esplanade, Australia *97*
Cairns Esplanade Lagoon 97
Campo, D. 4, 5, 7, 9, 144, 146, 152, 153, 225
Canadian Manufacturers' Association 86
Carta, M. 3

241

Index

case studies 3–5
Chang, T. C. 53, 198
changing waterfront 107–109
Cheonggyecheon, Seoul, South Korea *99*, 99–101
Choblet, Jean-Christophe 157–158
citizen engagement in placemaking: conceptualising 181–183; performance 181; sandpit 183; temporary use 182–183; urban pioneers and 'culturepreneurs' 182
citizen-initiated beaches 180, 194
citizen-led city beaches 12, 180
City and Port (Meyer) 7
'city beach' as new waterfront development model: beach as business opportunity 149–151; design of city beaches 140–142; enjoying looseness of urban waterfront 145–148; learning from beachmaking process 151–153; local spatial and developmental contexts 137–139; outside mainstream of waterfront masterplanning 143–145; overview 132–134; producing the beach 148–149; programming 142–143; spreading sand around 134–137
city beaches: citizen-led 12, 180; commercial 142, 184, 188, 192; community entrepreneurship 189–191; design of 140–142; 'events' 143; image management 142; internal layouts 142; key physical attributes of 132, 155; local spatial and developmental contexts 137–139; looseness 187–188; 'night time economy' 145; non-profit 143; palm trees and 141; performance 188–189; physical elements of 141; producing 148–149; programmed activities 142–143; 'public viewing' 143; religious services 143; sandpits and players 192–195; simple 186–187; specific design characteristics of 147; sports 143; 'sweat equity' 148; temporary use 191–192; types of sites used for 155
Civic Guild of Toronto 86
Clark, A. 74–76, 78, 83–84
commercial city beaches 142, 184, 188, 192
community-based beaches 183–184
Community Benefits Agreements 85, 89
community-driven city beach projects 189
community entrepreneurship 189–191
Community Land Trusts 85, 89
COVID-19 epidemic 3
Cox, K. 75
'creative milieu' 138
Cresswell, T. 87
cross-river links: design of new 32–35
Crown Casino, Melbourne *18*, 19, 29–30, 36, 115–116, *116*, 122–130, *128*
'culturepreneurs' 182, 228

Debbage, K. 175
de Certeau, M. 124
Delanoë, Bertrand 157
Deleuze, G. 127
Delirious New York (Koolhaas) 107
DEMOS 166, 168
Desfor, G. 2, 74, 76–78, 81–82, 84–86, 87
design: of city beaches 140–142; of new cross-river links 32–35
'Docklands' 25
Dodson, B. 22–23
Douglas, C. 210
Dovey, K. 4, 5, 7, 8, 109, 148
Dublin Docklands Development Authority (DDDA) 79

Eckstut, S. 22, 37
'Entertainment Zones' 152
entrepreneurial city beaches 150
entrepreneurialism 83
entrepreneurship: commercial 143; community 189–191
environmental experiences of leisure: dialectical tensions **23**; theoretical sources and spatialisation on urban riverfront **24**
Esso (Exxon) 62, 121, *121*, *122*, 129
Europe 3, 6, 17, 133, 155, 166, 175
European debt crisis 3
'Explosive Media' 120
Exxon *see* Esso (Exxon)

Fainstein, S. 118
Fang, Chloe 6
Featherstone, M. 126
Ferrari, M. 2
Festival of Britain, 1951 20, 29, 39, *41*, 42
flows of people 30–39; beyond the riverfront 37–39; design of new cross-river links 32–35; longitudinal pathways 35–37; new links to the city centre 31–32
Fluid City (Dovey) 4
The Fluid City Paradigm (Carta and Ronsivalle) 3
Flyvbjerg, B. 78
Freiluftrebellen 151

Gale, T. 176
Galerie Eigenheim 185, 194
Garreau, J. 31, 35
Gastil, R. 4, 5
Gates, Bill 129
Gehl, Jan 26, 30, 203
German city beaches: as business opportunity 149–151; map of Berlin's 'city beaches,' 2010 *135*; outside mainstream of waterfront masterplanning 143–145; Sandburg Cologne *146*; as small-scale interventions 138; Strand Pauli, Hamburg *133*; Traumstrand, Berlin *150*

242

Index

Germany 133; beach as business opportunity 149–151; entrepreneurial city beaches 150; Kasteler strand on Rhine River, Mainz *137*; map of Berlin's 'city beaches,' 2010 *135*; 'Media Harbour' scheme 139; Oststrand, Berlin *151*; *Strandbar Mitte,* Berlin 135, *136*; Traumstrand, Berlin *150*; Tropical Islands, near Brand, Germany *103*, 103–105
Gertler, M. 175
Gibson, Robin 21
Gidel, M. 53, 74, 75–76, 78–82, 83–84, 87
Global Financial Crisis of 2007–08 3
Gordon, D. 3, 5, 22, 48–49, 109, 198, 222, 223
'grassroots' beaches 183–184
grassroots waterfronts 228–229
Guattari, F. 127

Hack, G. 31
Hafenweg, Münster 139
Hall, P. 74, 75–76, 78, 83–84
Hannigan, J. 126
Harvey, D. 83
Haydn, F. 137
Heeg, S. 76, 78–79, 80, 81, 82, 84–87
Hoyle, B. 2
Huang, S. 53, 198

interactive robot play objects 207
International Network of Urban Waterfront Research conference, Hamburg 89
Ioannides, D. 175
Iveson, K. 128, 129

Jacobs, J. 37, 125–126
Jones, A. 5, 7, 9, 225

Kane, S. 74, 76, 77, 80, 84, 86–88
Kilian, D. 22, 23
King, R. 67, 69
Kistemann, T. 199
Kodak Corporation 98
Kuala Lumpur, Malaysia: founded in 53; informal murals painted on walls of Klang River *63*; Kuala Lumpur City Centre (KLCC) 54–59, *55*, *56*; major floods in 53; map of *56*; Masjid Jamek (Mosque) 53, *54*, *70*; summary of elements drawn in cognitive map of **60**
Kulturstrand, Munich *185*, 185–186

learning from beachmaking process 151–153
Lefebvre, H. 23, 94, 129–130
leisure, environmental experiences of **23**, **24**
local spatial and developmental contexts 137–139
London, Britain *40*, *41*, 93; Albert Embankment 20; cross-river links 35; Elizabethan 20; Jubilee Bridges 34; London Plan, 1943 20; Millennium Bridge 32, 39; riverfront spaces of 29–30; teenagers jumping from steps onto sand at river's edge *45*; Thames River 20
London Docklands Development Corporation (LDDC) 79
London Plan 1943 20
London South Bank 26; Gabriel's Wharf *29*; skateboarders using undercroft of Queen Elizabeth Hall *28*; staircase connecting Golden Jubilee Bridge to *36*
London Thames Gateway Urban Development Corporation (LTGUDC) 79
longitudinal pathways 35–37
looseness, of urban waterfront 145–148
Lynch, K. 31

Macarthur, J. 37
Macdonald, Elizabeth 6–7
Malaysia: analysing, showpiece waterfronts 54–59; analysing showpiece waterfronts 54–59; Economic Transformation Plan (ETP) 63–64; two capital cities 53–54
Malone, P. 2, 3, 8
Marshall, R. 6, 9
Mean, Melissa 166–167
'Media Harbour' scheme, Münster 139
Melbourne, Australia *44*, 93; CBD 31, 33; Crown Casino *18*, 19, 29–30, 36, 115–116, *116*, 122–130, *128*; Melbourne Exhibition Centre 31, 37; Southbank pedestrian bridge *43*; SouthGate 19, 29–32, 37, *116*, 119, *120*, *121*
Melbourne Docklands: intimate space on Victoria Harbour Promenade *202*; map of *203*; public spaces of 199–200, *201*–*202*; site analysis of existing water accessibility in 203, *203*–*204*; users appropriating benches in *201*; users appropriating berth pontoons and showing interest in marine life *204*; wooden structure on Harbour Esplanade *202*
Melbourne Exhibition Centre 31, 37
Melbourne Southbank 25; authority and resistance 127; busking at Esso entrance *122*; casino as fortress-as depicted in media *128*; circa 2002 *116*; Concert Hall and SouthGate *120*; concert hall undercroft *119*; cracks in the spectacle 124–125; Crown casino promenade *117*; figure-ground map *48*; local spaces/global politics 128–131; overflowing desire 126–127; Pedestals, Queensbridge Square *123*; pedestrian bridge looking towards SouthGate and Esso *121*; redevelopment of 35–36; skating the lugs, casino promenade *124*; Southbank overview from pedestrian bridge *116*; three dialectics 124; walk along waterfront 119–124

Index

Meyer, Han 7–8
'middle class escapism' 118
Mikkelsen, Jacob 224
Misselwitz, P. **172**
mobile vending trailers 142
modified shipping containers 142
Monacella, R. 210
Montag Stiftung Urban Räume and Regionale 2010 8
Münster 139

A Negotiated Landscape: The Transformation of San Francisco's Waterfront Since 1950 (Rubin) 4
neoliberalism 3, 72, 83–86
The New Waterfront: A worldwide urban success story (Breen and Rigby) 6
New World waterfronts 84
'night time economy' 145, 171
non-profit city beaches 143, 191
North America 17
Novy, J. 76, 78–80, 82, 84, 86–88

observing public engagement with installation 211–219
On South Bank: The Production of Public Space (Jones) 5
'ordered disorder' 126

Paris, France 12, 93, 107, 173, 178
Paris Plage(s) beach 133, 155–157, *157*, 157–159
passive leisure experience on urban waterfronts 23–24
Peck, J. 84
people, flows of 30–39
Pile, S. 127
Piscine Josephine Baker, Paris 159
place: adding new sense of 169–170; as a performance involving many actors 173–174
'place apart' defined 25
placemaking: adding new sense of place 169–170; conceptualising citizen engagement in 181–183; novel aspects of 169–174; place as performance involving many actors 173–174; temporary open space within long-range development process 170–172
plastic brick diorama *216*, 216–217
pools of use 26–30
pools (swimming) *see also* swimming pools; Badeschiff, Piscine Josephine Baker
positioning, waterfront 105–107
postcolonial waterfronts: city image 60–62; ecological performance 66–68; economic development 62–66; learning from local waterfront 68–69; Malaysia's showpiece waterfronts 54–59; Malaysia's two capital cities 53–54; overview 52–53

post-Fordist placemaking 174–178; *Blijburg aan Zee, Amsterdam 162*, 162–165; *Bristol urban beach 165*, 165–169, *167*; four pioneering city beaches 157–169; novel aspects of 169–174; overview 155–157; *Paris Plages* beach *157*, 157–159; post-Fordist placemaking 174–178; *Strandbar Mitte, Berlin 160*, 160–162
post-Fordist production methods 176
post-Fordist tourist development 175
post-Fordist tourist industry 176–177
Price, Emily 165–166, 168–169
producing, beach 148–149
programming 142–143; uses 226–227
public spaces: of Melbourne Docklands 199–200, *201–202*; for water engagements 198–199
Putrajaya, Malaysia: Ayer 8 commercial development *66*; government office buildings in *61*; Lake Putrajaya 57, 59, *59*, *67*; map of *58*; Putra Mosque and Prime Minister's Office as seen from Lake Putrajaya 57, *59*; open-sided waterfront restaurant in Taman Seri Empangan *65*; summary of elements drawn in cognitive map of **60**

Ramsey, K. 75, 80–81, 83, 87–88, 90
Rigby, D. 6
riverbank stage 39–42
Riverscapes: Designing Urban Embankments (Montag Stiftung Urban Räume and Regionale 2010) 8
Ronsivalle, D. 3
Roovers, Igor 162–164
Rubin, J. 4, 5, 76, 78–79, 82–83, 85, 86–88
Ryan, B. 152

sand 27, 45, *45*, 95, 104, 109, 111, 140–141, 147–148, 155, 158; concrete-making 148; dredged 162–163; spreading 134–137, *135*, *136*, *137*
sandbox 183; *see also* sandpit
sandpit(s) 183; and players 192–195; *see also* sandbox
sandpit urbanism: action and actors 189–195; avant-garde beaches 185–186; community entrepreneurship 189–191; conceptualising citizen engagement in placemaking 181–183; 'grassroots' beaches 183–184; overview 180; sandpits and players 192–195; spaces for action 186–189; temporary use 191–192
Savage, V. 53, 58
Scalmer, S. 128–129
Schaller, S. 76, 78–80, 82, 84, 86–88

Schubert, D. 74, 76, 78, 79, 82, 87
Schulz, Christian 160–161
scoping underwater environments 211–213, *212*
Seattle demonstrations 128
'second nature' 94, 99
Seoul, South Korea 93; Cheonggyecheon 99, 99–101
shifting waterfront: flowing and fixed aspects 73–74; interpreting waterfront change 86–88; overview 72–73; role and interests in waterfront change 79–81; scale and direction of fixities and flows 74–77; time and tide 78–79; turning of the political tide 81–83; whither neoliberalism 83–86
site analysis of existing water accessibility in Docklands 203, *203–204*
Skanska 166
'Skybeach' 151
Smith, H. 2
'social geology' 25
South Bank, Brisbane *see* Brisbane South Bank
South Bank, London *see* London South Bank
Southbank, Melbourne *see* Melbourne Southbank
Southbank Promenade, Melbourne 26, 30–31, 33, 45, 115–117, 121, 129–130
'Southbanks' 10, 105, 222; across the river 25–26; active leisure experience on urban waterfronts 23–24; Brisbane industrial waterfront area *18*; common history of waterfront regeneration 17–23; design of 'Southbanks' and people's needs for leisure **47**; on the edge 42–46; flows of people 30–39; improving waterfront image and integration 46–50; London industrial waterfront area *19*; Melbourne industrial waterfront area *18*; overview 17; passive leisure experience on urban waterfronts 23–24; pools of use 26–30; riverbank stage 39–42 *see also* Brisbane, London, Melbourne
SouthGate, Melbourne 19, 29–32, 37, *116*, 119, *120*, *121*
South West of England Regional Development Agency 166
spaces for action 186–189
spectacle: authority and resistance 127; casino as fortress – as depicted in the media *128*; casinos 117, *117*, 122–130, *124*; cracks in 124–125; local spaces/global politics 128–131; overflowing desire 126–127; overview 115–119, *116*, *117*; three dialectics 124; walk along the waterfront *119*, 119–124, *120*, *121*, *122*, *123*, *124*

spectacular design-oriented catalogues of 'waterfront success stories' 5–8
'Sphero' robots 207, 213, *214*, 215
stage(s) 40, 104, 121–122, *122*, 184–187, *185*
Strandbar Mitte, Berlin 151, 155–156, *160*, 160–162
Strandleben, Vaihingen an der Enz *187*, 187–190
Sungu-Eryilmaz, Y. 77, 79–80, 82, 84–85, 89
surface interaction, prompting 213–216, *214*, *215*
'sweat equity' 148
Swyngedouw, E. 76

taming, waterfront 94–103
Taşan-Kok, T. 77, 79–80, 82, 84–85, 89
Temel, R. 137
temporary open space, within long-range development process 170–172
temporary waterfront: creating temporary waterfront installation 205–211; future design perspectives for urban waterfronts 219–220; observing public engagement with installation 211–219; overview 197–198; public spaces for water engagements 198–199; public spaces of Melbourne Docklands 199–200, *201–202*; site analysis of existing water accessibility in Docklands 203, *203–204*
temporary waterfront installation: creating 205–211; data collection methods 210–211; diagrammatic overview of installation elements *207*; elements 206–207; prompting surface interaction 213–216, *214*, *215*; recruiting participants 208–210, *209*; scoping underwater environments 211–213, *212*; selected site 207–208; temporary installation 206–207; unfolding waterfront multiplicities *216*, 216–219, *217*, *218*; use of interactive robot play objects 207
Thatcher, Margaret 75
Theodore, N. 86
Tickell, A. 84
timber-framed huts 142
Toronto Harbour Commissioners (THC) 79
Toronto's Board of Trade 86
Transforming Urban Waterfronts (Desfor et al.) 2, 72–73, 75–76, 78, 80, 83, 86–89

underwater environments, scoping 211–213, *212*
Urban Development Corporations 83
urban managerialism 83
urban pioneers 182
'urban renaissance' 88
'Urban Renaissance' agenda 20

Index

Urban Waterfront Promenades (Macdonald) 6–7
urban waterfronts: active leisure experience on 23–24; enjoying looseness of 145–148; future design perspectives for 219–220; holistic understanding of waterfront activation 229–230; new actors and relationships 227–229; passive leisure experience on 23–24; shaping encounter with water's edge 223–225; successful planning and design of **22**; testing waters through design research 224–225; waterfront uses that attract and stimulate diverse users 225–227; waterfront visibility and access 221–223
urban waterfront transformations 2–8; collective perspectives 2–3; design-oriented catalogues of 'waterfront success stories' 5–8; detailed individual case studies 3–5

Vaihingen an der Enz *187*, 187–190
van Mierlo, Stanja 163–165, 174
Vienna 93, 107, 171
Völker, S. 199

Washington demonstrations 128
water 34–35, 42–46, *44*, 49–50, 121–122, 126–127; existing water accessibility in Docklands 203, *203*, *204*; fountains 64, 158; public spaces for water engagements 198–199; quality 64, 67–69, 136, 194
water access 140, 194, 203, 208; *see also* accessibility; waterfront visibility and access
water-based robots 213–216, *214*, *215*
water engagements, public spaces for 198–199
waterfront activation, holistic understanding of 229–230
waterfront change: interpreting 86–88; role and interests in 79–81
waterfront-inspired landscape 136
waterfront installation: observing public engagement with 211–219

Waterfront Landscapes (Fang) 6
waterfront masterplanning 143–145
waterfront multiplicities, unfolding *216*, 216–219, *217*, *218*
waterfront open spaces 146
Waterfront Promenade Design: Urban Renewal Strategies (Andersson) 6
waterfront regeneration: active leisure experience on urban waterfronts 23–24; common history of 17–23; passive leisure experience on urban waterfronts 23–24
Waterfront Revitalization: Experience in City-building (Smith and Ferrari) 2
waterfronts: artificial 223–224; augmenting 103–105; changing 107–109; 'culturepreneurs' 228; grassroots 228–229; image and integration, improving 46–50; overlapping pools of uses 225–226; passive and active leisure experience on urban 23–24; positioning 105–107, 223; programming uses 226–227; taming 94–103; uses that attract and stimulate diverse users 225–227; visibility and access 221–223
Waterfronts: A New Frontier for Cities on Water (Bruttomesso) 6
Waterfronts: Cities Reclaim their Edge (Breen and Rigby) 6
Waterfronts in Post-industrial Cities (Marshall) 6, 9
'waterfront success stories': spectacular design-oriented catalogues of 5–8
waterfront visibility and access 221–223
'wellness landscape' 104
Witham, Julie 165, 168–169
Wonneberger, A. 73, 75–76, 79, 85–87
World Economic Forum (WEF) congress 128
World Trade Organisation 128

YAAM (Young and African Art Market) 184, *184*, 191, 193

For Product Safety Concerns and Information please contact our EU representative GPSR@taylorandfrancis.com
Taylor & Francis Verlag GmbH, Kaufingerstraße 24, 80331 München, Germany